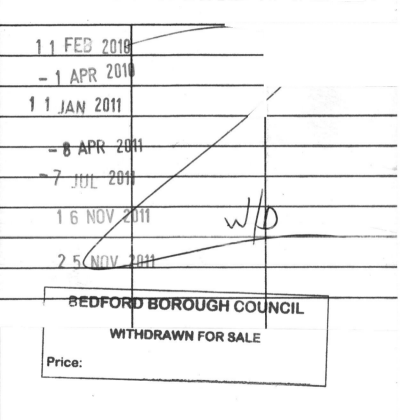

The Ministry of Defeat

The Ministry of Defeat

THE BRITISH WAR IN IRAQ – 2003–2009

RICHARD NORTH

continuum
LONDON • NEW YORK

Continuum UK
The Tower Building
11 York Road
London SE1 7NX

Continuum US
80 Maiden Lane
Suite 704
New York, NY 10038

www.continuumbooks.com

First published 2009

British Library Cataloguing-in-Publication Data
A catalogue record for this book is available from the British Library.

ISBN 9781441169976

Typeset in Adobe Minion by Tony Lansbury, Tonbridge, Kent.
Printed and bound in Great Britain by MPG Books Ltd, Bodmin, Cornwall

Having been summoned to London to attend the Ministry of Defence, a young officer was reputed to have been confused as to its exact location. Walking up Whitehall, he hailed a passer-by for directions. 'Which side is the Ministry of Defence on?' he asked. 'Ours, I hope,' came the response.

In southern Iraq in 2003, that hope was not fulfilled.

Contents

Acknowledgements

Very many people helped with the making of this book but, if I was to single out one person, it would be my wife, Mary, who provided so much support and my link with reality during the long period when I was gripped with the obsession required to embark on such a venture. In what was something of a family enterprise, I am also grateful to my son, Peter, who undertook some of the early research.

I must also thank my close colleague Christopher Booker for his encouragement and advice, particularly with the structure and the shaping of the narrative, advice I did not always take, which reflects more on me than on him.

Many others who helped in small ways, and a few who provided enormous assistance, prefer not to be named – or cannot be named – but they know who they are. I thank them for their input, without which the book would not have been possible. When, occasionally, I lapse into references to 'we' in the narrative, I am referring to one or other of those who gave me so much help.

Special thanks and appreciation go to Ann Winterton MP, an unsung hero in Parliament, who has laboured long and hard over many years to raise defence issues which otherwise would certainly not have been aired, and which vastly informed this narrative.

Also in Parliament, my thanks to Owen Paterson MP, who provided timely advice on framing, and also lodged a number of useful Parliamentary Questions which were of very great value. Mike Hancock MP, unbidden, also asked many questions in response to enquiries made in developing the themes covered and my appreciation is recorded.

I must also thank former Secretary of State for Defence Des Brown – a much under-rated minister – who, the one time I met him, gave me an extraordinary boost, which convinced me that much of the material on which I was working was well-founded.

Very special thanks must go to Sue Smith, mother of Pte Phillip Hewett, who was so tragically killed with his comrades in a Snatch Land Rover in al-Amarah in 2005. She gave freely of her time, gave me much information and made contact with others on my behalf, whom I was then able to consult. Of these, Pauline Hickey, mother of Sgt Christian Hickey, was of enormous assistance and I thank her for her time and patience.

I am also very grateful to freelance journalist Nigel Green who freely allowed me to use some of his photographs and gave me some insight from his experiences in Iraq and Afghanistan, to Thomas Harding, defence correspondent of *The Daily Telegraph*, whom I once called an 'idiot' and who proved to be anything but. That again is a reflection of me rather than of him.

On the production side, I must record my thanks to Robin Baird-Smith at Continuum who has taken the very great risk of agreeing to publish this book, and our typesetter, Tony Lansbury, whose assistance went far above and beyond the call of duty.

Finally, I had expected to record my thanks to the MoD, representatives of which approached me as the first draft was nearing completion, with an offer to review the book, correct inaccuracies and provide additional information.

In the event, that offer was withdrawn and instead I was faced – way beyond the agreed deadline – with a 'request' to remove or change significant portions of the book on the grounds that they breached 'OPSEC' (operational security). It says something of the MoD that one such offending section was based entirely on – and quoted from – information provided on the MoD website. This and other material remains.

It was suggested that yet other material, graphically describing the death of some soldiers, should be removed for fear of offending or disturbing relatives. Such material also remains as it was made clear to me by the relatives who provided me with accounts that they wanted readers to know of the suffering of these brave soldiers. I have respected their wishes.

That apart, the errors that the MoD might otherwise have corrected remain, as probably do others about which I am unaware – all of which are entirely my responsibility. However, that there should be some errors in a work of this nature is inevitable. It is too early yet to write a fully-sourced, accurate account of the British occupation of Iraq and, if the media writes the first version of history, this is the second. There will, I hope, be many more versions to come.

In any event, this is not so much a history as the 'case for the prosecution'. As I make clear in the body of the book, while there were many problems and flaws in the military campaign, no blame can attach to those on the ground who so bravely put their lives at risk. But, at High Command and political level, there were very clearly some major errors.

Acknowledgements

These may or may not be excusable or understandable, but such errors that were made need to be acknowledged. That the emphasis in 'high places' is now to present the campaign as a 'success' is a wilful distortion of the facts. Thus, warts and all, this book makes a case, one I believe needs to be answered. From the debate that I hope will ensue, perhaps a better book may emerge, in which case this will have achieved its purpose.

I apologise in advance to those whom I may offend or have unjustly – by accident or design – wronged. I hope that they will accept that the search for the truth is an endeavour which needs to be undertaken and to which this book is intended to contribute.

Bradford, Yorkshire
April 2009

Foreword

By Christopher Booker

Timed to coincide with the moment when the last British troops leave Iraq in 2009, this book is intended to serve two purposes.

The first is that it gives the first comprehensive account of Britain's military occupation of Iraq between 2003 and 2009. Even today few people in Britain realise the extent to which our intervention in south-eastern Iraq was an abject failure. The second purpose of this book is to explore what should have been the lessons of that defeat, and to suggest that, unless those lessons are properly learned, we now face the very strong possibility that our forces face a similar debacle in Afghanistan.

The British occupation of south-eastern Iraq lasted six years, a period longer than the Second World War. As Dr Richard North shows, despite the bravery of many individual soldiers, the British government enjoyed only one real success in all that time. Such was the extent to which it managed to hide from view how, thanks entirely to its own catastrophic misjudgements, this became one of the most humiliating chapters in the history of the British Army.

North is well qualified to tell this shocking story. Having worked closely with him for many years, I was aware that from 2005 onwards he was following events in Iraq increasingly closely. His attention had initially been drawn to what was going on in Iraq because, as a political analyst, he was carrying out an intensive study of a dramatic but little-reported revolution which was taking place at that time in Britain's defence policy.

In particular he was following the moves being made by the Blair government to re-equip Britain's armed forces, under the terms of the EU's 1999 Helsinki accords, to play a role in a future ERRF, the planned European Rapid Reaction Force.

Shrouded as it was in considerable secrecy, it was not widely understood at the time just how much between 2003 and 2006 this had come to dominate the priorities of the Ministry of Defence. The latter was committing a huge proportion of Britain's defence budget to a whole series of procurement and other projects relating to the needs of the ERRF.

Yet what North also observed, from his expert knowledge of defence equipment, was how strikingly this contrasted with the MoD's conduct of the operations in which British forces were at the same time engaged in southern Iraq.

In 2006, through his political and journalistic contacts, North played a key part behind the scenes in drawing to public attention the startling inadequacy of the equipment provided to British troops in carrying out their task. This had been supremely symbolised in the decision three years earlier to deploy nearly 200 Snatch Land Rover patrol vehicles, in which so many soldiers were subsequently killed or seriously injured.

How was it, North reflected, that the MoD was prepared to commit tens of billions of pounds to projects designed to equip Britain's armed forces to fight imaginary wars of the future when so little was being spent on properly equipping them in Iraq and Afghanistan for wars they were actually having to fight in the real world?

From there North developed an increasingly well-informed picture of what was really happening in Iraq, which was eventually to result in this book. Drawing on a wealth of published and unpublished sources, including private contacts with members of the forces who have served in Iraq and with high-level sources in the defence establishment, he has been able to reconstruct for the first time a detailed account of this tragic story. It was one which, like many another tragedy, was to unfold through five main 'acts' or stages.

The first act of the story began in April 2003, following those few weeks when 43,000 British troops took part in the US-led invasion which toppled Saddam Hussein. As the second largest component in the coalition forces, Britain had agreed to take on the responsibility of restoring order in the predominantly Shi'a south-east of the country, centred on Iraq's second largest city, Basra.

The British entered on their new task in a spirit of hubris, imagining that they would be welcomed by the local population as liberators. From their experience in Northern Ireland, they fondly imagined that establishing law and order would present no great problem. Almost immediately, however, British troops came under sporadic attack by armed local militias, notably the 'Mahdi Army' run by a militant cleric Muqtada al-Sadr. And here the British had already made two fatal mistakes. First, they had decided for political reasons on a very drastic reduction in their troop numbers to just 11,000. Secondly, they had dismantled all the existing structures of authority. The occupying forces therefore had nothing like enough men to fulfil what was their solemn legal duty under the Geneva Convention to maintain public order and safety.

This stage of the story culminated in the fateful decision in late 2003, endorsed by General Mike Jackson as head of the Army, to deploy 178 Snatch Land Rovers from Northern Ireland as the army's chief patrol vehicle. The intention behind this, as part of the bid to win over local 'hearts and minds', was to avoid more aggressive-looking vehicles for routine patrolling, such as armoured Warriors which looked like light tanks. But, as North shows, the decision to depend so heavily on the Snatch betrayed a fatal misreading of how serious the situation around Basra had become; a misreading that sowed the seeds of the disaster which was to follow.

The second act of the story began in 2004 when Muqtada's Mahdi Army launched a conventional uprising in several cities across Iraq, including Baghdad. This provoked a massive US response which led to Muqtada's defeat. But in Basra and the south this prompted the Mahdi Army, in turn, to resort to guerrilla tactics, notably through the use of roadside bombs. These caused havoc when employed against the hopelessly unprotected Land Rovers in which so many British soldiers were being asked to carry out their routine patrols.

By summer 2005, as yet more soldiers died, the British were forced to suspend Snatch patrols. But tragically, for want of any alternative, their use soon had to be resumed. As British units showed themselves inadequate either in numbers or equipment to maintain control, the cities of Basra and al-Amarah to the north effectively fell under the violent sway of the ruthless militias, in particular the Mahdi Army. It was during this time, as the remains of civil order collapsed, that the British finally lost the confidence of an increasingly terrorised local population.

The third act of the story in 2006 centred on an extraordinary, largely unreported drama surrounding al-Amarah and the Army's nearby base at Abu Naji, its largest outside Basra. Unable to keep control over the city, the British withdrew to Abu Naji, where they were subjected to constant mortar attacks to which they had neither the men nor the equipment to respond. In August they retreated, supposedly handing over the base to the Iraqi Army, only for it to be triumphantly looted by the Mahdi Army. By the end of October Muqtada's men had turned al-Amarah into a vast bomb-making factory, the chief source of supply for insurgents all over Iraq.

The story's fourth act in 2007 charts the attempt by the British to restore control in Basra and the progressive failure to recover lost ground. Eventually, impotently confined to just four bases in Basra, under constant attack from mortars, rockets and gunfire, the British could do little more than protect the convoys needed to keep them supplied. Forced ignominiously to abandon one base after another around the city to the Mahdi

Army, in September 2007 they were allowed by their enemies to retreat to their last remaining 'safe haven' in Basra airport. For the British, in effect, 'the war was over'.

The fifth and final 'act' of the story saw the Americans to the north, under General David Petraeus, launch their spectacularly successful 'surge'. This was the turning point of the entire allied occupation. The key to its success was not just President Bush's decision to draft in 20,000 additional men, but the fact that they were now properly equipped with hundreds of mine-protected vehicles of the type the British so conspicuously lacked. This did more than anything to quell the insurgency in the centre of the country and to build up the standing of the Iraqi government under the country's new prime minister, Nouri al-Maliki.

In March the newly resolute Iraqi government and the US Army, frustrated by the total failure of the British to carry out their responsibilities, and determined to end the flow of bombs and other weaponry flooding out of al-Amarah, launched the military operation known as 'the Charge of the Knights'.

Entering Basra in overwhelming force, they routed the Mahdi Army, restoring the city with remarkable speed to peaceful normality, In June 2008, Iraqi and US forces similarly liberated al-Amarah without a shot being fired. It was made embarrassingly clear to the British that their presence in Iraq was no longer relevant or wanted. In effect, an angry Maliki ordered the British to leave his country as soon as possible. Before Christmas 2008 it was announced that virtually all remaining British troops would have departed from Iraq by the summer of 2009.

Such is the unhappy story Dr North sets out for the first time in full in this book. The British Army had entered Iraq in 2003 with a reputation as 'the most professional in the world'. As it left six years later, it had failed to fulfil any of its allotted tasks and had earned the contempt of both the Iraqis and the Americans, after one of the most shameful defeats in its history.

The fault for this debacle lay not with the British troops on the ground, who had tried to do all that was asked of them, with wholly inadequate support from above. The blame lay almost entirely with Tony Blair, abetted by one or two very senior military commanders, who failed at any point after the invasion to provide the men and equipment needed to carry out the task to which Blair had vaingloriously agreed. Yet all the time this tragedy was unfolding, to a quite remarkable degree the British public was kept in the dark as to just how profound Britain's failure had been.

The reasons why it was possible to maintain such an effective cover-up of the full scale of the disaster were several. Partly it was a reflection of the London-based media's lack of interest in Iraq, which in turn reflected the British people's general unhappiness over Britain's involvement there in the first place. Partly it reflected the complete failure of opposition politicians to develop an informed understanding of what was going on. But more than anything, as Dr North so chillingly shows, it was a triumph for the news management skills of the Blair government in continually misleading the media, Parliament and the public as to the reality and seriousness of what was happening.

The most obvious price to be paid for this catastrophe was that which could be measured in the so often unnecessary deaths and injuries of our soldiers. But much wider and deeper than this, it lay in that destruction of the reputation of the British Army which will remain one of the most painful and lasting legacies of the Blair era.

What makes it all the more urgent that the true nature and scale of our defeat in Iraq should be recognised, however, is that so many of our soldiers are still engaged in an equally frustrating counter-insurgency war in Afghanistan. So many of the lessons which should have been learned from Iraq are still not being applied further east, where British troops continue to die because they are inadequately equipped for a task which the politicians have never properly defined or understood.

Such is the final message Dr North tries to put across in this remarkable book.

Introduction

Successful tactics did not only require sound training, instinctive ability, quick reactions and decisive leadership. They also depended on a correct combination of weapons immediately available.

GENERAL SIR DAVID FRASER[1]

Every single war in which our armed forces have engaged was either just about won, or even lost, not just because of poor leadership but because of poor procurement.

BRUCE GEORGE MP,
CHAIRMAN, DEFENCE COMMITTEE, 1979–2005[2]

At 11.13am on 11 September 2005, army intelligence officer Major Matthew Bacon was travelling from one of Saddam Hussein's former palaces to Basra air base when a roadside bomb exploded a few feet away from his Land Rover. He was killed instantly. Sitting with his back to the blast, Matthew, 34, stood no chance as a copper projectile sliced through the vehicle and went through his chest. Three other occupants of the vehicle were seriously injured.

This stark narrative is adapted from a *Sunday Times* 'Focus' report on 25 June 2006.[3] It highlighted the fact that soldiers were getting killed in Iraq in an armoured vehicle called a Snatch Land Rover that gave little protection from roadside bombs. The article was part of a campaign to get the vehicle replaced with something better.

Major Bacon had been the twelfth soldier to die in a Snatch-related incident since 4 October 2003. That was when these vehicles first arrived in Iraq, having been transported from Northern Ireland where they had been widely used during the Troubles. By the time *The Sunday Times* report was published, 10 more soldiers had died. By the end of 2008, 38 had lost their lives in Iraq and Afghanistan. Those deaths – those and the even greater number of serious injuries – motivated Christopher Booker and I to mount a campaign for better equipment.

That campaign is part of this story but, as it developed, issues came to light which suggested that the inadequacy of the Snatch Land Rover repre-

---

1. *And we shall shock them – The British Army in the Second World War* (London, Hodder & Stoughton, 1983), p. 159.
2. Hansard, 19 June 2008: Column 1140.
3. *The Sunday Times*, 25 June 2006, Focus: 'Is the army putting money before lives?'

sented something far bigger. It symbolised the whole approach of the Army and the British government to the war in Iraq. That was eventually to become the subject of this book, which sets out for the first time a comprehensive account of how a mindset symbolised by a single type of vehicle lost us the war.

In mid-2006, when I helped to raise the issue of Snatch Land Rovers to public awareness with the aid of allies in the press and Parliament, this seemed to be a relatively straightforward matter of troops being issued with inadequate equipment and dying as a result. It was only as we explored further that we saw that the Snatch represented something much wider and deeper than this: a failure of the political and military establishments to adapt to the realities of the most vicious insurgency war fought by the British Army in 40 years.

We saw how, following the successful allied invasion of Iraq in 2003, the British forces responsible for administering south-eastern Iraq had fundamentally misjudged the situation which confronted them.[4] An insurgency rapidly developed, as rival groups jockeyed to establish their own dominance over the British zone, notably that led by the Shi'a cleric, Muqtada al-Sadr. In their attempts to challenge British control, their tactics evolved from outright military confrontation to the more classic forms of guerrilla warfare. One of the insurgents' primary weapons became the improvised explosive device (IED), more commonly known as the 'roadside bomb'.

In the early days of the insurgency, these devices were often crude and largely ineffective. As they became more sophisticated and powerful, however, the Army failed to counter them with better vehicles, more advanced equipment and new tactics. The IED thus deprived the Army of tactical mobility to such an extent that it was no longer able to perform a useful role. When the Shi'a then launched sustained attacks on British bases, using mortars, rockets, rocket-propelled grenades and sniper fire, the Army was gradually forced to withdraw from them. Eventually, it was hunkered down, virtually impotent, in its one remaining major base at Basra's former International Airport.

This was why the Snatch became the central symbol of the British Army's tragic and culpable ill-preparedness and lack of flexibility in dealing with the Iraqi insurgency. Much the same was later to become evident in Afghanistan, where some of the same failures were to be repeated.

The deaths of soldiers and the dismal succession of military 'retreats' in

4. To be fair, so did all the other forces in post-invasion Iraq. In particular, as is acknowledged later, the US forces made serious errors.

Iraq also to a great extent reflected another very serious failure: the disarray in Britain's military procurement policy. The failings of the Army in Iraq seemed to support the widespread claims at home that the government was 'underspending' on defence. But the truth was that a large part of the defence budget was being earmarked for expensive prestige projects, such as equipping the Royal Air Force with Eurofighters and the Royal Navy with giant aircraft carriers. The Army was doing the bulk of the fighting, was losing the most men and had committed a larger proportion of its strength to the fight than the other services – yet it was getting palmed off with wholly unsuitable, second-hand equipment.

In Iraq and then Afghanistan, those 38 soldiers died because the protection given them was glaringly inadequate. Many more came home with life-changing injuries. Furthermore, thousands of Iraqis were killed and injured, simply as a result of the inability of the British to bring peace and stability to the region which was their responsibility. In that sense, the story of the Snatch is the story of the failure of the entire British campaign, as my colleague Christopher Booker calls it in his Foreword, 'one of the most humiliating chapters in the history of the British Army'.

As Christopher sets outs out in the foreword, there were five main 'acts' to this unhappy story. The first opened in May 2003, in the wake of the dramatically successful allied invasion, when the British took on the formal responsibility for running southern Iraq. That 'act' ended in October 2003, when it had become clear that the initial 'honeymoon' was over. Failing to recognise the signs that a full-scale insurgency was developing, the British treated the growing disorder around Basra primarily as a 'public order' issue, similar to that which they had faced in Northern Ireland. It was this which led, as described in Chapter One, to the deployment of the Snatch Land Rovers imported from Belfast.

The second 'act' of the story is covered in the four chapters which follow. Chapter Two deals with the emergence of the full-blown insurgency when the militias confronted the Army head-on – and lost. Chapter Three charts the militias' adoption of classic guerrilla war tactics, with the emergence of more sophisticated bombs. These forced the Army onto the defensive. Chapter Four covers the period when the militias rebuilt their strength. Faced with the prospect of a long-drawn-out campaign which it was not equipped to fight, the Army decided to pull out and began to reveal its intention to withdraw altogether. Chapter Five charts the descent of Basra into chaos, ruled by the fundamentalist militias. The Army had lost control.

We then break off from the narrative concerning Iraq itself for a chapter describing events back in Britain. As described in Chapter Six, a spirited political campaign was launched in 2006 in an attempt to force the government to provide British forces in Iraq with equipment more appropriate to their task and the conditions they faced. It was by then clear that the Blair government was not prepared to countenance the other prime requisite for that task, a substantial increase in the number of troops deployed.

Returning to Iraq, the third 'act' had now begun, as described in Chapter Seven. This centres on the city of al-Amarah north of Basra, where the Army, having shown itself unable to bring the militias under control, eventually decided on a disastrous tactical retreat. In order to concentrate its resources on Basra, it abandoned al-Amarah to the militias, who then turned it into the central armoury supplying the various insurgent groups across the rest of the country.

The fourth 'act', covered in Chapters Eight and Nine, marked the humiliating conclusion of Britain's involvement in post-war Iraq. The first of these chapters describes the Army's last-ditch bid at the end of 2006 to regain the initiative in Basra, amid growing violence and disorder. This was its last hope of regaining honour and a semblance of victory from the chaos which had developed continuously since the Army's arrival in 2003. Chapter Nine then describes how the Army's strategy collapsed, leaving the militias in virtually complete control of the city. This culminated in the Army being permitted by the militias to beat a peaceful but ignominious retreat to the comparative safety of Basra airport.

Then came the fifth and final 'act' of the story, described in Chapter Ten, which was to provide a dramatic conclusion to all that had gone before. With the British now almost wholly out of play, the focus shifted to the Americans and the Iraqi government, who between them were to transform the situation in southern Iraq.

Three separate but related steps made this transformation possible. The first, following President Bush's appointment of Robert Gates as his new Secretary of Defense, was Gates's decision to re-equip US forces in Iraq with a fleet of protected vehicles, the so-called MRAPs (Mine Resistant and Ambush Protected), precisely the type of vehicle the British had so conspicuously lacked. This was followed by Bush's courageous decision to overrule the advice of the Iraq Study Group by greatly stepping up the numbers of US troops in Iraq, in order to launch the 'surge', under the command of General David Petraeus. Finally, a series of astute political moves by Iraqi prime minister Maliki enabled him to neutralise the political power of the leader of the Shi'a insurgency, Muqtada al-Sadr.

All this made it possible for the US and Iraqi armies in March 2008 to make a dramatic intervention in southern Iraq, by launching the operation known as 'the Charge of the Knights'. This, with remarkable speed, wrested control of Basra from the militias. It was followed three months later by a second, equally important operation, 'Promise of Peace', by which US-Iraqi forces recovered al-Amarah. These remarkable victories, bringing southern Iraq for the first time under the control of Maliki's government in Baghdad, were followed by Maliki's decision to eject the British from Iraq.

Throughout this narrative, like lettering in a stick of Blackpool rock, lies the story of the Snatch, the supreme symbol of Britain's inability to face up to the realities of what it had taken on in Iraq. This failure brings us in Chapter Eleven to the story of the military campaign in Afghanistan, where we see many of the mistakes repeated.

Intentionally, the chief focus throughout this narrative is on the conduct of the Army – the Army as a corporate body and in particular the 'donkeys' that led some courageous 'lions'. The men and women on the ground performed admirably, fighting a vicious and unprincipled enemy while handicapped by poor strategy, inadequate equipment and insufficient resources. Without their perseverance, their skills and, in some cases, quite extraordinary courage, things might have been far worse. The sad fact though is that the Army was at the cutting edge of the conflict, the major player in a drama ordained by the politicians, and therefore the one whose record is most clearly illuminated. In important respects, however, the word 'Army' in this story could read 'military'. This was, after all, a combined operation. Many of the senior decision-makers were from other Services.

Where criticism is directed at military capabilities though, there is a tendency to focus on the Ministry of Defence (MoD). Better described as an amorphous collection of warring tribes, it inhabits a vast office block in Whitehall which, despite vast expense on its refurbishment, boasts an atrium that has the look and feel of a public lavatory. This is not inappropriate, considering what it does with much of the public money entrusted to it.

Beyond Downing Street, where the main responsibility lies, the failures in Iraq, grievous as they were, lie at the door of the MoD, rather than with the men on the ground, far too few in numbers and hopelessly ill-equipped for the task the politicians had set them. Of the two, the poor equipment was probably more important. While procurement and deployment decisions are ultimately made by government as a corporate entity, the MoD is the executive decision-maker and has huge influence. As such, the finger points firmly at the MoD – better named, we feel, the Ministry of Defeat.

A central thesis in this book is that, long before the invasion of Iraq, the government, the MoD and the Army, separately and as a group, made some disastrous choices. As a group, it ensured that the counter-insurgency

11

in Iraq was grievously handicapped. Further decisions ensured it remained so throughout the occupation. All this is explored in the final chapter. The evidence presented there points to an issue of some considerable importance – that procurement and equipment deployment decisions have major effects on campaigns and thus need more scrutiny than they are often given.

This brings into focus a third major player – the media. A counter-insurgency campaign is a very different kind of war from conventional conflict, public opinion playing a vital part in sustaining the effort. The media plays its part in shaping and informing that opinion. It says something of their activities – or lack of them – that the bulk of the narrative was constructed from sources other than the British media, much of it from Arab news agencies and foreign media – guided by sources close to the ground who added vital interpretations and explanation of events, which allowed the material to be analysed in context.

Views will vary as to the precise role the media should assume, but we believe that in a democracy it has a duty to inform the debate. It is largely through the media that ordinary people gain some appreciation of what is happening in areas of British interest – southern Iraq obviously being one. The media therefore is – or should be – more than a branch of the entertainment industry. It is an essential part of a functioning democracy. During the occupation of Iraq, however, it is fair to say that the British media failed in many ways to inform. It rarely explored the types of issues which were discussed widely in the US media and which shaped the way the US campaign was conducted. In consequence, the media – and its lack of engagement – became part of the story and, throughout this narrative, we follow closely its activities.

Thus, of the many parties involved in the Iraqi campaign, we focus on the three groups outlined: the British government; the MoD and military leaders as a collective; and the media. Wherever the fault lies, what is not acceptable is the extent to which the MoD and the military – where they can be distinguished – have been re-inventing the narrative to cast the campaign as an unalloyed success. Individuals and units performed well and some heroically, but their successes do not a victory make. In the terms set at the beginning of the occupation, it was a failure. It did not achieve its objectives. By any rational meaning of the word, that was a defeat.

While so much can be put down to the politicians and the media, the MoD at the highest level bears a huge responsibility for the failure. Its refusal to recognise this is deeply disturbing. The purpose of recognising and evaluating failure is not to apportion blame, but to prevent it from being repeated. As long as the failures in Iraq remain unexplored, a repeat is not only possible but also very likely in Afghanistan.

That sentiment was reflected by Rudyard Kipling at the end of the Boer War. He wrote a poem, 'The Lesson', arguing that we should admit the mistakes made there and learn from them. Although the defeat was clearly the result of some of the most egregious examples of military incompetence in history, Kipling had an even more trenchant and altogether uncomfortable message. 'It was our fault,' he wrote, 'and our very great fault.' We made an Army in our own image. It 'faithfully mirrored its makers' ideals, equipment, and mental attitude'. So, 'we got our lesson: and we ought to accept it with gratitude'.

There is great truth in that sentiment. The Army is but an instrument – we make it and shape it. In that sense, its failures are indeed our failures. We are the fourth 'player' in this defeat. But if the failures are ours as well, then we share the responsibility for putting them right. That is why this writer, a political analyst rather than a military specialist, feels entitled to enter the debate. If war is too important to be left to Generals, its study is too important to be left to military historians. Moreover, the outcome of the war was shaped by an amalgam of domestic, international and Iraqi politics – not the province of a military historian – and heavily influenced by public opinion. Mine is a voice of a member of that public – a public that had its part to play in the war.

It is Kipling, then, who sets the frame for this book. Its purpose is to draw attention to the urgent need for an open and honest debate about what went wrong in Iraq and why – and then to learn the lessons. Insofar as it can, the book also stands testimony to the courage and dedication of the men and women of our Armed Forces, many of whom, in the opinion of this writer, died needlessly.

Chapter 1 – Losing the peace
The build-up to the insurgency:
May–September 2003

You fought the battle, you won the battle, and you fought it with great courage and valour. But it didn't stop there. You then went on to try to make something of the country you had liberated. And I think that's a lesson for armed forces everywhere, the world over.

TONY BLAIR, 29 MAY 2003
SPEAKING TO BRITISH TROOPS IN BASRA

Spearheaded by US forces, backed by British, Australian and Polish troops, on 20 March 2003 an invasion force crossed from Kuwait into Iraq to commence Operation Iraqi Freedom. Over 240,000 Americans were committed, with 43,000 British and smaller numbers from the other contingents. After an amphibious assault on the southern port of Umm Qasr, where unexpectedly stiff resistance was encountered, the British 7th Armoured Brigade (Desert Rats) first surrounded and then fought its way into Iraq's second city, Basra, entering on 6 April. On 9 April, Baghdad was formally occupied by coalition forces and the power of Saddam Hussein was declared ended, marked by the memorable toppling of Saddam's statue in Baghdad's Firdos Square.

Victory was achieved after only two weeks of conflict, which included the biggest tank battle by British forces since the Second World War when the Royal Scots Dragoon Guards destroyed 14 Iraqi tanks on 27 March. Casualties were light, with only 11 British soldiers killed in action. The war was formally declared at an end on 1 May by President Bush on the aircraft carrier *USS Abraham Lincoln*. Clearly visible in the background was a banner stating: 'Mission Accomplished.'

Britain then took formal control of what became known as Coalition Provincial Authority South, comprising the four southernmost provinces of Iraq: Basra, Muthanna, Maysan and Thi Qar. The sector was about 275 miles wide and 260 miles from north to south, covering some 60,000 square miles – about a quarter of Iraq's whole area. It included around 600 miles of borders with Iran, Kuwait and Saudi Arabia, 30 miles of coastline, the ports of Umm Qasr and az Zubayr, the Marsh Arab area east of Nasiriya and large areas of desert covering much of Muthanna. Ninety per cent of the population was believed to be Shi'a Arab, with mixed Sunni and

15

Shi'a populations in Muthanna, and small communities of Christians in Basra, amongst other groups.

The occupation brought obligations under international law, specifically the Hague Regulations of 1907 and the fourth Geneva Convention of 1949. They set out the responsibilities of the occupying power, which Britain now was. Amongst these was the requirement to restore and ensure as far as possible public order and safety.[1] This was an absolute obligation. But if British prime minister Tony Blair took it seriously, there was no attempt made to ensure that the resources were available to honour it.

This put the Army in a difficult position. It was being asked to do a job without the necessary tools. The requirement was wildly over-ambitious. Having deployed 43,000 men with their equipment, it was in the throes of winding down. The administration of organising, assembling and then returning surplus troops and *matériel* was in itself a major burden. In addition, faced with the task of organising an occupation of indeterminate length, it had to select and equip suitable bases and then arrange for their manning, their defence and their supply.

THE EARLY DAYS OF OCCUPATION

British troops were widely spread. In Basra alone there were five major bases, the headquarters in the former Basra International Airport, which became Basra Air Station, later renamed the Contingency Operating Base (COB). To the south-east of the city, there was the Shaibah logistics base, using a former airfield which the British had only vacated in 1958 after their last occupation.

In the city itself, to the south, the Army took over one of Saddam Hussein's former palaces, on the banks on the Shatt al-Arab waterway. This became known as Basra Palace. In the north of the city, it requisitioned the Shatt al-Arab Hotel, a sprawling complex also alongside the waterway, formerly part of the now disused Maqal city airport. Roughly in the centre was the Old State Building. Then there were various outposts, in the former Naval Academy, in the port of Umm Qasr and in az Zubayr, a Sunni stronghold 22 miles south of Basra, near the Kuwaiti border.

In the most populous of the other provinces, Maysan, a base was set up in the former Iraqi Army barracks, five miles outside the provincial capital, al-Amarah, known as Abu Naji. A city centre compound was taken over,

---

1. For a summary of these obligations, see: Military occupation of Iraq: I. Application of IHL and the maintenance of law and order, produced by Relief Web, 14 April 2003.

the site occupied by the former governor's residence known as the Pink Palace and an administrative building called CIMIC House. Troops were also stationed in the now vacant prison. As President Bush extended the 'coalition of the willing', other national contingents were drafted in, which all had to be organised and accommodated. In the British sector, to add to the Australians, new arrivals included Spanish, New Zealanders, Japanese, Dutch and Danes. In terms of just sorting out its own arrangements and those of the coalition members, the Army – and the military generally – was fully stretched. It was also supposed to run a major part of the country.

One can, therefore, have a little sympathy with General Sir Richard Dannatt, Chief of the General Staff between 2006 and 2009. In 2008, after the all-but-final withdrawal of British Forces from Iraq had been announced, he sought to defend the performance of 'his' Army and the military generally. Speaking specifically of Basra, he said:

It's a city of huge size, however many British troops or coalition troops have been there we would never have been able to impose a regime and we had no intention of doing that. It was always going to be an Iraqi solution to an Iraqi problem, and what we had to do was to enable that to happen …[2]

Such words do not reflect the world of May 2003. Nothing said or written at that time suggested that the military was simply 'holding the line' to buy time for an Iraqi solution. Moreover, that could not have been the case. The Hague Regulations and the Geneva Convention are very clear. From the beginning, though, there was a mismatch between what was expected of the Army and what it could actually do.

In May 2003 establishing control looked easy, which was to have the unfortunate effect of lulling the occupiers into a false sense of security. The mainly Shi'a population in the south largely welcomed their liberators and did not show the degree of antagonism experienced by the US forces further north. The Americans were having to deal with the minority Sunni sect which had dominated the more populous but oppressed Shi'a and which very quickly mounted an organised resistance to the occupation. In the south, British troops patrolled in soft hats, without body armour. They travelled in open vehicles and even hired civilian cars, going freely about their business with little fear of attack. The main security concern was renegade supporters of Saddam Hussein.

The media largely bought into the euphoria – although there was con-siderable and perhaps over-blown coverage of the looting in the immediate aftermath of the liberation. We thus saw a trickle of feel-good stories such

2. MoD website, 23 December 2008, CGS on Iraq: 'We have achieved what we set out to achieve.'

as the tale of the Northumberland soldiers who liberated a 'unique symbol of Iraq's fresh hope for the future' – a litter of puppies. Born in the week that British soldiers had occupied Basra, the five puppies had been adopted by 'sentimental soldiers' and taken under their protection.[3]

While a few lucky puppies might have prospered, the British as a whole did not get off to a good start in forming a new government. The plan was pragmatic. The military – closely guided by anonymous officials from the Foreign and Commonwealth Office (FCO) who were never very far away – was to set up a civilian interim administration and gradually to shift power and responsibility to it. Once things had stabilised, there would be democratic elections from which would emerge a legitimate government, enabling a grateful (and peaceful) population to run its own affairs. The military would then depart in orderly fashion.

This set the scene for the troubles to come. It defined the role of the military, and especially the Army. Neither the Army nor the British government actually wanted to run southern Iraq. Both were highly sensitive to accusations of invading Iraq for its oil or other nefarious purposes. Thus, in something of a policy vacuum, the Army (and the military in general) was allowed to cast itself in a role with which it was familiar, one it had performed in Northern Ireland. Effectively, it saw its task as the 'support of the civil power'.

PROBLEMS EMERGE

Therein lay the main problem. The whole apparatus of civil administration had melted away leaving nothing even remotely approximating to a functioning government. One had to be created from scratch. Casting around for an experienced Iraqi to head an interim administration, British Army intelligence 'talent-spotters' picked a tribal sheikh by the name of Muzahim Mustafa Kanan al-Tamimi. He was considered to have clean hands, and to be sufficiently distant from the former regime to be acceptable to the people of Basra. It turned out that he had been a former brigadier in Saddam's army and a member of the ruling Ba'ath Party.

News of his impending appointment had hundreds of protesters marching through the city centre waving banners. A rival clan staged a near-riot outside his home while al-Tamimi was holding talks with other local leaders. In what was to become a wearisomely familiar routine, troops were forced to intervene.[4] The British quietly dropped al-Tamimi but the final

3. BBC, 13 April 2003, 'Puppies are symbol of Iraq hope'.
4. *The Daily Telegraph*, 11 April 2003, 'Britain's chosen sheikh found to have Ba'ath link'.

shape of the 'interim council' still dismayed the Basrawis. They noted that half of the dozen members had held prominent places in the fallen regime. As news of the council's make-up filtered through to the streets, 'some appointments drew fire'.[5]

At this stage the 'fire' was verbal. Although the forces were being wound down, there were still enough to contain demonstrations. That was to change. In late April, it had been announced that the force level would be reduced to around 11,000.[6] Many thought that too low.

Nevertheless, while the Sunni-led insurgency in the US-held zones gathered pace, Basra remained relatively quiet – reinforcing the sense that the occupation would be trouble-free. A number of commentators made favourable comparisons, although many were motivated by anti-Bush sentiment.[7] Unfortunately, flattered by the compliments and buoyed by an innate sense of superiority over their gauche American cousins, many in the Army began to believe the propaganda. Hardly a meeting between the coalition forces went by without, at some stage, a British officer referring to the Army's counter-insurgency skills, honed by experience in Northern Ireland.

Behind the scenes though, Basra was undergoing a terrifying change, almost completely unnoticed. Shi'a fundamentalists were taking control, pursuing a form of ethnic cleansing, driving out Sunni and other minority groups.[8] Some would have it that the occupation caused this process. But it started immediately after Saddam's regime had been deposed. Had the occupation forces left immediately, ethnic cleansing would have been even worse than it was to become. One tenable scenario is of a dark, terrible civil war, matching the worst days of Lebanon.

THE POLITICAL MAKE-UP

Initially, some sort of order prevailed. Many attest to the relaxed atmosphere, the freedom of movement and relative safety. That was in a city of 1.3 million with an estimated 150 political and tribal factions. It is relatively easy now to categorise the main political players. It was not so easy back in 2003, when little was known about the different factions and the battle lines in the coming insurgency were far from clear.

5. *The Daily Telegraph*, 18 April 2003, 'British anger Basrans by bringing back Ba'athists'.
6. *The Daily Telegraph*, 23 April 2003, 'Britain calls home bulk of ground forces'.
7. For instance, on 29 May 2003, the US tabloid *USA Today* ran an editorial headed: 'British postwar approach provides model for US', noting that, while in Baghdad, US soldiers in full combat gear sit nervously atop tanks scanning the horizon through gun sights, 'the atmosphere in Basra is more relaxed'.
8. *The Daily Telegraph*, 9 May 2003, 'Murder of Catholics selling alcohol raises fundamentalist fear'.

Best established of the Shi'a groups was the Supreme Council for the Islamic Revolution in Iraq (SCIRI), with its own paramilitary wing known as the Badr Corps. This was an Islamic fundamentalist organisation, strongly pro-Iranian and violently anti-American, wanting the Kurdish north of the country split off, leaving a pro-Iranian Islamic rump. It boasted a strength of between four and ten thousand, although in the shifting sands of Arab politics, loyalties and affiliations could change with bewildering speed. Under the leadership of cleric Mohammed Bakr al Hakim, SCIRI was to become part of the *de facto* government in Basra. Much of the Corps was incorporated into the official security forces and ranks of the administration. This move was tolerated by the British, who saw in SCIRI an organisation capable of maintaining a semblance of government.

The hegemony of the SCIRI in Basra was challenged by two rivals. The first was the party of Said El Sadr, led by Muqtada al-Sadr, son of the founder Mohammed Sadeq al-Sadr, who had been murdered by Saddam in 1999. Although he was to become the main player, Muqtada al-Sadr and his movement was in 2003 largely unknown, often dismissed as a 'firebrand dissident cleric' of little importance.

An Islamic fundamentalist, Muqtada opposed the formation of a British provisional authority, volubly opposed any form of occupation and was passionately anti-American. But he was an Iraqi nationalist, rejecting Iranian rule. In the early days, the Sadrists were the minority in Basra. With their own militia, the Mahdi Army (known as the Jaysh al Mahdi or JAM), their strength lay in Sadr City on the outskirts of Baghdad, in the holy cities of Najaf and Karbala – all in the US zone – and in al-Amarah in Maysan province.

The other main player was the Fadhila (Virtue) Party. An offshoot of the original Sadrist movement, it was rapidly to emerge as a major Shi'a faction in southern Iraq. Basra was its main power base but it had a minority presence in Maysan province. It took control of the oil production and much of the economic activity, making it a prime target for Shi'a insurgents and SCIRI. Nevertheless, in the early days, it enjoyed the support of the city's professional class.

In contrast with the Sadrists, who sought control over the whole of Iraq and therefore presented a direct – but initially unrecognised – challenge to the authority of Baghdad, Fadhila, like SCIRI, was pro-Iranian and pursued a separatist agenda. It had more local ambitions though, seeking autonomy for the southern provinces, including Basra and Maysan. Fadhila was led initially by Ayatollah Muhammad Yaqubi, based in Karbala.

Because of its overtly separatist agenda, with a regional bias, the faction never enjoyed the support of the British.

THE MILITIA THREAT

In the early stages, al-Hakim, representing the SCIRI, made the most noise and was given the most attention. On 12 May, huge crowds greeted his return from exile in Iran and his message that US-led forces should leave the country. In what Stephen Farrell of *The Times* called a 'nuanced' message, al-Hakim declared: 'We must never permit the presence of foreigners and we must not be their slaves. We must show that we can rule ourselves.' The speech created, 'an effect akin to drums of war'.[9]

There was certainly no shortage of war-making materiel. It was estimated that every household in Basra had two or three guns. Heavier weapons such as rocket-propelled grenades (RPGs) were common. There was an endless supply of explosives, looted from deserted Iraqi Army ammunition dumps left unguarded after the invasion. Nor, despite their legal obligations, were the British able to take the place of 16,000 police deserters. Basra was being policed by just 48 armed British military policemen, plus 900 unarmed locals. Militias, mainly from Badr and Fadhila, were to fill the gaps but as the police force expanded it was heavily infiltrated by Sadr activists.

Under the pressing burdens of organising the occupation, the British failed to recognise the militia threat and stuck to their plan of devolving government to local administrations, thereby ceding power to them. Fadhila were the beneficiaries when they handed over control of Umm Qasr to an interim council.[10] For Basra as a whole, the British were forced temporarily to abandon the idea of handing over their responsibilities. Unable to find leaders with widespread support, they set up a 'utilities' committee to sort out the reconstruction. It was headed by Brigadier Adrian Bradshaw, commander of the British Seventh Brigade. Additionally, they set up a civic forum of political leaders.[11] These developments were not popular in some quarters. Clerics led a crowd of 5,000 to the military headquarters carrying banners proclaiming: 'No to British rule over Basra' and 'We can rule ourselves'.[12]

The faction which the crowd represented was not identified, but it cannot be asserted that it spoke for the people of Basra as a whole. The clerics

9. *The Times*, 12 May 2003, 'Foreign forces must go, insists Shia ayatollah'.
10. *The Daily Telegraph*, 16 May 2003, 'Army hands over control to town council'.
11. BBC, 26 May 2003, 'UK forces disband Basra council'.
12. BBC, 1 June 2003, 'Basra protests against UK leader'.

and their followers were highly voluble, but the city of Basra was by no means a religious centre. Like many port cities, it had a cosmopolitan flavour with a large secular population, more interested in business and commerce than the finer points of Islam. Most Baswaris were fearful of the way the fundamentalists were moving in and were expecting the British to check their zeal.

THE UNSTATED OBJECTIVES

That the British did not and let the situation get out of control, is perhaps the major indictment over the handling of the occupation. But the lead was given by Blair. In late May, he visited British troops in Basra and gave no sign that he understood what was happening. Instead, he professed to be satisfied with progress. He praised the troops for the way they had taken the city. He then told them they were rebuilding in relative peace. The term 'relative' is, of course, relative. It was quieter in Basra than elsewhere, but then the situation there was different from elsewhere.

Instead, Blair offered one of his uplifting speeches. 'You fought the battle, you won the battle, and you fought it with great courage and valour,' he told the troops. 'But it didn't stop there. You then went on to try to make something of the country you had liberated. And I think that's a lesson for armed forces everywhere, the world over.'[13] In that speech was a sense of smug self-satisfaction. Less than a month into the formal occupation, it was somewhat premature to be congratulating the troops on having made 'something of the country'. But there was also implicit the expectation that the Army would continue the process of 'nation building' it had begun.

Nowhere officially will you find any such clear statement. Blair was locked into a false paradigm, where he had sought to justify the invasion on grounds acceptable to the United Nations Charter, choosing the 'weapons of mass destruction' as his *causus belli*. That the coalition did not gain UN approval, and that in October the Security Council only reluctantly legitimised the 'occupation', is not part of this story. What is relevant is that the real objective of 'regime change' could not be admitted. Therefore, its formal sequel, 'nation building' could not either. That this was the task of the British Army was clearly understood, but it explains in part why the resources were never properly allocated.

13. *The New York Times*, 30 May 2003, 'After the war: the Britons; Tony Blair, visiting Basra, tells of challenges ahead'.

SECURITY DETERIORATES

Whatever the impact of Blair's speech on the troops, Basrawis were not impressed. More than anything, they wanted security and it was by no means evident that this was on offer. After dark, gunfire could be heard across the city. Looting of government buildings, businesses and homes continued.

The British were not helped by news of a scandal over 'shocking pictures' of soldiers abusing male Iraqis at a base, codenamed 'Camp Bread Basket'. The story flashed around the world with lurid details translated into Arabic and posted on a number of websites, remaining to this day.[14] This coincided with another story, just three days later, of the MoD police investigating the death of two Iraqi civilians in British custody.[15,16] The fragile relationship being built up between the occupiers and the Iraqis was considerably damaged, giving much comfort to those who wished to oust the British.

Sectarian violence was also bubbling to the surface. On 6 June, the head of the al-Saadun tribe was shot dead by four hooded assailants close to the Basra office of the SCIRI. The tribe had close ties with Saddam and Badr involvement was suspected. That was one of the many signs that there was a reckoning going on.[17] Other malign forces were at work. In a deliberate attempt to undermine the British administration, saboteurs targeted the power grid in order to shut down the Basra Refinery. They mounted a series of destructive attacks on carefully selected power lines around Basra, the effect of which was to cut off vital petrol supplies.[18] Such sabotage was to have a serious effect. With many Iraqis judging the occupation on its reconstruction efforts, the failure to deal with it was to damage the authority of the British.

At this time, every section of society seemed to be involved in some form of dissent. Even lawyers took to the streets. Their complaint was the reinstatement of Ba'athist judges. Everywhere there were Shi'a groups with Sadr clerics in evidence. Some 2,000 staged a march to the British military headquarters at the same time that the lawyers were protesting. Theirs was a more political message, expressed by their slogans: 'No to Tony Blair, no to Satan,' and 'Leave peacefully lest we expel you through our jihad'. They handed in a petition demanding that the British withdrew to the outskirts of the city.[19]

14. See for instance: *www.albasrah.net/maqalat/english/kelly/iraqi_pow.htm.*
15. *The Daily Telegraph*, 4 June 2003, 'MoD police investigate Basra civilian deaths in custody'.
16. *The Sun-Herald*, 1 June 2003, 'Soldier's war snaps show British troops abusing prisoners'.
17. Reuters, 6 June 2003.
18. KRT News Agency, 7 June 2003, 'Systematic acts of sabotage in Basra aim to create chaos, officials say'.
19. BBC, 7 June 2003, 'Basra protest against British presence'.

Despite the obvious Shi'a involvement, the British still tended to believe – and perhaps wanted to believe – that the rump of the deposed regime was causing the sporadic violence. With Saddam Hussein and his sons still at large, this was not entirely unreasonable. Furthermore, a cell of Fedayeen militia had been uncovered. One member, after his arrest, confessed he had been sent to Basra to gather information in preparation for launching attacks. The captive claimed that the new 'resistance' cell had a large network of activists in Basra province as well as a cache of arms in one of the villages in the area.[20]

In the south though, the real threat was from Shi'a fundamentalists. They were united in one thing. They wanted the British to leave, clearing the way for them to battle it out for control. In a sense, this was a low-grade civil war, with insurgency overtones. The factions were vying for power while opposing attempts to create a unifying central government. The occupation forces, representing that government, were resented for their interference. That said, in the immediate aftermath of the invasion, the Shi'a were disorganised, lacking in skills and structures. Resistance to the occupation was largely confined to demonstrations and to stoning British military patrols, the latter becoming a daily occurrence. But the demonstrations were also getting bigger. One on 15 June had 10,000 demanding self-government. Again they were led by Shi'a clerics.[21]

Of more immediate concern to ordinary people was the dire state of the utilities.[22] Only weeks into the occupation, even taxi drivers in Basra were worried. Some wanted Saddam back. 'At least under him we had security', was the refrain. Few people dared go out at night. During the day there were carjackings and armed robberies. Nor were the hospitals safe. A gang attacked the infectious diseases unit of Basra General Hospital, firing automatic weapons and hurling grenades as doctors and patients scattered. They stole the air-conditioners.[23] Out of the spotlight, there were increasing signs that the hard men were taking over. A local newspaper was attacked by Shi'a fundamentalists for carrying photographs of glamorous Western women.[24]

The British were aware that the situation was deteriorating. They had already experienced unrest from the cadres of former soldiers, thrown destitute onto the streets after the US administrator in Iraq, Paul Bremner, had disbanded the Army. That had left 400,000 men jobless. In an attempt

---

20. *The Age*, 8 June 2003, 'Iraq militia cell uncovered'.
21. *The Daily Telegraph*, 15 June 2003, 'Demonstrators stone Army vehicles as 10,000 protest in Basra'.
22. *USA Today*, 16 June 2003, 'Iraqis still frustrated by disabled telephone system'.
23. *New York Times*, 17 June 2003, 'Cheers to Jeers'.
24. *The Guardian*, 16 June 2003, 'News from Baghdad'.

to keep the lid on this potential flashpoint, the British paid monthly wages to thousands of these men, part of a 'hearts-and-minds campaign'. The 'unspoken desire' was to reduce the threat of the Shi'a taking up arms. That much was recognised. The Shi'a could turn against the occupation.

As the demonstrations and unrest gathered pace, with the discovery of leaflets calling on the people to rise up against the British, Brigadier Bradshaw claimed to be unconcerned. 'What we are seeing here is a new emerging democracy starting to flex its muscles,' he said. 'I think we should expect to see a certain amount of expression of opinion … We don't feel threatened in southern Iraq. That is because we have won the people's trust by being open with the Iraqis we meet.' [25, 26] This almost smug complacency was the single most important factor in preventing the British from recognising what was going on.

MAJAR AL-KABIR – THE SLAUGHTER OF THE MILITARY POLICE

Nevertheless, Bradshaw's confidence was about to be shaken. A hundred miles or so north of Basra, in Maysan, lay the small town of Majar al-Kabir, 15 miles south of al-Amarah. A Shi'a stronghold which had suffered greatly under the rule of Saddam, British troops were welcomed when they had first entered, the town then held out as an example of progress. Unwisely though, British forces had also been trying to disarm the population, carrying out a programme of house searches and road blocks in their hunt for weapons. This had been extremely unpopular, so much so that on Monday 23 June an agreement had been reached with local leaders that searches would be suspended.

On the Tuesday morning, 12 Paras arrived in the town in two light trucks, together with a group of local Iraqi militia. This was a 'routine joint patrol' and no searches were planned. Some 500 angry residents, unaware of this, surrounded the soldiers. Stones were thrown. One soldier retaliated with a baton round (rubber bullet) and shooting erupted on both sides. A small force of paratroopers failed in a rescue attempt and the fire became so intense that the soldiers abandoned their vehicles and sought shelter. Another relief force in an RAF Chinook was driven off by heavy gunfire, injuring seven on board. On the ground, a fierce firefight lasted for three hours, the gunmen 'so frenzied' that as soon as one was shot, another

25. *The Daily Telegraph*, 24 June 2003, 'Wild West town a haven for exiles and smugglers'.
26. KUNA News Agency, 19 June 2003, 'Demonstrations "do not pose threat to British soldiers" – commander Military and Security'.

would take his place. The 12 soldiers were eventually rescued by troops in Scimitar light tanks, backed by air cover.

Unfortunately, at the local police station there were six Royal Military Police. With the Paras gone, the crowd turned on them. Their Land Rovers were torched, destroying their radios. With limited ammunition and no communications, the RMPs were unable to save themselves. They were slaughtered.[27, 28, 29, 30]

A CULTURE OF DENIAL

When there should have been real alarm, back in London, Tony Blair was soothing. Despite media and opposition party pressure to increase troop levels, he insisted that there was no need. He had been told, so he said, by Chief of Defence Staff Sir Michael Walker that British commanders inside Iraq felt they had enough troops. Of the situation of a whole, he declared, 'Progress is being made but it is a job literally of rebuilding a country and it will take time. I think it is necessary to take the time to get the job done.'[31] If Blair had not recognised what was happening, neither – it seems – had the Army. Walker's refusal to send more troops was matched by a concerted effort to demonstrate that it was 'business as usual'. A show was put on for the BBC, the local correspondent being enlisted to run a 'feel good' piece about a soft-hat patrol in Basra.[32]

On Saturday 28 June, when the Paras returned to Majar al-Kabir, it was anything but business as usual. They turned out in force, 500-strong, backed by 100 armoured vehicles including Challenger tanks, and helicopters.[33] Freshly-painted banners greeted them, in both Arabic and English, denouncing the British Army. The display of force was largely symbolic. The Paras stayed for barely an hour and carried out no weapons searches.[34]

Contrary to the soothing words of the politicians and Army 'brass', some were convinced the honeymoon was over. Major Charles Heyman, Editor of *Jane's World Armies*, felt there were not enough coalition troops. The death of the six RMPs 'was bound to happen'. 'This could become a nasty, long, drawn out campaign across the whole of the country', he wrote. The

27. *The Daily Telegraph*, 25 June 2003, 'Six British soldiers die in Iraq'.
28. *The Daily Telegraph*, 24 June 2003, 'Wild West town a haven for exiles and smugglers'.
29. BBC, 26 June 2003, 'Majar al-Kabir: From quiet to carnage'.
30. *The Times*, 23 April 2004, 'The gunmen were so frenzied that as soon as one was shot, another would take his place'.
31. Agence France Presse, 25 June 2003.
32. BBC, 26 June 2003, 'Business as usual for British forces in Iraq'.
33. *The Daily Telegraph*, 28 June 2003, 'Paras storm town where mob killed British soldiers'.
34. *The Daily Telegraph*, 29 June 2003, 'Paras' show of force brings new Shia threat of bloodshed'.

Government had two options: 'either reinforce or withdraw.' He concluded, 'I can look at the evidence and say that the security situation is likely to worsen during the coming months.'[35]

Inevitably, opinion was split.[36] Michael Clarke, of the Department of War Studies at King's College in London, did not rule out the idea of the Shi'ite community becoming restive with the occupation. But neither did he rule out Saddam loyalists establishing a guerrilla presence in the south. Philip Mitchell, of the London-based International Institute for Strategic Studies, thought the attack could have been carried out by smugglers profiting from the general lawlessness. His 'gut reaction' was that the attack had been a one-off.

Patrick Cockburn, writing for the *Independent on Sunday*, was pessimistic.[37] Majar al-Kabir was 'one of the most dangerous towns in Iraq', he wrote. Guerrillas had harried Saddam Hussein's army for decades from hideouts in the district. Tribesmen were convinced that the US and Britain wanted to stay a long time in Iraq and were waiting for their religious leaders to issue a fatwa against the occupation, when they would fight. Cockburn suggested that the US and Britain faced many dangerous enemies in Iraq, other than from the surviving supporters of Saddam Hussein.

Perhaps, at this point, the politico-military establishment could have taken stock. The 'noise' level was high and the signals were ambiguous but there were ominous signs. One would like to think that there had been a powerful and influential unit analysing the flow of reports and intelligence, warning of possible chaos. But the indications are that information-gathering was fragmented and ill-coordinated, with little in the way of a clear picture being presented.[38]

There was also a sense that the politicians did not want to know. In early July, the then foreign minister Jack Straw visited Iraq. He, like Blair, was determinedly upbeat. Treading a well-worn path, he attributed the violence to elements of the Ba'ath Party and the Fedayeen. He did concede that they were 'operating in a relatively organised way' but, reacting to media comment about the need for more troops, he relied on Blair's mantra. There had been no request for reinforcements.[39] Also, the then Chief of the General Staff, General Sir Mike Jackson, had other concerns. He was

35. *The Times*, 25 June 2003, 'Lack of troops leaves force vulnerable to further attacks'.
36. *Asia Times*, 27 June 2003, 'Alarm bells over attack on British soldiers' (originally published by Radio Free Europe).
37. *Independent on Sunday*, 29 June 2003, 'We promised them peace but the killings and chaos spread'.
38. See: Russell W. Glenn, S. Jamie Gayton, November 2008, *Intelligence Operations and Metrics in Iraq and Afghanistan* (RAND National Defense Research Institute) – one of a series of studies which illustrated a chaotic system, lack of preparedness and wholly inadequate intelligence.
39. BBC, 2 July 2003, 'Straw upbeat on Iraqi authority'.

embarking on a fundamental reorganisation of the Army and planning a massive re-equipment programme, directed at transforming the Army into a lean, high-tech airmobile expeditionary force.[40] Iraq, as we will see in the final chapter, was a sideshow.

MISSING THE SIGNS OF THE INSURGENCY

If the Army's public pronouncements in theatre are any guide, the prospect of a prolonged insurgency was certainly not being taken seriously. In early July, a soldier was injured in a Basra 'blast'. A spokesman put this, and an attack on one of the oil pipelines in the Faw Peninsula, down to 'subversive elements'.[41] Similarly, when on the same day a sniper shot and wounded a soldier on the northern outskirts of Basra, this was an 'isolated incident'.[42]

The incident was not reported in the British media. Through the remainder of the year and beyond, there were many such which also went unreported, even if reports were carried by local Arab media and international press agencies. The media thus, by its lack of reporting, supported the myth of 'isolated incidents'. There was no attempt to discern a pattern which, perhaps, might have indicated something more sinister.

What should have rung more alarm bells was that relief agencies were also having trouble. The UN's World Food Programme was losing trucks to armed hijackers on the road between the Kuwaiti border and Nasiriya. Food from Kuwait had to be transferred to Iraqi trucks at the port of Umm Qasr. The port itself had been affected by looting in mid-June for some days after the withdrawal of Spanish troops. The 1,300-strong Spanish contingent had been ordered home by a newly-elected Socialist government, honouring pre-election commitments.[43] British forces, with the aid of Iraqi guards, had to provide security.[44] Some of the attacks were put down to general disorder and criminality, others attributed to Sunni dissidents. Whether that was the complete picture remains to be seen. Criminality and insurgency are not mutually incompatible. Often, they go hand in hand.

Furthermore, there had been between 10 and 15 kidnappings in the first two weeks of June, partly for money, partly tribal disputes and sometimes

40. House of Commons Select Committee on Defence, 24 April 2004, Examination of witnesses (Questions 220–239).

41 Asia Africa Intelligence Wire, 3 July 2003, 'British Army spokesman confirms one soldier injured in Basra "blast"'.

42. CNN, 8 July 2003, 'First sniper attack on UK soldiers'.

43. BBC, 18 April 2004, 'Spain PM orders Iraq troops home'.

44. United Nations World Food Programme, Press Release, 10 July 2003.

people taking hostages to swap for one of their own. A spate of armed robberies as well as the kidnappings had prompted the UN in Basra to ban its staff from going out after 8pm. Walking anywhere was prohibited and cars had to travel in pairs. There had also been 7 to 10 homicides a week connected with revenge against members of the former regime.[45]

Still the Shi'a were cleaning out the Sunni. The Sunni Waqf Directorate (an Islamic charitable foundation) found itself under armed attack by 40 Sadrists who took control of its building and expelled the employees after threatening to kill them. They stole all the documents and records. Director Haqqi Isma'il launched an appeal to 'Islamic governments, religious institutions and academic circles'. He urged them to intervene. The aggressors' persistence in their attacks, he warned, 'might result in a sectarian crisis that could be hard to settle at such a delicate time'.

Isma'il also referred to a previous incident in which groups had broken into five Sunni mosques and taken control of them, expelling worshippers. He complained that the British had refused to intervene, had disregarded all the appeals and had 'confined themselves to holding some meetings, which were fruitless'.[46] Patience was running low, a theme voiced by one café owner. 'Liberation has brought insecurity and crime to Basra – robbers, mugging, kidnappings for ransom,' he said. 'And they can't even provide us with reliable electricity.'[47]

This once again illustrated the hands-off approach of the British, and their refusal to confront the reality. While they could do little immediately to improve the electricity supply, neither were they providing even the most basic protection to the citizens of Basra. And, while the lack of security and the very obvious lack of progress in reconstruction was spasmodically picked by the media, it was presented more as a curiosity than as a high-level political issue. There was no criticism at that time of the failure of the British to take a firm grip of a deteriorating situation.

Nevertheless, the Army did respond with a 'crackdown', setting up security roadblocks in Basra and neighbouring districts.[48] But events elsewhere were to take a hand, stepping up the tension. In Najaf, where Muqtada al-Sadr had established his base, action by US troops led to rumours that he had been arrested. As these spread to Basra, between 2,000 and 3,000 protesters took to the streets. British troops were again forced to intervene,

45. *The Guardian*, 15 July 2003, 'Kidnappers and robbers make most of police shortfall'.
46. Asia Africa Intelligence Wire Service, 18 July 2003, 'Sunni figure protests over seizure of religious building in Basra'.
47. BBC, 19 July 2003, 'Patience runs low in Basra'.
48. *Voice of the Mujahidin*, in Arabic, 19 July 2003, via BBC Monitoring International Reports.

shots were fired and Sadr's representative in Basra was among the three wounded.[49]

The contrast with what happened next – or did not happen – perhaps offered the best clue as to what was going on. Saddam Hussein's sons Uday and Qsay were killed in an American raid on a house in northern Iraq.[50, 51] Despite an Arab satellite broadcaster playing a message from Saddam ordering his former soldiers to rise up against the occupation, there was no sign of mass unrest in Basra.[52] The only recorded incident around that time was an attack on a Czech field hospital in Basra, when three shots were fired, slightly injuring one Iraqi patient. This was dismissed as an 'occasional shooting'.[53]

More serious incidents occurred on 27 July. In Basra centre, unidentified men attacked a liquor store with RPGs, wounding five people and causing substantial damage.[54] A British military base was also attacked. Some parts of the building were destroyed and the electricity supply to the district was completely cut off.[55] On 6 August, four Iraqis were wounded in a bomb attack targeting British forces at a petrol station just over a mile south of Basra.[56] About 50 miles north of Basra, near the village of al Uzayr, six soldiers on a night-time patrol were fired on from a village. The next night, another patrol took heavy fire from the same village. Troops returned fire. The following morning they returned, supported by Scimitar light tanks. After a heavy firefight, in which a number of Iraqis were killed, they drove the attackers from the village.[57]

THE AUGUST RIOTS

In Basra that same day, 9 August, a British military vehicle came under attack in front of another petrol station, with reports of a grenade thrown. The vehicle caught fire and when reinforcements arrived, they were stoned by a gathering crowd. Soldiers fired shots in the air and baton rounds into the crowd, wounding – it was claimed – at least four Iraqis, including a child. The crowd grew to more than 2,000. Protestors erected barricades of burning tyres in the streets and stoned passing cars.[58]

49. *The Age*, 20 July 2003, 'Shi'ites erupt in protest'.
50. *The Independent*, 22 July 2003, 'Saddam sons "may have died" in major firefight'.
51. Associated Press, 24 July 2003, 'US releases photos of bodies of Saddam's sons'.
52. Associated Press, 23 July 2003, '"Saddam message" heralds fresh attacks on US troops'.
53. CTK News Agency, 23 July 2003.
54. *Voice of the Mujahidin*, in Arabic, via BBC Monitoring International Reports, 28 July 2003.
55. Agence France Press, 28 July 2003.
56. Agence France Press, 5 August 2003.
57. Dan Collins, *In Foreign Fields* (Monday Books), pp. 62–73.
58. Agence France Press, 9 August 2003.

This was the start of two days of rioting as Iraqis protested against power cuts and petrol shortages. In the baking heat, reaching 122°F, with no electricity for air conditioners, tempers had snapped.[59] The military had to use Warriors to safeguard fuel deliveries. At least one Iraqi was killed and an ex-Gurkha, working for a private security contractor, was shot while riding in a car, dying shortly afterwards. Officially, this was a 'terrorist attack'.[60] In the thick of the action was Sadr's Basra representative. The military suspected him of orchestrating the trouble but conceded that, without water, wages, fuel and power, few people in Basra need much encouragement to turn to violence.[61]

Washington Post correspondent Anthony Shadid forecast that the 'worst may be ahead', citing a fishing net salesman Sabah Khairallah: 'One month,' said the gaunt, unshaven and angry Khairallah. That's how long he gave the British forces occupying Basra to bring electricity, water and fuel. After that, more riots would ensue. 'But not with rocks ... with guns.'[62] A young man, Sa'id Ali, echoed this comment. He said, 'If the situation continues like this we are willing to give up our women and children to be martyrs. We will stop buying petrol and start buying weapons to fight.'[63] Fadhila leaders gave the British their own ultimatum, warning them that they had a week to sort out the severe electricity and petrol shortages. But they only threatened more protests.

In complete contrast to the picture offered by the politicians and the emollient official spokesmen ensconced in comfortable and relatively secure quarters in Basra air base, troops were finding it necessary to patrol in Warriors – the antithesis of the preferred 'hearts and minds' approach – only to be greeted with stones and the occasional shooting or RPG attack. Even when it was deemed safe enough for forays in Land Rovers, these had to be escorted by Warriors. Patrolling al Haritha, one of Basra's poorest and toughest neighbourhoods, troops noted constant gun battles between rival factions.[64]

Although Fadhila and the Sadrists were fighting for control of the area, much of the violence was still put down to 'Saddam loyalists'. Hardly at all did it register that Islamic militants were moving into the poorer neighbourhoods, stirring up an already angry and frustrated population against the coalition. It was perhaps unfortunate, therefore, that there had been

59. CNN, 10 August 2003, 'Iraqis riot again in Basra'.
60. *The Daily Telegraph*, 11 August 2003, 'Ex-Gurkha shot dead as Basra rioters protest at power cuts'.
61. *The Daily Telegraph*, 11 August 2003, 'Armoured cars guard petrol stations'.
62. *The Washington Post*, 12 August 2003, 'In Basra, worst may be ahead'.
63. *The Independent*, 13 August 2003, 'Sort out shortages within a week or face more protests, British troops told'.
64. BBC, 15 August 2003, 'Troops' tough challenge in Basra'.

wholesale rioting as this confused the picture, disguising the political activism behind it. It seemed to confirm to the British that they had a 'public order' problem, one they understood and one with which they were comfortable. It was certainly the scenario they wanted to believe.

THE FIRST ROADSIDE BOMB

One day after Sa'id Ali's strident comments, a military ambulance was travelling from Basra, taking a soldier and medical officer Captain David Jones to the hospital in Shaibah. It never arrived. En route, it was hit by a bomb hidden next to a lamp post. Captain Jones was killed, two others were injured and the vehicle was badly damaged.[65, 66]

This was the first time a British soldier had been killed in a bomb attack. It could not have been interpreted as a 'public order' issue. Defence analyst Paul Beaver told the BBC that the incident looked like 'a pre-meditated act of terrorism'. He feared it could signal a change in the way groups opposing the coalition operated in the south. The BBC's correspondent, Mike Donkin, agreed. 'The Basra area will now be considered a dangerous potential flashpoint,' he said.[67] The use of the term 'terrorists' was perhaps instructive. The term 'insurgency' was not then being used – not then and rarely later in public statements.

Without doubt, tension was rising. On Sunday, 17 August, a Danish soldier was killed during a routine overnight patrol after his unit had stopped a truck carrying several Iraqis.[68] This was later reported as a 'friendly fire' incident but it was symptomatic of troops on edge. Almost in passing, it seemed, Ali Hassan al-Majid – 'Chemical Ali' – one of Saddam's most brutal henchmen, had been captured. He was number five on the US forces' most-wanted list.[69]

Quickly following that, on 23 August, three more Royal Military Police were killed, these in an ambush in central Basra. Another soldier was seriously injured. They had all been riding in a Nissan sports utility vehicle, part of a two-vehicle convoy, when it had come under attack from men in a pick-up truck.[70] This brought to 10 the number of British soldiers killed in action since the formal cessation of hostilities.

Dominic d'Angloe, spokesman for Basra's Coalition Provisional Authority, was 'shocked'. 'We thought things had been calming down in the

65. *The Daily Telegraph*, 15 August 2003, 'British officer killed in Basra attack'.
66. BBC, 16 November 2005, 'Officer died in Iraq bomb attack'.
67. BBC, 14 August 2003, 'British soldier killed in Basra'.
68. BBC, 17 August 2003, 'Danish soldier killed in Iraq'.
69. Associated Press, 21 August 2003, '"Chemical Ali" captured by American troops'.
70. *The Observer*, 24 August 2003, *http://observer.guardian.co.uk/iraq/story/0,,1028670,00.html*, online edition.

region,' he said.[71] To military spokesman Lynda Sawyers, it was 'a very unusual and unfortunate incident'. 'We have very good relations with the people of Basra,' she said.[72] At the headquarters at Basra Air Station, officers were 'confident' that British troops were not yet facing an 'established pattern' of attacks.[73] Once again, the mantra of the 'isolated incident' was to the fore. A pattern of denial was emerging.

Experts in London were still divided. Major Charles Heyman thought the attack had been 'just a matter of time'. There was already 'a low-level insurgency campaign against the occupying forces', he said. The word insurgency had emerged. Defence expert Michael Yardley argued against this. 'We were always going to see an extended guerrilla and terror campaign against Allied forces,' he said, adding, 'We can't be sure who is responsible – "holy war" Jihadists, remnants of Saddam Hussein's intelligence or Fedayeen militia.'[74]

For sure, the signals were confused. But the idea of the attack representing the dying spasms of a deposed regime was clearly more acceptable to the Army. It was preferable to the prospect of a Shi'a insurgency. In the former eventuality, the casualty rate, distressing though it was, could be expected to fall. The consequences of an insurgency were unthinkable – even if the signs were there and others could see them. Gary Marx for the *Chicago Tribune* observed: 'More than two weeks after deadly riots hit this southern city, residents are simmering with discontent.'[75]

TROOPS 'DELIBERATELY TARGETED'

On 27 August, Fusilier Russell Beeston died. His six-vehicle patrol had been returning from arresting what were described as – but were unlikely to have been, in a strongly Shi'a area – 'two Saddam loyalists' in Ali al-Gharbi. This was not far from Majar al-Kabir. The patrol had found the road blocked by vehicles and had diverted through a nearby village. The Iraqis anticipated their arrival, an angry crowd blocking their route. When a second group of Iraqis sealed the road behind them, the soldiers fired warning volleys into the air. The Iraqis responded, killing Fusilier Beeston.[76, 77, 78]

71. *The Sunday Mirror*, 24 August 2003, 'No armour, no chance'.
72. *San Francisco Chronicle*, 24 August 2003, '3 British soldiers killed in ambush in Basra'.
73. *The Daily Telegraph*, 26 August 2003, *op. cit.*
74. *The Sunday Mirror*, 24 August 2003, 'No armour, no chance'.
75. *Chicago Tribune*, 26 August 2003, 'Faith in coalition forces fades in wake of Basra ambush, riots'.
76. Associated Press, via *The Independent*, 28 August 2003, 'British soldier killed in Iraq'.
77. BBC, 28 August 2003, 'Sadness at soldier's Iraqi death'.
78. *The Independent*, 31 August 2003, 'On a dusty road 3,000 miles from home, a young unemployed Briton is cut down'.

This was the 50th British death since the start of the invasion, yet an Army spokesman appeared to make light of it. It was the first attack on British forces in that area of Maysan province, he said. 'There is no indication that this attack was deliberately targeted.' Instead, 'it came as the result of a crowd who, we suspect, were orchestrated into expressing their anger at the arrest of a well-known local figure'. Another army spokesman disagreed. He said it appeared the convoy had been lured into an ambush.

The Scotsman was in no doubt, and neither should have been the Army. It was a 'premeditated attack on British troops which reinforced the impression that they are now being regarded as viable targets by Iraqi opposition fighters'. The attack, it wrote, suggested that the low-key British tactics were 'no guarantee of long-term success'.[79] *The Guardian* was of a similar mind, also arguing that 'anger at power shortages, high crime levels and the slow evolution of an Iraqi government' was triggering riots and increasingly violent attacks.[80] The same day, an explosion 'rocked' a British military base in Basra.[81]

At last, or so it seemed, the authorities woke up. Tony Blair gave a 'cautious response to a call for 5,000 extra British troops'. His defence secretary Geoff Hoon admitted the situation was 'serious'.[82] By the end of the week, a 120-strong company was under orders to fly out from Cyprus to spearhead a new deployment. Hoon was expected to announce that about 1,200 soldiers were to be sent and 'defence sources' were saying that another 1,800 would be put on standby to join the mission.

That weekend the Shi'ite Islamic Dawa party – to become a key player in national politics – was targeted. Two men armed with Kalashnikovs had opened fire from a car on its headquarters at 8am in the morning, before coming back three hours later and firing again. After the attacks, a dozen armed party activists set up a road block in full view of British soldiers.[83] They did not intervene – another clue as to the stance of the British. They were showing no enthusiasm whatsoever for holding the ring between rival factions. The militias were going to be allowed to fight it out.

THE SNATCHES ARE ON THEIR WAY

There now came the best clue to the thinking. During the night of 10/11 September, 3,000 miles away in Belfast, convoys of military vehicles were

79. *The Scotsman*, 29 August 2003, 'British troops are prime target in Iraq'.
80. *The Guardian*, 29 August 2003, 'Territorial Army soldier killed in Iraq'.
81. *The Daily Telegraph*, 29 August 2003, 'Blast rocks British military base'.
82. RFE/RL, 4 September 2003, 'Iraq: Blair says security situation is "serious"'.
83. Asia Africa Intelligence Wire, 7 September 2003.

being driven to the docks. Snatches, 178 of them, were on their way to Iraq. The vehicles were drawn from reserve stock or surplus to requirements.[84] In many ways, the equipment the military fields reveals the underlying thinking – a window into the mind of the military. The deployment of the Snatch was very revealing. The Army defined it as a protected patrol vehicle, intended for general patrolling in low-threat areas of Northern Ireland, where heavier armoured personnel carriers could not travel.

Armoured with lightweight Kevlar armour, they were 11 years old, having replaced the steel-reinforced Armoured Patrol Vehicles (APVs) also built on a Land Rover chassis by the now defunct Southampton firm Glover Webb Ltd. For defence, they had a hole in the roof, wide enough for two soldiers to keep guard as 'top cover'. These soldiers had only their personal weapons and occasionally a light machine gun, either impossible to fire accurately from a moving vehicle.

The Snatch was better than the APV, which was also to find its way to Iraq, but not in Army colours. At just over three tons 'combat weight' – nearly two tons lighter than the APV – it was indeed 'nimble' and 'manoeuvrable' but even in Northern Ireland it had been excluded from the 'badlands' such as Armagh and Crossmaglen as being too fragile. There, the tools of the trade had been helicopters and foot patrols. Clearly, the British were not preparing for the possibility of an insurgency in Iraq. Additional troops notwithstanding, they were locked into the idea that they were dealing primarily with a public order situation – peacekeeping rather than fighting a war.

84. BBC, 11 September 2003, 'Land Rover fleet for Iraq'.

Chapter 2 – A very secret war

The shooting phase:
October 2003–June 2004

Our rulers want us to believe that southern Iraq is stable. In fact, Britain is fighting a very secret war.

STEPHEN GREY, *THE NEW STATESMAN*, 31 MAY 2004

The Snatch deployment drew from *The New Statesman* what they thought was an obvious parallel. Iraq would be 'Blair's Northern Ireland'. [1] From a purely practical point of view, though, it looked as if the Snatches were needed. Troops were having to rely on their open 'Wolf' Land Rovers. As had happened in the early days of the Troubles, they were fitting steel mesh to stave off the constant barrages of stones with which they were increasingly greeted.

Unfortunately, the British media was more concerned with the wider political issues of the invasion. This was to dog the reporting. Most of the attention was given to what had been, rather than what was happening. At this time, the obsession was with the 'dodgy dossier', the intelligence that Tony Blair had used to justify going to war. What news did emerge was mainly from the US zone.

There was one exception. As the Snatches docked in Umm Qasr on 4 October, news was breaking of an investigation into the death of an Iraqi national, Baha Musa, killed while in the custody of British troops. [2] Bizarrely, a day before the news broke, *The Independent* in London had run a 'puff' on the Army, headed: 'Charm offensive: the Army's secret weapon in the battle for Iraqi hearts.' The strap proclaimed: 'British soldiers in Iraq have been much praised for their tact.' [3] In some ways, this illustrated the disconnect between the media and reality.

A SHIFT IN MEDIA POLICY

More importantly, it signalled a shift in official media policy. During the invasion and its immediate aftermath, there had been a fairly free flow of

1. *New Statesman*, 20 October 2003, 'Iraq will be Blair's Northern Ireland'.
2. *The Times*, 4 October 2003, 'British soldier questioned over captive's death'.
3. *The Independent*, 3 October 2003, 'Charm offensive: the Army's secret weapon in the battle for Iraqi hearts'.

information. Now, it seemed, an attempt was being made to play down the violence and emphasise the positive aspects of the occupation. It seemed also that the Army was actively collaborating with the politicians in talking down the emerging crisis. The military has substantial resources and capabilities for disseminating publicity, and contacts with many journalists. Had it wanted to convey a message of growing chaos and impending disaster – with the inevitable consequence of raising the political temperature and invoking demands for more resources – it could have done so. It did not. Journalists at the time recall being asked (with more than a hint of pressure) to avoid references to attacks on troops. The dog rolled over and did not bark.

Sweeping through Iraq then was a rumour that the administration was running out of money, leaving compensation to former Iraqi soldiers unpaid. US and British troops found themselves confronting rioting ex-soldiers in both Baghdad and Basra. They were forced to open fire, killing one man in each city.[4] Turmoil in Basra lasted two days. Soldiers fired baton rounds to disperse rioters who had set fire to tyres and were bombarding vehicles with stones. Five people were wounded on the second day.[5]

Two days after these riots, the British headquarters was mortared. It was a minor incident but a sign that the situation might develop into something rather more serious than Northern Ireland. There was also more evidence of an official determination to play down problems. Major Charlie Mayo, the British military spokesman, claimed that the mood in Basra had been 'very calm' in recent days.[6] The next day, a bomb was defused in the residential district of the university of Basra.[7] The following week there was yet another bomb attack on an Army Land Rover, injuring one soldier, and another attack on an Army base, slightly injuring three.[8]

A PROGRESSIVE BREAKDOWN OF LAW AND ORDER

It was now over six months since the British Army had entered Basra. In that period, the British had been unable to set up a credible civilian administration and were attempting to manage the city themselves, a task for which they had neither the resources nor the capabilities. Law and order was deteriorating and the gap left by the absence of security forces was

4. *The Independent*, 5 October 2003, 'Troops kill rioters in Baghdad and Basra'.
5. *The Independent*, 6 October 2003, 'British fire baton rounds to quell riot'.
6. BBC, 8 October 2003, 'Attack on British Basra base'.
7. *Al-Ta'akhi*, Baghdad in Arabic, 9 October 2003.
8. BBC, 13 October 2003, 'Four soldiers hurt in Basra blast'.

being filled by Shi'a militias. These were fighting to establish their own territories and driving minority groups out of the city. At the same time, they were establishing a fundamentalist Islamic regime, challenging a weak and under-resourced administration in Baghdad. Gradually, they were beginning to turn their attentions to the British occupiers, with a nascent insurgency emerging. Army vehicles were routinely being attacked, although little of this was being reported. In the absence of recent fatalities – which were always reported – there was little to trouble the British public. Neither the Army nor the politicians were minded to disturb them.

Nevertheless, the progressive deterioration in law and order was eroding local confidence in the occupation. In October a forlorn band of university academics gathered outside Basra Palace to protest at the inaction over the murder of a colleague. They knew who the killers were but complained, 'The British drive around, but they aren't protecting us'. Frustrated at the lack of security, Basrawis were calling for the British to be tougher. Eventually, it was not the occupiers *per se*, but the failure to stamp out the violence, which became a driver of the insurgency. Lacking protection from the British, the population turned to the militias, supporting those who could provide them with the security they needed.

They had an ally in Sir Hilary Synnott, Britain's senior administrator in Basra, recently appointed head of a new body, the Coalition Provisional Authority in southern Iraq. Under the aegis of the Americans in Baghdad, this had become the – ill-resourced – temporary government. He acknowledged that the security situation was 'tense'. 'We're all targeted', he said.[9] Another ally was Assistant Chief Constable Stephen White, on detachment from Northern Ireland. His assessment was blunt, if self-evident. The UK government was not providing the necessary help to maintain law and order. He had expected a contingent of about 1,500 international recruits. He had a team of just 15.[10]

Yet again this illustrated the 'hands-off' approach – a progressive abrogation of legal duties. Instead of an aggressive attempt to impose law and order, the emphasis was on avoiding confrontation, a strategy of appeasement. Less aggressive vehicles like the Snatch admirably fitted this ethos. Even then, there were more signs of problems to come. On 19 October, further north in Karbala, Sadrists fought with US troops, killing three of them.[11] Five US soldiers had been killed by Shi'a fighters in the past 10 days, when previously the only casualties had come in fighting with

9. *The Independent*, 12 October 2003, 'Crime-racked Basra calls on British troops to get tougher'.
10. BBC, 14 October 2003, 'UK "failing" to police Basra'.
11. *The Independent*, 19 October 2003, 'Shias fight back as resistance spreads'.

Sunnis. If the Shi'a were challenging the occupation, the implications for the British zone were serious. The British could not assume that violence in the north would not eventually be visited on them. The signs are, though, that this is precisely what they did.

That possibility certainly should not have been ruled out when British troops discovered two bomb-making factories and interrupted a major oil smuggling ring, impounding boats and dozens of trucks carrying bootleg oil destined for Iran. They were part of a lucrative 2,000-ton-a-day racket. Significantly, large caches of weapons were also seized.[12] Apart from warning of a nascent insurgency, this also pointed to links between arms and oil smuggling, the finance from the latter being used – quite possibly – to buy arms from Iran.

As further harbingers, that same day, a British soldier was slightly wounded in southern Basra when a bomb detonated as his patrol was passing. Two Iraqis, a contractor and a civilian, were also injured, the contractor seriously. It had been the third incident that week.[13] The evidence of a growing insurgency was mounting. This could not have been renegade Saddam supporters.

A ROSE-TINTED VIEW

Despite this, the military and political establishments held to their rose-tinted view of the occupation. Another example came in the last day of October when Corporal Ian Plank, attached to the SAS, was killed, 'out of area' near the northern town of Mosul. The MoD, as is usual in these cases, refused to comment, saying simply that Cpl Plank had been killed during 'a coalition operation'. When the news of his death emerged on 4 November, it brought extraordinary statements from Geoff Hoon, the defence secretary.

'In most parts of Iraq and in most parts of Baghdad,' he said, 'the security situation is very calm.' He was not, he claimed, complacent about the 'tragic attacks' on coalition forces but was not depressed by the rising casualty rate. UK forces would stay until the Iraqi people were able to take over. They had been welcomed with a 'positive reaction' by Iraqis and more local people were being trained to help with patrols. 'The security situation in and around Baghdad continues to be a cause for concern. But many aspects of normal life in British areas of operation in the south have returned to normal and I've managed to see that for myself when I visited Basra.'[14]

12. AP Online, 25 October 2003.
13. AP, 28 October 2003.
14. BBC, 5 November 2003, 'Iraq situation "calm" says Hoon'.

This was delusional, but may have been delivered purely for domestic consumption. On the other hand, if the military or politicians were preparing worst-case scenario contingency plans, they were keeping them extremely well concealed. The evidence indicated that the strategy of playing down incidents was now locked in, even to the extent of denying incidents when they were reported.

Thus, when four days after the Hoon statement, news broke of yet another bomb attack on a Land Rover in Basra, the MoD denied knowledge of it, admitting only to a minor traffic accident.[15] When reports persisted, the MoD conceded 'an incident involving two vehicles and an improvised explosive device' but denied any injuries.[16] There had, in fact, been a serious attack on two unarmoured Land Rovers, with two injured.[17] The IED had not landed a mortal blow but the attack highlighted the vulnerability of military vehicles. Unless security miraculously improved, it could only be a matter of time before there were more attacks. And there was every reason to expect insurgents to use larger bombs or modify their techniques until they achieved lethal results.

There were certainly no signs of security improving. A day after the Land Rover incident, the Red Cross suffered an attack in Baghdad and closed all its offices in Iraq, including its outpost in Basra. There was now an exodus of aid organisations.[18] *Medecins Sans Frontieres* had already withdrawn from Basra after attacks on its vehicles and buildings. After a major car bomb attack on the UN headquarters in Baghdad the previous month, there was little doubt that aid agencies were being deliberately targeted. 'We are used to working in theatres of war,' said the Red Cross spokesman in Baghdad, 'but this is something else.'[19]

Even then, the insurgents were still targeting the military. On a route frequented by British military vehicles, a bomb had detonated prematurely killing four. Iraqi civilians including two policemen and the man planting the bomb were killed. Nine people, some of them schoolchildren, were injured. There were unconfirmed reports of a second explosion a few hours later.[20] The 'calm' looked somewhat tenuous. Furthermore, while British troops had again escaped, risks were obviously increasing. Yet there were no signs that the Army was taking any specific precautions.

---

15. *Ireland on Line*, 9 November 2003, 'Troops injured in traffic accident in Basra'.
16. BBC, 9 November 2003, 'UK troops targeted in Basra blast'.
17. *Manchester Evening News*, 15 November 2003, 'My brush with death'.
18. *The Daily Telegraph*, 9 October 2003, 'Exodus of aid workers as lawless Iraq becomes too perilous'.
19. *The Independent*, 28 October 2003, 'Red Cross rethinks mission to Iraq in wake of "targeted" suicide bomb attack'.
20. BBC, 11 November 2003, 'Four Iraqis killed in Basra bomb'.

Instead – in public, at least – the official rose-tinted view prevailed. November saw a rash of 'feel good' stories, one telling of how 'the British forces have succeeded in establishing a relatively stable security situation and as a result have found a population that seems mostly welcoming'.[21] On 19 November, though, there was an unconfirmed report that 'a British Army jeep was blown up by a roadside bomb on the road to Safwan, with claims of serious injuries'.[22] A 'resistance' website then claimed that, on 13 December, a 'battle' had taken place in Basra between several tribes armed with RPGs and small arms. A British patrol in the area had been attacked by these groups.[23] On 19 December, Ray Hurst was patrolling outside Basra in a Snatch when it was hit by an RPG. The vehicle rolled over, trapping Hurst. With a badly damaged leg, he was flown back to Britain to have it amputated on Christmas Eve.[24]

On 13 December, Saddam Hussein had been captured by US forces, but – as with the killing of his sons – there had been little street reaction. This further indicated that the violence against British forces came not from Saddam loyalists but from within the Shi'a community. Had that minimal response been tied in with the intensity of attacks, the conclusion can only have been that a new situation was developing. But there was no such analysis. *The Guardian* captured the falsity of the mood with a report headed: 'All quite quiet on the British front.'[25]

Its report was a travesty. On Christmas Eve, Shi'a fundamentalists publicly executed a 48-year-old Christian liquor merchant in Basra's main market place. This was an open, brazen murder, carried out without fear of intervention. Better evidence would be hard to find of how the British had failed to maintain 'public order and safety'. That made at least nine Christian alcohol dealers killed since April. Others had been kidnapped, or had received death threats and beatings. Another alcohol dealer lost two of his Muslim associates to militiamen who had arrived *en masse*, cornering and killing the men. Journalists were also warned that they too would be killed if they were seen again at the house of 'those Christians'.[26]

PROPAGANDA FROM BLAIR VERSUS REALITY

It is hard, then, not to regard a lightning visit by Tony Blair to Basra early in the New Year as a propaganda exercise. Thanking troops for working for 'a

21. *Boston Globe*, 16 November 2003, 'British forces govern Basra with an expert's touch'.
22. *Voices in the wilderness*, 19 November 2003, 'A week in occupied Basra'.
23. Albasrah, 11 December 2003, Resistance report.
24. *The Guardian*, 21 January 2006, 'We drove past ... they detonated an IED. They got me in the leg'.
25. *The Guardian*, 29 December 2003, 'All quite quiet on the British front'.
26. *The Times*, 3 January 2004, 'Smiles for British troops mask bigotry in Basra'.

noble and a good cause' – and saying, incidentally, that British forces would have to remain until at least 2006 – he told the servicemen and women that their help in transforming a dictatorship into a prosperous democracy meant they were the 'new pioneers of 21st century soldiering'. But they had to 'win the peace' before they could consider going home.[27] Once again we had seen the refrain – 'winning the peace'. The military task, in Blair's mind, was clear. He was focused on what he imagined the situation to be, not on what it was becoming. Two days after his peroration, Iraqi police fired at former Iraqi Army soldiers in Basra. At least four people were injured.[28] There were no signs that the 'new pioneers' were anywhere near winning that peace. More to the point, they were not winning the war. They had not yet admitted there was one.

They were also very far from winning in al-Amarah. On 10 and 11 January, the Light Infantry were confronted by major riots in the town which left six Iraqis dead, two shot by British troops after home-made bombs had been thrown from the crowd. At least 11 were wounded. Warriors had to be brought in to quell the violence.[29, 30] On the second day, in an incident which was to have major repercussions, soldiers grabbed two young rioters, dragged them into their compound and administered a beating. This was filmed by a colleague. The mood on that day was recorded by Stephen Farrell: 'the mob was as hostile as any he had seen.' He, his photographer and an Iraqi interpreter had sought refuge with the Army in Abu Naji.[31]

As before, though, greater influences were at play. On 16 January, the Shi'a were again on the march in Basra, this time mustering between 20 and 30,000, demanding early elections for an Iraqi national assembly.[32] Days later in Baghdad, they were doing the same. Over 100,000 protesters marched to the University, their greatest show of political strength since the war.[33] Crucially, the demonstrations were supported by the highest Shi'ite authority in Iraq, the reclusive Iranian-born Grand Ayatollah, Ali al-Husseini al-Sistani. The marchers represented the whole Shi'ite religious establishment, radical and conservative alike.[34] This was no longer a few hundred activists led by dissident clerics. This was a mass movement in the making.

27. *The Independent*, 5 January 2004, 'Blair hails troops in Iraq as "new pioneers of soldiering"'.
28. *Al-Jazeera* TV, Doha, in Arabic, 6 January 2004.
29. *The Independent*, 11 January 2004, 'Iraqi protesters killed in clash with UK troops'.
30. Light Infantry website, undated, 1 LI Operations in OP Telic 3.
31. *The Times*, 14 February 2006, 'On the spot in al-Amarah on day abuse video was filmed'.
32. *The Independent*, 16 January 2004, 'Iraq's Shia Muslims march to demand early elections'.
33. *The Independent*, 20 January 2004, 'Shia protesters step up demand for Iraq elections'.
34. *The New York Times*, 1 February 2004, 'The Shiite surge'.

There were other disturbing signs. A week later, Patrick Cockburn, then in American-occupied Falluja, wrote how roadside bombs had 'become the Iraqi guerrillas' most dangerous weapon'.[35] The specialist military magazine, *Jane's*, agreed. The 'weapon of choice' for the southern insurgents was 'the roadside improvised explosive device or the suicide car/truck bomb', it said.[36] Two days later in Basra, as if to prove the point, a four-year-old Iraqi boy was seriously injured by an IED exploding close to the court of justice, just as a British military convoy was passing.[37] Shortly afterwards, a bomb was used to target a car belonging to a Danish relief organisation, Danchurchaid, wounding two aid workers and several Iraqis.[38] At the end of February, there was another bomb attack on a British Army vehicle.[39]

Before that, there had been a pitched battle when masked men had shot at a group of street alcohol vendors. The attackers pulled up in two police trucks wearing police uniforms and a gun battle ensued in which British troops had intervened, killing two of the 'policemen'.[40] This, though, did not stop the Prince of Wales calling in during the second week of February. He nibbled Welsh cakes and sipped tea from a china cup in Basra Palace but he did not go walkabout.[41] Sir Jeremy Greenstock, the British representative on the CPA, admitted that, 'although largely peaceful', Basra was still full of risks. 'This is not a safe theatre for any visitor,' he said. Underlining that, later in February assailants killed a former judge at his home in Basra, wounding his daughter and son.[42]

March saw a new development – a foiled bomb attempt on a mosque in central Basra as tens of thousands of worshippers were celebrating the festival of Ashura. Later in the day, police arrested two women wearing suicide vests as they marched in a procession. Worshippers in Baghdad and Karbala were not so lucky. At least 170 of them were killed by a series of bombs. US military officials suspected al-Qaeda attempts to foment civil war between the Sunnis and Shi'a.[43] That possibility gravely aggravated the security situation. British forces were now having to contend with the very real possibility of a civil war *and* an insurgency, running side by side.

35. *The Independent*, 26 January 2004, 'How roadside bombs have become the Iraqi guerrillas' most dangerous weapon'.
36. *Jane's*, 20 February 2004, 'The insurgency threat in southern Iraq'.
37. *Middle East online*, 29 January 2004, 'Twin attacks target Iraqi Civil Defence Corps'.
38. *The Washington Post*, 1 February 2004, 'Two attacks kill 14 Iraqis, wound 49'.
39. *AP Online*, 28 February 2004, 'Homemade bomb damages British Army vehicle in Basra'.
40. *The New York Times*, 19 February 2004, 'Killings of vendors in Iraqi city drive alcohol sales off streets'.
41. *The Times*, 9 February 2004, 'A nice day for tea and cakes on the terrace'.
42. *USA Today*, 21 February 2004, 'Bremner: Iraq elections could be 15 months away'.
43. *The Scotsman*, 3 March 2004, 'Bombers kill 170 in bid to spark Iraq civil war'.

Nor was there any let-up in Maysan province. On 5 March, troops on a routine patrol in the village of Qal at Salih, south of Amarah, came under small arms fire. They arrested a gunman and a hostile crowd several hundred strong gathered, the patrol then coming under sustained heavy fire from machine guns and an RPG. A nearby patrol was called in to help, which was joined by a helicopter-borne quick reaction force and four Warriors. In the ensuing firefight, which lasted for several hours, three Iraqis were believed to have been shot dead, four soldiers were injured and two Land Rovers were destroyed.[44, 45] Days later, on 10 March, the Mahdi Army paraded in al-Amarah chanting anti-US and anti-Israel slogans.[46] A 'soft top' Land Rover travelling to Abu Naji was hit by a 'mine'. Four soldiers were injured, one losing a leg.[47] That week, one battalion reported suffering seven combat casualties in al-Amarah.

Back in Basra, two Iraqi washerwomen working for American forces were attacked while going home in a taxi. Four gunmen had surrounded their car, ordered the driver out and shot the women.[48] A week passed and there was another car bomb, this one killing four Iraqis and injuring 15.[49] The following week, troops were dealing with yet another riot. Fourteen soldiers were injured, three seriously. A MoD spokesman spoke of attackers deliberately targeting coalition forces.[50] A week later, British troops were again battling rioters. At least one protester and two soldiers were wounded.[51] Then, to round off the month, another three British soldiers were injured – one seriously – when their vehicle was hit by an IED in az Zubayr.[52]

WHAT THE F*** ARE WE DOING HERE?

That day, a piece by *Times* columnist Matthew Parris was published, its trenchant headline asking: 'Basra: What the f*** are we doing here?'[53] British rule in Basra, Parris wrote, is a sham, conducted from behind sandbags in a deal with Shi'a leaders:

The place is a stinking mess and the townsfolk are unemployed and desperate. There is far less to show for a year's occupation than there should be, and if our (undoubted) attempts to make friends with the locals seem to have brought peace, then that will be because their

44. BBC, 6 March 2004, 'Army inquiry into Iraq firefight'.
45. Light Infantry website, undated, 1 LI Operations on OP Telic 3.
46. BBC Monitoring, *Al-Jazeera*, 10 March 2004.
47. *Northern Echo*, 24 March 2004, 'Family of Iraq bomb blast soldier tell of tears for pal'.
48. *The New York Times*, 12 March 2004, '2 Iraqi women working for US are shot to death in taxi'.
49. *USA Today*, 18 March 2004, 'Basra car bombing kills four'.
50. *The Daily Telegraph*, 22 March 2004, 'British soldiers hurt in Basra blasts'.
51. *The Daily Telegraph*, 30 March 2003, 'Troops fire baton rounds in Basra clash'.
52. BBC, 31 March 2004, 'British soldiers injured in Basra'.
53. *The Times*, 31 March 2004, 'Basra: What the f*** are we doing here?'

Shia leaders have yet to stir the mob against us. Bigger forces are at work than can be tamed with a handshake, and all that goodwill could disappear in a puff of smoke.

Parris, an outsider, could see it, and events were to prove him right. But there was no significant reaction in the UK. While Basra and the southern provinces were sinking deeper into anarchy, at a critical moment – and not for the last time – attention was diverted elsewhere. On 1 April, the world was horrified by the sight of the dismembered and burnt corpses of US civilian contractors hanging from a bridge in Falluja.[54]

Falluja was Sunni heartland, but Najaf was not. It was the centre of the Sadr movement and, on 4 April 2004, in what was part of a coordinated uprising across central and southern Iraq, the Mahdi Army attacked the Spanish-Salvadoran base in Najaf. This was an overt attempt to seize control of the country ahead of a planned transfer of sovereignty on 30 June to a new Iraqi provisional government. By 14 April, a 2,500-strong US force, backed by tanks and artillery, had massed on the outskirts of the city, the start of a series of battles which was to last well into August.[55] Moreover, this was a Shi'a insurgency. The war had started for real and it was only going to be a matter of time before it spilled over into the British sector.

Nevertheless, for a short time, Basra remained relatively quiet. A few hundred demonstrators demanding jobs assembled, but it was left to the local police to control them. British troops kept their distance, although they had armour on standby. The calm was false though, bought by a 'deal' that had British troops returning to their bases.[56] That was the British way – negotiation rather than confrontation. But it did not stop about 150 Sadrists occupying the governor's office in the centre of town, leading to a gun battle with British troops who had surrounded the building. That led to more negotiations, a three-way discussion between the Army, Islamic parties and the governing council. The occupation ended.[57, 58]

Until the 'deal' took effect, on or around 13 April, British troops were still carrying out routine duties. L/Cpl Christopher Balmforth was thus engaged on 8 April, visiting Jameat police station. On leaving in a four-vehicle convoy comprising three unarmoured Land Rovers and one Snatch, his detachment ran into a well-prepared ambush, sustaining small arms and RPG fire. Balmforth's Land Rover was in the lead. His driver was hit twice and the vehicle disabled. After a brisk firefight, in which at least

54. BBC, 1 April 2004, '"Horrific" Iraq deaths shock US'.
55. *The Age*, 14 April 2004, 'Troops mass for Najaf showdown'.
56. *Independent Online*, 3 April 2004, 'Iraqi cops and protesters clash in Basra'.
57. *Bloomberg*, 5 April 2004, 'Iraqi Shiites Occupy Governor's Office in UK-Run Basra'.
58. *The Independent*, 5 April 2004, 'Governor's office stormed in Basra'.

one Iraqi was killed, the insurgents fled. Interestingly, the Snatch was hit by at least 14 rounds, the occupants surviving uninjured.[59] In broader terms, this confrontation illustrated a willingness of the militias to take the Army head-on. But when they did, they were defeated by the superior firepower, training and discipline of British troops. They were to learn, but it was to take some time.

As had become usual, media coverage was slight. The only report at the time seems to have been a very brief item by the BBC.[60] More prominently reported was the street violence. On 21 April, five simultaneous suicide car bombs tore through Basra, targeting police installations. The death toll was estimated at 68. Three city police stations were hit and the police training academy at az Zubayr took two bombs. Four British soldiers were injured there, two seriously. Seventeen Iraqi children died – kindergarten pupils and girls from a local school.[61, 62]

THE MAHDI UPRISING IN AL-AMARAH

Further north, a different tragedy was being played out. From the beginning of April, Maysan province had been bubbling. In al-Amarah, order had broken down. But with the city off the beaten track for most journalists, initial press coverage was minimal. There were only vague references to 'clashes' and troops coming under fire from 'criminal elements'.[63] The BBC offered a one-liner tucked into another story remarking, '… there are reports suggesting that British troops have killed 15 people in two days of violence in al-Amarah'.[64]

There was little more coverage later. *The Times* of 7 April wrote of 'two nights of street battles' which had transformed the town 'from a model of British softly-softly occupation to a dangerous battleground'. Soldiers of the 1st Battalion The Light Infantry, protected by Warriors, had come under fierce attack, six had been injured and the 15 Iraqis killed. This had been 'the highest number killed by British troops in one location since the war ended last year'.[65]

It took the bestselling book, *Sniper One*, first published in 2007, to paint a more accurate picture. Its author, Sgt Dan Mills, wrote:

59. Dan Collins, *In Foreign Fields* (Monday Books), pp. 74–82.
60. BBC, 9 April 2004, 'Commons call after Iraq violence'.
61. *The Guardian*, 21 April 2004, '68 dead in Basra blasts'.
62. PBS NewsHour, 21 April 2004, 'Suicide bombings'.
63. *The Independent*, 5 April 2004, 'Governor's office stormed in Basra'.
64. BBC, 6 April 2004, 'British troops feel the heat in Basra'.
65. *The Times*, 7 April 2004, 'British troops kill 15 in southern fighting'.

The Light Infantry had had two weeks of misery. The main base in the city centre had been repeatedly surrounded by more than 3,000 demonstrators. It started as just an angry protest, but the mob – which was constantly chanting the name of Moqtada al-Sadr – had got increasingly violent. Blast bombs were now regularly coming over the base's walls and armoured Warriors had to be deployed on the streets. Over the last two nights, troops had also fought a series of clashes with Mehdi Army gunmen after coming under small arms fire. Six British soldiers had been injured, and they had killed at least fifteen enemy in return. It was the worst violence British-controlled southern Iraq had seen since the end of the war.

And, wrote Mills, 'it showed no signs of abating at all'.[66] Yet nothing of this was reaching the popular media. It was not even reaching the troops about to be deployed. Mills and his colleagues had been under the impression that they were facing 'peacekeeping duties'. They had intended to leave their heavy weapons back in their UK depot. Only once the advance party had arrived at al-Amarah had they learned of the real situation.

The media were part of the problem. The 8th April saw the BBC recording the departure for Iraq of the very unit to which Sgt Mills belonged, the Princess of Wales's Royal Regiment (PWRR). Its tone was reassuring, referring to 'a tense but calm situation'. The report quoted an armed forces spokesman who only mentioned Basra, stating: 'The coalition forces in this area are starting to let the Iraqis run the area. It is not quite business as usual but we are trying to let them carry on. From what we see on a daily basis we still have the consensus of the population of this area.'[67]

The upsurge of violence moved two 'anti-war' Labour MPs to request a recall of Parliament, then in Easter recess. Like the media, though, they were concerned with the American sector. Hardly mentioned by the media was another attack on a British Land Rover in Basra.[68]

The lack of reporting was partly because no journalists were based in al-Amarah, or even Basra full-time. No one was concentrating on the British sector. The press corps generally stayed in Baghdad, reporting from the relative security of the heavily guarded 'green zone'. Most of their energies were expended on the deteriorating situation in Baghdad and the rest of the US sector. No one was in a position to know much more than what the Army was prepared to divulge – and that was very little. There were even indications that the British were not keeping their US allies fully informed. An American press briefing on 16 April, relying on information supplied by the British, informed reporters that, 'Down in Multinational Division Southeast [it] remains very, very quiet'.[69]

66. Mills, Sgt Dan, *Sniper One* (Michael Joseph, 2007), p. 18.
67. BBC, 8 April 2004, 'Hundreds of UK troops have set off for duty in southern Iraq'.
68. BBC, 9 April 2004, 'Commons call after Iraq violence'.
69. Coalition Provisional Authority briefing, 16 April 2004.

That very day, Muqtada al-Sadr – with Najaf still under siege and the US Army poised to arrest him – appeared in the mosque of the nearby town of Kufa. Pledging to continue the fight, he proclaimed: 'I am ready to face martyrdom.' He was wearing a white shroud, a sign that he was willing to face death.[70] This was a signal for a major escalation in the Mahdi uprising. The British kept it quiet. There was an official report of two soldiers injured in al-Amarah after their convoy had come under fire but an MoD spokesman 'denied there was fierce fighting in the area'.[71]

The BBC also offered low-key reports. One told of three soldiers in al-Amarah injured, one seriously, their Land Rover blown on its back.[72] There was only a brief reference to Lt-Colonel Jonny Gray, commanding officer of the Argyll and Sutherland Highlanders. He had been involved in a 'security incident', his vehicle hit by an RPG which had failed to detonate. But for the presence of Gethin Chamberlain, chief reporter for *The Scotsman*, little more would have been revealed at the time. In a remarkably graphic report published the day after the incident – which happened on 18 April – he tried to bring home the reality. In al-Amarah, there was a war going on.[73]

It took until 2007 for more details to emerge, via Sgt Mills. Colonel Gray had been in a small convoy driving to the relief of a two-Snatch patrol. This had been led by Mills who, with his men had stopped, unwittingly, in front of the Mahdi headquarters and dismounted, then to be attacked by numerous fighters. A Snatch had been disabled and set on fire by an RPG round. A two-Snatch relief force had been ambushed and prevented from getting through. Colonel Gray's 'multiple' had helped keep the attackers at bay long enough for a Warrior-mounted rescue force to arrive.[74]

Mills's account underlined the fragility of the Snatch. But, apart from unarmoured Land Rovers, the only alternative was the Warrior. A thirty-ton tracked war machine, boasting a tank-like turret and a 30mm cannon, this was not exactly designed for routine urban patrols. People, said Mills, hated it. 'It was a beast of a thing, it knocked down their buildings, churned up their tarmac and made a hell of a din. I couldn't blame them.' Nevertheless, after his experience and that of the others on their patrol, along with the 'ever increasing roadside bomb threat', it was decided that Snatches were 'too vulnerable'. They were banned from leaving the base.[75]

70. *The Independent*, 17 April 2004, 'Rebel leader warns US: I am ready to face martyrdom'.
71. *The Daily Telegraph*, 18 April 2004, 'Two British soldiers injured in Iraq'.
72. BBC, 19 April 2004, 'Soldiers caught in roadside bomb'.
73. *The Scotsman*, 19 April 2004, 'Caught in the middle as al-Amarah explodes'.
74. Mills, Sgt D, *op. cit.*, Prologue and pp. 47–73.
75. Mills, Sgt D, *op. cit.*, p. 104.

Nothing of this was made public in early 2004, concealing the marked deterioration in the situation. News coverage continued to be slight. The one useful contributor was Gethin Chamberlain, who wrote another piece, this one based on an exclusive interview with Brigadier Nick Carter the commanding officer of British forces in Basra. It retailed Carter's views that that British troops might have to stay in Iraq for up to 10 years to ensure security.

As so often with pieces of this type, a detail was tucked into the story. In this case, it revealed that, in addition to attacks in the centre of al-Amarah, there had been a separate attack 'just north of Basra'. A large convoy carrying Warrior armoured vehicles had been attacked on the main Route 6 highway running up to Baghdad. A British soldier had lost a leg to an RPG.[76] This was yet another attack on a Land Rover, to add to the many others.

Al-Amarah was to become the epicentre of the Mahdi uprising in the British-occupied zone. Action centred on the compound enclosing the 'Pink Palace' and CIMIC House. From the start of the uprising on 18 April to the end of June, troops faced 320 'contacts' – around five a day. More than 30,000 rounds were fired, a dozen vehicles were lost and 28 soldiers were wounded. Over 100 insurgents were killed.[77] After a short ceasefire in July, hostilities recommenced on 5 August. Until 28 August when another ceasefire was negotiated, the compound took 595 mortar bombs, 57 separate RPG attacks and five barrages of rockets. The troops fought 25 firefights in the city and repelled 86 assaults on the compound.[78]

During this period Pte Johnson Beharry, on two occasions, extracted his Warrior from ambushes, gaining a Victoria Cross for his heroism. So intense was the fighting that by 15 May the BBC noticed something was amiss. 'UK troops in increased fighting,' it reported. There had been a series of ambushes on troops driving from Basra to al-Amarah. One convoy had passed unscathed but a second and third had been attacked. Reinforcements were hit by an IED, mortar fire, RPGs and machine guns. Then, at Friday prayers in Basra, Sheikh Abdul-Sattar al-Bahadli, one of Muqtada's men, called for suicide attacks on coalition forces and offered money for the capture or killing of coalition troops.[79] Anyone who captured female soldiers could keep them as slaves.[80]

On 20 May, a BBC correspondent was reporting that 150 Mahdi Army fighters had ambushed two convoys of Land Rovers. The PWRR battle

---

76. *The Scotsman*, 19 April 2004, 'British troops "in Iraq for ten years"'.
77. *The Sun*, 30 Jun 2004, 'Our boys' unseen war'.
78. Mills, Sgt D, *op. cit.*, p. 338.
79. BBC, 15 May 2004, 'UK troops in increased fighting'.
80. *Voice of America*, 8 May 2004, 'Al-Sadr militia attacks British troops in Basra'.

group had fought back with the help of reinforcements in Warriors.[81] This was the famous 'Battle of Danny Boy', triggered by the inability of Snatches to extricate themselves from the ambushes. Although the PWWR had banned them, not so the Argyll and Sutherland Highlanders. They had been attacked near Majar al-Kabir, close to where the six Military Police had been slaughtered the year before.[82]

Then fighting slackened. With the transfer of sovereignty to the provisional Iraqi government now close, the Americans wanted a peaceful handover. They agreed to lift the siege on Najaf and a truce was negotiated with Muqtada. He promised to abandon violence and engage in the political process, turning his movement into a political party. The Mahdi in al-Amarah then negotiated a ceasefire with Colonel Maer, commanding the PWRR. He promised that no armoured vehicles would be sent into the city unless in self-defence. Also, the number of troop movements would be cut. An agreement was concluded by 18 June and read out in all the mosques.[83] The ban on Snatch patrols was lifted. In time, this was to have fatal consequences.

Resumption of these patrols had been tried in early May, after a massive armoured foray into al Amarah had cleaned out the Mahdi Army headquarters. Troops made bets on how long they would last. The most pessimistic had been 11 minutes, others allowing 24 and 25 minutes. The first (and only) patrol lasted 8 minutes, forced back by an IED attack followed by prolonged gunfire. The ban was immediately re-imposed, not to be lifted again until June.[84]

A few weeks before the ceasefire, journalist Stephen Grey had noted the lack of information coming out of Iraq. He wrote: 'Our rulers want us to believe that southern Iraq is stable. In fact, Britain is fighting a very secret war.' At the height of the fighting, Colonel Maer had told him that nothing too serious was going on. Grey was unconvinced. Writing of the actions in al-Amarah, he concluded, 'The British don't want any of this reported. The impression is of orders from "on high", maybe even from Downing Street, that this kind of fighting is not really happening.' There was, he concluded, 'intense pressure, from Downing Street and Whitehall all the way down, to portray only a rosy view of life'.[85]

This media silence puzzled troops in CIMIC House. But Sgt Mills observed: 'the papers weren't writing about us because they hadn't a

81. BBC, 20 May 2004, 'War "not over" in southern Iraq'.
82. *The Times*, 11 July 2004, 'British soldiers tell of heroics in textbook attack'.
83. *Ibid*.
84. Mills, Sgt D, *op. cit.*, pp. 156–157.
85. *The New Statesman*, 31 May 2004, 'Why you don't hear about our brave boys'.

Scooby any of this was going on. The MoD was doing an excellent job of simply not telling them. The government had local elections in June. The last thing they needed was pictures of big old tanks on the streets of southern Iraq.'[86] Attempts to control the media agenda were also picked up by *The Independent*. Reporting that 800 troops were being sent to Iraq to counter increasing attacks on British forces, it remarked that Tony Blair had delayed the announcement, 'until after the local and European elections on 10 June'. Downing Street denied involvement but former cabinet minister Clare Short alleged there had been a delay because of fears of a voter backlash.[87]

This was the smaller part of it. For months, the politicians and the Army had conspired to keep off the front pages some of the most vicious and extensive fighting in which British forces had been engaged for decades. They had concealed the emergence of a major uprising and the fact that there was now a full-blown insurgency in southern Iraq. They had downplayed the seriousness of events and stifled debate and analysis of a situation which was far from resolved. They were to pay the price, as indeed were the Iraqis. Failing to admit there was a war on, the politicians and the Army could then hardly ask for the resources to fight it. They had sown the seeds of their own failure.

THE FIRST SNATCH FATALITY

Amid the disjointed, patchy coverage of operations, it had been easy to miss an historic event on 28 June 2004. Then, Fusilier Gordon Gentle, aged 19, was killed by an IED in a blast that also injured two other soldiers. He had been riding 'top cover' in a convoy from Basra Palace. Not all the contemporary reports mentioned a vehicle type, and the BBC identified an 'armoured Landrover'.[88, 89] Fusilier Gentle was the first soldier to be killed in a Snatch. The 'very secret war' had claimed its first victim.

86. Sgt Dan Mills, *op. cit.*, pp. 173–174.
87. *The Independent*, Friday, 28 May 2004, 'Blair deploys marines as attacks intensify'.
88. *The Independent*, 29 June 2004, 'British soldier killed in Basra bomb attack'.
89. BBC, 28 June 2004, 'UK soldier killed in Basra attack'.

Chapter 3 – Hit and run

The emergence of guerrilla tactics:
the scourge of the IED

We also need to consider less conventional forms of threat. For instance, impro-
vised bombs have obvious advantages for hostile groups who cannot hope to
prevail in an outright military confrontation.

MINISTRY OF DEFENCE – JULY 2002[1]

Although the main action was in al-Amarah during the first phase of the Mahdi uprising of April 2004, it is tragically ironic that the first soldier to be killed in action during that period had been stationed in Basra. This under-lined the fact that Basra was also a very dangerous place for British troops.

Fighting had erupted in Basra in early May after Sheikh al-Bahadli had offered money for the capture or killing of coalition troops. Several hun-dred Mahdi Army fighters had taken to the streets, attempting to seize key buildings and setting up checkpoints. Media coverage of events in Basra had, at the time, been as thin as the coverage of al-Amarah. The impression conveyed was of occasional 'skirmishing' and isolated outbreaks of violence. One report gave the flavour of this, telling of four British soldiers injured, three in a 'grenade attack' on a vehicle, and of Iraqis killed – but with no context or attempt to paint the bigger picture.[2]

Such reports belied the intensity of the fighting. The nature of an insur-gency – at least in its early stages – is that fighting tends to be sporadic, heavily localised and on a small scale. But it is still an insurgency. An unre-ported engagement took place on Saturday, 8 May 2004 when L/Cpl Darren Dickson was part of a detachment escorting six water tankers from Shaibah to Basra Palace. On the outskirts of Basra, the convoy had met with two ambushes in quick succession. This was not the only convoy to be attacked. 'Everything was kicking off that morning,' said Dickson, 'everyone was getting hit.'[3] That indeed was the case. Over the weekend, there were more than 100 engagements. Eleven British soldiers and one Dane had been injured.[4]

1. Ministry of Defence, Strategic Defence Review: A New Chapter – July 2002.
2. BBC, 9 May 2004, 'Basra "calm" after grenade attack'.
3. Dan Collins, *In Foreign Fields* (Monday Books), Darren Dickson, pp. 127 *et seq*.
4. Hansard, 10 May 2004, Column 21.

In addition, an oil pipeline had been attacked, slowing the flow of Iraqi oil for export by 25 per cent. This sabotage could have been economically motivated. To feed the thriving smuggling racket, oil pipelines were often attacked simply to force oil producers to use road tankers, giving smugglers more opportunities to hijack consignments.[5] Nor had this been the only attack on oil installations. In late April, there were three suicide boat attacks on the offshore oil terminal, killing at least two US sailors and injuring four more.[6]

Adding to the general misery, internecine strife had also continued. On 4 June, 16 people were killed in clashes between the Badr-dominated local police and guards of a mosque held by Sadr activists. This came hours after another car bomb explosion, this one near an outdoor market in the city centre, killing about 27 people and wounding over 60 others.[7]

MORTARING AND ROADSIDE BOMBS BECOME MORE FREQUENT

Nevertheless, to the relief of the British, attempts by the insurgents to take control of Basra by direct confrontation failed – as they had in al-Amarah where they had sustained heavy losses. But there was an unwarranted self-congratulation on the part of the British, with some suggestion that the Mahdi Army was a spent force.[8] Once again the signs were being misread. The lack of success had more to do with the Badr Corps and Fadhila, neither of which had been prepared to back an uprising.

Furthermore, not immediately recognised by the British, the insurgents were taking time out to rebuild their strength, and had learned from their experience. Increasingly, they would rely on hit-and-run tactics in the classic guerrilla war mould. Evidence of this came on 14 June, as defence secretary Geoffrey Hoon visited troops in Basra. There was a mortar attack on an Army base at the former naval academy. Two British soldiers were wounded.[9] Then, on 19 June, a Portuguese security guard and an Iraqi policeman were killed when a bomb hit a car. The blast flipped the car over several times, a sign that the attackers were using more powerful bombs.[10] Thus, when Fusilier Gordon Gentle's Snatch had been targeted, it should not have come as a surprise.

5. *The New York Times*, 11 May 2004, 'US destroys headquarters of rebel cleric in Baghdad'.
6. *The Independent*, 25 April 2004, 'Suicide bomber boats explode in attack on Basra oil terminal'.
7. *Xinhua* News Agency, 4 June 2004, 'Sixteen people killed in clashes in Sunni mosque in Basra'.
8. *The Daily Telegraph*, 27 May 2004, 'The Army's stern words beat Sadr's men in Basra'.
9. AFP, 14 June 2004, 'NZ Army comes under mortar attack in Iraq'.
10. *Independent Online*, 19 June 2004, 'Policeman, guard killed in Basra bomb blast'.

Nor was this attack on a British military vehicle a one-off. On 3 July, a British soldier was wounded when a Land Rover escorting a convoy had been attacked near az Zubayr. It was on its way to Basra along a road specially built to avoid potential ambush areas.[11] More evidence of the hit-and-run strategy came when insurgents fired rockets at a government building in central Basra.[12] By then, British forces had been under frequent mortar bombardment for the past three months, 'despite assurances from the Army' that the situation was 'quiet'. In the latest incident, a local businessman had been killed and several other Iraqis seriously injured, including a two-year-old boy. In three months, the Cheshire battlegroup based in Basra had suffered 93 separate attacks from rockets, mortars, RPGs and gunfire. On the night of the latest mortar attack, there had been rockets fired at three military camps in and around the city. Only 'a combination of luck and vigilance' had kept casualties low. Many believed the attacks were becoming more expert and potentially more lethal.[13]

Despite this, in a gesture of supreme optimism the British opened a new consulate in the Basra Palace complex. It symbolised, said Ambassador Edward Chaplin, 'a new relationship for Britain with Iraq: a relationship based on partnership; on a shared vision for a peaceful, prosperous and democratic Iraq; and on friendship and co-operation between the peoples of two sovereign nations ...'[14] The insurgents promptly assassinated the interim Basra governor.[15] Within the week, two Iraqi women working for British forces as cleaners at Basra Air Station were murdered on their way to work. Two others were injured. This was part of the general 'reign of terror' – anyone working for coalition forces was targeted.[16]

The attacks on the British were nonetheless going through a transitional stage. The insurgents were still occasionally taking on the troops in open gun battles. On 5 August, for instance, when British troops arrested four Sadr activists as part of a 'routine security check,' militiamen took to the streets. Troops responded in armoured vehicles and tanks, parking them around Sadr's offices and elsewhere in the city. Shortly afterwards a fire-fight broke out lasting 15 minutes.[17] *Al-Jazeera* claimed that three militia had been killed, with three British military vehicles damaged. That latter claim was denied by a British spokeswoman.[18] Unlike on previous occasions,

11. *Al-Jazeera* TV, 3 July 2004.
12. *Associated Press*, 4 July 2004.
13. *The Independent*, 6 July 2004, 'British forces face frequent mortar bomb attacks in "quiet" Basra'.
14. *Iraqi News*, 23 July 2004, 'British Consulate General opens in Basra'.
15. *The Age*, 21 July 2004, 'Gunmen assassinate Basra governor'.
16. AP Worldstream, 21 July 2004, 'Insurgents kill two Iraqi women working for British forces in Basra'.
17. BBC, 5 August 2004, 'UK forces fight militia in Basra'.
18. *Al-Jazeera* TV, in Arabic, 5 August 2004.

though, mass attacks on military bases did not materialise, leaving the situation 'tense but calm'. However, direct confrontation did continue, four days later killing a British soldier, the first in action since Cpl Plank the previous October.[19]

The casualty was Pte Lee Martin O'Callaghan. He had been part of an operation to rescue a patrol ambushed by Mahdi militiamen. That patrol, in two Snatches, had come under heavy small arms and PRG fire in an elaborate and carefully planned ambush. The soldiers had to abandon their vehicles and hold out in nearby buildings. Pte O'Callaghan had been standing up in the back of a Warrior as his detachment fought their way towards the stranded patrol when he had been hit and killed. Others were injured.[20] Triumphant Mahdi fighters captured the Snatches and set them alight, the results photographed by local media and beamed round the world.

A mere three days later, on 12 August, the violence claimed another soldier's life – Pte Marc Ferns. This time it was a radio-controlled IED packed with ball-bearings. Ferns was driving a Warrior, normally reckoned to be safe, but one of the ball-bearing had shattered his skull.[21, 22] This exposed the fatal weakness of the Warrior. With no air conditioning, in the heat of the Iraqi summer, drivers had to keep their hatches open for ventilation. It took only five days more before the next fatality, the third in less than 10 days. The soldier was L/Cpl Paul Thomas, killed when his patrol had been attacked – another open confrontation.[23] The engagement had started when a convoy of two Snatches had been forced to halt after one of the vehicles had broken down. Very quickly, they had been 'pounced on' by Shi'a militiamen. Lt Will Follett, in the second Snatch, took up the story:

There were around 60 militiamen armed with heavy machine-guns, RPGs, and AK47s. We had 24 men. We were almost surrounded. Our only exit route was back the way we came. We were outnumbered by a determined enemy only too happy to die for their cause. There were rounds flying all over the place and one grazed the back of my helmet – which I didn't realise at the time.

In this firefight, Thomas was shot in the neck. The patrol was eventually rescued by a Warrior but not before Cpl Tony Wilson had engaged enemy RPG positions 15 feet from his Land Rover, despite a missile having struck his windscreen and failing to detonate. Another soldier, Pte Naz Qureshi, had cleared a building of gunmen using grenades. 'That was the hairiest

19. BBC, 9 August 2004, 'UK soldier dies in Basra battles'.
20. *Soldier* Magazine, October 2004.
21. *The Scotsman*, 17 November 2005, 'Scottish soldier who died as he wrote home'.
22. *The Daily Telegraph*, 13 August 2004, 'Mother calls for troops' return'.
23. *The Independent*, 19 August 2004, 'British soldier killed in Basra was his platoon's "backbone"'.

situation I've been in in Iraq – and there's been quite a few like it,' said Lt Follett.[24] Nor had it been the only 'situation' that day. Earlier, what were described as 'foreigners' travelling in three British vehicles had to be rescued by British troops after their convoy was hit by a bomb in the centre of the city. No one was hurt in this incident.[25]

As the siege of Najaf came to a climax, the Basra commander of the Mahdi Army threatened to attack the oil infrastructure of southern Iraq, saying: 'We will not leave a single coalition base untouched and we will attack oil wells.' To emphasise the threat, the Mahdi Army torched the offices and warehouses of the Southern Oil Company.[26] Meanwhile, the new British consulate was taking a hammering. It had been under siege almost as soon as it had opened, suffering almost daily mortar attacks. The only way in or out of the mission, sealed off by 12ft-high concrete walls, was by military helicopter and the British Army now moved around Basra only in armoured vehicles. There had been a 'lockdown' at the mission as Sadr militiamen had taken control of large areas of the city. The 50 members of staff were protected by 60 former Gurkhas and a company of soldiers. A further detachment of troops from the Black Watch was also guarding the area, with more than a dozen Warriors in reserve. The roofs of containers, converted to accommodation, were protected by sandbags and blast walls. At night, everyone had to wear body armour.[27]

The emphasis on force protection inevitably meant that the effort devoted to routine patrols was reduced. But as the Army progressively vacated the streets, the insurgents were able to go onto the offensive. British bases started to suffer continuous hit-and-run attacks. In the three months to mid-August, they had suffered more than 1,000 individual bombardments, causing two serious injuries. What was also evident was that Basra residents were feeling abandoned. In the absence of British troops, the militias had stepped into the power vacuum, roaming the streets with RPGs and AK47s. Vital reconstruction had been halted and the citizens were suffering deprivations daily. But, the military was insisting that its strategy of waiting out the barrage was preferable to attacking the Mahdi Army. This, they argued, 'would lead to an inevitable escalation of violence and the deaths of civilians'.[28]

Soon, though, the worst of the violence was over – for the time being. The siege at Najaf was lifted. Muqtada concluded his agreement to demo-

24. *Soldier* Magazine, October 2004.
25. *The Scotsman*, 19 January 2004, 'Soldier dies as British troops clash with Sadr's Basra army'.
26. *The Age*, 20 August 2004, 'Al-Sadr refuses to disarm'.
27. *The Daily Telegraph*, 27 August 2004, 'British envoys under siege in Basra'.
28. *The Daily Telegraph*, 30 August 2004, 'British trapped in Basra vacuum'.

bilise his militia and engage in the political process preparatory to fighting elections scheduled for the January. Crucially, there had been no direct agreement between the provisional Iraqi government and Sadr. There thus had been no Iraqi government decision to declare a ceasefire. That had been the initiative of Sistani, brokered directly with Sadr.

As the dust settled, disturbing evidence emerged that the Mahdi Army was no longer relying on salvage from abandoned army dumps. New Iranian-made mortars, RPG launchers, machine-guns and explosives had been found in Najaf.[29] Similar weapons had been found on rooftops of state-run offices in al-Amarah. There was also growing evidence of an extensive weapons-smuggling network across the Iranian border. Rifles, pistols and munitions were being hidden under consignments of water melons and tomatoes, while launchers, rockets and mortars had even been placed in coffins.[30]

With this, few believed the Mahdi uprising had ended. It had not – for Muqtada, this was merely a tactical retreat. His objectives had not changed and he had no intention whatsoever of disbanding his militia. Yet, despite the robust line taken by the Iraqi government, the British met with representatives of Muqtada and formally signed another truce agreement in al-Amarah on 3 September.[31] Part of the deal, repeating the agreement to keep Warriors out of al-Amarah, had been to suspend legal suits filed against many prominent supporters of al-Sadr.[32] After their murderous rampage, the insurgents were walking away with an indemnity from the British, free to rebuild their strength.

A CHANGE IN POLICY

Nor did it take long for the streets of Basra to see violence again. This time, it was initiated by the British, but it was not directed at restoring law and order to the streets. The underlying objective was force protection.

The first event, in a sequence, was when a company of the PWRR had surrounded Sadr's offices on the eastern bank of the Shatt al-Arab waterway. Iraqi policemen then stormed the compound, the first move against one of his buildings.[33] A few days later, on 18 September, British troops were

---

29. *Al-Sharq al-Awsat*, London, 31 August 2004, 'Iraqi defence minister says Iranian-made weapons found in Al-Najaf'.
30. *Al-Mada*, Baghdad, 12 September 2004.
31. BBC, 21 September 2004, 'Basra: British troops in Iraq's "peaceful" city'.
32. *Al-Manar* Television, Beirut, 3 September 2004, 'Al-Sadr supporters, British troops sign truce accord in southern Iraq'.
33. *The Daily Telegraph*, 29 September 2004, 'Fatal attack on troops "revenge for Sadr raids"'.

again out in force, briefly occupying the main Sadr offices in Basra.[34] It took the entire Cheshire battle group, some 500-strong, supported by Warriors and Challenger tanks. This, though, had been provoked by the Mahdi Army's response to the earlier raid. Incensed by the intrusion, its fighters had attacked from their own building a passing military supply convoy, showering it with RPGs and small arms fire, seriously injuring a soldier.

The British, in the interests of their own self-defence, could hardly have not reacted. What began as an operation to arrest the gunmen ended with the battle group uncovering an 'Aladdin's cave of arms'. The grounds of the building had been booby-trapped with remote control bombs which had to be defused before troops could enter. Not a single fighter was found inside the building although, on the streets, gunmen engaged British troops in a series of skirmishes lasting nearly 16 hours.

The intent was revealed by Capt Stuart Macaulay, who had taken part in the action: 'This was an own-goal by the militia,' he admitted. 'If they hadn't attacked our convoy British forces wouldn't have raided the building and we wouldn't have found this goldmine of weapons.'[35] It also says something of the attitude of the Army that it expected the weapons seizures to have dented the Mahdi Army's ability to fight. The extent of the insurgency was still being underestimated.

Predictably, the attacks continued – they were inevitable. The initiative had been ceded to the insurgents. On 24 September, the unremitting bombardment of the British Consulate caused a small fire while, in northern Basra, a British patrol came under mortar attack.[36] This time there were no casualties, but the luck was not to hold.

By 28 September, despite no evidence that the insurgency had in any way been contained, Snatches had been back on the streets for a fortnight. Come what may, it seemed, the Army was determined to go through with its 'softly-softly' policy. Inevitably, the Mahdi Army struck. Targeting a supply convoy escorted by two Snatches in the south-west of Basra, fighters hit the leading vehicle with an RPG. Soldiers trying to rescue the injured then came under fire. Cpl Marc Taylor and Gunner David Lawrence were killed.[37, 38] There was no doubt that the attack had been carried out in revenge for the raid on the Sadr HQ.

---

34. *The Age*, 18 September 2004, 'British troops take al-Sadr's Basra HQ'.
35. *Soldier* Magazine, October 2004.
36. *Al-Diyar* TV, Iraq, 24 September 2004.
37. BBC, 28 September 2004, 'British soldiers killed in Iraq'.
38. BBC, 30 September 2004, 'MoD names second killed soldier'.

THE 'SOFT HAT' POLICY CONTINUES

Still an Army spokesman pledged to continue the 'soft hat' policy. Security had improved significantly in the past month, he claimed, even though two or three incidents involving improvised explosive devices were still being reported every week. But the real plan, revealed the spokesman, was to concentrate on supporting the Iraqi security services. Troops were training the Iraqi National Guard to 'take on the responsibility of all security'. More and more, the Army was relinquishing the initiative. With it went its authority and its grip on the situation.

The 'improving security', therefore, was not a sign of success. It was exactly the opposite. A *Washington Post* journalist, commenting on a similar 'calm' in the US sector, revealed why such claims were illusory. 'There are fewer attacks here because we're out on the road less,' a Marine officer had told him. 'But you shouldn't conclude from that that things are any safer.' That strategy, officials noted, had allowed insurgent cells to expand.[39]

That analysis was, in part, shared by *The Times*. It viewed the latest attack as dispelling any notion that the occupation of Iraq would be benign. The paper also observed that British troops had 'in the past' retreated to their bases to avoid confronting the militants and inflaming the insurgency. On the other hand, the 'militants' had already shown that they would make Iraq ungovernable, leaving Britain to face a 'new Iraqi conflict'.[40] But, if casualties were to be reduced, pulling troops back to their camps and handing over security to the Iraqis – whether they were ready or not – was the preferred option.

As long as the British were out and about, they were attacked with monotonous regularity. But the roadside bomb was now becoming the major threat. On 6 October, such a bomb exploded as a patrol was crossing a bridge leading to Basra airport. The blast sent an Iraqi taxi tumbling off the bridge onto railway tracks below. The driver and his six passengers were killed and four Iraqi police in a patrol car were hurt. The troops escaped injury.[41] The intended targets were just as fortunate six days later when a bomb was planted in a rubbish bin outside the British Consulate. It blew up as a British convoy of three civilian cars drove out. No casualties were reported.[42]

The end of October saw the Black Watch regiment sent north for a month into the US zone. They assumed a blocking position outside Falluja

39. *The Washington Post*, 26 September 2004, 'Violence in Iraq belies claims of calm, data show'.
40. *The Times*, 29 September 2004, 'More British soldiers die in Iraq keeping peace than in war'.
41. AP Worldstream, 6 October 2004, 'Suicide car bomb kills 10 Iraqis northwest of Baghdad'.
42. AP Worldstream, 12 October 2004.

to prevent insurgents escaping from advancing American troops. This deployment was to cost them four dead. Three were killed on 4 November by a suicide bomber at a vehicle checkpoint protecting an operation to recover two Warriors, one disabled by a roadside bomb and another by RPG fire. Eight were also hurt by mortar rounds.[43] The fourth, Pte Pita Tukatukawaqa, was killed by an IED while riding in a Warrior on 8 November, the blast so powerful that it blew the vehicle off the road, taking the wheels off one side.[44]

Pte Tukatukawaqa was the last British soldier to be killed in action in 2004, but he was not the last Briton – nor indeed the last Iraqi. On 1 November, the insurgents launched rockets at Basra air base. Fortunately, there were no injuries to British troops. Two members of the Iraqi national guard were considerably less fortunate when they were blown up by a car bomb in Basra on 3 November. Another three policemen were wounded by a bomb targeting the police chief. Seven national guardsmen were injured when yet another car bomb targeted the National Guard commander.[45] On 7 November, a British civilian security employee and a South African colleague were killed in a bomb attack near Basra.[46]

Around this time, there was beginning to be evidence of Iraqi police action, independent of their British 'minders'. On 3 December, there was a gun battle between police and gunmen in az Zubayr. Two gunmen were killed and one arrested after they had been found riding in a booby-trapped car. There was also violence being directed at the coming election when, in a district west of Basra, 'unknown assailants attacked an election centre, throwing a hand grenade at the centre and firing a machine-gun from a speeding car'.[47]

There was also a revealing event the following week, on 8 December. Iraqi National Guard and police forces stormed the house of a member of the Association of Muslim Scholars in Basra, a Sunni organisation and also a hotbed of extremist religious supporters of the insurgency. This was not merely – or even – part of the factional 'ethnic cleansing' but an attack on the heart of the Sunni insurgency. Their 'target' was not at home, but this raid was part of a bigger operation. Raids were also made against several members of the association in the city. They were coordinated with the storming of the al-Imam al-A'zam College in northern Baghdad, also by

43. BBC, 5 November 2004, 'Blair tribute to Black Watch dead'.
44. BBC, 9 November 2004, 'MoD names soldier killed in Iraq'.
45. *The Age*, 3 November 2004, 'Two killed in attacks on Iraqi forces'.
46. Kuna News Agency, 7 November 2004, 'Briton killed in Iraq car bomb attack'.
47. *Al-Jazeera* TV, 3 December 2004, 'Two gunmen killed, one arrested; Basra election centre attacked'.

Iraqi security forces. In the south, there seems to have been no involvement by the British.[48]

ACTION IN MAYSAN

Despite the reactive stance in Basra, British forces had not been not idle in Maysan, where something of a proactive policy still survived. The PWRR had been replaced by the Welsh Guards and, with the Iraqi police, they had enjoyed early success in intercepting an insurgent convoy loaded with anti-tank mines, mortars and rockets headed for al-Amarah.[49] They were also preparing to re-enter Majar al-Kabir, which had been left largely to itself since the murder of the RMPs back in June 2003, a 'no-go area' for coalition forces. The Mahdi Army had taken over and it had become a 'haven for bandits and fighters'.[50]

The Iraqi police were also active. On 14 December, they shot dead two 'road bandits' on the infamous Route 6 between al-Amarah and Basra. They arrested 12 others after a pursuit that led to the seizure of large quantities of arms.[51] The attacks on the British continued. The British Consulate had suffered another mortar attack late in the evening on 12 December. There were no casualties, but the sense of siege intensified. A police station had also been mortared earlier in the day, followed by a gunfight between attackers and police.[52] A day later, British troops arrested the driver of a sewage tanker after explosives had been discovered in the vehicle by sniffer dogs. It had been heading to the British Consulate.[53]

A MEDIA FAMINE

What was still remarkable, though, was how little of this was getting to the British public. Significant events were happening almost daily, such as on 19 December. Then, British troops fought a major gun battle with insurgents in az Zubayr. A police captain was caught in the crossfire and killed. There had also been an 'incident' involving 'a multinational convoy and a civilian vehicle'. That much detail was recorded, oddly enough, by the Irish media.[54]

48. *Al-Jazeera* TV, 8 December 2004.
49. *Western Mail*, 6 December 2004, 'Welsh troops intercept weapons convoy'.
50. *The Daily Telegraph*, 12 December 2004, 'Welsh Guards seek justice for Redcap killings'.
51. Kuna News Agency, 14 December 2004, 'Iraqi police kill two bandits and arrest 12 others in Amarah'.
52. MENA News Agency, Cairo, 12 December 2004.
53. *Al-Diyar* TV (Iraq), 15 December 2004.
54. *Ireland Online*, 19 December 2004, 'Police officer killed in clashes'.

Had there been more media coverage of operational issues, perhaps history might have been different. That was not to be. For instance, not for the British public was the news that, the same day of the az Zubayr clash, Iraqi police and British troops had seized a cache of missiles and other weapons in the centre of Basra. The arsenal included more than 450 mortar rockets and 'cannonballs' – according to a local agency report – and a number of other weapons. A military spokesman pointed out that a large number of missiles were ready to be used. Also, Iraqi police backed by multinational forces seized arsenals in the al-Sharsh village in northern Basra. These included a large number of 'explosions', mines, equipment for manufacturing bombs 'and more than 5,000 different bullets'. [55]

Similarly, on 23 December, nothing was reported in the UK when seven armed men were arrested and large stockpiles of weapons seized from a farm in Maysan province. A search operation by Iraqi police had led to the discovery of a number of RPG launchers, 52 rounds, 35 grenades, a light machine gun, 107mm mortar rounds and a mortar, in addition to explosives and automatic weapons. The detainees, the police said, were responsible for major arms smuggling, supplying operations in southern Baghdad. [56]

These events were reported by an obscure Kuwaiti news agency. Although the seizures were regarded as success, as with drug smuggling to the UK, this did not indicate that trafficking was being prevented. For every one consignment detected, many more got through. These reports, therefore, simply confirmed that there was a major flow of arms coming through the highly porous Iraq–Iran border. It also positioned Maysan province, and the city of al-Amarah, as a key supplier to the Shi'a insurgency throughout Iraq. And, if arms were being supplied, they were going to be used.

Evidence of that was ever-present. On 31 December, in al-Amarah, two military vehicles were damaged by an explosion in front of the British headquarters, which also came under mortar attack. [57] The same day, a British base in Basra was attacked. Insurgents fired three RPGs and two mortar bombs, fortunately causing no injuries or damage. [58] Then a bomb wounded four people including two policemen, also in Basra. The blast damaged a police car and another vehicle. [59]

---

55. Kuna News Agency, 19 December 2004, 'Multinational forces seize missiles, other weapons in Basra'.
56. Kuna News Agency, 23 December 2004, 'Seven armed men arrested, stockpiles of weapons seized in Basra'.
57. *Al-Jazeera* TV, 31 December 2004, 'Raid on UK vehicles in southwest Iraq'.
58. Kuna News Agency, 31 December 2004, 'Multinational forces position attacked in Basra'.
59. Kuna News Agency, 31 December 2004, 'Four wounded in Basra blast'.

A NEW YEAR AND NO RESPITE

Nor did the New Year bring any respite. On 1 January, a bomb went off near the al Khawrah Park in Basra, seriously wounding three civilians.[60] The British Consulate was mortared again.[61] More weapons caches were found, two in central Basra on 9 January, but the bombing continued.[62] On 10 January, two nearly simultaneous suicide car bombs exploded near Iraqi police stations and a suicide bomber drove his car into the head-quarters of the Fadhila party causing extensive damage.[63, 64]

What confused the issue though was the 'bigger picture' in Iraq. The number of incidents in Basra and the rest of the British zone was relatively modest by comparison with the rest of Iraq, where they were approaching 70 a day. But, while the Americans were actively taking on the insurgents, in Basra, the militias were in charge. Badr, for instance, had been formally recognised as a legal entity. Many of its officials were in high positions in the police and administration. Much of the lower-ranking police corps had been taken over by the Sadrists, while Fadhila had maintained its grip on oil production.

Any hiatus in the level of violence, however, was not attributable to the activities of the British forces. Simply, Muqtada was not yet strong enough to challenge either of the established militias and had lost too many men to take on the British in open battle again. He needed to rebuild the strength of his milita. Thus, in the British sector, he was consolidating his grip over Maysan province. There were not, therefore, the same dynamics in the south – as long as the British did not interfere, which they were being careful not to do.

That left the ordinary citizens of Basra, and particularly the secular middle-classes, without a champion. They not only had to suffer a rising tide of violence, they were also suffering from fuel shortages and power outages. Residents now received electricity only four hours a day, the least in anyone's memory, before or after the invasion.[65] Although there were still the occasional demonstrations, they were small-scale and without the passion which had characterised the unrest of the previous year. Many of those who might have protested were either cowed into submission or had fled, joining the ever-growing ranks of refugees.

60. *Al-Diyar* TV, Baghdad, 1 January 2005.
61. *Al-Jazeera* TV, 2 January 2005.
62. Radio Dijlah, Iraq, 9 January 2005.
63. CNN, 10 January 2005, 'Car bombs target Basra police stations'.
64. *Al-Sharqiyah* TV, 12 January 2005.
65. *New York Times*, 19 January 2005, 'Rebuilding of Basra progresses, but it's harder than expected'.

The progenitors of the violence were not always easy to pin down. On 16 January, three Basra voting centres, slated for use at the end of the month for the elections, were blown up. Mortar bombs were lobbed at a brace of others. There were also political assassinations. The 18 January saw one of the candidates from interim prime minister Allawi's party murdered.[66] This was not unexpected and, that day, 650 additional British troops arrived in Basra to help maintain security.[67] Attacks on police stations continued, one on 20 January when armed men exchanged fire with its guards.

That day, 10 days before the elections, past actions were to revisit the British. Soldiers involved in the Camp Bread Basket abuse incident in May 2003 were being court-martialled in Germany. Photographs were released to the media.[68] Next day, a car approached the main entrance of the Shaibah logistics base. Two British military vehicles tried to stop it but a bomb hidden in the car detonated, injuring nine troops and several Iraqis. The al Qaeda group led by Abu Musab al Zarqawi claimed responsibility.[69] Significantly, the attack had been out in the desert, rather than in Basra where the militias were dominant.

As the elections approached, al Zarqawi declared 'a fierce war on this evil principle of democracy', threatening those who voted with death. He held little sway in the south. Sistani issued fatwas instructing all Iraqis, including women, to vote. That ensured a fair wind for the elections in the south.[70] When they arrived on 30 January, they were peaceful. In time – it took until 7 April to appoint him – they were to bring a new prime minister, Ibrahim al-Jaafari, formerly the main spokesman of the Dawa Party and one of the two vice-presidents under the interim government. But he had won the prime ministerial nomination by only one vote, thanks to the support of Muqtada al-Sadr.

Overshadowing the elections for the British was the loss of an RAF Hercules C-130 transport. It had been shot down on an 'administrative' flight from Baghdad to Camp Anaconda, the huge US airbase in Balad, about 20 miles north-west of Baghdad. Ten servicemen were killed, the largest loss of life in one incident to date.[71] This was in part attributed to the failure to fit the Hercules with fire-retardant foam in the fuel tanks.[72]

---

66. *Albawaba News*, 18 January 2005.
67. *The Daily Telegraph*, 18 January 2005, '650 British troops arrive in Basra for poll security'.
68. *Los Angeles Times*, 20 January 2005, 'Basra prison photos show graphic scenes of inmates wronged'.
69. *The Times*, 21 January 2005, 'Nine British troops injured by revenge bombing in Basra'.
70. *The New Statesman*, 31 January 2005, 'Threats won't stop the Shias of Basra from going to vote'.
71. *The Times*, 1 February 2005, 'Deadly blasts that could prove terrorists remain a real threat'.
72. *The Daily Telegraph*, 21 September 2007, 'Hercules inquest leaves families "in limbo"'.

MORE EVIDENCE OF INSURGENT
TACTICS CHANGING

The 'success' of the elections did not stop the violence, and nor should any diminution have been expected. But there was evidence that insurgent tactics were continuing to change – IED attacks, and mortar attacks on bases, were beginning to predominate. On 5 February, a bomb exploded beside a British military convoy near the port of Basra. The British Consulate took five 82mm mortar rounds. Such attacks were occurring 'virtually on a daily basis'.[73] Also, four Iraqi military were killed by a motorcycle bomb. Their pick-up truck had been thrown a few hundred yards down the road by the force of the blast.[74] There was another bomb two days later, injuring one civilian, this making four since the election.[75]

Lt-Col Phil Lewis, commander of the Duke of Wellington's Regiment, noted that security forces were being attacked more frequently. 'Those who feel the election has challenged their power base can, unfortunately, very easily plant roadside bombs and cause destruction,' he said.[76] He was soon to speak from experience. Three days later, a Snatch 'multiple' from his regiment was hit by a car bomb on a canal bridge in the central al Tuwaysa district. It was claimed that no soldiers were hurt but a civilian was taken to hospital after being hit by shrapnel.[77]

The bombings were not the only sinister development. With his three-year-old son, Abdul Hussein al-Basri, a Shi'a journalist, was shot dead as he left his home. He had worked for a US-funded television channel *al-Hurra*. Al-Basri was a member of the Dawa Party, and the editor of a local news-paper in Basra. He was also head of the press office at Basra City Council.[78] Basra was now a very dangerous place not only for British troops but for journalists as well.

That knowledge had influenced *New Statesman* journalist Lindsey Hilsum, in Basra to cover the elections, to opt for embedding with British forces. Later, writing of how the pictures of happy voters showed a reality that could not be denied, she also noted that the reluctant choice that she and 70 colleagues had made reflected 'the other Iraqi reality'. She fingered yet another. The year 2005 was a general election year in Britain. Blair would be trying to downplay the lack of security. The success of the Iraqi poll would help his own re-election, as he tried to portray Iraq as a triumph

73. *Free Arab Voice*, 5 February 2005, Resistance report.
74. *Middle-east Online*, 5 February 2005, 'Iraq violence continues to escalate'.
75. *Western Daily Press*, 7 February 2005, 'Bombs and bloodshed continue after election'.
76. *The Daily Telegraph*, 6 February 2005, 'Troops "under more under threat" in Iraq'.
77. *The Daily Telegraph*, 8 February 2005, 'British soldiers ambushed by Iraq car bomb'.
78. *The Times*, 9 February 2005, 'Shia journalist murdered in Basra'.

for his policy. 'I came to Basra to report on one election,' Hilsum wrote, 'but I fear that my stories may be used in the campaign for another.'[79]

Guardian journalist Jonathan Steele had a different 'take'. He saw the embed as a Downing Street operation 'to ensure ample coverage of joyful Iraqis going to the polls'. Blair had been disappointed that no roses had been showered on the troops who toppled Saddam Hussein in April 2003. 'The Iraqi election would be a second chance to get liberation-style pictures with huge enthusiastic crowds. Coming shortly before Blair himself went to the polls, it might finally crush public doubts about the war', he wrote.[80]

The two views were not incompatible. A lack of security and the determination of the Blair government to paint a rosy picture would ensure that the already minimal flow of information would all but dry up. That which did emerge would be highly controlled.

Something of that was already evident further north. Sadr, having kept a low profile in Maysan in anticipation of the election, was confident he would end up holding the political reins in the province.[81] There, the Welsh Guards were adopting a low-key approach. Reverting to Snatches, they conducted a full range of patrols, concentrating on the infamous Route 6. Finally, they re-entered Majar al-Kabir, 'guns in one hand, cash in the other' after having pumped money into the outlying villages, showing residents the benefits of becoming 'law-abiding'. The troops went in with just Iraqi police, while the tanks stayed outside. Recorded Capt Robert Gallimore, 'We got a couple of stones thrown, but that was it. It used to be the bogeyman town; now it is fairly under control.'[82]

Based at Abu Naji, the Guards nevertheless suffered rocket attacks and mortars. But, returning to Britain in March 2005 with every single person who had deployed with the battle group, they regarded their tour as a 'tremendous success'. The hearts and minds of the locals 'were certainly captured by the smiling, upbeat Welsh Guardsmen' and they had 'forged a strong working relationship with the local population'.[83]

What the Guards had actually done was poke a stick in a hornet nest. In re-entering Majar al-Kabir, they had got too close to the heart of a bomb-making centre serving the Shi'a insurgency. Their replacements were the Staffords battle group, comprising elements of the Staffordshire Regiment, the 1st Battalion The Coldstream Guards and the King's Royal Hussars. They were to pay the butcher's bill.

---

79. *The New Statesman*, 7 February 2005, World view – Lindsey Hilsum.
80. *The Guardian*, 7 March 2005, 'Polls apart from reality'.
81. *The Sunday Times*, 30 January 2005, 'Only Iraqi democracy for Iran'.
82. *San Francisco Chronicle*, 17 February 2005, 'Troops tread softly in "Wild East"'.
83. Welsh Guards website, undated.

THE EFP EMERGES IN AL-AMARAH

The first instalment came on 2 May. The battle group had been tasked to seek out and arrest 'subversive elements' in al-Amarah. On the evening of 1 May, there were several patrols out. One, a two-Snatch unit, was on the northern outskirts, driving along a poorly lit road leading out of town. Top covers in the second vehicle were Guardsmen Anthony Wakefield and Gary Alderson. At 23.37 hrs, as the Snatches drove along the road lined by a few buildings and shops but dominated by waste ground, there was a loud explosion and 'a fireball' to the right side of the second vehicle. Alderson fell down, injured. He would survive. Wakefield would not. A projectile had entered his neck, severing one of four main arteries to the brain. Fragments from the blast passed through his chest. They hit a lung and his heart, causing massive internal bleeding. He was flown by helicopter back to Abu Naji where, at 00.50 hrs on 2 May 2005, he was declared dead.[84]

Guardsman Wakefield had been hit by a weapon new to the British sector – an explosively formed projectile or EFP. Also known as an 'off-route mine', the basis of the bomb was very simple. It was made from a steel cylinder (often a sawn-off pipe), sealed at one end and filled with explosive. Into the open end was fixed a shallow dish, usually made of copper. When the bomb was detonated, it blew out the dish, the force of the explosion inverting it and converting it into a high-speed slug of metal which – in theory – could penetrate several inches of armoured steel.

The EFPs had an added refinement. Each had a passive infra red sensor which could detect the heat from the engine of a passing vehicle. This triggered the charge, slightly offset to hit its intended target. This type of sensor bypassed all the electronic counter-measures then fitted to British military vehicles. These could only block out radio devices or mobile telephones which might be used to trigger a bomb. The Snatches were defenceless. The minimal armour and the exposed position of the 'top cover' soldiers made them fatally vulnerable. The EFP was to transform the battle, giving the Shi'a an advantage which was eventually to contribute significantly to the defeat of the British and their eventual withdrawal from Iraq.

At the time, this was hardly appreciated. Commenting on the death, BBC Iraq correspondent Jim Muir – from the safety of Baghdad – said it was 'fairly unusual' for the British, who were not targeted in the same way as the Americans, to take casualties.[85] He did not know the half of it.

The attack could not have happened at a worse time for Blair. With three days to go before the general election, Wakefield had been the 50th soldier

84. O'Hagan, Andrew, *London Review of Books*, Wakefield, 2 May 2005.
85. BBC, 2 May 2005, 'UK soldier dies in action in Iraq'.

to be killed in action in Iraq (the 87th fatality of the overall British military operation). That iconic milestone, *The Independent* suggested, had dashed his hopes of evading Iraq as an election issue.[86] The paper was wrong. A single death, without context – the MoD misleadingly describing Wakefield as having 'died after being hit by shrapnel' – had no significant electoral effect. Blair got his third term with a comfortable majority.

On 5 May – the day of the election – Lt-Col Andrew Williams, commanding officer of the Staffords, was free to decide on a robust response. His full battle group launched a raid on al-Amarah, positioning Warriors on the outskirts of city. This evoked outrage from the civic leaders, themselves militia supporters. The provincial governor used the 'insult' as an excuse to withdraw 'all co-ordination and co-operation with multinational forces'. Williams caved in and renewed the promise to keep Warriors out of town.[87]

Nevertheless, Abu Naji became a target for increasingly intensive mortar and rocket fire, the battle group in turn responding with more patrols, aimed at detecting and deterring attacks.[88] In a deadly game of tit-for-tat, the insurgents upped the ante. But there was to be no uprising in the style of the previous year. Their new weapon was the EFP. They struck again on 29 May, targeting a three-vehicle Snatch convoy driving south along Route 6. Near the small town of Qal at Salih, there was a flash and a loud explosion. L/Cpl Alan Brackenbury was riding 'top cover' in the first vehicle. He died instantly. Four others were injured.[89, 90, 91]

How many more attacks there were we do not know. With no journalists present, the Army had absolute control over the flow of information. Very little escaped. We do know that Colonel Williams himself was targeted by a bomb, some time before 23 May.[92] We also know that, for every fatality, there were multiple 'near misses', some with serious injuries. One Stafford soldier recorded:

I was at the medical centre one day. I had just come off QRF [quick reaction force]. Four Snatches pulled up. Three blokes were carried out, brought in on stretchers. There was blood everywhere, all over the floor. It made me feel sick. They had shrapnel wounds to their legs and arms. An IED had gone off. People are not told what is happening to our blokes out there.[93]

86. *The Independent*, 3 May 2005, '48 hours to go: Iraq, the issue that won't go away'.
87. Axe, David, *The Razor's Edge*, 28 June 2005, 'In relatively calm southern Iraq, people chafe under the occupation'.
88. *The Times*, 17 July 2005, 'Iraq road blast kills three British soldiers'.
89. *The Independent*, 31 May 2005, 'Latest British fatality in Iraq identified as 21-year-old corporal'.
90. *The Daily Telegraph*, 30 May 2005, 'British soldier killed in bomb attack on convoy'.
91. BBC, 14 September 2007, 'British soldier unlawfully killed'.
92. *Birmingham Evening Mail*, 23 May 2005, 'Lucky escape for army chief'.
93. *The Independent*, 14 January 2006, 'Basra: What really happened'.

Operational officers became extremely concerned at the vulnerability of the Snatch. An e-mail written by an officer in Abu Naji at the time, stated baldly:

Commanders on the ground had no choice but to use what equipment they were provided with … That led to terrible decisions having to be made, decisions that have caused untold anguish and mental suffering that you can only guess at. I have seen very senior commanders cry because of it.[94]

If the officers were anguished, some senior NCOs were close to mutiny. One, on being ordered to take out a Snatch patrol, demanded the order in writing, together with a formal 'risk assessment'. It was never delivered and the Snatches remained on the base.[95]

With this situation developing, on 6 June, a patrol from the Staffords led by Lt Richard Shearer was mentoring Iraqi Highways Police while they carried out vehicle checkpoint practice. Having demonstrated how to conduct a checkpoint, Shearer's team secured the location from where the police were to operate. The soldiers dismounted to carry out standard security checks and 'sharp-eyed Pte Adam Mills' saw a small antenna sticking out of the top of a mound of earth with wires buried on the side.[96] Capt Simon Bratcher, a young and only recently qualified bomb disposal officer, was called in to what turned out to be 10 linked EFPs. Despite the extreme danger, he disarmed the bombs, which were then sent for forensic analysis. This 'moved the countermeasure process on significantly'.[97,98]

If indeed the 'countermeasure process' was moved on at all, it was not fast enough for Lt Shearer. About midnight on Friday, 15 July 2005, he was leading a three-Snatch patrol in al-Amarah. Its task was to help reduce the 'substantial threat' against Abu Naji from the constant barrage of 120mm mortars and rockets. This had reached crisis point. With others, the patrol was intended to deter attackers.

There had been 'a spate of incidents in this area over recent weeks' – at least five. In Lt Shearer's largely residential patrol area, there had been an attack as recently as 20 June.[99] Thus, the Snatches had been escorted to the edge of the city by Warriors. At that stage, 'there had been no intelligence' to suggest that an insurgent would use an IED within a residential area, 'thereby threatening his own people'. Once the Snatch multiple arrived at

94. *The Sunday Times*, 25 June 2006, 'Focus: Is the army putting money before lives?'
95. Author's interviews with serving soldiers, plus access granted to private e-mails.
96. Army website, 15 June 2005, 'Staffords soldier thwarts roadside bomb attack'.
97. MoD website, 23 March 2006, 'George Cross awarded to bomb disposal expert'.
98. *The Dorset Echo*, 7 December 2007, 'It was exposed and dangerous ... I put it to the back of my mind'.
99. Unpublished. Weapons Intelligence Section, Headquarters Multinational Division (South East), 17 July 2005, Explosion – IVO Yellow 2, al Amara.

its patrol area, therefore, it was on its own. With Lt Shearer was driver Pte Philip Hewett. Pte Leon Spicer and a Fijian soldier nicknamed 'Pax' were 'top covers'. Later, they were joined by Pte Stephen Baldwin, who manned the command radio.

At 01.20 hrs, now on the morning of Saturday 16 July, a small explosion was heard by the patrol – thought later to have been a decoy. The convoy stopped to allow the patrol's interpreter to question bystanders. He was directed to the football stadium on the edge of town. The patrol set off to investigate, driving down the main road, divided – as was common in the city – by a drainage ditch. Within minutes, from the area of the ditch came 'a flash and loud bang'. A cloud of dust covered Shearer's vehicle.

Inside the Snatch, Pte Baldwin was thrown to the middle. Pte Spicer landed on top of him. The vehicle was full of smoke and Baldwin realised it had been hit by an IED. He kicked open the back doors and stumbled out. He was one of the lucky ones. 'Pax' survived, but with leg injuries. Lt Shearer had been decapitated. Hewitt and Spicer had also been killed – by another EFP.

At last, Williams took the Snatches off the streets. 'We really needed to buy some time for the technological experts to ascertain what was the threat and what were the best means of countering it,' he later said. Until then, 'I had to mitigate the risk to our soldiers and I did so by declaring that Warriors would be used'.[100] In fact, he had no option. He had to promise the Staffords that they would never again be required to operate Snatches. Had he not done so, his battalion would have fallen apart.

And for the insurgents, unlike with the open confrontations, 'hit and run' tactics had prevailed. This was a significant victory – they had not only regained the initiative, but kept it.

---

100. Account compiled from unpublished proceedings of the Coroner's inquest, 30 January 2007, contemporary witness statements and Army incident reports.

Chapter 4 – The seeds of betrayal

The Army plans its withdrawal:
June–December 2005

Has he [Blair] not noticed that in Basra and the other two south-eastern provinces where British forces are based the insurgency barely exists? … Suicide bombers are conspicuous by their absence. Attacks on British forces are rare, and fatalities even rarer.

JONATHAN STEEL, *THE GUARDIAN*, 9 MAY 2005

While new tactics – and technology – were being exploited by the insurgents in Maysan, Basra again took on a mantle of calm. Again, it was a false calm, sustained only by the passivity of the British forces. A 'silent and largely undocumented social revolution' had transformed the south, turning it into a virtual Islamic state. In Basra's courthouses, Sharia law was routinely used. Politicians worked with the tacit approval of Shi'a clergy and referred many important decisions to religious leaders. Control of the security forces was often shared between local police and party militia.[1]

The process had been strengthened by the elections. The militias had been able to rely on block votes, swamping interim prime minister Allawi's secular party. They had forged an uneasy alliance of the largest Shi'a parties, relying on the backing of Sistani as the cement to hold it together. A beneficiary had been Muqtada. Although his party had gained 23 seats in the new National Assembly, it only took 12 of 41 city council seats in Basra, against SCIRI which had won 20. But Sadr formed a coalition with factions which had been soured by the thuggish behaviour of the Badr brigades. By late April, the Sadrists were highly organised. They were beginning to gain control of Basra, and becoming a formidable force.[2]

In early March, the British had other problems. The Dutch had used the excuse of the elections to pull out of Muthanna province. The Queen's Dragoon Guards had to fill the gap. They were struck by the 'lack of fanfare about what they were doing'. No British media had been present – unlike in earlier events. 'It was a surprise,' said Lt-Col Tim Wilson, the Guards' commanding officer, 'as this is Britain effectively taking over another province and British soldiers are doing a bloody good job.' His

1. *The Daily Telegraph,* 14 February 2005, 'Clerics become powerbrokers in the south'.
2. *Asia Times,* 21 April 2005, 'The shadow Iraqi government'.

71

number two, Major Alan Richmond, noted that, with a general election coming, the government did not want reports of 'mission creep'.[3]

NEWS FROM BASRA BURIED

Nevertheless, evidence of the growing disaster in the British sector was there, albeit hard to find. In a crowded news agenda with UK politics gearing up for the election, Iraq had to compete for attention. With most of the focus on the US sector and the broader political issues, news from Basra was buried even more deeply.

Thus, in a story in *The New York Times* of 20 March headed 'Bomb kills 3 Iraqi policemen in procession', the substantive news was of tens of thousands of war protesters demonstrating across Europe to mark the second anniversary of the 'American invasion'. Only briefly was there a reference to hundreds of students protesting in front of the governor's office in Basra, 'in the latest show of anger against the Shi'ite parties and militias that largely run the city'. The demonstrations had begun when Sadr's militiamen had beaten a group of students dressed Western-style, with uncovered hair and jeans, as they had eaten a picnic lunch in a park. Police officers standing by did not intervene.[4]

Behind that was the ever-present street violence, some of it sectarian, some of it militias engaged in their turf wars, some tribal vendettas and plain criminality. A selection of 'snippets' from the period illustrates how fragile the situation had become.

In one month, April, a car bomb destroyed a police car in downtown Basra. A policeman was killed and three were wounded. That was on the first day of the month. Another police car was destroyed opposite the University on the 5th. The following day, a professor of education and Sunni preacher was shot dead as he came out of a meeting of his department. On the evening of the 7th, an Iraqi Army Major was eating in a restaurant in Basra when three masked men burst in and killed him. Earlier that day, another police car was targeted by a bomb. On the 8th, a British soldier had been shot while on foot patrol in the centre of Basra. The following day, there was a bomb attack on a British military convoy.

Thousands of Sunnis were out in az Zubayr on 11 April to protest against 'the wave of sectarian repression and violence'. The town was 90 per cent Sunni. The demonstrators marched on the offices of the Shi'a-

---

3. *The Daily Telegraph*, 13 March 2005, 'Britain's troops take the strain as Dutch pull out'.
4. *The New York Times*, 20 March 2005, 'Bomb kills 3 Iraqi policemen in procession'.

dominated Interior Ministry, chanting slogans and complaining about arrests and harassment. An Iraqi policeman was killed and six others wounded when roadside bombs exploded in Basra on the 18th. Three went off near a mini-bus as the policemen were travelling to az Zubayr. A British vehicle patrol was attacked the same day in a market area west of Basra. On the 19th, a police car was destroyed by a bomb in the az Zubayr area, with four policemen claimed dead.

Gunmen then assassinated a tribal leader on his farm in az Zubayr on the 20th. On the 22nd, another police car was destroyed by a bomb. Four policemen were injured. The next day a 'booby-trapped car' exploded near a mosque, wounding seven people and damaging a nearby house. Two young girls were injured. The 24th saw a bomb attack on military vehicles, and a car bomb also exploded outside a Shi'a mosque. The 27th saw another attack on a police car and, on the 28th, in the village of Safwan, the local commander of the Badr Brigade was killed when an RPG was fired at his car. On the 29th, a bomb targeted an Iraqi border guard patrol west of Basra, killing one and wounding two.[5]

There was also endemic corruption in the oil industry, undermining the entire economy of Iraq – to which the oil-rich south contributed nearly 80 per cent of the wealth. The scale of black market trading was so vast that 20 illegal taps were found on just one oil pipeline, allowing tankers to top up their loads at will. It was estimated that only 60 per cent of trucks carrying oil products from wells reached their destination. The remainder were attacked and hijacked. Organised gangs were heavily involved, often with the cooperation of the police and the authorities. So brazen had they become that operations were often carried out in the open.[6]

The one bright spot, which was to have far-reaching implications – but not for the moment – was on 6 May. The headquarters of the Iraqi Army's 10th Division 'Zulfiqar' unit was set up at Basra airport, under the watchful eye of the British Army, which was expending considerable resources in training and 'mentoring' the unit. Comprising 7,000 troops, the Division was later slated to be ready to take on the insurgents by the end of the year.[7] This, to say the least, was optimistic.

Unfortunately, the UK political and media focus remained on the invasion. Too little attention was being given to what was actually happening, and there was no public recognition of how far the situation had changed,

5. Agencies and various – culled from contemporary reports. See also: Free Arab Voice on the Albasrah website. Although these reports often exaggerate casualties from attacks, triangulation with other sources suggests that their actual reports of incidents are accurate.

6. ENS Newswire, 21 April 2005, 'Corruption Draining Iraq's Oil Industry'.

7. *The Daily Telegraph*, 1 August 2005, 'Iraqi troops who hold key to Army's way out'.

and how different it was now from the heady days in the early stages of the occupation.

It is not as though Iraq was not being discussed. Simply the focus was on the continuing controversy over the legality of the war.[8] Even grieving relatives of dead soldiers were looking backwards. They delivered a letter to No. 10, threatening legal action unless they were granted an inquiry, vowing to pursue Blair for his 'lies' about the war.[9, 10] Blair, following his re-election, responded that it was 'time to move on'. He was much derided for that comment, even if he was right – in principle. But his was not an acknowledgement that we should 'move on' to confront the insurgency. In Blair's world, that did not exist.

The absence of comprehensive media reporting of events on the ground sustained the false impression given in London. This was reinforced by some journalists. Jonathan Steele, writing for *The Guardian*, actually declared that the insurgency barely existed. Basra has been 'quiet for months', he wrote. 'Suicide bombers are conspicuous by their absence. Attacks on British forces are rare, and fatalities even rarer.'[11] The mistake was the choice of measurement – troop fatalities. For some time, in Basra if not al-Amarah and more by luck than judgement, there had been no British deaths. It was, therefore, 'quiet'.

Taking over from Geoff Hoon as defence secretary after the election was John Reid. He flew into Basra on 17 May to visit troops and, significantly, to meet members of the newly formed 10th Division. He used the visit to highlight a '£27m package of security assistance given by Britain'. This included guns, ammunition and 'armoured Land Rovers'. Those Land Rovers were Glover Webb APVs. They were to become somewhat contentious.[12]

MILITIAS AND SECTARIAN KILLING

In early June, a prominent Shi'ite cleric was gunned down in Basra after he left his mosque to go home with his son. *The New York Times* assumed this was another sectarian killing.[13] On the other hand, a report by a correspondent on the spot suggested he was the 'latest victim of sporadic

8. Richard Beeston, Foreign Editor of *The Times*, was to write: 'Of all the parochial, navel-gazing, non-issues surrounding the Iraq war, the endless debate about the lead-up to it has wasted more time and energy than any other.' See: 'The war went wrong. Not the build-up', 26 February 2009.
9. *The Daily Mail*, 29 April 2005, 'I want Blair locked up'.
10. *The Daily Telegraph*, 4 May 2005, 'Blair dogged by Iraq while grieving families demand public inquiry into legality of war'.
11. Jonathan Steel, *The Guardian*, 10 May 2005, 'Britons want troops out of Iraq'.
12. BBC, 17 May 2005, 'Reid on first Basra troops visit'.
13. *The New York Times*, 3 June 2005, 'New attacks highlight growing sectarian divisions in Iraq'.

assassinations which are blamed on rival militias and crooked police officers'.[14] The two attackers had been wearing black, the uniform of the Mahdi Army.[15] This was Shi'a infighting, something not seen to anything like the same extent in the rest of Iraq. Basra was experiencing a very different type of war and the signs were being misread.

Michael Rubin of the US *National Review* picked up the militia theme, contrasting the US and British approaches. While the US was actively engaging with the militias in the pursuit of a constitutional democracy, 'British forces empowered them for the sake of tranquillity'. Basra is far more peaceful than Baghdad, he wrote, 'but posters of Ayatollah Khomeini hang in the University of Basra and militant gangs impose Islamist social mores. To British diplomats, stability trumped democracy.'[16]

Steve Vincent, a freelance American journalist, living in Basra after the absence of a year, also wrote a piece for the *National Review*. It was curiously upbeat about normality being restored.[17] A day after its publication, gunmen murdered the dean of the city's police academy.[18] Vincent was in print again on 13 July, now remarking on the writ of the 'extremist Shi'ite Muslims' who were dominating Basra. He wrote of the influence of Iran on the militias and of nearly 1,000 people – most of them Sunnis – having been killed in the past three months, with 100 murdered in one week in May alone. But he still injected a note of optimism, suggesting that many in Basra were tired of the increasing 'Iranification' and planned to vote in December – when the next round of elections was due – for secular candidates.[19]

The next time he wrote it was on the last day of July. Again he referred to the increasing control of the Shi'ites but this time added, 'the British seem unable or unwilling to do anything about it'. He also recorded an anonymous Iraqi police lieutenant who confirmed 'widespread rumours' that a few police officers were perpetrating many of the hundreds of assassinations. There was even a sort of 'death car': 'a white Toyota Mark II that glides through the city streets, carrying off-duty police officers in the pay of extremist religious groups to their next assignment.' 'The British know what's happening but they are asleep, pretending they can simply establish security and leave behind democracy,' the police lieutenant had said.

This was the last piece Vincent wrote. Two days later he was abducted and murdered. His translator and fiancée, Nouriya Itais, was shot four times

14. *The Guardian*, 4 June 2005, 'Ravaged "Venice of the east" seeks to regain status as tourist magnet'.
15. *Swissinfo*, 3 June 2005, 'Iraqi Shi'ite cleric assassinated in Basra'.
16. *National Review*, 7 June 2005, 'Our ally Down Under'.
17. Vincent, Steven, *National Review*, 9 June 2005, 'Back in Basra'.
18. Council on Foreign Relations, 13 October 2005, Iraq Timeline 2005.
19. Vincent, Steven, *The Christian Science Monitor*, 13 July 2005, 'Shiites bring rigid piety to Iraq's south'.

and seriously wounded. Few had any doubts as to the reasons. But there were also strong suspicions that the issue which had hastened his death had been his open criticism of Muqtada al-Sadr and his supporters' infiltration of the police.[20]

Vincent was the last independent Western journalist in Basra. Another blow came in September when Fakher Haider, a 38-year-old Shi'a reporter, was abducted by masked men claiming to be police. He was found later, dead with his hands bound and a bag over his head. Haider had covered Basra for *The New York Times* and other Western media. He too had been critical of Muqtada. With his murder, Basra effectively became a closed city to investigative journalists.[21]

Responding to Vincent's death, *The Guardian* accused Britain of having 'bought a way out by abandoning Basra to intolerance'. It recorded how the chief of police in Basra had revealed that he had 'lost control of 75 per cent of his officers' and that sectarian militias had infiltrated his force. The militias were 'using their posts to assassinate opponents'. Half of his 13,750-strong force was secretly working for political parties and some officers were involved in ambushes. Other officers were politically neutral but did not follow his orders. 'I trust 25 per cent of my force, no more,' he said. And although Basra was still a 'relatively peaceful' city, that peace had been bought 'by ceding authority to conservative Islamic parties and turning a blind eye to militia corruption scams and hit squads'.[22]

THE BRITISH CONSIDER TROOP WITHDRAWALS

Completely ignoring the reality on the ground, in what should be marked in history as one of the most egregious examples of political myopia and self-deception, Blair was now actively planning troop withdrawals. Details were leaked in July, heralding a cut from 8,500 to 3,000 by the middle of 2006, handing over Muthanna and Maysan provinces to Iraqi control by October 2005.[23] This was only a reasonable proposition if the fact of an ongoing insurgency was ignored and if the metric of progress was confined to troop fatalities. By the end of July, compared with almost daily American deaths, there had been five in the previous three months. The base outside Basra had not been attacked with mortars since the previous November.[24] That was enough to maintain an illusion of progress.

20. *The Times*, 3 August 2005, 'Basra blogger is abducted and murdered'.
21. *The Times*, 20 September 2005, 'Second journalist probing Basra police killed'.
22. *The Guardian*, 27 August 2005, 'A bloody trade-off'.
23. *The Guardian*, 11 July 2005, 'UK plans to slash Iraq force over the next year'.
24. *The Daily Telegraph*, 28 July 2005, 'Colonel tells of concerns over trial decisions'.

The effect of this 'leak' was soon to become apparent. Rival militia factions took it as a signal to redouble their efforts to assert their own control of Basra and to cement their credentials as fighters against the occupiers. Each was seeking the credit for driving the British out and thereby staking a greater share in the coming division of spoils. Early in the first half of July, a 'prominent commander' of the Badr Brigade was killed by 'resistance fighters' and an officer of the directorate of police intelligence was ambushed while driving his car, dying in a hail of bullets. Iraqi national guards living in Basra received death threats, telling them to quit work.[25]

A SELF-LICKING LOLLIPOP

On 13 July, 'resistance fighters' claimed to have shot dead a British soldier on foot patrol in the al Haritha area of northern Basra, offering an account of British troops rushing to seal off the area, conducting house-to-house searches.[26] There is no official record of a soldier having been killed. He may have been wounded. Certainly, there was an attack the next day, leaving one Iraqi policeman dead and another wounded.[27] A Sunni university professor was shot dead in the street on 17 July, and two of his associates wounded.[28]

For the British, there was a more deadly attack on the penultimate day of July when a bomb hit a three-vehicle convoy carrying consulate staff. The lead vehicle manned by security contractors took the full force of the blast, killing the two occupants. As a crowd gathered another bomb went off, seriously injuring two children.[29] Lt-Col Williams, still at Abu Naji, acknowledged that the insurgents had changed their tactics. 'Last year,' he said, they had 'fought pitched battles in the open, with AK47s and RPGs.' They had learnt from this. 'The guerrillas now carefully orchestrate their attacks after tracking every move of British patrols by mobile phones.'[30]

Security forces were quick to interpret the bomb attack as evidence of an 'elevated threat'.[31] They were not wrong, but again there was no evidence that the British were dealing with the threat. Thus, on 6 August, the lead vehicle of a three-Snatch patrol was hit by a bomb on the northern outskirts of Basra. A soldier was seriously injured and the Snatch was

---

25. *Free Arab Voice*, 12 July 2005, Resistance Report 340.
26. *Free Arab Voice*, 13 July 2005, Resistance Report 341.
27. *Free Arab Voice*, 14 July 2005, Resistance Report 342.
28. *Free Arab Voice*, 17 July 2005, Resistance Report 345.
29. *The Times*, 31 July 2005, 'Security guards hit by Basra road blast'.
30. *The Independent*, 31 July 2005, 'Sophisticated strikes threaten British withdrawal from Iraq'.
31. Iraq – South, Security Briefing MNF, 1 August 2005.

destroyed. Two weeks later, another Snatch was hit while travelling through the city. A soldier was hurt.[32] Then fighting erupted between the Mahdi Army and rival militias on 24 August. Initially in Najaf, it spilled over into Basra where Sadrists took on the Badr militia. They attacked the SCIRI offices in at least four neighbourhoods and a radio station belonging to the party. The war was coming back out into the open.[33]

In Baghdad, politicians were interminably discussing the shape of a new constitution. It would have to be approved by the Shi'a majority and would set in stone the weakened position of the formerly dominant Sunni minority. Towards the end of August, they had failed yet again to agree to a draft. This could not help but to increase instability. Crucially, while it pointed to the federalisation of Iraq – an option preferred by the Iran-backed SCIRI – it was violently opposed by the Sadrists and by the Sunni, who were finding common cause.

The Mahdi, meanwhile, were fighting the Badr Brigade in six cities.[34] One of those was al-Amarah, where they mortared the Badr headquarters. British troops in Abu Naji logged around 70 explosions, describing the fighting as 'extraordinarily violent'. It would have been 'impossible' for local Iraqi forces to quell it and the British would normally have intervened. Yet, much to their surprise, troops were ordered to stand down. Army officials insisted that intervention was 'not required', motivated – it was charged – by increasing pressure to leave things to local security forces. Few believed the latter were ready to do the job properly. Control of the city was being lost.[35] These charges were hotly disputed by Major Gen Jim Dutton, now commanding British forces. There was no 'deliberate policy' to shift the burden to Iraqi security forces. Rather, the British forces only intervened when asked. But troops readily intervened when seeking to prevent attacks on their base.[36] That had become their main interest and the activity which was absorbing most of their resources. The British presence was becoming what the military were calling a 'self-licking lollipop'.

MORE SNATCH DEATHS

Unsurprisingly, the insurgents continued to attack the military. Their next targets were Fusiliers Donal Meade and Stephen Manning. On the morn-

32. BBC, 21 August 2005, 'British soldier wounded in Basra'.
33. *The New York Times*, 25 August 2005, 'Shiite cleric's soldiers battle rivals in Najaf and Basra'.
34. *The Daily Telegraph*, 27 August 2005, 'Iraq on brink of meltdown'.
35. *The Daily Telegraph*, 28 August 2006, 'Troops told to stand aside as Shia factions grip Iraqi city'. Online copy withdrawn. Available on the United Jerusalem Foundation website.
36. *The Sunday Telegraph* (letters), 3 September 2005, 'The view from within Iraq'.

ing of 5 September, they had been top cover in the leading vehicle of a two-Snatch patrol, near az Zubayr. Their vehicle was hit by an IED. Both were killed.[37] Despite the ongoing attacks on Snatches, their vulnerability demonstrated again and again, they were still on the streets.

Two days later, 16 people died and 21 were injured when a car bomb exploded outside a restaurant near a market in the centre of Basra. Two police cars and several shops were destroyed.[38] Three American security contractors were killed and one injured by a bomb which hit a convoy they were escorting from the US Consulate.[39, 40] On 11 September, in an attack similar to that which had killed Meade and Manning, L/Cpl Craig Short and Fusilier Aveuta Tuila were caught in the blast. 'We just drove past a rural community and they detonated an IED ... they got me in the leg,' said Tuila. Both survived but needed amputations.[41, 42]

That day, Major Matthew Bacon was murdered. Three other soldiers with him in the Snatch were badly injured. Major Bacon had been a passenger on his way back to the air base from Basra Palace. Tragically, he had been due to make the journey by Merlin helicopter but it had developed a hydraulic fault. There had been no spare helicopters so he had been forced to go by road, with tragic results.[43, 44] Still the militias had not finished. After dark, four rockets slammed into the US Consulate compound.[45]

Over the following weekend, in an attempt to staunch the attacks, British troops launched a series of raids. They arrested the local leader of the Mahdi Army, his brother, his aide and about 200 others. There were no qualms about intervening here but, in fighting between rival militias, the British stood aside. On the Monday, the militia retaliated by blocking roads with burning furniture and tyres, crowding into the city centre to demand the release of their people. Troops were stoned. Fire bombs were thrown, memorably setting fire to a Warrior, forcing the crew to evacuate. One suffered severe burns. The soldiers were pelted with stones as they escaped.[46]

In an unrelated incident initially linked to the violence, Iraqi police had arrested two plain-clothes soldiers driving an unmarked car on the grounds that they had refused to stop at a checkpoint and had fired at the

---

37. MoD website, 5 September 2006, 'Deaths of two British soldiers in Iraq'.
38. *The Independent*, 9 September 2005, 'Insurgents open "southern front" with deadly car-bomb in Basra'.
39. *The Times*, 7 September 2005, 'Westerners killed in Basra as Saddam "confesses"'.
40. *The Daily Mail*, 7 September 2005, 'Basra roadside bombing "kills contractors"'.
41. Army website, undated, the Royal Regiment of Fusiliers.
42. *The Guardian*, 21 January 2006, 'We drove past ... they detonated an IED. They got me in the leg'.
43. *The Times*, 25 June 2006, 'Focus: Is the army putting money before lives?'
44. Roger and Maureen Bacon, Channel 4 website, 18 September 2006.
45. Kuna News Agency, 12 September 2005.
46. *The Guardian*, 20 September 2005, 'Day of violence in Basra exposes myth of trust between British and Iraqi forces'.

police. They were taken to the infamous Jameat police station. After a tense stand-off when the police refused to surrender their captives, British tanks smashed through the walls of the station in a bid to free their men. They were not there but intelligence revealed they were in a nearby house. With fears that they were about to be handed over to the insurgents, a swift raid was mounted and the soldiers were rescued.[47, 48]

Richard Ingrams, writing for *The Observer* that weekend, had some interesting observations. Charging that: 'The Secretary of State for Defence is still doing his damnedest to hide the truth about Iraq,' he noted how hard it was, even for a compulsive newspaper reader like him, to find out exactly what was going on in Basra. What you can deduce, he wrote, is that the situation there is considered so dangerous now that journalists daren't go there any more. But he also averred: 'The army, taking its instructions from Dr John Reid and his Ministry of Defence, is making it difficult, if not impossible, for anyone to find out what is going on, even if they manage to get there in the first place.'[49]

In the wider public, there was a sense of weariness which translated into a 26 September ICM poll which had 51 per cent of respondents calling for troop withdrawals. This was not surprising as all the public was getting was an unremitting diet of news about British casualties. Nevertheless, Blair insisted that the troops would not leave 'until the country's emerging democracy and its armed forces were strong enough to cope alone'.[50, 51] He was, however, not prepared to reinforce the Army or insist on new equipment. As for the troops, plans for withdrawal were unchanged.

If the poll sent a message to the militias, they were quick to acknowledge it. On 1 October, a Danish soldier was killed and two others wounded when a bomb blew up alongside their vehicle in al Harta, just north of Basra.[52] They were in a convoy of two Mercedes 'G-wagons', equivalent to the Snatch.[53] The British were not the only Army to leave their troops dangerously vulnerable.

The British Army had its own messages, but they were mixed. On the one hand, it passed control of a small military camp over to the 10th Division of the Iraqi Army. This was Camp Chindit at az Zubayr. About 100 British soldiers had been training Iraqi troops there.[54] On the other hand,

47. *The Guardian*, 19 September 2005, 'British soldiers arrested over alleged killing'.
48. *The Times*, 20 September 2005, 'Iran blamed as militias step up Basra violence'.
49. Richard Ingrams, *The Observer*, 25 September 2005, 'Dr Reid's barmy army'.
50. *The Guardian*, 21 September 2005, 'Pressure grows for troop withdrawal'.
51. *The Guardian*, 26 September 2006, 'Blair out of step as voters swing behind Iraq withdrawal'.
52. Iraq page – individuals, Denmark, undated.
53. Nyhederne, 1 October 2005, 'Irak: Dansk soldat dræbt i angreb'.
54. *The Scotsman*, 2 October 2005.

it continued its raids, on 7 October arresting 12 police officers and suspected militia commanders.[55] Although it was feared that this would enrage the militias further, there was no immediate response. Instead, the internecine fighting continued. On 13 September, a senior leader of the Dawa Party, Sheikh Mahdi Al-Attar, was kidnapped and killed.[56] On 9 October, a suicide bomber struck the local headquarters of the Badr organisation, killing a child and her mother and wounding five others. The target had been a former governor of Basra and current leader of the Badr Brigade.[57]

A new constitution having finally been agreed by the National Assembly, the Iraqis were now voting on it. The event went peacefully although one Iraqi complained that the British Army had 'handed the city to the Islamist groups as a gift'. The BBC's defence correspondent noted that the British army had scaled down its patrols in Basra. Convoys had been cut and most journeys were undertaken by helicopter. The reason was 'a new, more lethal kind of roadside bomb'.[58] This was yet more evidence of the insurgents retaining the initiative.

Michael Evans, defence editor of *The Times*, remarked on these 'new' bombs. He argued that the expertise for their infra-red triggers came from 'outside Iraq', noting that the 'complex technique' used had been mastered by Hezbollah in Lebanon. By extension, suspicion had fallen on Iran which funded, armed and trained them.[59] *The Guardian* reported that British forces had 'no answer' to these sophisticated bombs.[60] The narratives, undoubtedly officially inspired, had two messages: that Iran was responsible and that the bombs were 'unstoppable'. Evidence of government 'spin' was most definitely there.

Whatever the origin of the bombs, the Army was fully aware that Iraq was no longer a safe place for Snatches – if it ever had been. Yet they were still on the streets. The Army, though, was building up an alibi to explain its failure to confront the threat. If the bombs were 'unstoppable', it could not be blamed for not stopping them.

One Snatch commander was 30-year-old Coldstream Guards Sergeant, Christian Hickey. Close to midnight on 18 October, he was leading a convoy of two Snatches, just short of a roundabout on a road dubbed 'IED alley'. The place was ideal for an ambush. The spotlight on his vehicle was not working, making it difficult to see the verges ahead, so he called the

---

55. *The Daily Telegraph*, 8 October 2005, 'British Army strikes back against the Shia renegades in Basra'.
56. Dawa Party website, undated, Party History.
57. *The Washington Post*, 9 October 2005, 'Suicide bomber strikes Basra'.
58. Wood, Paul, BBC, 16 October 2005, 'Shia militants gaining strength in Basra'.
59. *The Times*, 6 October 2005, '"Infra-red" bombs based on tactics used by Hezbollah'.
60. *The Guardian*, 6 October 2005, 'UK's Iraq forces face Hizbullah-style roadside bombs'.

convoy to a halt. Dismounting, he went forward to clear a route. As he bent down to examine a suspicious object, there was a huge explosion. Hickey took the full force of an EFP which tore off his legs, shattered his skull and peppered his body with shrapnel. Infra-red activated, the bomb had probably been triggered by his body heat. It had been destined for the leading Snatch, packed with men, their lives undoubtedly saved by their Sergeant's heroic action.[61, 62, 63]

The incident was chronicled by Mike Smith, defence correspondent of *The Sunday Times*. He claimed that Hickey's CO, Lt-Col Nick Henderson, had resigned, furious that Hickey's death had been 'a direct result of the failure to supply "armour protected" Land Rovers for his men'. There were no direct quotes from Henderson, but Smith had the MoD saying that 'frontline troops cannot have the armoured Land Rovers because they are not suitable for use off-road'. He added: '… but six weeks ago Britain supplied a number of the vehicles to Iraqi police in Basra.'[64] Indeed Britain had.[65] They were the old Glover Webb APVs.[66] Of those, 79 had been renovated for the Iraqis. The extra weight of their steel armour prevented their off-road use.

Smith did usefully add that, because of the vulnerability of the Snatch, British troops were using tanks or convoys of up to 12 Warriors to mount patrols. Some areas were deemed too dangerous to be patrolled at all. 'We're in survival mode right now, we can't do anything at all,' his defence source had told him. As for Lt-Col Henderson's allegation, it was not repeated. Nor did Henderson ever refer to it.

The charge having been made, it was to remain like a virus in the system. When questions might have been asked about the inadequacy of the Snatch, and why the Army was not confronting the threat of the EFP, the attention was instead focused on undefined 'armoured' Land Rovers, these wrongly being seen as an answer. So it was that on 14 November, Lord Astor of Hever – the Conservative defence spokesman in the House of Lords – tackled the government. He asked whether giving armoured vehicles to the Iraqi police force had contributed to their non-availability to UK forces. The answer was 'no', but no explanation was given.[67] The

61. MoD website, 20 October 2005, 'Sergeant Chris Hickey of 1st Battalion the Coldstream Guards killed in Iraq'.
62. *The Times*, 15 December 2005, 'Deadly stalkers follow patrols in "bomb alley"'.
63. *The Times*, 19 October 2005, 'British soldier killed by roadside bomb in Iraq'.
64. *The Sunday Times*, 23 October 2005, 'Colonel quits as troops are denied armoured land rovers in Iraq'.
65. MoD website, 17 May 2005, 'UK hands over equipment to Iraqi security forces'.
66. Hansard, 16 September 2003: Column 705W.
67. Hansard, 14 November 2005: Column WA122.

government did not attempt to explain that these too would have been useless against the EFP threat.

Lord Astor also wanted to know whether the government would equip the Army 'with armour-plated vehicles similar to those provided to United States Armed Forces'. The answer from procurement minister Lord Drayson was disingenuous. He claimed that, 'UK Armed Forces always deploy with a mix of armour in order to suit the range of conditions and threats encountered on operations ....'.[68] Had there been plans then to upgrade the protection or take on the EFP threat, this would have been an opportunity to say so. That there was not even a hint of any change indicated that it was business as usual.

THE BUFFALO – AN EARLY US RESPONSE TO THE IED

What Astor had picked up was that the US forces were suffering exactly the same IED onslaught as the British – in fact more so. In May alone they had been attacked more than 700 times and were likewise experiencing the EFP.[69] One US response had been progressively to add armour to their vehicles, especially their Humvees. This was to prove fruitless. Another response was to have profound significance. Already there were appearing what were later called Mine Resistant Ambush Protected (MRAP) vehicles. These in 2005 were available in small numbers and a testament to the effectiveness of one type was being recorded by spray-painted graffiti appearing on Baghdad walls. It read: 'Kill the claw.'[70]

The target of the graffiti-writers was a 23-ton, six-wheeled armoured truck – twice the weight of a London bus – called the Buffalo. Introduced in 2003, it was equipped with a 16-foot hydraulic arm, ending in an artic-ulating 'claw' – hence the insurgents' sobriquet. This was used to investi-gate suspect packages, accumulations of roadside rubbish and other debris which might conceal bombs. What especially marked out the vehicle was its design. It had a 'v-shaped hull', more like a boat than a vehicle, which deflected blast rather than attempting to stop it by a mass of armoured plate. It could withstand the force of six anti-tank mines exploding simul-taneously, any one of which could destroy a tank three times its weight.

Lord Astor had not registered this war-winning machine, even though its success was being widely hailed.[71] The crew of one, in four months, had found 24 IEDs. Six had gone off, including two in which the Buffalo had

68. Hansard, 14 November 2005: Column WA122.
69. *The New York Times*, 27 June 2005, 'Insurgents getting better at what they do'.
70. Defense Tech, 13 September 2005, 'Bomb-busting buffalo'.
71. Defend America (DoD), 1 September 2005, 'Buffalo roams supply routes in Iraq'.

taken direct hits. The windows and sides of the vehicle had been damaged and tyres had blown out. No one had been seriously injured.[72] This, the British Army could have used for what is known as 'route clearing'. Had it done so, Sgt Hickey could still have been alive. Yet, when Conservative backbencher Ann Winterton asked the MoD whether it would be introduced, the response was disappointingly negative. A 'broad assessment' had been carried out. There were 'no current plans' to procure it.[73]

Nevertheless, there was still unease about Snatches. Conservative shadow defence minister Gerald Howarth claims he took up the issue with Reid in September 2005, later stating:

I think I was the first to raise the issue of armoured vehicles which I did on my return from Iraq in September 2005. I told John Reid privately that he had to do something to get better protection for the troops facing roadside bombs (privately because I represent a garrison town and know how careless politicians can cause increased anxiety). He told me that they were aware of the problem and actively seeking solutions, but would not be specific.[74]

In November 2005, Foreign and Commonwealth Office security manager, John Wyndham, took a stand. He prohibited his staff from riding in Snatches. Major General Dutton opposed the decision but was overruled.[75] There was, though, no public hue and cry. Thus, in 2005, a major opportunity to save lives was missed. Equally importantly, with the vulnerability of the Snatch seriously limiting tactical mobility, the opportunity to restore the initiative to the British Army in Iraq was lost.

Meanwhile, back in Basra, British forces continued their raids and weapons searches, successfully finding a cache on 22 October and arresting nine suspects. The action had been carried out under the authority of UN Security Council Resolution 1546, which required Coalition forces 'to conduct security and stabilisation operations in support of the political process' – when, of course, it suited them.[76]

On the last day of October, a massive car bomb exploded in Basra. The car had been parked in a busy thoroughfare in the centre of the city used by shoppers. Shi'a officials attributed the bombing to Sunni insurgents from central Iraq.[77] In retaliation, many Sunni clerics were killed, continuing the thread of sectarian murder and violence.[78] Elsewhere in Basra, gunmen

---

72. *The Washington Post*, 29 October 2005, 'Where the IEDs lie, the Buffalo roams'.
73. Hansard, 9 November 2005: Column 553W.
74. Defence of the Realm (blog), 13 January 2007, 'The shadow minister responds'.
75. *The Sunday Mirror*, 9 November 2008, 'Indefensible – pen-pushers banned from death-trap Land Rovers, but they're still OK for our heroes'.
76. MNF press release, 25 October 2006, 'Coalition forces conduct search operation in Basrah'.
77. *The Independent*, 1 November 2005, 'Basra bomb kills 20 as Iraq violence escalates'.
78. *The Washington Post*, 26 November 2005, 'Police in Basra find body of second Sunni cleric killed in a week'.

burst into the home of an intelligence official from the defence ministry and killed him. Two Iraqi police officers, one a colonel, were killed when a bomb struck their convoy on 8 November. Four were injured.[79]

With a clearly deteriorating security situation, even a casual observer might have felt that more troops were needed. There was no question of that. Despite Blair's assurances of support for the Iraqis, the political imperative was unchanged. Troop reductions were going ahead. This gave rise to more leaks, by which means *The Guardian* 'learned' that a phased withdrawal was possible by the middle of 2006. The timing would be linked to the elections scheduled for 15 December. They were the first under the new constitution, and would establish a government for a full span of four years. Voters were choosing 275 members of parliament from among 7,655 candidates running on 996 tickets. The successful candidates would appoint a prime minister for a 'national unity' government. The occasion would also mark the Sunnis joining the political process. Blair and George Bush would then claim they had introduced democracy, making it easier to begin talking openly about withdrawal.[80]

Out in Basra, Army commanders, in what can only be described as a triumph of hope over experience, had deemed it was quiet enough for the Snatches to come out again. On patrol on 20 November were Sgt John Jones with L/Cpl Mark Dryden as his driver. As they drove over a railway line leading into the old port, there was a loud explosion, then a second. Sgt Jones was killed and four others, including Dryden, were seriously injured.[81] To no one's surprise, this was another EFP strike.[82]

Since it happened in a public place, media photographers captured numerous pictures of the wrecked Snatch. These were quickly to be seen on the internet throughout the world. What was less visible was the wider impact of the bombing. The Army, once again, took a defensive stance, retreating from contact with the population at large, thereby taking on the mantle of a distant, occupying force. The only time most inhabitants saw British troops was when they passed through in heavy armoured columns. Foot patrols by soldiers wearing berets were history, except in a few safe areas on the fringes of the city. Routine movements between bases were now entirely by helicopter. The majority of troops spent their time at their bases. Yet imposing this isolation was the only way to halt the politically sensitive deaths and injuries.[83]

79. AP Worldstream, 8 November 2005, 'Senior police officer killed in Basra'.
80. *The Guardian*, 16 November 2005, 'Troops may start to leave Iraq in May'.
81. *The Independent on Sunday*, 9 November 2008, 'Casualties of war: a soldier writes'.
82. BBC, 20 November 2005, 'UK soldier killed by Iraq blast'.
83. *The Independent*, 13 December 2005, 'From flowers to armoured vehicles: British forces in Basra'.

A NEW DOCTRINE EMERGES

To rationalise this policy, there started to emerge an insidious yet seductive doctrine. Security for British forces in Iraq, it was argued, had deteriorated while it had improved for local people. By any measure, this was not true. There had been no improvement for local people. But it offered a spurious justification for the British withdrawal. Remove the troops and the violence would diminish still further. The very presence of the troops, rather conveniently, had become the cause of the violence.

According to this mantra, Iraqi security forces taking over should have resulted in reduced violence. Yet on Friday 26 November the Iraqi National Guard – the proto Iraqi Army – mounted a night raid to arrest an insurgent group. The result was a fierce, seven-hour battle in which 10 Guards were killed.[84]

Nor were the security forces trustworthy. That same Friday, a Sunni Imam had been found dead after being arrested in a police raid on his home. It was the second killing of a Sunni Imam that week.[85] This was but a continuation of the killing that had started the moment the British had entered Basra in 2003. Now, it was being done by militias in police uniform.

The British, though, had other preoccupations, particularly in al-Amarah. There, Abu Naji was under siege. Activity was increasingly limited to sallies in Warriors backed by Challenger tanks. One soldier said: 'We go out in armoured Land Rovers which are barely armed and we're getting minced.' In the camp, the days were punctuated by sirens warning of rocket and mortar attacks, 17 in the month the battle group had taken over. The city was even less safe. A soldier, fixing a radio antennae on the roof of a communications centre, was shot by a sniper.[86]

Basra province also remained hazardous. On 1 December, a bomb destroyed 'a British Jeep' on the Faw Peninsula, wounding four soldiers, one seriously.[87] The small base on the peninsular was then attacked on 9 December, eyewitnesses speaking of a 'powerful bomb' with smoke rising over the camp as sirens wailed.[88]

The effect was to concentrate British minds still further on force protection. Thus, as the elections drew close, the militia rivalry continued unchecked – there was nothing to constrain it. The British were mainly

---

84. *Free Arab Voice*, 26 November 2005, Resistance Report 350.
85. *Free Arab Voice*, 26 November 2005, Resistance Report 350.
86. *The Daily Record*, 29 November 2005, 'Iraqi rockets landed outside the camp … the boys turned back to their Chicken Kiev'.
87. *Free Arab Voice*, 1 December 2005, Resistance Report 355.
88. *Free Arab Voice*, 9 December 2005, Resistance Report 363.

interested in protecting themselves, not stopping the violence. As long as it was not directed at them, it could continue. Thus there was a drive-by shooting in the Sadr-controlled area of Hayaniyah in the pre-dawn hours of Sunday 4 December. Three officials of the Badr-controlled Internal Affairs Directorate were killed. In another incident, a member of the Directorate was arrested while tearing down election posters of Sunni candidates.[89] Nevertheless, when the election arrived, the British Army suspended patrols in order to avoid accusations of influencing the process. The day passed off peacefully.[90]

Had there been a clinical analysis of the results, no comfort could have been drawn from them. The electoral battle in the south had been a contest between the pro-Shiite, Islamist United Iraqi Alliance (UIA) and the secularist, National Iraqi List. The Islamists had swept to victory. They took 77 per cent of the vote in Basra and 87 per cent in Maysan.[91] This gave Muqtada another boost. His party had become one of the largest single groups in the National Assembly and had effectively gained political control of the south. The elections, therefore, had not brought Iraq closer to peace. Attacks on British troops were not going to stop. On 16 December, a bomb exploded near a British convoy close to the Old State Building.[92]

BLAIR ANNOUNCES WITHDRAWALS

Despite the continuing violence, Blair was determined to misinterpret the electoral results, ignoring the victory of the extremists. On 22 December, therefore, he made a 'surprise' visit to Basra, declaring the situation 'transformed'. Exactly as expected, he then signalled troop withdrawals, to begin in six months. Thus, 800 troops in Maysan province and 300 in Muthanna province had been switched to 'tactical overwatch' – going out on patrol with the Iraqi security forces only when asked for help.[93] Otherwise, they were going to sit in their bases.

With his statements, Blair had given the green light to Sadr and spelt the death knell of moderation. There was no need to work with the British – they were leaving. Sadr was going to do the best he could to hasten the process – and claim the credit.

89. *Free Arab Voice*, 4 December 2005, Resistance Report 358.
90. *The Times*, 15 December 2005, 'Ballot papers run short as Sunnis turn out to vote'.
91. Reider Vissar, 22 December 2005, Histories of political imaging.
92. *Free Arab Voice*, 16 December 2005, Resistance Report 370.
93. *The Times*, 23 December 2005, 'Iraq troops sent back to bases ahead of pullout'.

Chapter 5 – Descent into chaos

Basra and al-Amarah:
January–June 2006

Basra is calm and British forces are working hand in hand with their Iraqi and coalition partners. Suggestions that the city is, in some way, out of control are ridiculous.

DES BROWNE, SECRETARY OF STATE FOR DEFENCE,
BASRA, 18 MAY 2006

Less than one month into the New Year, L/Cpls Allan Douglas and Colin Meikle were standing on the roof of a police station in al-Amarah. Their commander was in the building below and they had been keeping watch. Just as they were about to leave, a shot rang out. Meikle heard the crack of the rifle. He looked up and heard the thump as the round passed. Allan Douglas fell back unconscious. He died later that day.[1]

On the home front, that marked out this war. Every death was personal, every name known. Each time a soldier died, the prime minister and defence secretary offered their condolences at the despatch box in the Commons. That ritual alone served to magnify the impact of the losses, personalising them in a way never seen before. Then the media kept a running count. Alan Douglas was the 99th to die. The 100th came on 31 January when Cpl Gordon Pritchard died in a blast in Umm Qasr. Three other soldiers were injured, one seriously. All four had been in a Snatch.[2,3] Predictably, the media made a meal of the event, a completely artificial landmark that included non-combat injuries.[4] The distinction gave the media two hits. They could highlight the '100th death' – with 77 killed in action – and then come back for the 100th combat fatality. Pritchard's death had an added twist. He had been one of the soldiers whom Blair had met on his flying visit to Basra in December. The media also made much of that.[5]

Meanwhile, Blair's withdrawal plans were taking shape. Foreign Secretary Jack Straw paid a brief visit to Basra early in the New Year, to shore up the agenda. He 'indicated' that 'one or two provinces' outside Basra could

1. BBC, 17 November 2006, 'Justice hope for soldier's family'.
2. MoD Website, 31 January 2006, 'Corporal Gordon Alexander Pritchard killed in Iraq'.
3. Associated Press, 30 January 2006.
4. BBC, 31 January 2006, 'UK forces suffer 100th Iraq death'.
5. *The Independent*, 2 February 2006, 'The corporal who met Tony Blair. A month later, he was killed in Iraq'.

soon be 'stable enough to pull some troops out'. His trip was spent entirely inside the British compound. It was too precarious for him to venture into the city.[6] There was, of course, the bigger picture. The newly elected Iraqi politicians were in Baghdad, now haggling about the shape and composition of a government upon which the plans for troop withdrawal were to depend. That was to become a protracted affair.[7]

THE IRANIAN DIMENSION

Over the border there was the brooding presence of Iran, locked in 'negotiations' with the Western powers over its nuclear weapons programme. The fear was that if a tough line was taken with Tehran, support for the Shi'a insurgency would increase, with deadly consequences for the troops.[8] For whatever reason, after the strident accusations about Iran supplying EFPs, a statement was quietly slipped out which effectively ruled out Tehran's involvement.

Michael Evans of *The Times* reported it, writing that officials were now 'merely' saying that the new technology matched bomb-making expertise traditionally found in Syria and Lebanon. Although the devices or the technology to construct them 'must have been smuggled to Iraq across the Iranian border into Maysan province in the south', there was no longer any intelligence linking the bombs to Tehran or even to elements of the Iranian Revolutionary Guard.[9]

The claim that the technology *must* have come from Iran was disingenuous. The French had made a very similar off-route mine, which had been sold to Iraq.[10,11] Furthermore, it had been fitted with infra-red initiation. There is, therefore, a possibility that the technology was already in Iraq, perhaps copied by a disaffected Army specialist working for the insurgency.

THE BOMBING CONTINUES

Nevertheless, the EFP issue, and the relationship between the different militias with Iran, were to be running themes, confused, confusing and unresolved. In the meantime, on the ground in Basra and elsewhere, bombing and killing continued. An egregious episode occurred on 18 January,

6. BBC, 6 January 2006, 'First UK troops "may leave Iraq"'.
7. *Taipei Times*, 8 January 2006, 'Straw urges Iraq to form an "inclusive government"'.
8. *The Independent*, 14 January 2006, 'British troops could be victims of Iran's nuclear stand-off with West'.
9. *The Times*, 2 January 2006, 'Bomb allegations withdrawn'.
10. Produced by Giat Industries, designated the MIACAH F1.
11. Mine Action Information Center, Ordata online, undated, French landmine, ID 1655.

when a roadside bomb hit a convoy carrying a US security team, killing two American civilians and seriously wounding a third.[12] The military continued to be targets. An attempt was made on a British patrol the following day, slightly wounding a soldier.[13] This was the Thursday. On the Friday, *Mafkarat al-Islam* reported that a roadside bomb in northern Basra 'disabled a British tank and wounded or killed four or five British soldiers'.[14]

The British, on the other hand, were continuing to devote their resources to force protection. On 24 January, they mounted a series of dawn raids detaining several police officers and others linked to the killings, bombings and kidnappings. In all, 14 were taken. Brigadier Patrick Marriott put a gloss on the action, saying it was aimed at 'ridding rogue elements from Basra's security services'.[15] In that the police were mounting many of the attacks on British forces, that much was true. And it had been a major effort, deploying more than 400 troops, including 150 Danish soldiers, and air cover.[16] But nine of the suspects were subsequently released. Nevertheless, this suggested that new tactics were being employed. As the bomb attacks on the British had intensified, gradually the emphasis had shifted to raids which specifically targeted the bomb-makers.

The tactics had little effect. The same day as the latest raid, insurgents attacked another British patrol. Riding in a Snatch, Bombardier Sharron Taylor was hit by shrapnel when a bomb exploded near her vehicle. She suffered minor wounds but the real victims were the 22 high school students wounded by the blast, two of them seriously. Two teachers had also been injured.[17] There may also have been another British patrol attacked, with two British soldiers and two Iraqi policemen injured. Four rockets were fired into the Basra Palace complex.[18]

POLITICAL REPERCUSSIONS

The British raids had political repercussions. Basra governor Mohammed Waeli, a Fadhila member, hostile to the occupation and close to Iran, had been constantly demanding the withdrawal of British troops. He and the provincial council 'composed entirely of Shi'a, many of them former

12. AP, 18 January 2006, 'Two US civilians killed in Iraq bombing'.
13. AP Worldstream, 19 January 2006, 'British soldier lightly wounded in southern Iraq roadside bombing'.
14. *Free Arab Voice*, 20 January 2006, Resistance Report 404.
15. *Ireland Online*, 24 January 2006, 'British troops detain Iraqi police officers in raids'.
16. *The Daily Telegraph*, 25 January 2006, '400 British troops in swoop on "corrupt" Basra police'.
17. *Manchester Evening News*, 28 January 2006, 'I want her home, says mother of bomb victim'.
18. *Free Arab Voice*, 24 January 2006, Resistance Report 409.

Iranian residents', issued a statement denouncing the arrests and calling on the British to release its captives. Observers noted that the council had never protested about 'the killings, abductions, sectarian imprisonment, and incidents of torture of Sunni individuals in the province'. [19]

The previous September, after the Jameat incident, the governor had threatened to withdraw cooperation from the Army and now this was what he planned to do. He called for mass demonstrations unless the British freed the policemen and sent an ultimatum calling for their release. As he was framing his demands, a bomb exploded in a crowded Basra market, killing at least one woman and wounding three others. It had been planted by a man who had got out of a traffic police vehicle. [20]

Lt Gen John Cooper, then commander of the British-led multinational force, responded to al-Waeli with an open letter addressed to the citizens of Basra. He described those arrested as 'the most dangerous and corrupt people in Basra'. Many of them were believed to have had strong ties with neighbouring Iran, exerting broad control over all areas of city life, enforcing strict Muslim codes of dress and behaviour with beatings and shootings. Those arrested had included a police major from the Department of Internal Affairs – which had been accused of running torture cells under the aegis of the Criminal Intelligence Unit and the Serious Crimes Unit.

Cooper said that his men were acting at the behest of the Interior Ministry, which had 'instructed the chief of police to remove the most dangerous and most rotten elements from the police service'. He added: 'They can no longer intimidate and attack those officers who wish to uphold the Iraqi law and protect the Iraqi people. Now a long-term strategy of reform can truly begin.' [21] But this was wishful thinking, motivated by a vague sense that, if the attacks stopped – of their own volition – then the kindly British could get down to some reconstruction. But there was no reconciliation in the offing, and never likely to be. This was akin to pleading with the IRA to be nice people – and about as effective. Waeli and the council had their own agenda – and building his strength was Muqtada, his militias soon ready again to take the Army on full-frontal.

'SIMMERING TENSIONS COMING TO THE SURFACE'

At this time, the wider world intruded. The previous September, the Danish newspaper *Jyllands-Posten* had published cartoons of the Prophet

---

19. *Free Arab Voice*, 25 January 2006, Resistance Report 410.
20. *The Independent*, 27 January 2006, 'Basra governor threatens to stop liaison with British'.
21. *The Times*, 28 January 2006, 'Basra governor threatens British'.

Mohammad. It had taken Moslem communities to the end of January to be offended by them but they were now demonstrating all over the world. In al-Amarah, 1,000 Sadr supporters turned out. And there was a Danish contingent in the area. With weary predictability, a joint Danish-Iraqi military patrol was targeted. They were hit by a roadside bomb. One unfortunate Iraqi policeman was wounded.[22]

By the end of January, therefore, there had been no let-up in the violence. The 100th British military death, though, saw a number of reflective – if superficial – pieces in the UK media. James Hider in *The Times* noted: 'In Basra there is a suppressed undercurrent of violence.' There were far fewer car bombings than in Baghdad but there were daily reports of assassinations, kidnaps and murders by the militias. There was, he added, 'an overriding atmosphere of fear'. That was not necessarily the British Army's fault. 'The British only have 8,000 troops in Basra and they could not use the American tactic of tackling the militias head-on. They could not afford to get into a showdown with the Shias.' He concluded: 'It looks like the simmering tensions are coming up to the surface.'[23]

That much was a false picture. The tensions had never been under the surface. Nevertheless, Hider offered a useful antidote to the false optimism of the politicians. Almost to prove the point, on 2 February, two officers from the 'police intelligence division' were gunned down while driving an official car.[24] The following day, 'resistance fighters' attacked a motorcade conveying the director of intelligence in a district south of Basra. He was severely injured and his driver was killed. In another incident, armed men opened fire on the prayer leader at a mosque in az Zubayr, seriously wounding him.[25]

That February, vicious fighting had broken out in Afghanistan. Even though Iraq was crying out for more troops, Blair had pledged 3,000 additional troops to this theatre (where, famously, they would perform their mission without a shot being fired). This made it even more important that Iraq should be a 'success'. Only then could there be the much anticipated 'drawdown'. Only this would reduce the Army's 'overstretch' and allow Blair – now considering fresher fields after nearly 10 years in office – to retire in triumph. His 'success', though, could not be declared until provincial elections had been held, which could not be until six weeks after a national government had been formed. More than seven weeks since the December poll, politicians were still bickering about this.

22. AP, 30 January 2006, 'Bomb targets Danish-Iraqi military in Iraq'.
23. *The Times*, 31 January 2006, 'On the spot: bubbling tension in Basra'.
24. *Free Arab Voice*, 2 February 2006, Resistance Report 418.
25. *Free Arab Voice*, 3 February 2006, Resistance Report 419.

Yet, on 5 February, British military chiefs were urging a reduction in the troop levels.[26]

That day, another bomb exploded, this one by a British convoy on the road linking az Zubayr with Safwan. Iraqi police claimed the bomb had 'disabled a British tank, wounding three British troops'. Also, the deputy director of prisons in Basra was murdered.[27] Elsewhere, insurgents shot at Danish soldiers while they were giving first aid to a group of children injured in a traffic accident.[28] Children hurled stones at another Danish patrol and a bomb was defused near their base in Qurnah. 'All these things add up to the idea that we might not be as popular as we have been as a result of the Prophet Muhammad drawings,' observed a rueful Danish forces Capt Filip Ulrichsen.[29]

On 6 February, the Shatt al-Arab Hotel came under mortar bombardment. The next day, four policemen were wounded when a bomb targeted their patrol. On the 11th, armed gunmen shot dead the Iraqi Army spokesman in Basra as he was on his way to work.[30,31]

Already fragile, the prospects for peace were looking even bleaker a few days later. While Shi'ite leaders had again been meeting in Baghdad to discuss the next prime minister, the *News of the World* published a video showing four young Iraqi males, including a child, being beaten by British soldiers. This was the footage taken during the al-Amarah riots in January the previous year.[32] As Arab satellite television stations replayed the video alongside images from the Abu Ghraib prisoner abuse, Abu Naji was attacked by a barrage of more than 20 rockets. Hundreds of troops were forced to take cover. In another incident, a British patrol was fired on by a hidden gunman.[33]

This was the excuse the provincial council needed to break off contact. It framed a litany of demands, including the withdrawal of Danish troops and an apology to Muslims worldwide from the Danish government. It also demanded that soldiers accused of beating 'innocent Iraqis' were brought to justice.[34] Demonstrators took to the streets to burn British flags.[35] Muqtada's representative vowed that if British forces continued

---

26. *The Independent*, 5 February 2006, 'Generals call for faster Iraq pull-out'.
27. *Free Arab Voice*, 5 February 2006, Resistance Report 421.
28. ABC News, 7 February 2006, 'Danish soldiers come under attack in Iraq'.
29. Associated Press, 6 February 2006, 'Al-Sadr grabs Iraqi political limelight amid prophet picture protests'.
30. RTE News, 7 February 2006, 'At least seven die in double blast in Baghdad'.
31. AFP, 11 February 2006, 'Iraq Army spokesman in Basra shot dead'.
32. *The Times*, 13 February 2006, 'Battalion involved in Army abuse video is named'.
33. *The Sunday Telegraph*, 18 February 2006, 'Troops came under attack within hours of beating video'.
34. CNN, 14 February 2006, 'Basra council breaks ties with coalition'.
35. *The Independent*, 15 February 2006, 'Basra demonstrators burn British flag as victims of army abuse threaten to sue'.

'their actions against our people, we will make Basra a mass grave for them'.[36] Even the foreign minister of Iran joined in, accusing British forces of having 'destabilised security in the city'.[37] Then the chairman of the Maysan council gave notice that all contacts with the British would be suspended.[38]

The head of the Islamic Party in Basra intervened in a different way. He wrote of the bemusement of the people of Basra by reports that, since 2003, they and their city had enjoyed 'a state of calm and stability under the command of the British forces'. Their 'smug superiority' is an insult to those of us who live here, he added. Until recently, Britain had been admired and respected by Iraqis. 'The past three years have seen to it that that respect has been obliterated,' he said.[39] He was wasting his breath. The British were beyond shame. They had their agenda and what a mere Sunni Arab was telling them was of very little importance.

All the while the insurgents continued attacks on support personnel – Iraqi and foreign – two Macedonian contractors working with coalition forces being kidnapped.[40] And, on Sunday, 19 February, a Badr Brigade commander was shot dead at a food stall in central Basra. Shaibah was treated to a salvo of four rockets on 20 February. Next day, Danish troops came under attack.[41]

A LURCH TOWARDS CIVIL WAR

The seeds of neglect were now to reap a deadly harvest. Wednesday 22 February saw an event which shocked the whole of Iraq. Men dressed in Iraqi security force uniforms broke into the Askariya shrine in Samarra, about 65 miles north of Baghdad. In one of the Shi'ites' holiest shrines, they had planted a huge bomb which blasted the famous gilded dome 'into naked steel and gaping blue sky'. The intention was to provoke civil war and the Shi'a response was quick in coming. More than 20 Sunni mosques across Iraq were hit. At least 18 people were killed, including two Sunni clerics.[42]

That much could not have been prevented by the British. But in Basra, where their responsibilities lay, Shi'a protestors filled the streets. Civil order

36. *The Washington Post*, 26 February 2006, 'An end to the soft sell by the British in Basra'.
37. *The Washington Post*, 18 February 2006, 'Iran demands British troops leave Basra'.
38. *The Times*, 20 February 2006, 'Council cuts ties with forces'.
39. Jasem al-Aqrab, *The Guardian*, 16 February 2006, 'The Basra video should lay to rest a scurrilous lie'.
40. BBC, 18 February 2006, 'Seven killed in bombings in Iraq'.
41. Details in this and the preceding paragraphs also from: *Free Arab Voice*, undated, 'The Other War in Iraq'.
42. *The Washington Post*, 23 February 2006, 'Bombing shatters mosque in Iraq'.

collapsed. Gunmen attacked the Sunni al Ashara Mosque, firing three rockets directly into it. Three other mosques were also attacked. Armed gangs stormed the headquarters of the Islamic Party, setting it on fire and slaughtering the occupants. Police, largely Badr militia, prevented anyone from intervening. Mobs also attacked the Sunni Waqf Directorate. They beat up the guards, burst into the building, and hurled hand grenades into the rooms, setting them ablaze.[43] On the outskirts of the city, dozens of armed Shi'ites stormed a Sunni shrine.[44] In the centre, gunmen dressed as police officers entered Mina prison and seized 11 suspected Sunni insurgents, including several foreigners. Their bodies were later found in the city, amid reports that they had been tortured before being shot.[45]

The following day, the violence spent, the city was 'quiet but uneasy'. On the Friday, 24 February, Basra airport was blasted by mortars. Local people reported ambulances and a helicopter arriving.[46] In the city, gunmen kidnapped three children of a Shi'ite assembly member, Qasim Attiyah al-Jbouri – a member of the Dawa Party and former head of Basra's provincial council. They were released unharmed a few hours later. Meanwhile, police found the bodies of two bodyguards for the Basra head of the Sunni Waqf Directorate. Like the Sunni prisoners, they had been shot.[47]

A particularly worrying aspect of the wave of violence was that sectarian killers often disguised themselves as army or police officers or really were soldiers or policemen. This meant that both Shi'a and Sunni would be forced to rely on their own powerful militias for security. Patrick Cockburn, writing for *The Independent*, felt that this development marked 'a new stage in the disintegration of the Iraqi government'.[48] It also marked a new low point in the conduct of the occupation.

LOSING CONTROL IN AL-AMARAH

That 'disintegration' was even more advanced in al-Amarah where the BBC's Jane Corbin was making a *Panorama* documentary. The British, she found, were increasingly leaving it to the new provincial council and to Iraqi security forces to keep the peace. But a 'respected local tribal leader' had told her, 'there is chaos in town, assassinations and a lack of discipline and leadership among local forces'. Clearly, the local security forces were not coping.

43. *Free Arab Voice*, 22 February 2006, Resistance Report 438.
44. AP, 22 February 2006, 'Basra: Shi'ite rioters set fire to Sunni shrine'.
45. BBC, February 2006, '"Sunni militants" killed in Basra'.
46. *Free Arab Voice*, 24 February 2006, Resistance Report 440.
47. *International Herald Tribune*, 24 February 2006, 'Iraq imposes curfew in attempt to stem unrest'.
48. *The Independent*, 24 February 2006, 'Ten imams murdered in Iraq as sectarian killings intensify'.

On her arrival, the atmosphere had been tense. Corbin attributed that to a gunman having been killed by a rival militia and the video of the pictures of British troops beating up Iraqi youths. There was more to it. Something pretty big had been 'going down' just before she had arrived, big enough for US and RAF aircraft to have been called in to provide close air support to troops 'in contact with anti-Iraqi forces'.[49] Nevertheless, on 28 February, she had been taken to the city by Capt Richard Holmes. After nearly an hour, he had felt it dangerous to stay. 'Quickly but calmly' he had escorted her to the army vehicles and left. Corbin recalls that as she reached Abu Naji 15 minutes later, there had been a flurry of activity: 'a helicopter racing overhead en route into al Amarah – Warriors being scrambled and jets roaring overhead.'

Capt Holmes and another soldier, Pte Lee Ellis, had been killed by an IED placed in an abandoned car.[50] Another soldier had been injured. As he had staggered from the wrecked vehicle, he had been attacked by a mob of around 30 locals hurling bricks.[51] The vehicle had been a Snatch. Before he had died, Ellis had told his sister that the city was dangerous. 'You didn't go out in that town unless in a Warrior,' he had said. In January, though, as had happened so many times before with tragic results, it had been 'deemed safe enough to travel in Land Rovers (death traps)'.[52] Despite the troops in Abu Naji being on 'high alert' after the video release, Snatches had continued in use.

The Army really should have known better. Each time there had been accusations – real or invented – of British soldiers involved in the abuse of Iraqi citizens, there had been a violent backlash. Faked pictures of abuse had appeared in the *Daily Mirror* in May 2004 and 11 soldiers had been injured in 100 engagements with Iraqi gunmen in and around Basra and al-Amarah.[53] A Snatch must have been a very obvious target.

John Reid was unapologetic. There was 'simply too much at stake' to allow British casualties to affect an early hand-over. 'Despite all the blemishes we have to deal with the reality as it is in Iraq today and it is a far better reality than it was only a few years ago,' he said. Many would have disagreed. But Corbin had caught the mood. 'The truth,' she said, 'is the British believe they have gone as far as they can in Maysan. It is "good enough", as one British army officer put it, for troops to start leaving soon.'[54] Defeat had taken over the minds of the military.

49. Air Force Link, 23 February 2006, 'CENTCOM releases daily airpower summary'.
50. BBC, March 2006, 'A British tragedy in a volatile province'.
51. *The Times*, 1 March 2006, 'Tributes paid to British soldiers killed in Iraq'.
52. Military Families Against the War website, 4 December 2004, 'RIP Private Lee Ellis – Killed for a war based on lies'.
53. *The Scotsman*, 1 March 2006, 'Mob violence after bomb kills UK troops'.
54. BBC, March 2006, 'A British tragedy in a volatile province', *op. cit.*

As for Reid's 'blemishes', that was a novel way of describing a full-blown insurgency and a nascent civil war, but he was allowed to get away with it. There were more of his 'blemishes' to follow. Another Sunni cleric was gunned down in Basra as he left a mosque after dawn prayers.[55] The consulate at Basra Palace was mortared again, injuring one civilian.[56] Qasim Attiyah al-Jbouri, who had had his children kidnapped 10 days previously, was seriously wounded when gunmen fired on his car. An aide was killed. Two bodyguards were injured.[57] A Danish soldier was shot in the leg while his unit was sealing off an area after finding a roadside bomb.[58]

The following day there was another 'blemish' – an attack on a Snatch patrol mounted by the Royal Scots Dragoon Guards, seven miles south of Basra. The IED missed its intended target and exploded only after the convoy had passed. As bomb disposal teams made the device safe, a second was discovered. A third device was found some miles away.[59] The Guards were not to be so lucky next time.

Lucky also was a group of plain-clothed soldiers. In an incident redolent of the capture of the two soldiers in September which had led to the Jameat siege, Iraqi police claimed they had 'tried to stop a group of British intelligence officers wearing civilian clothes, in two cars'. According to the Iraqis, they had driven off without providing identification. After a chase and as police had tried to surround one of the vehicles, the occupants had opened fire, wounding four people. British troops arrived and helped them escape.[60] A major incident had been averted. Almost by way of light relief, a bomb exploded at the Basra headquarters of Iraq's Southern Oil Company, causing minor damage but no casualties.[61]

THE ARMY SETS THE WITHDRAWAL AGENDA

The Army was now to intervene very publicly in the political debate. Lt Gen Nick Houghton, the most senior Army officer in Baghdad, revealed an intention to withdraw most British troops from Iraq by the summer of 2008. The withdrawal was prompted, said the General, by confidence that Iraq's 225,000 soldiers and police officers 'could soon maintain order without assistance'. As events were to demonstrate, this was wildly optimistic.

55. CBS News, 2 March 2006, 'Bomb rips through Baghdad market'.
56. *Free Arab Voice*, 2 March 2006, Resistance Report 446.
57. *USA Today*, 4 March 2006, 'Blast at terminal kills 7 in Iraq, breaking one-day calm'.
58. *AP Worldstream*, 7 March 2006, 'Danish soldier shot in leg in southern Iraq'.
59. BBC, 6 March 2006, 'Roadside device targets UK troops'.
60. AFP, 8 March 2006, 'UK troops shot at policemen, say Iraqis'.
61. *Fox News*, 8 March 2006, 'Dozens of security workers kidnapped in Baghdad'.

But the prospect of an early departure has the insurgents rejoicing. Muqtada's Baghdad spokesman happily announced that the departure of the troops was 'our aim and our goal'.

Houghton was clearly happy to oblige Muqtada. To justify his stance, however, he offered a carefully crafted and superficially reasonable explanation. There was a need, he said, for a 'gradual withdrawal' to ensure that the Iraqi people understood that British troops had no intention of staying for ever. 'There is a fine line between staying too long and leaving too soon. A military transition over two years has a reasonable chance of avoiding the pitfalls of overstaying our welcome but gives us the best opportunity of consolidating the Iraqi security forces,' he said.[62]

By then, the Army was openly briefing that the presence of British and American troops was becoming part of the problem. The line was that foreign soldiers driving tanks in towns, as they had to do for their safety, did not create a peaceful environment.[63] What it was actually admitting was that the absence of a vehicle safer than a Snatch, yet less aggressive than a Warrior, was having a strategic effect on the campaign, threatening its very continuation. Not being able to engage with the population without suffering casualties, the Army was having to use heavier armour and in so doing distancing itself from the population, thereby increasingly alienating itself and attracting more attacks. But rather than address the root cause of the problem, it was drawing entirely the wrong conclusions – the conclusions it wanted to draw. It chose to interpret the problem as a reason for leaving.

Iraqi president Jalal Talabani did not welcome Houghton's intervention. His spokesman stated: 'If the multinational forces leave too quickly the consequences could be very bad ... It is very important that these troops are in Iraq. They help ensure stability. In order for the Iraqi Army to be able to combat external interference will take many years.'[64] Despite that, John Reid announced that Britain was cutting troop levels from 8,000 to 7,200. He described this move as 'the end of the beginning'. For many Iraqis, those to be murdered in the streets by the militias, it was to be their end.

The timing was dictated entirely by domestic politics. Blair had been facing a difficult week over his reform agenda and, marking the third anniversary of the invasion, large anti-war demonstrations were expected. He was under strong pressure to withdraw troops, not least from the families of the 103 British soldiers killed in Iraq. Articulating his worst

---

62. *The Daily Telegraph*, 8 March 2006, 'British troops out of Iraq in two years, says general'.
63. *The Daily Telegraph*, 7 March 2006, 'Time is now right to begin withdrawing troops'.
64. *The Daily Telegraph*, 8 March 2006, 'Iraqis fear more violence if soldiers are withdrawn too quickly'.

political nightmare was Reg Keys, whose son Tom had been one of six RMPs killed in Majar al-Kabir. 'The honeymoon period ... is well and truly over,' Keys warned. 'It is just going to be a constant trickle of flag-draped coffins until the Government starts a phased withdrawal.'[65]

The danger the British were quite blatantly ignoring was highlighted by a Washington insider. The greatest threat to stability was Muqtada al-Sadr and his militia, he said. Sadr was riding a 'wave of tremendous popular support'. His movement, with its arsenal of weapons and radical ideology, posed a threat to any central authority and inspired other political movements to take up arms. A high-level US official thought the Sunni-led insurgency was troublesome but not a threat to the whole order of Iraq. Basra, increasingly under the control of Sadr, was. A senior Western diplomat noted: 'It is not an acceptable answer to succumb to the presence of a militia to protect a particular neighbourhood or a city's security.'[66] That was precisely what the British were doing.

The troops were paying the price – and were to continue to do so. On 13 March, Danish troops were attacked twice, taking small arms and RPG fire.[67] Two days later, another British military convoy was targeted, a bomb injuring two civilians and a British soldier, also destroying a civilian car. A damaged Warrior, skewed across an urban carriageway, had a set of its road wheels blown off and scorch marks up its side.[68] Snatches had been part of the convoy but the Warrior had taken the hit. Some in the military were beginning to suspect that the Mahdi Army was beginning to target Warriors, looking for a 'spectacular' which would grab the headlines. It would succeed.

This attack had been in Basra, visible to local journalists. In al-Amarah, there was no such visibility and only rarely did the military lift the curtain. On one such occasion, the MoD revealed how Tornado GR4s on a routine sortie had been diverted to the city. A Warrior-mounted patrol had taken fire, a crowd had gathered and the detachment commander had called for help. A Tornado flew over the crowd at 250ft 'causing people to run for cover', allowing the patrol to extract.[69] That alone should have been sufficient to warn that security was fragile.

Some were thinking through the consequences of withdrawal, among them Terri Judd, writing for *The Independent*. 'Overshadowing everything

---

65. *The Independent*, 14 March 2006, 'Withdrawal of 800 troops from Iraq takes heat off Blair'.
66. *Los Angeles Times*, 13 March 2006, 'Radical Iraqi Cleric Expands His Reach'.
67. BBC Monitoring, 14 March 2006, 'Danish troops attacked in Iraq'.
68. AP Photo/Nabil Al-Juarni, 15 March 2006.
69. BBC, 17 March 2006, 'Low-flying bomber disperses mob'.

else is a security situation which is far worse than three years ago,' she wrote. There was some respect for the 'new and increasingly professional-looking Iraqi army', but little faith in the police who were believed to be responsible for much of the crime. A resident told Judd: 'Whether we like them or dislike them, the majority want to keep a British presence.' The collapse of the former regime had created a political vacuum and the security forces were still unprepared. The MNF [Multi-National Force] was vital for security.[70]

During the night of 21 March, 300 British troops provided security while several platoons carried out precisely timed arrests at nine different addresses on the outskirts of the city. Seven insurgents suspected of smuggling arms from Iran were taken. Notably, the arrest teams had met with no resistance. The officer in charge, Major Jonny Crook, observed: 'When we go in with overwhelming force, the locals tend to react positively.' Ordinary people had had enough of the lawlessness. With the security of large numbers of troops around them, they were prepared to give information. 'People have the perception that everybody is against us, but it is completely not the case,' said Crook.[71]

That was an authentic voice, pointing the way to what needed to be done. Past experience had often showed that when an area was saturated and security re-imposed, the hard men melted away. But the voice was ignored.

As might be expected, the smaller units continued to be attacked. The penny packets that were put out on the streets to maintain a token presence were easy targets for the insurgents. Thus, on 22 March, a bomb wounded two soldiers on a foot patrol and killed an Iraqi interpreter.[72] That same day, insurgents killed a Danish soldier with an IED, near the town of al Harta, the site of the first Dane to be killed in action. After that, the Danes took to patrolling in US-built M-113 tracked armoured personnel carriers.[73] The British continued to use Snatches. They might just as well have painted bulls-eyes on the sides.

BASRA PLUMBS NEW DEPTHS

Basra, meanwhile, was about to plumb new depths. On 26 March, a 13-year-old boy was killed by a bomb placed outside his school. It exploded

70. *The Independent on Sunday*, 19 March 2006, 'Whether we like them or not, the British can't leave us in a vacuum'.
71. *The Independent*, 21 March 2006, 'British troops swoop on Basra "smugglers"'.
72. *Aswat al-Iraq*, 22 March 2006, 'Iraqi interpreter killed, British soldier wounded in Basra blast'. AP Photo/Nabil Al-Juarni.
73. *Xinhua* News Agency, 24 March 2006, 'Danish soldier killed by roadside bomb in Iraq'.

just as the children were arriving for their classes. There was little doubt that they had been deliberately targeted.[74] Days later, a prominent woman lawyer was shot dead as she got out of a taxi in the centre of the city.[75] Then, in broad daylight in the middle of the city's main market place, six members of a prominent Sunni family were murdered in a drive-by shooting. The dead included a four-year-old child.[76] A policeman was also shot dead and another officer wounded.[77] Then two Sunnis – a professor and an ambulance driver – were gunned down in the streets.[78] Between 29 March and 8 April, 50 people were murdered in Basra – doctors, teachers, officials and students. By the 11th, 30 more had been killed. Steve Vincent's 'death car' featured prominently in reports. The locals called it 'Bata' – 'Swan' in English – a car with four armed men inside. Another car always followed, 'with more invisible ghosts sitting inside'.[79]

This lurch into darkness, mirrored by similar events happening elsewhere in Iraq, had the *Independent*'s Patrick Cockburn writing: 'a cruel and bloody civil war has started in Iraq.' George Bush and Tony Blair, he declared, have for the past three years continually understated the gravity of what is taking place.[80] Iraq's deputy interior minister agreed. 'Actually Iraq has been in an undeclared civil war for the past 12 months,' he said.[81]

This made the appointment of a new Iraqi prime minister all the more urgent. The United States and the UK wanted rid of Jaafari but the dominant Shi'a group in the parliament were split over the choice of a successor. Jaafari was standing his ground and, without a leader, chaos ruled.[82] A confidential assessment of the security situation confirmed this to be the case. Carried out by US officials, it portrayed a country beset by violence and sectarian division. The stability of 6 of its 18 provinces was considered 'serious'. One was said to be 'critical'. The situation in Basra was 'serious' and the report repeated that which was all too obvious: crime, intimidation, assassinations and smuggling were commonplace.[83]

Still the killing went on. On 10 April, gunmen murdered the Mayor of Qurnah and wounded his wife.[84] A professor in the College of Agriculture was gunned down while heading for work. Eleven employees of a building

---

74. *USA Today*, 26 March 2006, 'Bombing at Basra school kills student'.
75. BBC, 30 March 2006, 'Eight oil workers killed in Iraq'.
76. CNN, 3 April 2006, News roundup.
77. *Dawn*, 3 April 2006.
78. *Independent online*, 4 April 2006, 'At least 21 killed in Iraq – officials'.
79. NPR, 14 April 2006, 'A witness to horror in Basra'.
80. *The Independent*, 8 April 2006, 'Iraq three years on: Don't look away'.
81. *The Independent*, 9 April 2006, 'It's a "state of civil war", admits Iraqi government official'.
82. *The Times*, 4 April 2006, 'Strong ruler needed, not a stunt team'.
83. *The Independent*, 10 April 2006, 'Three years after Saddam's fall, US report says Iraq is in turmoil'.
84. *Aswat al Iraq*, 'Iraq-Basra-Assassination'.

company in Basra, all Sunni Arabs, were kidnapped and slaughtered. In all, 42 people were killed in Iraq over a 24-hour period.[85] Gunmen also killed the chief of Basra's traffic police and wounded his driver. An official from the riot police division was shot, his bullet-riddled body later found under a bridge.[86] Three employees of a state-run electrical company on their way to work were kidnapped and, near Basra, gunmen attacked a convoy carrying the deputy culture minister. His bodyguards had exchanged fire with the assailants and, this time, there had been no casualties.[87]

Amid the violence, mortar and rocket attacks on Abu Naji had been intensifying, with rocket strikes virtually every day.[88, 89] Rockets were also launched at Basra airport. The consulate was hit on 5 April, disrupting a party to celebrate the Queen's coronation. A report on 7 April claimed that the British forces were taking back responsibility for security, 'after it had been proved that puppet policemen had been involved in attacks on British troops as well as incidents of murder and arrest of local citizens'. An overnight curfew was declared.[90] On 14 April, a suicide bomb exploded near a British military convoy on the main road near Shaibah. Four British soldiers were injured. Two Iraqi civilians were killed. One was wounded.[91]

The very next day, the insurgents, having failed in their attempt on the Royal Scots Dragoon Guards in March, succeeded in killing with an IED one of the Regiment's 'talented and popular' young men – Lt Richard Palmer. He had been leading a Snatch patrol near ad Dayr, 22 miles northwest of Basra. The explosion slightly injured three others.[92] This had been a joint patrol with the Iraqi Army, although Lt Palmer's platoon had been attached to the Danish contingent. He had been warned about heightened tensions arising from the Muhammad cartoons and also about a possible bomb in his area the day before his last patrol. He had taken out a Snatch to investigate but had found nothing. Possibly, he had been caught by the very bomb he had been hunting. A Warrior would have saved him but it would have been too heavy for a bridge in the patrol area.[93]

Throughout this period, Saddam Hussein's trial was being held. It excited little interest. Even when he was later found guilty and hanged, there was no great public response. At this time, people were more concerned with

85. AFP, 14 April 2006, '11 abducted, shot dead in Basra'.
86. *The New York Times*, 15 April 2006, 'Dozens of Iraqi Police Still Missing Days After Night Ambush'.
87. Associated Press, 17 April 2006, 'US death toll in Iraq hits 47 for April'.
88. Uruknet, 27 March 2006, Resistance Report.
89. Uruknet, 6 April 2006, Resistance Report.
90. *Free Arab Voice*, 7 April 2006, Resistance Report 482.
91. *The Guardian*, 15 April 2006, 'Seven British soldiers injured in Iraq and Afghanistan'.
92. BBC, 16 April 2006, 'UK soldier killed in Iraq named'.
93. *The Scotsman*, 7 May 2008, 'Controversial cartoons heightened Iraq tension prior to officer's death'.

'the most absorbing Iraqi soap opera: the bungling attempts by the country's powerbrokers to agree on a prime minister'.[94] The 20th April saw
some movement when at last Jaafari agreed to step down.[95] The logjam
broken, parliament nominated the 'veteran politician' Jawad al-Maliki.
Leader of the Dawa Party, he had spent years living in exile in Iran during
Saddam's rule, having been sentenced to death. Despite that, the violence
continued.

As before, little of this was being reported by the media. Basra news
was still being buried, again most often in reports headlining something
completely different. On 21 April, for instance, *The New York Times*, in a
report on Jaafari dropping out, embedded the detail that, 'In Basra, a car
bomb killed two civilians and wounded five others ...'.[96] Likewise, in an
item about al Qaeda, the *International Herald Tribune* informed of three
men in Basra being abducted in two different incidents. In one case, the
kidnappers had worn commando uniforms.[97] These reports were absent
from the British media. The previous day, *Mafkarat al-Islam* reported that
'resistance fighters' had driven a car bomb into a British armoured column
near al Haritha. 'As is their usual practice,' the newspaper noted, the
British 'released no information regarding their losses.'[98] This was not
reported in the British media either.

What did get into *The Sunday Times* was a plea for more troops in
Afghanistan. There had been an upsurge in violence in Helmand province
and the Army was demanding reinforcements. In more than one way,
Afghanistan was affecting the Iraqi operation.[99] Most obviously, it was
making demands on limited resources. But there were other effects.
Afghanistan and Iraq, although both insurgencies, were very different
wars. The military was being asked to split its intellectual capacity. Also,
the media was splitting its resources and giving even less attention to
Basra.

One thing an alert media might have picked up was an incident reported
by a local Iraqi agency on 4 May. A US lieutenant-colonel had been killed
and two other US citizens wounded as they had travelled through the
British sector, some 25 miles north of Basra, when an IED had exploded
near their convoy. An official spokesman was keen to stress that it had been
a civilian convoy, but the local agency nevertheless noted that US forces

94. *The Times*, 18 April 2006, 'Iraqis switch off Saddam trial to watch government soap opera'.
95. *The Independent*, 21 April 2006, 'Iraq's PM agrees steps down to break political stalemate'.
96. *The New York Times*, 21 April 2006, 'Shiite drops bid to keep post as premier'.
97. *International Herald Tribune*, 21 April 2006, 'Al Qaeda video hails Iraq insurgent leader'.
98. *Free Arab Voice*, 20 April 2006, Resistance Report 495.
99. *The Sunday Times*, 23 April 2006, 'Army pleads for more troops after Afghanistan firefight'.

had recently been reported moving to Basra.[100] For some time, there had been rumours that development of the Basra airport base into a permanent camp was on a scale that far exceeded British requirements. Was this incident evidence of a planned US takeover?

This information famine obscured the fact that the situation in the south was very different from the rest of the country. There were now three simultaneous conflicts. There was a 'civil war' element, but that was not so much a war as a continuation of the ethnic cleansing of non-Shi'as which had started back in 2003. None of these minorities was sufficiently powerful to mount an armed struggle against the huge and well-armed Shi'a majority. The second element was the internal Shi'a rivalry and in particular a battle between the Mahdi Army and the other militias for the control of the south.

ATTACKS ON THE ARMY ESCALATE

Running through this was the third element – the attacks on the 'occupiers'. The British had long since lost their grip, resembling a somewhat ineffectual referee in a game where the players had abandoned the ball and were beating up each other. With the city on the point of collapse, they were almost an irrelevance. They pootled about in their Snatches, handing out sweets to children and being 'nicey-nicey' to people who were trying to kill them. Occasionally the Army made itself a nuisance with sporadic sallies from their fortresses, but the militias, although taking a steady toll, were not yet expending all their energies on attacking the 'occupiers'. They had been too busy fighting each other. That was to change. Things were about to get very nasty.

The first shock came on 6 May. At about 2pm local time, a Royal Navy Lynx was flying towards the Old State Building. Five hundred yards short, it exploded, crashing in flames onto a residential building in the centre of Basra. It had been struck by an anti-aircraft missile, fired at extreme range.[101] All five on board died instantly, including the first woman to be killed in action in Iraq, Flight Lieutenant Sarah Mulvihill.

On the ground, all hell broke loose. Troops from the OSB, backed by armoured vehicles, rushed to the scene. They were met by a hail of stones from a crowd of several hundred, shaking fists and dancing as the smoke rose. Others, 'hysterical with delight', shouted, 'Victory to the Mahdi army', while looters stripped as many parts from the burning wreck as they could.

100. *Aswat al-Iraq*, 4 May 2006, 'Iraq-Basra-US'.
101. MoD, Board of Inquiry Report into the loss of Lynx XZ614 on 6 May 2006.

Bloody battles were fought on the streets as the crowd hurled petrol bombs at troops trying to reach the blazing wreckage. At least three British vehicles were set on fire, one a Warrior. After using batons against the crowd, some of the soldiers opened fire. Four Iraqis – including a child – were killed. Only when a curfew was imposed from 8pm local time was something like calm restored.[102]

What shocked troops was the jubilation with which their misfortune was treated. They should not have been surprised. It stemmed, it was said, from the city's descent into misery. Locals warned that the violence could be repeated. There was one very small consolation. Mohammad Waeli agreed to resume cooperation with the British in an effort to defuse tension.[103] This was hardly a sign of *rapprochement* though. What had just been seen was a raw demonstration of the growing power of the Mahdi. Even Waeli was worried.

The British army spokesman in Basra said he hoped the crash had been an 'isolated incident', once again parroting the mantra. It was to become so – no more helicopters were shot down. The price was heavily limited use. Other than for the most urgent missions, flying was done at night. That put more pressure on ground patrols, exposing them to even greater risk from attack. That, it seemed, was acceptable. Losing troops in badly protected vehicles was tolerated, but precious aircraft could not be exposed to danger.

Attacks there were – in just over a fortnight, British forces were to endure 41. One was on 13 May, close to midnight, when another IED hit a Snatch. It killed two men, Ptes Joseva Lewaicei and Adam Morris. They had been on another 'routine patrol' in the second of a four-vehicle convoy crossing a bridge at al-Halaf, near Basra airport. As they had done so, the bomb had exploded, triggered by a command wire. Most military vehicles still carried electronic counter-measures which blocked signals from remotely activated bombs – the mobile phone being commonly used for this purpose – but this had rendered their ECM useless. Both soldiers had died instantly. Another had been seriously injured.[104, 105] It says a great deal for the circumstances that senior officers thought it too dangerous to send officers from the Army's Special Investigation Bureau to the scene to investigate.[106] Yet it had been 'safe' enough to send out men in unprotected Snatches.

102. *The Guardian*, 7 May 2006, 'British soldiers die as helicopter is shot down'.
103. *The Guardian*, 8 May 2006, 'British tactics reviewed as Basra erupts'.
104. BBC, 15 May 2006, 'Four troops injured at Iraq camp'.
105. *The Times*, 15 May 2006, 'Two British troops killed at end of bloodiest week'.
106. AFP, 28 February 2007, 'Inquest told Basra not safe enough for British investigators'.

On 15 May, Abu Naji suffered its heaviest attack for months. During a pounding from 56 mortar bombs and rockets, three female soldiers received shrapnel injuries. A fourth soldier was seriously injured and five more female soldiers had to be treated for shock. One officer described the scene as 'carnage'.[107] Troops were now calling their base 'Camp Incoming'.

Another Snatch was bombed on 20 May. This time the crew escaped with two of their number slightly injured, rescued by the ubiquitous Warriors. The vehicle, stalled under a road bridge, was looted and set on fire. A large group of youths entertained themselves throwing stones at the vehicle, pouring petrol on it from the bridge parapet to feed the flames.[108] This was swiftly followed by a mortar attack on the Basra airport.[109] Another British patrol was attacked on 27 May.[110] The following day, a bomb exploded by a British patrol on the road to the Shatt al-Arab Hotel. This was followed by a mortar attack on the base.[111] On 28 May, one more Snatch was hit. This time, two soldiers were slaughtered, Lt Tom Mildinhall and L/Cpl Paul Farrelly. Two others suffered minor injuries.[112]

If the Army was still using Snatches in Basra, that was no longer the case in al-Amarah. It was using Warriors. Then, it was risky. There had been heavy fighting in the centre on 12 April, when a night raid had been launched to arrest suspected insurgents. A Warrior had been disabled.[113] Even 'normal' visits were hazardous. On 23 May, Capt James Knight was making a daytime visit to a police station when his platoon of four Warriors came under attack by up to 50 insurgents using RPGs and small arms. After a brisk firefight, he was ordered to withdraw, subsequently to be awarded a Military Cross.[114] That was the measure of the situation. A routine liaison visit could end up with a medal for gallantry. If there was any pretence that this was 'peacekeeping', that was long gone on the streets of al-Amarah.

If the Army was not prepared to change its order of battle in Basra, back in the UK a change was afoot which would in time bring that about. A cabinet reshuffle on 5 May replaced Reid with Des Browne in Defence. Equipment would have to wait though. Pitched into the middle of the crisis, Browne had to hold the line against growing domestic opposition to the war. Conservative deputy leader, Michael Ancram, broke ranks with his

107. *The Independent*, 31 May 2006, 'Bloodiest month: UK suffers largest post-war losses'.
108. BBC, 20 May 2006, 'Roadside bomb targets UK troops'.
109. *The Independent*, 21 May 2006, 'British soldiers hurt in Basra bombing and attack by mob'.
110. *Free Arab Voice*, 27 May 2006, Resistance Report 532.
111. *Free Arab Voice*, 28 May 2006, Resistance Report 533.
112. BBC, 30 May 2006, 'MoD names troops killed in Iraq'.
113. *Free Arab Voice*, 12 April 2006, Resistance Report 487.
114. MoD website, Princess of Wales's Royal Regiment (Brochure).

party, demanding British withdrawal from Iraq. 'If there is a civil war,' he said, 'which all the indications are that there is now, then it is not a place where we should be.'[115]

Ancram did not speak for his party, but he reflected the views of a significant minority within it. Browne was further undermined by two of his own. One of them, Peter Kilfoyle, a former armed forces minister, said: 'A decision has to be made very shortly whether we are serving any useful purpose in Iraq any longer. I don't believe that is the case.'[116] In terms of what the troops were achieving, he had a point. But he did not stop to ask what it would take to enable troops to serve a useful purpose.

PUBLIC ORDER IN BASRA DISINTEGRATES

As to security in Basra, by mid-May one person was being murdered in the city every hour – a level close to that of Baghdad. Public order was disintegrating. Police no longer dared attend murder sites for fear of attack and the governor of Basra was trying to sack his police chief – who was himself later the target of an assassination attempt.[117] When the leader of the Karamsha clan was killed by men dressed in police uniforms on 15 May, his heavily armed clansmen stormed a police station in north Basra, killing at least 11 policemen. They also burned down two SCIRI buildings. Police and army did not intervene.[118, 119] Three days later, Browne made his first visit to Basra 'for a series of briefings with military commanders'. Amazingly, he then proclaimed: 'Basra is calm and British forces are working hand in hand with their Iraqi and coalition partners. Suggestions that the city is, in some way, out of control are ridiculous.' While he was there, he was to enjoy a boat trip along the Shatt al-Arab waterway.[120] He survived the experience. In November, others would not.

In Baghdad, Maliki, sworn in as prime minister on 20 May, was flexing his muscles. Determined to break the grip of the Fadhila Party on the economic artery of Basra's oil, he had stripped the Oil Ministry portfolio from it and handed it to an independent. Fadhila retaliated by refusing to join Maliki's government and threatening to halt oil exports. Meeting Tony Blair in the Iraqi capital on 22 May, Maliki then announced that he expected British troops to hand over responsibility in two provinces to Iraqi security forces

---

115. *The Independent*, 22 April 2006, 'Ancram calls for Britain to pull out of Iraq'.
116. *The Independent*, 31 May 2006, 'Bloodiest month: UK suffers largest post-war losses'.
117. *Independent Online*, 18 May 2006, 'Basra chief walks away after close encounter'.
118. *The Independent*, 17 May 2006, 'Basra carnage escalates as one person killed every hour'.
119. *Aswat al-Iraq*, 15 May 2006, 'Iraq-Basra Attack'.
120. MoD website, 18 May 2006, 'Defence Secretary praises forces' resolve on first visit to Basra'.

by the following month. US, British and other foreign troops should be out of 16 of the country's 18 provinces by the end of the year.[121]

This was rhetoric for domestic consumption. The new prime minister was having to play to his domestic audience, in particular his political allies, of which Muqtada was the most potent. It did not represent reality – it did not even approach reality. The violence was continuing unabated. On 26 May, 10 bullet-riddled corpses were found in al-Moqal district of Basra. Their hands were bound and there was evidence of torture.[122]

In the absence of British intervention, Maliki had to do something. On the last day of May – less than a fortnight after Des Browne had proclaimed Basra to be 'calm' – he declared a one-month state of emergency in Basra. 'We shall use an iron fist against the leaders of the gangs or those who threaten security,' he declared.[123] He set up a security committee independent of the governor, strengthened Iraqi security service arrest powers and imposed an evening curfew. He also ordered the half-trained and ill-equipped 10th Division onto the streets.[124, 125] Another British convoy was attacked.[126]

The state of emergency made little difference. On 2 June, a drive-by shooting killed a prayer leader at a Sunni mosque. On 3 June, a car bomb exploded in a popular market, two miles from the centre of Basra, killing 27 and injuring 62.[127] Next day, gunmen attacked the al-Arab Mosque in Old Basra, kidnapping nine and killing seven people. On 6 June, gunmen were roaming the streets of downtown Basra in pick-up vehicles, shooting 'heavily and randomly' at pedestrians. Eight were killed and many more wounded.[128] Five Italian soldiers, operating 20 miles south of al-Amarah, were wounded when an explosive device went off near their patrol vehicle.[129] There was also an attack on a British vehicle.[130]

The following day, the Speaker of the Iraqi parliament met a delegation of British MPs, afterwards stating, 'I made it clear … that the British troops have failed in Basra because maintaining security there was their responsibility.'[131] Yet the British had abandoned this task. Their overriding concern was their own security. Attacks on British forces in 2006 had escalated to 60 a month, a 26 per cent increase on the previous year. In January, there

121. *The Guardian*, 23 May 2006, 'Host springs surprise for PM'.
122. *Arab News*, 27 May 2006, 'Shi'ite faction menaces Iraq's Basra oil exports'.
123. CBS News, 31 May 2006, 'Iraq PM vows "Iron Fist" in restive Basra'.
124. Associated Press, 1 June 2006, 'State of Emergency declared in Basra, Iraq'.
125. *Aswat al-Iraq*, 31 May 2006, 'Iraq-Basra-Emergency-Update 1'.
126. *Free Arab Voice*, 31 May 2006, Resistance Report 536.
127. *Aswat al-Iraq*, 3 June 2006, 'Iraq-Basra-Carbomb'.
128. *Aswat al-Iraq*, 6 June 2006, 'Basra-Shooting'.
129. *Aswat al-Iraq*, 6 June 2006, 'Basra-Italians'.
130. *Free Arab Voice*, 6 June 2006, Resistance Report 542.
131. *Aswat al-Iraq*, 7 June 2006, 'Mashhadani-British'.

had been 36, in February 41, in March 57 and in April 103 – the latter split between 71 in Basra and 23 in Maysan province. The total for the first three months was 237, contrasting with 562 in the whole of 2005.[132] To contain losses, troops were again patrolling in Warriors. The routine was punctuated by occasional large-scale raids, aimed largely at protecting bases from attack.

Nowhere more so was this the case then with Abu Naji, under incessant mortar and rocket fire. Air support had been called in on 8 June.[133] On 9 June, there was another rocket attack and, on 10/11 June, the Army launched a night raid on the residential quarters of al-Amarah, the aim to find mortar and rocket teams and 'take them out'. There was no longer a hint of a 'hearts and minds' agenda. Warriors were now reinforced by 65-ton Challengers. But the raid went badly wrong when a Warrior bogged down in a sewage ditch in the centre of a main highway. What followed was the most intense battle in Iraq since 2004, lasting six hours. Over 200 Mahdi fighters attacked, using the narrow alleyways and rooftops as cover as they engaged with RPGs, heavy small arms, snipers, blast bombs and grenades. Superbly professional fighting enabled the British troops to extract with only one man wounded.

Courageously fought though it was, the raid was a strategic failure. Sadr's fighters had successfully defended their turf. The British position was becoming untenable – the 'self-licking lollipop' meant that most of their energies were almost entirely devoted to protecting their own bases. So far had the situation deteriorated that they could no longer even do that effectively. By Friday 16 June, attacks resumed. Local reports claimed five rockets fired that night, triggering 'six explosions so powerful they had been felt in nearby villages'. The insurgents followed up with mortars.[134] Many more attacks were to come. Inevitably, thinking began to concentrate, to the exclusion of all else, on that seductive premise. Remove the bases and the attacks would stop.

This brought Des Browne back to Iraq. A month after he had declared Basra 'calm', on 19 June he made a surprise visit to Baghdad for discussions with the Iraqi government on a new security plan for the city.[135] Whatever his ideas, there were others who had their own about what should be done, their primary concerns being to protect the troops from the violent attacks they were enduring. At the centre of those concerns was the Snatch.

132. *The Independent*, 29 May 2006, 'Sixty attacks a month on British forces as 1,000 soldiers go Awol'.
133. *Global Security*, 8 June 2006, 'CENTAF releases airpower summary'.
134. *Free Arab Voice*, 16 June 2006, 'Resistance barrages drive British troops out of their base and into animal pens for the night'.
135. *Aswat al-Iraq*, 19 June 2006, 'British-Basra'.

Chapter 6 – The Campaign
The political battle to replace the Snatch

The Snatch Land Rover provides us with the mobility and level of protection that we need.

LORD DRAYSON, HOUSE OF LORDS, JUNE 2006

The government lied systematically, until the very end of the war, about the Allies' tragic failure to produce tanks capable of matching those of the Germans.

MAX HASTINGS
IN: 'OVERLORD' – D-DAY AND THE BATTLE FOR NORMANDY

The home front is always ill-informed. We are not on the front line. We have very little information on what is going on and we are not – most of us – in the military. Yet, it is on the home front that counter-insurgency campaigns are won or lost. Arguably, that was the case with Vietnam, where a critical analysis suggests that US-backed forces had been winning militarily; but public support had evaporated. Without that, even the most bellicose of governments are forced to bring the troops home.

So it was in June 2006 – or very close. What we know now, we did not know then. And, while some in the popular press invoked forebodings, there was no coherent picture – just a vague feeling that things were going wrong. Nevertheless, that June, one thing did stand out – Snatch Land Rovers. An awful lot of soldiers seemed to be getting killed in them.

It had taken a long time for this issue to emerge, after many false starts. Back in August 2003 when the three RMPs had been killed in a Nissan SUV, the media had called for *more* armoured Land Rovers. *The Sunday Mirror* had argued that their deaths had been attributable to 'a shortage of armoured jeeps'. The men's comrades 'in an armoured Land Rover on the same patrol, we were told, escaped unharmed'.[1] This was perverse. There had been no armoured Land Rovers in theatre until the Snatches had arrived.[2]

Most newspapers at the time were concentrating on the Hutton inquiry but *The Daily Mail* had protested that the life-saving 'armoured Land Rovers' were being sold off as Army surplus.[3]

---

1. *Sunday Mirror*, 24 August 2003, 'Chaos in Iraq: The real price of Blair's war of words'.
2. Hansard, 9 December 2008: Column 51W.
3. BBC, 26 August 2003, 'Papers focus on Hutton inquiry fall-out'.

These Land Rovers were to emerge as a *cause célébre* in October 2005, after the death of Sgt Hickey.[4] They were the Glover Webb APVs which had been superseded by the Snatches, but that did not stop *The Scotsman* complaining that they were, 'specifically designed to withstand the kind of attack which killed the three military policemen in Basra'. It noted that they had been classed as 'army surplus' – 'despite having air conditioning' which would make them ideal for use in southern Iraq. The criticism had been led by Conservative defence spokesman Gerald Howarth who had claimed 'the sell-off was part of the Labour Government's desire to cut Britain's defences to the bare bones'.

In response, the MoD argued that it had been 'a deliberate decision' to use ordinary cars. Its rationale, now dreadfully familiar, was that they were an important part of the battle to 'win the hearts and minds of local people'. Using armoured vehicles all the time was 'inappropriate' to this aim. Civilian vehicles had been used with considerable success in places such as Bosnia. This was countered by the editor of *Jane's World Armies*. 'Any commander would welcome a hundred or so of these Land Rovers as it gives more options, especially when you are seriously short of manpower,' he said.

A foretaste of the Snatch controversy came from Lianne Seymour, whose husband Ian had been killed in the invasion. But, as with the media, she complained about the lack of armoured Land Rovers. 'The Government is far too quick to judge things in terms of cost when it's not them who face the dangers,' she said. 'If our guys are still at risk we should be doing our utmost to protect them.'[5] From *Northern Echo* reporter Steve Parsley, who had just returned from Basra, came a different perspective. 'The real problem,' he said, 'was that the Nissans and similar vehicles were not open-topped, making it harder to respond quickly to enemy fire.'[6] That, at least, the Snatch could offer. Then, so could the standard Land Rover.

The issue died. After the Snatches had arrived in Iraq, Gerald Howarth returned briefly to the subject, asking the government how many armoured Land Rovers had been deployed and whether the number would be affected by the MoD's decision to sell off some of them. He did not distinguish between the APV and the Snatch.[7] In fact, no armoured Land Rovers of any description had been sold after May 2003.[8]

4. *The Sunday Times*, 23 October 2005, 'Colonel quits as troops are denied armoured land rovers in Iraq', *op. cit.*

5. *Evening News* – Scotland, 26 August 2003, 'Defence chiefs face civilian cars storm'.

6. *The Northern Echo*, 25 August 2003, 'Hunt for the killers of hire-car soldiers'.

7. Hansard, 20 November 2003: Column 1253W.

8. Hansard, 16 September 2003: Column 705W.

It was to be March 2006, nearly 18 months later, before there was any further focus on Land Rovers. This came initially in a letter delivered to 10 Downing Street by Pauline Hickey, mother of Sgt Hickey, working with an organisation called Military Families against the War. A version was published in *The Guardian* headed, 'Mr Blair, you sent my son to die in a war based on lies', asserting that it was 'time to bring our troops home and let the Iraqi people decide their own future'. Mrs Hickey revisited the issue of 'fibreglass Jeeps', complaining that there had been 'no armoured Land Rovers'. The British government, she wrote, had given some to the Iraqi police prior to her son's death. His commanding officer had also requested some 'but was turned down on the basis that they were not suitable for the roads'.[9]

Mrs Hickey was once again referring to the APVs. But she had no idea of the relative merits of the APV versus the Snatch.[10] Nevertheless, her emotional appeal gained considerable traction.[11] The issues of inadequate equipment and soldiers' deaths were becoming inextricably bound up with the anti-war movement.

Another entrant into the debate that March was a Conservative front-bencher who asked the government how many British soldiers had been killed and seriously injured in Iraq in armoured and unarmoured Land Rovers. There had been 16.[12] Once more, there was no follow-up. The next MP to dip his toe in the water was David Taylor, a Labour backbencher. In oral defence questions on 22 May – shortly after the deaths of Ptes Lewaicei and Morris in a Snatch – he referred to 'a Land Rover protected only by composite fibreglass'. But this was a foil for his substantive question, whether 'a large majority in both the UK and Iraq wanted an early withdrawal of foreign troops'.[13] He did not press the point on the Land Rovers.

Following the deaths of Lt Mildinhall and L/Cpl Farrelly, Snatch vulnerability was briefly aired on BBC television news. But the focus was on the difficulties in dealing with 'shaped charges' – EFPs.[14] Lack of suitable armour was then rehearsed by Max Hastings in *The Daily Mail*. 'The armoured Land Rover is not remotely adequate for patrolling in areas where insurgents are using landmines', he wrote. Until a new vehicle is provided, 'our soldiers will continue to be blown up …'.[15] The temperature was rising.

9. *The Guardian*, 2 March 2006, 'Mr Blair, you sent my son to die in a war based on lies'.
10. Telephone interview with Mrs Hickey, 14 November 2008.
11. For instance: *The Daily Telegraph*, 20 April 2006, 'Should we pay more to protect our troops?'
12. Hansard, 21 March 2006: Column 359W.
13. Hansard, 22 May 2006: Column 1183.
14. BBC, 30 May 2006, 'British soldiers killed in Iraq named'.
15. Max Hastings, *The Daily Mail*, 30 May 2006, 'Our soldiers are being exploited and mistreated by a political leadership unfit to lick their boots'.

A further response to the recent Snatch deaths came in a reader's letter in *The Sunday Telegraph*. Martyn Pocock asked:

On how many more missions will our troops have to go in vehicles that were essentially designed for Northern Ireland? How many more deaths will there be before the Government is held to account for not providing the money for equipment that is fit for the role? The 'Snatch Land Rover' may have been armoured in the context of Northern Ireland, but it certainly is not in the context of Iraq and Afghanistan.[16]

Three days later, on 5 June, David Taylor MP was back on the case, asking, 'what assessment has been made of the effectiveness of composite fibreglass in protecting the occupants of Land Rovers …'. The impenetrable answer told of the 'overall protection level' having been assessed in March 2005. That had been 'part of a number of ongoing assessments to ensure the suitability of a range of equipment used on current operations'. The results of these assessments were withheld. Their disclosure 'could prejudice the safety of the armed forces'.[17]

THE PARLIAMENTARY BATTLE

It was here that this author played a small part in the ongoing drama. Pocock's letter had struck a chord and triggered an online investigation into possible alternatives to the Snatch. That brought to light an incident that had happened in January, near Camp Taqaddum, 50 miles west of Baghdad.

Then, four US Marines and one sailor had been on patrol. There was a 'bump' in the road, which had turned out to be an IED. It had detonated directly underneath their vehicle, throwing it into the air. Both front wheels were blown off, the hull had been buckled and extensively charred. But the crew had only suffered minor injuries. They had been in an RG-31, a South African-designed 'mine-protected vehicle' brought to Iraq in 2004. Like the Buffalo, the lower part of the hull was 'v-shaped'. The IED blast had been deflected, dissipating harmlessly.[18] There was a photograph of the wrecked machine. This, with other data, was sent to the Conservative Parliamentary defence team and to Christopher Booker.

The Conservatives reacted. Lord Astor of Hever, still the defence spokesman in the Lords, was already planning to raise the issue. But, while previously he had been arguing for 'armour-plated vehicles' he now had a more potent line of attack – the RG-31. On 12 June, he tackled Lord Drayson, cribbing almost exactly Max Hastings' line in *The Mail* two weeks earlier.

16. *The Daily Telegraph* (Letters), 2 June 2006, 'Armour in Iraq'.
17. Hansard, 5 June 2006: Column 624W.
18. USMC website, 13 January 2006, 'Protective gear keeps Marines safe'.

The Snatch, he declared, was 'not remotely adequate for patrolling areas where insurgents use landmines'. Then he asked about the RG-31. Drayson set the tone for the controversy that was to follow:

I do not accept that Snatch Land Rovers are not appropriate for the role. We must recognise the difference between protection and survivability. It is important that we have the trade-offs that we need for mobility. The Snatch Land Rover provides us with the mobility and level of protection that we need.

We had 14 RG-31s in Bosnia, which we took out of service some time ago due to difficulties with maintenance. We have looked at the RG-31 alongside a number of alternatives for our current fleet and concluded that the size and profile did not meet our needs. Size is important in the urban environment. The RG-31 cannot access areas that Snatch Land Rovers can get to.

The reliance on size and mobility as the rationale for the Snatch was surprising. In many instances where Snatches had been withdrawn, they had been replaced by Warriors and even Challengers. These were now routinely used in al-Amarah. But when Gerald Howarth also asked about the suitability of the RG-31, the MoD responded: '… its size and profile did not meet our needs.'[19] That was to become the battleground.

These exchanges were just the opening shots. Christopher Booker ran a story about the RG-31 in his column on 18 June with the picture of the Camp Taqaddum machine, its first appearance in the British press.[20] One reason British troops continued to be killed and injured in southern Iraq, he wrote, was that their 'lightly-armoured Land Rovers' gave them no protection against roadside bombs and rocket-propelled grenades, unlike their American counterparts with RG-31s.[21]

Thursday, 22 June, saw a defence debate in the Commons. But the issue was ignored by the opposition front benches. It was raised by back-bencher, Lee Scott.[22] Ann Winterton joined in, focusing on Afghanistan where Snatches had also been deployed: 'Our forces appear to be winning the firefights in Afghanistan,' she observed. Did the Minister expect the enemy to revert to the use of IEDs? If so, she asked, what vehicles would be used to counter the threat? Defence Minister Adam Ingram was non-committal. Where we identify a threat, he claimed, 'we identify a quick way to deal with it'.[23] Yet troops had been facing the threat of IEDs in Iraq, one which the MoD had anticipated in 2002. It showed no signs of dealing with it.

Moreover, the MoD was beginning to look isolated. No only were the US and Canadians buying RG-31s, Australian forces in Iraq were equipped

19. Hansard, 16 June 2006: Column 1528W.
20. Christopher Booker, *The Sunday Telegraph*, 18 June 2006, 'How Blair is destroying our forces'.
21. BAE Systems website: Land Systems OMC.
22. Hansard, 22 June 2006: Column 1554.
23. Hansard, 22 June 2006: Column 1501.

with their own purpose-designed vehicles called the Bushmaster. German forces in Afghanistan had their equivalent, the Dingo II. In early July, they were to be attacked three times in one week, including a suicide attack that failed to inflict harm on the crew. As a result, the German defence ministry placed an order for 149 extra vehicles.[24] The Dutch contingent in Afghanistan were by then borrowing RG-31s from the Canadians and were shortly to acquire their own fleet of Bushmasters. They bought directly from the Australians who supplied them from their Army inventory to avoid any delay getting them into theatre.[25]

THE SUNDAY TIMES INTERVENES

In view of the negative response of the MoD, the weekend after his initial article, Booker returned to the Snatch.[26] Jonathan Ungoed-Thomas of *The Sunday Times*, with defence correspondent Michael Smith, visited the issue for the first time.[27] Their report was given a front page 'teaser' and accompanied by a robust leader entitled: 'Pay up and save lives.'[28]

Michael Smith, though, was not convinced about the RG-31. Writing on his blog, he cited Brigadier Bill Moore, the MoD's Director, Equipment Capability (Ground Manoeuvre), who argued that the use of heavy armour had to be balanced with the need for soldiers to interact with local communities. Smith agreed. At 20 inches wider than the Snatch, 'the RG-31 was not manoeuvrable enough to be used in the streets of Basra'. It had the wrong profile for peacekeeping and an earlier version had been used in Bosnia where it had proved to have maintenance problems. 'Its profile is all wrong and it's just that bit too big for Basra,' Smith concluded.[29]

THE ISSUES – PROTECTION VERSUS MOBILITY

This reflected a very real divergence of opinion within the military. Some of the controversy was played out on the unofficial Army forum, where there was no agreement on the relative merits of protection *versus* mobility – the issues identified by Lord Drayson. But another recurrent theme was

24. *Defence of the Realm*, 11 July 2006, 'Let's see now'.
25. *Defence of the Realm*, 24 October 2006, 'An odd sense of values'.
26. *The Sunday Telegraph*, 25 June 2006, ' "Europe-first" procurement has left our soldiers unprotected in Iraq'.
27. Jon Ungoed-Thomas and Michael Smith, *The Sunday Times*, 25 June 2006, 'Focus: Is the army putting money before lives?'
28. *The Sunday Times* (leader), 25 June 2006, 'Pay up and save lives'.
29. Mick Smith blog, *Times Online*, 25 June 2006, 'Too big for Basra'.

the EFP. Since no amount of armour could protect against it, claimed some, it was better to rely on manoeuvrability and tactics.[30] At no time though did the government officially argue that the RG-31 would not provide enhanced protection to the troops. It never mentioned the EFP.

Why it did not was something of a mystery. Its dangers were being rehearsed widely in the media. The very day Booker and *The Sunday Times* were complaining about Snatches, *The Sunday Telegraph's* defence correspondent, Sean Rayment, wrote about, 'The precision-made mine that has "killed 17 British troops"'. He asserted that the EFP could 'penetrate the armour of British and American tanks and armoured personnel carriers and completely destroy armoured Land Rovers'. The MoD, though, had 'attempted to play down the effectiveness of the weapons', suggesting that they were 'crude' or 'improvised' devices which had killed British troops 'more out of luck than judgement'.

A source cited by Rayment said: 'If you are travelling in an armoured Land Rover which is attacked by one of these things, you are in trouble. You have a better chance of surviving if you are in a tank or an armoured vehicle but it will "kill" the tank.' Soldiers who had recently served in Iraq believed lives were being put at risk by senior officers insisting on the use of armoured Land Rovers even though they provided little or no protection from EFPs. Patrolling in Land Rovers and on foot in preference to the better-protected Warrior armoured vehicles was 'costing lives', a policy, in part, foisted on the Army by a lack of more heavily armoured vehicles. Rayment noted:

… whenever possible, the Army prefers to adopt the lowest patrolling profile which the prevailing security conditions allow because of the belief that heavily armoured vehicles tend to alienate the local population. But, with eight servicemen and one women killed by insurgent attacks in May, many troops believe that the battle to win the hearts and minds of the Iraqis is 'all but lost'.[31]

The contradiction was evident. If an EFP would 'kill' a tank and, by inference, the less-protected Warrior, it mattered not whether a Snatch or a tank – or anything in between – was used. Nevertheless, in debates behind the scenes, the potency of the EFP was frequently cited as a reason for not procuring RG-31s. So the argument went, these vehicles had been designed to counter mines and offered no protection against the EFP, not least since they were less thickly armoured than Warriors.[32]

At the time, this issue was never resolved, but it later emerged that the threat of the EFP had been overstated. At that particular time, it was not a

30. Army Rumour Service forum, Snatch thread.

31. *The Sunday Telegraph*, 25 June 2006, 'The precision-made mine that has "killed 17 British troops"'.

32. Army Rumour Service forum, Snatch thread, *op. cit.*

Above: A Snatch Land Rover, seen here in central Basra in a typical role, supporting a raid. In the background is a Warrior, guarding the end of the street.

Below: The aftermath of an explosively formed projectile (EFP) attack which killed a soldier and wounded two others, one seriously. Apparent is the relatively modest damage compared with a blast bomb, and the multiple, jagged entry points, suggesting imperfect formation of the projectile, reducing its penetrative power.

Above: The weapon of choice – the 'classic' improvised explosive device (IED): artillery shells salvaged from Iraqi Army munitions dumps. The fuze cavities are filled with plastic explosives, with detonators inserted, linked by wires to a trigger mechanism. The object on the right is an anti-tank mine.

Picture: Wikipedia Commons

Below: An explosively formed projectile (EFP) device. Although such devices have been used by Iranian-backed Hamas and Hezbollah, this device is not dissimilar in size and appearance to the French weapon, designated the MIACAH F1, which was sold to Iraq.

Picture: US Department of Defense

Above: The initial response to the IED: an 'uparmoured' Humvee. The added weight of armour reduced manoeuvrability, shortened the vehicle life and afforded limited extra protection. The object projecting from the front of the vehicle is a 'Rhino' – an extendible heat emitter designed prematurely to trigger bombs linked to infra-red sensors.   Picture: US Department of Defense

Below: The US Marine RG-31 at Camp Taqaddum, after an IED had detonated directly underneath the vehicle. The blast had been successfully deflected by the v-shaped hull, allowing the crew to escape with very minor injuries.   Picture: USMC

Above: A Warrior armoured vehicle in Basra. In the absence of a mine-protected vehicle, the Army was forced to use these heavy tracked vehicles for routine patrols. Despite their heavy top armour, they provided less protection from IEDs than specifically designed vehicles.

Picture: Nigel Green Media: *info@nigelgreenmedia.com*

Below: A Force Protection Buffalo route clearance vehicle. While the British Army was relying on men to go ahead on foot to search for hidden IED, US forces were employing this equipment, with its extendible arm, to do this dangerous work. Picture: US Department of Defense

Above: The British way: a Tellar 'munitions disposal vehicle'. Unarmed, unarmoured and expensive, it required a heavy escort to allow it to attend incidents.

Below: The American way. A Cougar MRAP of a type used by the US for ordnance clearance. Heavily armoured, armed and capable of autonomous action, crews have three times more chance of surviving an IED 'hit' than if they were in a main battle tank at six times the weight.   Picture: US Department of Defense

These men should be dead. When the British Army finally acquired the Mastiff (background), they were to save many lives. The three soldiers pictured, Ptes Stephen MacLauchlan, Lee Ashton and Lee Jones, all owe their lives to the vehicle. Picture: Nigel Green Media: *info@nigelgreenmedia.com*

MRAP vehicles awaiting delivery to units at Camp Taqaddum, Northern Iraq, in September 2007, just as Robert Gates's MRAP programme was getting underway. This batch alone, mainly Cougars but with a few Buffaloes, totalled more than the entire fleet of protected vehicles fielded by the British, yet was only a fraction of the 10,000 vehicles that were to be delivered.
Picture: US Department of Defense

Above: The British Way. A Nimrod MR2 maritime reconnaissance aircraft. Six were fitted with advanced video cameras to provide land surveillance in Iraq and Afghanistan, costing £30,000 an hour to operate.

Picture: Wikipedia Commons

Below: The Iraqi Way. A Sama CH2000 surveillance aircraft operated by the Iraqi Air Force. Fitted with exactly the same video equipment, its purchase price is roughly equivalent to the cost of a 12-hour Nimrod sortie. The aircraft is flying over Basra Air Station. Visible is the control tower which was used as an aiming point for insurgent rocket attacks.

Picture: Jordan Aerospace Industries

'super-bomb'.[33] The most compelling evidence was the fate of Snatches hit by EFPs. Crucially, for weapons that produced high-speed slugs of molten copper, entry points should have been small, neat holes. Against the light armour of the Snatch, they should have continued through the vehicle, leaving similarly neat exit holes. In most instances, there were large, jagged entries and no exit holes. The 'projectiles' had insufficient power to punch their way through.

This was in part explained when EFP components were discovered in captured arms caches. In many instances, their construction was crude. To function properly, the weapon did require precision manufacture and a uniform, well-packed explosive charge. Imperfections caused the copper 'dish' to fragment, projecting shards of copper rather than a projectile. These, against the thin armour of the Snatch, caused the jagged holes. The fragments were lethal to their crews but lacked penetration power.

Having been fielded by Hezbollah and Hamas, in Lebanon and Gaza, Israeli bomb disposal experts had already met them. They had found that the initial types had been 'relatively ineffective against armoured vehicles'. Even the heavier versions caused 'catastrophic results' only against 'softer or lightly armoured vehicles'.[34] Most armoured vehicles – including the RG-31 – would be relatively immune to these early bombs. Gradually, bomb-making techniques improved and EFPs were eventually able to penetrate Warriors. By then, armour was being developed which could block them.

The EFP's infra-red trigger mechanisms bypassed the electronic counter-measures but the US forces had quickly developed an alternative called the 'Rhino'. A glow plug – a pencil-shaped object with an electrical heating element, often used in diesel engines – was placed inside a metal ammunition box and attached to the end of a 10ft metal pole fixed on the front of each vehicle. The heat decoyed the infra-red sensor into firing prematurely. Within four to six weeks, insurgents began offsetting the aiming point to strike 10ft back from the Rhino. This provoked a variation called Rhino II with a telescopic pole that allowed the distance to be varied. It was not complete proof against the weapon, but reduced its effectiveness.[35]

This counter-measure was not used on Snatches. The vehicles' electrical systems were already over-burdened. Thus, after the death of Guardsman Wakefield in May 2005, and the recovery in June of an intact EFP system – including its trigger mechanism – the Army must have known the Snatch

---

33. *Defence of the Realm* (blog), 15 September 2006, 'The myth of the "super-bomb"'.
34. *Defense Update*, 18 October 2006, 'Shaped charges IED in the Middle East'.
35. *The Washington Post*, 2 October 2007, 'You can't armor your way out of this problem'.

could not be protected. Furthermore, EFPs were by no means unfamiliar to the Army. They had been on the British inventory until 1994.[36] They were not, by any means, new weapons. The attacks on the Snatch pointed to the Army being unprepared to meet a predictable threat, perhaps explaining why the government preferred to rely on its 'size and profile' argument. Entertaining a debate on the EFP could have revealed its unpreparedness.

ARMY RESISTANCE

Even then, the government's obduracy remained puzzling. In time, it emerged that the opposition was not coming from the politicians but from the Army. The high command did not want the RG-31, or any other mine-protected vehicle, for two reasons. One was visible. The other, darker reason was not evident until very much later, centred on a project known as the Future Rapid Effects System (FRES). We deal with that in that final chapter.

The visible reason was that, with its eyes on Afghanistan, the Army had already decided on a replacement for the Snatch. This was a 'protected' version of a 6×6 Pinzgauer truck known as the Vector. With slightly greater capacity than the Snatch, the unarmoured vehicle had legendary off-road performance. For the Army, an armoured version was its choice. Already, in April 2006, an order had been announced for 80 Vectors at a cost of £35 million. The armour – very similar to that fitted to the Snatch – was claimed to 'protect troops from automatic fire, landmines and fragmentation bombs'.[37] The Army wanted more. Money spent on RG-31s could prejudice that ambition.

Allowing for that, there was an option called the Urgent Operational Requirement (UOR), whereby urgent purchases could be made, funded directly by the Treasury in addition to the defence budget. However, while that money covered the original purchase price, it did not meet the whole-life costs of operating and maintenance – often considerably more than the capital cost. The Army did not want to be 'saddled', as it thought, with specialised equipment of limited value, eroding its general operational budget for many years after the equipment was no longer being used for the purpose for which it was purchased.

There was also, however, one aspect of FRES that is directly relevant to this stage of the narrative. At the heart of that project, as far as the Army was concerned, was a new armoured vehicle which re-introduced into the

---

36. Hansard, 26 November 2008: Column 1532W – Designated the L114A1 and the L131A1.
37. *The Sunday Telegraph*, 29 April 2006, 'Army gets £35m vehicles to protect patrols from suicide bombers'.

Army inventory a much sought-after 'medium' capability. As had become all too evident in the Iraqi campaign, between the Snatch and the Warrior there was nothing. The Army hoped to use FRES to fill that gap – not wanting an alternative. On 11 July, Browne gave evidence to the Commons Defence Committee, admitting to the capability gap. But that day, there was also an announcement that the projected in-service date of 2009 for FRES had been pushed back. There was no longer a timetable. Since FRES was not going to provide an immediate answer, the case for a 'stopgap' was unassailable.

Despite their importance, these issues were to remain in the background, as did the technical debate over EFPs. But *The Sunday Times* had ignited a very public controversy. The day after its report during Commons defence questions, five opposition MPs challenged Browne on the safety of Snatches, including Liam Fox, his Conservative counterpart. Browne's answer was to announce a review.[38] That was a breakthrough. Sky News then carried a lengthy report featuring a Snatch patrol in Basra, interviewing a soldier who roundly declared: 'These Land Rovers are no use to any one.' This was a good sign.

THE RG-31 SAGA

Because it had been brought up so early in the debate, much of the ensuing discussion centred on the RG-31. It was a logical alternative to the Snatch. It had been used by the United Nations in Lebanon and Bosnia, for its 'high mobility and good crew comfort' and – confounding Mick Smiths's opinion of the machine – for its 'non-aggressive appearance'.[39] The USMC had 148 in Iraq and Canadian forces had 50 in Afghanistan, chosen for its '… proven performance in a range of climates and terrains, relatively small size'. [40, 41] There was no obvious logic to the MoD's rejection of this particular machine.

Much like an onion though, the story had multiple layers. It had become 'murkier' according to Christopher Booker on 25 June when he reported on two issues.[42] One was the MoD's evaluation of the RG-31; the other was the claim that they had previously been used in Bosnia.[43]

38. Hansard, 26 June 2006: Column 4 *et seq.*

39. Originally referenced to in the Wikipedia entry on the RG-31 Nyala, although the copy has since been amended and the reference removed. The original text was copied verbatim and is reproduced in EU Referendum (blog), 'How Blair is killing our soldiers', *op. cit.*

40. Aerospace and Defense Network News, 29 November 2005, 'General Dynamics awarded $60 million contract'.

41. Canadian American Strategic Review, undated, 'Background – armoured patrol vehicles'.

42. *The Sunday Telegraph*, 25 June 2006, *op. cit.*

43. Hansard, 12 June 2006: Column 2, *op. cit.*

The 'evaluation' had been part of the selection process for contract to supply a 'Future Command and Liaison Vehicle'. Five different vehicles had been submitted by three firms. One had been the RG-31.[44] It was acknowledged to have the highest protection against anti-tank mines.[45] When it came to the trials in 2003, though, there was an unexpected development. One of the bidders was asked to submit an Italian-built machine dubbed the 'Panther'. The MoD, having specifically asked for it to be included then, rather unsurprisingly declared it the winner. A contract was placed in November 2003 for 401 vehicles at a cost of £166 million.[46]

Thus, the MoD in 2003 – shortly after the first Snatches had been delivered to Iraq – had rejected the opportunity to buy large numbers of RG-31s. It had preferred a then untried vehicle, which was more expensive and offered significantly less protection. Furthermore, five years after the contract had been signed, the Panther itself was found 'wanting'. Beset with technical problems, it still had not been issued to units.[47]

As to the use of RG-31s in Bosnia, this claim was untrue. The vehicles had been an earlier and much less capable version called the Mamba.[48] The MoD had purchased 14 of them for £4.5 million and in 2004 – the year after the Snatches had been deployed to Iraq – had sold them for £448,000, approximately one-tenth of their original price. Nine went to Estonia, four to a US company and one to a company in Singapore.[49]

More damning, the Mambas had originally been bought for 'route proving'. This was a process of driving down roads to check for mines and other explosive devices before allowing vulnerable vehicles through. The technique, pioneered by the British Army, had been so successful that it had been copied by US and Canadian forces, who were employing their RG-31s for similar purposes. Furthermore, in Bosnia, the British had met the Russian-made TMRP-6, a mine with a shaped charge very similar in effect to EFPs. They had developed armour to deal with it, which had been fitted to some of the Mambas. It was the extra weight of that armour that had caused the 'maintenance' problems, straining primitive braking systems and steering.

The story did not end there. The US company which had acquired four of the Mambas was the security consultant Blackwater. It had refurbished them and taken them to Iraq. They were used to transport American and

44. *Defence Systems Daily*, 13 September 2001, 'Vickers reveals its FCLV solution at DSEi'.
45. *Jane's*, 14 May 2001, 'UK FCLV contest down to three'.
46. Hansard, 6 November 2003: Column WA143.
47. *The Daily Telegraph*, 21 February 2008, 'Iveco LMV: Dangerous World'.
48. Hansard, 29 June 2006: Column 1356.
49. Hansard, 8 November 2006: Column 1546W.

other VIPs from Baghdad International Airport to the Green Zone in central Baghdad along 'one of the most dangerous roads in Iraq'.[50, 51] There, they had taken at least two IED hits, from which passengers and crew had escaped unharmed. Of the nine Mambas sold to Estonia, there was an added irony. The Estonian Army brought them to Afghanistan to work alongside the British. While British forces were required to ride in Snatches and the even less protected 'Wimik', Estonian soldiers were enjoying cut-price protection courtesy of the MoD.

There was another twist to this convoluted story. In November 2001 replacements for the Mamba had been bought by the MoD – 4×4, heavily armoured 'mine-protected' trucks, with the classic v-shaped hull, produced by a US company that was to become Force Protection Inc. The design was based on South Africa principles, drawn from the same well-spring as the Mamba and the RG-31. Officially the Mine Protected Vehicle (MPV), the unofficial name was 'Tempest'. Eight were bought for £2.7 million. Some were sent to Bosnia from January to May 2004. Others were in Iraq from July 2003 to November 2004. They were withdrawn only months before the EFP emerged in theatre – the very weapon for which they had been developed to counter.[52]

Meanwhile, the design had been refined and a new vehicle called the Cougar emerged, available in four- and six-wheel configuration. The USMC and the US Army were using it to hunt IEDs in Iraq, alongside Buffaloes and RG-31s – the latter, confusingly, the Marines were also calling the Cougar. Thus, as the Tempests were being withdrawn from Iraq, their successors were being employed with huge success by the Americans. The British, on the other hand, who had *pioneered* the techniques for which these vehicles had been designed, were sending men on foot ahead of their vehicles to search for roadside bombs.

Furthermore, one thing of which the US forces did not complain was the size or lack of mobility of their new fleet, which remained the core of the MoD's objections to better-protected vehicles. Those objections were in part countered when it was shown that the majority of roads were well capable of handling the larger vehicles. Photographs from theatre showed Land Rovers and other military vehicles deployed in wide-open spaces. Some showed the Saxon wheeled APC, similar in size to the RG-31, used extensively in the early days of the occupation. The MoD's public arguments were unsustainable.

---

50. *The Washington Post*, 22 April 2005, 'Private security workers living on edge in Iraq'.
51. *Popular Mechanics*, April 2005, 'Riding shotgun in Baghdad with Blackwater's security detail'.
52. Hansard, 31 October 2006: Column 335W.

BROWNE ORDERS PROTECTED VEHICLES

The first intimation of success came when Michael Smith reported that Browne's review, less than a month after it had started, had been concluded and '100 new heavily armoured patrol vehicles had been ordered'.[53] They would be upgraded versions of 'the armoured Cougars used by US marines in Iraq', with 'additional armour, making them the most protected vehicles of their kind in the world'. It appeared that the MoD was going to buy RG-31s.

On Monday, 24 July, details emerged. There were to be more Vectors, the number increased to 166, as well as more up-armoured FV432s, the tracked APCs that had preceded the Warrior to be called the Bulldog.[54] Additionally, 100 'Cougars' were to be purchased, but they were the Force Protection vehicle, based on the Tempest design pioneered by the British. They were to be called Mastiffs. As to why he had rejected the RG-31, Browne answered:

> We chose [the Cougars] because up-armoured, with electronic counter-measures added and with Bowman radios fitted, we believe that they would be the best protected mid-range vehicles in theatre … Had we chosen the RG-31s, we would have had to fit ECMs and Bowman to them and possibly to up-armour them.[55]

However, for the Cougars to become Mastiffs, they had to be 'up-armoured', as indeed Browne had indicated. They also needed ECMs and Bowman. Furthermore, the MoD was buying the 6×6 version.[56] It was four feet longer than the RG-31, nearly a foot wider and two feet taller, making a mockery of claims about 'size and mobility'. But troops were getting life-saving equipment. For all its size and weight, the Mastiff was a superb vehicle. The only disappointment was that so few had been ordered, with the batch to be split between Iraq and Afghanistan. Nevertheless, after being deployed in a record-breaking 23 weeks, it was to save many lives.

53. *The Sunday Times*, 23 July 2006, 'Bombproof vehicles for troops in Iraq'.
54. BBC, 24 July 2006, 'More armoured vehicles for troops'.
55. Hansard, 24 July 2006: Column 591.
56. *Defence News*, 'Defence Secretary orders new vehicles for troops in Iraq and Afghanistan'.

Chapter 7 – Running away

The retreat from al-Amarah:
June 2006–October 2007

Armies have notoriously short memories for the realities of warfare, and despite various attempts to codify or disseminate 'lessons learned', they often become fixated on one particular aspect or procedure and institutionalise it rigidly, while neglecting a broad band of other considerations.

PADDY GRIFFITH, 1981[1]

As we left it, on 19 June, Des Browne was in Basra discussing a new 'security strategy'. Before the details became public, Maliki announced that Britain would hand over responsibility for patrolling Muthanna province. Maysan would follow. This was confirmed by a new British Foreign Secretary, Margaret Beckett, putting a time scale of two months on the withdrawal, evidence she said of 'mission accomplished'.[2] Gen Houghton was at the same time telling the Commons Defence Committee that security in Basra had deteriorated.[3]

Then, as reports came in on 20 June 2006 of gunmen in al-Amarah assassinating six police and army personnel, including two officers, and wounding a seventh, *The Independent* ran a story based on a *Washington Post* 'scoop'. This gave the lie to Beckett's optimism, completely supporting Houghton. The US ambassador in Baghdad had painted a grim picture of a disintegrating country 'in which the real rulers are the militias, and the central government counts for nothing'.[4] But there was an ulterior motive in Houghton's pessimism. The Army wanted to concentrate on Basra because there was 'a real sense to sort out the place once and for all'. To do that, the Army had to abandon al-Amarah.

A SECURITY PLAN FOR BASRA

Details of Browne's security plan were now emerging. Iraqi forces would in future answer directly to Maliki, removing all responsibility for security

1. Paddy Griffith, *Forward Into Battle* (Navato, CA: Presidio Press, 1991), p. 173.
2. *The Times*, 20 June 2006, 'Beckett unveils timetable for British troop withdrawal'.
3. *The Independent on Sunday*, 25 June 2006, 'British "helpless" as violence rises in southern Iraq'.
4. *The Independent*, 20 June 2006, 'Leaked memo reveals plight of Iraqis'.

from Muhammad al-Waeli. Maliki was, in effect, to acquire his own militia. New measures were to be taken against corrupt police and, over the coming months, the 10th Division would provide the main security presence.[5] In a characteristically optimistic statement, Browne referred to 'anecdotal evidence' that suggested security in Basra had improved since more Iraqi troops had starting patrolling. Setting out the parameters for British involvement, he then said:

There are militia and others who have infiltrated the police for malign purposes and we need to create the space to deal with those people and we will deal with them. And when I say we will deal with them, I mean the Iraqi forces will deal with them with our support.[6]

The next day, in an horrific attack, an 18-year-old Sunni suicide bomber struck an old peoples' home in Basra, blowing himself up as a group of elderly Iraqis lined up to collect their pensions. Two elderly women were killed and three wounded.[7] In a separate attack, a car bomb killed at least five people at a petrol station.[8] Military and diplomatic 'sources' warned that British forces were facing rising violence among Shi'a factions but were 'powerless to contain it'. They were largely keeping out of the centre of Basra and in many of the sectarian clashes had been 'bystanders'. Now, for the first time, they were coming under pressure from political factions to leave areas of the south so that their militia allies could move in.[9]

If British troops were preparing to abandon the peripheral provinces in order to concentrate on Basra, even there there was to be a retreat from the streets. With the 10th Division taking over routine patrolling, British troops would step up the tempo of raids. These, as before, would be aimed at clearing out known insurgents and intercepting weapon supplies. In terms of activity, the effect was dramatic. Over the next four months, the 20th Armoured Brigade reserve company travelled nearly 4,000 miles in Snatches in and around Basra on strike operations. The tempo became relentless: the company routinely went 72 hours with limited sleep in temperatures of up to 50°C. In total they participated in 39 operations, detaining 44 suspects.[10]

Disastrously, what had not been factored in was the role of Maysan province – and al-Amarah in particular – as a sanctuary, also serving as the armoury for the insurgency. Bombs were being manufactured on an industrial scale while weapons and ammunition were stored and distrib-

5. *The Times*, 22 June 2006, 'British to adopt lower profile in Basra'.
6. BBC, 22 June 2006, 'Security in Basra "has improved"'.
7. *The Daily Telegraph*, 22 June 2006, 'Pensioners die in Basra bomb blast'.
8. *The Age*, 24 June 2006, 'Mosque bombing kills 10 in Iraq'.
9. *The Independent on Sunday*, 25 June 2006, 'British "helpless" as violence rises in southern Iraq'.
10. Army website, undated, Princess of Wales Royal Regiment (Brochure).

uted to both Basra and Sadr City. The Army was taking a 'downstream solution', leaving the pipeline open – mopping the floor without first turning off the tap. This was a major strategic error, which was to cost the British the entire campaign.

In planning to depart from Maysan, though, the British were not entirely free agents. The Americans were convinced that the province was the weapons conduit for the Shi'a insurgency, with arms being smuggled over the border from Iran.[11] They insisted that the British kept a force in the province to interdict the flow. Plans were modified in order to humour the Americans, which were to be rolled out in the August.

IRANIAN SUPPORT FOR MUQTADA

Whether Iran was actively supporting the Sadrists is not clear. Muqtada regarded himself as an Iraqi nationalist and opposed the Iranian-backed SCIRI. He had no loyalty to Iran. Nor were his relations good with Sistani although, while the Grand Ayatollah was so influential, no Sadrist could openly oppose him.

Furthermore, Basra – despite a strong Iranian presence – had an uneasy relationship with its neighbour. Basrawis had not forgiven Iran for repeatedly shelling their city during the war of 1980–1988. Hostile sentiment was never far away and, on 14 June, a violent crowd had stormed the newly built Iranian consulate in Basra. It had destroyed one of its wings and planted an Iraqi flag on top of the main building.[12] The trigger for the violence had been an attack on Iranian television – widely watched in Basra – on the anti-Iranian ayatollah Mahmud al-Hasani. Virtually unknown in the West, Hasani was a Karbala-based cleric. His ultimate goal was to establish an Iran-like Islamic theocracy in Iraq, but wholly independent of Iranian influence.[13]

Both Hasani and Muqtada opposed the Iran-backed idea of partitioning Iraq. They were contenders for leadership of the Shi'ite community but they were also potential allies. And, while Muqtada found his constituency in the urban poor, Hasani appealed to the urban rich and middle classes – sectors that had previously gravitated towards SCIRI. The attack united them. Furthermore, Muqtada had been building alliances with the Dawa Party, the oldest political Islamic group in Iraq – and the power base of prime minister Maliki. This gave him considerable political leverage in

11. *The Guardian*, 11 August 2005, 'Iranian arms intercepted at Iraqi border'.
12. *Fox News*, 14 June 2006, 'Iraqis attack Iranian Consulate in Basra'.
13. *Asia Times*, 22 June 2006, 'The facade of Shi'ite unity crumbling'.

Baghdad. For all his strong words, Maliki was in no position to move against Muqtada. Now allied with Hasani, Muqtada was able to build a formidable power base in Basra and was poised to take control of the city, wresting it from SCIRI and the Badr Brigade.[14]

Iran, therefore, was not a natural ally of Muqtada. Most likely, it found the Sadr organisation and its allies useful in that they helped destabilise the coalition and the Baghdad government. It tolerated it rather than actively supported it – as long as it did not get too powerful. There was also a financial incentive. Iran had built up a significant weapons industry and would sell to all comers for cash.[15] The Sadr organisation had considerable revenues from oil smuggling. Additionally, in the areas it controlled, it imposed 'taxes' on businesses, rather like the sectarian groups in Northern Ireland and the Mafia.[16] It could afford to buy its arms.

How much of this the British military and political establishments knew at the time, or even cared, is not clear. But all the evidence is that, whatever the bigger picture, the Army wanted out – at any price. Pressed by the commitment to Afghanistan, convinced that it was under-resourced, ill-equipped and largely unappreciated, it had decided that it had done all it could. It was time for the Iraqis to resolve an Iraqi problem. The pessimism of Houghton and his ilk was simply to reinforce the argument that nothing further could be done.

CAMP ABU NAJI UNDER SIEGE

This was especially the case in al-Amarah where the situation had become very difficult. There, the King's Royal Hussars 2005 detachment, like its predecessors and successors, had been charged with policing the Iranian border as well as keeping order in the city. But, with only two routes from Abu Naji to the border, transit from the camp had become highly dangerous. Not least of the problems was 'dickers' – Army slang for insurgent observers. At one point, commanders had resorted to using Merlin helicopters to lift fully crewed Land Rovers out to the Iranian border, from a pre-arranged rendezvous some miles outside the camp, to avoid ambush and observation. By then, it had become too dangerous permanently to station helicopters at the base. Even landing there had become extremely hazardous, attracting a blizzard of mortar and rocket fire.[17]

14. *AlterNet*, 21 September 2007, 'Basra. After the British'.
15. *Global Security*, undated, 'Iran – defence industry'.
16. Council on Foreign Relations, 28 June 2006, 'The challenge in Iraq's other cities: Basra'.
17. *Defence of the Realm*, 21 June 2006, 'Canaries down the mine'.

At this stage, there was a complete media blackout. Despite Abu Naji suffering constant bombardment, little was reported in the British media. Road movement in the environs of al-Amarah was also very dangerous, yet only the occasional fragment of information escaped. There was, for instance, a report of an incident on 3 July – two lines buried in a news agency round-up – recording that an 'armoured vehicle' had been hit by a bomb south of al-Amarah. According to British spokeswoman Capt Kelly Goodall, nobody had been wounded.[18] Capt Goodall may have been misinformed, or there may have been attacks on armoured vehicles on successive days. The day before, there had definitely been an IED attack on a Warrior. The driver sustained severe leg injuries. The vehicle commander, L/Cpl Phillip Baines, was knocked out for a few seconds.[19]

The next day, an Arab source claimed a bomb had completely destroyed a truck in a supply convoy, between al-Amarah and Basra, severely wounding its driver.[20] The source was a 'resistance' site, obviously partisan and of suspect reliability – although perhaps no more so than Capt Goodall. On 30 June, it claimed that four heavy mortar bombs had been fired at Abu Naji, 'sending clouds of black smoke rising into the sky, followed by a powerful explosion that shook the entire facility'. One British soldier was killed and five more wounded went the report, with an account of helicopter evacuations of the wounded.[21] Another attack was claimed for 8 July, this one with four medium-range 'Katyusha' rockets, the barrage setting off 'explosions' followed by 'plumes of smoke rising into the sky'.[22]

The claim of a soldier killed was obviously an exaggeration – the MoD would have disclosed that. But it did not report incidents involving injuries. Occasionally, although rarely, official sources revealed the scale of the carnage. One retailed how four Guardsmen had evacuated a seriously injured soldier to the medical centre within Abu Naji, with mortar bombs exploding around them. One bomb had detonated nearly 21,000 gallons of aviation fuel.[23]

A supposedly reliable source, the BBC, on 26 July reported that a British 'armoured vehicle' had been attacked in Maysan, with no casualties. The forces had come 'under fire from rocket-propelled grenades which did not detonate'. Troops had returned fire.[24] The incident was more serious than

---

18. *USA Today*, 3 July 2006, 'Blasts across Iraq kill 12'.
19. Army website, undated, Honours and Awards, Iraq 2004–2007, The Princess of Wales's Royal Regiment.
20. *Free Arab Report*, 3 July 2006, Resistance Report 569.
21. *Free Arab Voice*, 30 June 2006, Resistance Report 566.
22. *Free Arab Voice*, 8 July 2006, Resistance Report 574.
23. Multi-National Force website, 10 August 2006, 'British soldier helps save life of fellow soldier'.
24. BBC, 26 July 2006, 'Army vehicle is attacked in Iraq'.

indicated, bad enough for F-16 Fighting Falcons to have provided support 'to troops in contact'.[25] *Aswat al-Iraq* told of 'clashes' (plural) between gunmen and British forces. Fighting had started at 11.30am after a patrol vehicle had been attacked with mortars and light weapons. The agency reported: 'Blasts echoed in Amarah, but there was no official word on what was going on.'[26]

Neither was there any 'official word' when, on 30 July 2006, L/Cpl Baines again came under attack in his Warrior, this time by 20 Mahdi Army militia.[27] There was, though, an 'official word' on 10 August, when a 'resistance' source claimed a British helicopter had been shot down in al-Amarah.[28] *Aswat al-Iraq* reported that it had been 'exposed to fire by unidentified gunmen', citing 'a British forces release'. The attack, according to this source – whether it was Capt Goodall was not specified – 'did not result in any damage'.[29] The 'resistance' claimed another victory the following day, recording that a bomb had exploded by a British patrol in al-Amarah. Eyewitnesses claimed that 'the blast disabled a vehicle, wounding three puppet troops, one of them seriously'.[30]

Back in London on 14 August, the cat was out of the bag on the withdrawal plan. *The Times* reported that British forces were to leave al-Amarah 'this month' and 'instead patrol the Iranian border to prevent weapons-smuggling in one of the largest redeployments the Army has undertaken in Iraq'. Security duties in al-Amarah would be handed over to Iraqi forces.[31]

As always, the violence continued. British Forces in al-Amarah came under mortar fire on 18 August.[32] Four mortar rounds and one Grad (Katyusha) rocket were fired, according to local sources, with three secondary explosions. The previous day, according to the same sources, 'a mortar shell blasted into the camp while two others landed in residential areas nearby, killing five local citizens'.[33] Then, on 22 August, there were reports that an Iraqi woman and a child had been killed with two other people wounded in clashes between British forces and gunmen. Eight 'citizens' had been detained. British forces had surrounded a neighbourhood in downtown al-Amarah. About '65 tanks had blocked all roads leading to the city, supported by fighters and helicopters'. The civil and security authori-

25. Air Force Print News, 27 July 2006, 'CENTAF releases airpower summary'.
26. *Aswat al-Iraq*, 26 July 2006, 'British forces clash with gunmen in Missan'.
27. Army website, undated, Honours and Awards, Iraq 2004–2007, The Princess of Wales's Royal Regiment.
28. *Free Arab Voice*, 10 August 2006, Iraq Resistance Report 607.
29. *Aswat al-Iraq*, 12 August 2006, 'British helicopter exposed to fire in Amara'.
30. *Free Arab Voice*, 11 August 2006, Iraqi Resistance Report 608.
31. *The Times*, 14 August 2006, 'Handover sets up British troops to stop gunrunners'.
32. Bahrain News Agency, 18 August 2006, 'British forces in Amarah come under mortar fire'.
33. *Free Arab Voice*, 18 August 2006, Iraqi Resistance Report 615.

ties had not been notified in advance and the British had not issued a statement.[34] 'Resistance' sources claimed that 'men armed with light and medium weapons attacked the British occupation troops, damaging one of the British tanks and disabling an armoured vehicle'.[35]

Something had been going on. A USAF F-16 had again provided support.[36] In fact, there had been a major and, for the British, worrying development. The report of a British tank 'damaged' had been accurate. It had been hit by a powerful rocket-propelled grenade, the Russian-made RPG-29, the first time it had been seen in Iraq. Fitted with a double-charge, the warhead was capable of defeating the frontal armour of a Challenger tank. It had penetrated the compartment and blown off half the driver's foot.[37]

As in the aftermath of the 12 June raid the 'resistance' attacked Abu Naji again, this time claiming six heavy 120mm mortar bombs fired, with 'direct hits', causing material damage and wounding five British troops, one of them seriously.[38]

THE FIRST STAGE IN 'REPOSITIONING'

Then it was over. On 24 August, a breathless report proclaimed: 'British occupation troops abandon Camp Abu Naji.' This was after 'having more than 70 rockets rain down on them within fewer than 40 days'. Hundreds of vehicles with equipment and troops had abandoned the base, heading for Basra.[39] Locals rushed in. Men, women and children were seen carrying loot. Police tried to impose a security cordon to protect what was left.

The Washington Post informed its readers the next day.[40] It recorded the scenes of looting and the jubilation of the Mahdi, but it also conveyed the views of the British Army, via Major Charlie Burbridge. The Army was not quitting Maysan. It was trading its heavy Challenger 2 tanks and Warriors for lightweight Land Rovers, to become a flexible, mobile force with no fixed base. It would receive supplies by airdrops. Hinting at the reason for the force remaining, Burbridge stated: 'The Americans believe there is an inflow of IEDs and weapons across the border with Iran ... Our first objective is to go and find out if that is the case. If that is true, we'll be able to disrupt

34. *Aswat al-Iraq*, 22 August 2006, 'Four casualties, eight arrested in British forces raid in Amara'.
35. *Free Arab Voice*, 22 August 2006, Resistance Report 619.
36. *Global Security*, undated, 'CENTAF releases airpower summary for Aug. 23'.
37. *The Sunday Telegraph*, 12 May 2007, 'MoD kept failure of best tank quiet'.
38. *Free Arab Voice*, 23 August 2006, Resistance Report 620.
39. *Free Arab Voice*, 24 August 2006, Resistance Report 621.
40. *The Washington Post*, 25 August 2006, 'British leave Iraqi base; Militia supporters jubilant'.

the flow.' He also acknowledged that the constant shelling was part of the reason the camp had closed.

It took until the next day for the British public to be told, and then only in *The Daily Telegraph*. It had the Army stressing that the redeployment had been 'a tactical move, not a withdrawal'. But, said *The Telegraph*:

> ... this was not how Iraqis viewed it. As news spread through Amarah that the British had gone, locals rushed on to the streets shouting 'God is great' and drivers sounded their horns in celebration. Hundreds gathered around the local offices of Muqtada al-Sadr ... whose followers had fired 281 mortar rounds and rockets at the camp, to offer their congratulations. A loudspeaker repeatedly broadcast the triumphant message: 'This is the first Iraqi city that has kicked out the occupiers.'

The police failed to protect the camp, even with the aid of Iraqi soldiers from the 10th Division. The following morning a mob of between 2,000 and 5,000 returned, hundreds of them armed with machine guns and RPGs. After sporadic fighting, the Iraqi troops had retreated. The base had been stripped. Here was more than adequate evidence that the Iraqi security forces were not ready. And it got worse. A day after the British departure, a battalion of the 10th Division in Maysan mutinied after being told it was going to Baghdad. Men had surrounded their officers and fired shots. Discipline was only restored when the order was rescinded.[41] This had not been the first mutiny. In April, Iraqi troops had refused to take orders when deployed in Falluja.[42] Yet, on this fragile plank rested the entire British exit strategy.[43]

Four days later, the MoD deigned to post the news of what it called the 'first stage in the repositioning' of British troops. There was no mention of the looting, nor the failures of the 10th Division. Rather, the MoD asserted that the change reflected 'the British Forces growing confidence in the Iraqi Security Forces and their ability to provide routine security in urban areas'.[44]

A few thoughtful commentators thought the move a mistake. One was British journalist Ronan Thomas. He called it a 'misstep'. He also noted that a baleful 90th anniversary had passed largely unnoticed, the defeat on 29 April 1916 of the British Army at Kut-al-Amarah. Further north than the base just abandoned, nevertheless, the name al-Amarah had not lost its ability to haunt British military planners.[45] However, while the Army in 1916 had lost to three Turkish divisions, the loss of al-Amarah had been precipitated by a small number of irregulars firing mortars and unguided

41. *The Daily Telegraph*, 26 August 2006, 'Army's best troops mutiny'.
42. MSNBC, 17 April 2006, 'The Iraqi Army: Mutiny in the ranks'.
43. *The Daily Telegraph*, 26 August 2006, 'Jubilant Iraqi looters strip military base after British forces pull out'.
44. MoD Website, 30 August 2006, 'Change of role for Queen's Royal Hussars in Iraq'.
45. *Asia Times*, 30 August 2006, 'Britain takes a misstep in Iraq'.

rockets. It did not seem possible that such a force could defeat a modern, technically sophisticated army.

COUNTER-MEASURES THAT WERE NEVER USED

What puzzled observers was the inadequate nature of the response. Such attacks (known in Army jargon as indirect fire – or IDF) had been experienced during the Oman/Dhofar War of the early 1970s. There, the base at RAF Salalah had come under sustained attack from insurgents using very accurate 82mm Chinese-made mortars.

The first requirement was to identify firing points, to which effect RAF Salalah had been equipped with 'counter-battery' radar known as 'Green Archer'. This could pick up, very rapidly, their locations. The responses then could vary. One was counter-battery fire – either mortars or guns – to fire back at the insurgents. Both were used in Oman.[46] In al-Amarah, updated radar had been available, the Mamba – an acronym for Mobile Artillery Monitoring Battlefield Radar. Three sets had been deployed since 2004.[47] They could pick up mortar bombs or rockets while they were still in the air, predict where they would land and identify precisely the points of origin. Counterfire, though, was rarely an option. The Mahdi would fire from built-up areas, preventing retaliation for fear of killing or injuring civilians – so-called collateral damage. Thus said Sgt Patrick Murray, a Mamba operator, 'we have to pass on the map coordinates to a patrol who will deal with the attackers'.[48]

Another problem was the 'hit and run' tactics. A team could set up a mortar, fire two or three bombs, dismantle the equipment and leave a site within minutes, often in a civilian vehicle, merging with other traffic to become completely anonymous. An option used with rockets was to set them up on cheap, home-made launchers, fired by a simple timing mechanism – something as basic as a domestic washing machine or oven timer.

The Queen's Royal Hussars had thus been forced to rely on patrolling or on a 'quick reaction force' sallying out from the base – plus the occasional large-scale raid. These activities had not been successful. Said commanding officer, Lt-Col David Labouchere: 'Young soldiers would slip out of base at night to try to find the attackers. They would return in the morning as frustrated as when they left. The boys felt they were powerless.'[49]

46. Royal Artillery Historical Society, 11 October 2006, 'Cracker Battery and the Dhofar War'.
47. *Defence Management Journal*, December 2004, 'Mamba'.
48. *Ibid.*
49. *The Washington Post*, 4 October 2006, 'British find no evidence of arms traffic from Iran'.

There was more to this than being 'powerless'. As Lt Shearer and his team back in 2005 had found to their cost, patrolling al-Amarah in Snatches was extremely hazardous. Using Warriors was neither practical nor acceptable to the residents. Raids invited swift and bloody counters. Either destroyed any semblance of 'hearts and minds' engagement with the population. The weakness of the Snatch had been instrumental in forcing the base to be abandoned.

UNMANNED AERIAL VEHICLES

In fact, ground patrols on their own were always inadequate. More was needed, graphically illustrated by American freelance journalist Michael Yon, well over a year before Abu Naji had been evacuated.[50] He wrote of the effectiveness of the unmanned aerial vehicle (UAV), recounting the response to a mortar attack on the US forward operating base (FOB) Gabe near Baquba in northern Iraq.

The UAV, a 'Shadow', was patrolling the base perimeter when a mortar attack started. Fed coordinates from anti-mortar radar, it arrived over the attack site in time to send back pictures of the team departing in an anonymous civilian van. Then – as its name so aptly described – it shadowed the van. When some of the team were dropped off at various points, the Shadow operators were able to note the locations, meanwhile vectoring in two US Army Kiowa light attack helicopters. These joined the chase while ground forces were guided in to intercept. Becoming aware that they were being followed, the team drove to an Iraqi police station and surrendered. The intelligence gathered from the incident enabled several raids to be made, with the capture of considerable amounts of bomb-making materials and more insurgents apprehended.

Such technology had been available to Lt-Col Labouchere. The British had an equivalent UAV – the Phoenix. But it under-performed most of the time and for some of the time it was completely useless. Phoenix had been deployed on 1 February 2006 to Iraq, initially to Shaibah where operational problems were encountered. It was, therefore, redeployed to al-Amarah where it completed 'over 60 successful missions'. But UAVs designed for northern Europe could not fly in the Iraqi summer. They last flew in Maysan in May. By early June, as the temperatures reached over 40°C, they were returned to the UK.[51,52]

50. Michael Yon, 14 March 2005, 'Shadows of Baquba'.
51. Army website, 22 (Gibraltar 1778–1783) Bty, undated, Op TELIC 7/8.
52. MoD Website, 25 March 2008, 'Unmanned Air Vehicle Regiment bids farewell to the Phoenix'.

This was its final deployment. It had been introduced in 1998, with a minimum 15-year in-service expectation. During its short life, it had cost approximately £345 million.[53, 54] An Army complaining of being under-resourced was also saddled with expensive equipment that did not work. Interestingly though, the Artillery unit which had operated the Phoenix retrained on the US-built RQ-11, a miniature UAV with a wingspan of five feet. Easy to dismiss as a model aircraft – which it resembled – this was to become a potent and highly regarded reconnaissance tool.[55] With that equipment, the unit was to return to Iraq.

THE LACK OF HELICOPTERS

In the meantime, what applied to the Phoenix, to an extent also applied to helicopters, the other half of the partnership which Michael Yon had described. The British Army had no direct equivalent to the Kiowa, which was based on the Bell Jet Ranger commercial helicopter. Instead, it had the Lynx multi-role helicopter. Its size had been optimised for anti-submarine operations onboard then current Royal Navy frigates. Consequently, it could perform reconnaissance and attack duties but was too small to carry a section of men. An Army version had been produced to keep down unit costs for the very limited runs that the British military needed. But it was still far more expensive to run than a converted commercial model, costing approximately £23,000 per hour.[56]

This was not the only type operated by the Army. It also flew Bell 212s, more powerful and capable versions of the Huey immortalised by the Vietnam war. These were on lease, costing 'in the region of £2,000 per hour to operate'.[57] Very similar helicopters were operated in Iraq by the USMC and by the Iraqi Air Force, but not by the British Army, which used its 212s only to support detachments in Belize and Brunei.[58] They had acquired them for their 'unique abilities', which included 'flying in hot and often humid conditions whilst also being able to carry considerable loads'.[59]

There was a considerable irony here. The aircraft had replaced the Lynx, which had proved, like the Phoenix, to be incapable of operating in these

---

53. The rise and fall of the Phoenix (website), 1 June 2001.
54. Hansard, 17 July 2006 : Column 214W.
55. Army News Service, 16 February 2005, 'Small UAV provides eye in the sky for battalions'.
56. Hansard, 16 April 2007: Column 161W.
57. Hansard, 16 April 2007: Column 144W.
58. British Army website, undated, 'Joint Helicopter Command'.
59. British Army website, undated, 'Bell 212'.

conditions. Yet they had been sent to Iraq where they could not fly during daylight hours during the summer. When they did, the load capacity was often reduced. Worse still, only six were available. Even when they could take to the air, there were too few of them. Counting all types, including the transport fleet – some of which could be used for surveillance – the British forces were fielding less than half the maximum of 72 that had been available in Northern Ireland at the height of the Troubles. Ulster was roughly the size of Maysan province.[60]

Clearly, without tactical helicopters, an essential component of any counter-insurgency operation, Labouchere was being forced to fight with one hand behind his back.[61] And, despite continuing claims of 'under-funding', this was not a matter of cost. Somewhere in the system, a blockage was preventing the necessary resources from getting through to the troops in the field.

What was particularly significant was that the world was awash with second-hand Hueys, which could be refurbished to 'as new' condition at a relatively modest cost. In 2007, to equip the re-born Iraqi Air Force, that was precisely the option taken by the United States. Sixteen airframes were donated by Jordan which were then fitted with modern avionics and new engines, plus Kevlar armour and missile defence systems. The unit cost was $3.5 million.[62] The same option – of upgrading existing airframes – was later taken by Canada when it needed more helicopters for Afghanistan.[63]

Although helicopter shortages became a *cause célébre*, it was nothing to do with shortage of funds as was frequently alleged.[64] The real reasons were far more complex. Lynx helicopters were nearing the end of their useful life. As with the armoured vehicles – where the Army had blocked the purchase of protected vehicles, fearful that a 'stopgap' solution might compromise other projects – a similar dynamic was at play. A replacement was planned, a considerably more capable version called the 'Future Lynx'. A formal order had long been delayed and there was considerable nervousness as to whether it would go ahead. The feeling was that, if a workable 'interim solution' was found, Future Lynx would be further delayed or perhaps cancelled altogether. There was also considerable concern in the Navy. Without the Army order to bring down the unit airframe price, the

---

60. Hansard, 29 June 2006: Column 1357.
61. The effectiveness of light battlefield helicopters in US hands was graphically illustrated by Michael Yon is his report of 4 June 2005: 'Battle for Mosul, Part III'.
62. *Defence of the Realm*, 5 March 2007, 'Value for money'.
63. Hansard, 21 July 2008: Column 513.
64. For instance, see: BBC, 18 March 2005, 'Troops "face helicopter shortage"'.

Naval aircraft would be too expensive, again adding pressure for the project to be scrapped.[65]

The cost, even by modern standards, was colossal. A sum of £1.9 billion had been approved for a mere 60 helicopters shared between the Royal Navy and the Army – averaging more than £30 million each.[66] The Blackhawk – the successor to the Huey and the mainstay of the US battlefield helicopter fleet – cost £3–4 million, with greater load-carrying capacity and proven performance. Furthermore, they were available off-the-shelf. The Future Lynx was scheduled for delivery 'before the end of 2016', but certainly no earlier than 2014.[67]

Here, though, there was also a substantial element of 'pork barrel' politics. The Future Lynx was to be made by Augusta Westland in Yeovil, Somerset, the last military helicopter manufacturer in Britain. The order would safeguard at least 3,000 jobs and, without it, the firm would probably have to close. Jobs came before operational capability.[68]

There was also another factor. The aviation wing of the Army, the Army Air Corps, felt itself under threat and had linked its survival to the Future Lynx order. If a heavier alternative was procured, such as the Blackhawk, this might be operated by the RAF, putting Army aviation at risk. The Corps had a high-level champion in General Dannatt. In 2005, he was Commander-in-Chief, Land Command but he was also Colonel Commandant of the Corps. He fiercely defended the Future Lynx order and would not accept an alternative.[69]

Arguably, had Labouchere and previous battle group commanders based in Camp Abu Naji been equipped with properly functioning surveillance UAVs and a fleet of tactical helicopters, plus suitable protected vehicles, history might have been different. Maybe, though, these alone would not have been enough. Yet, more could have been provided.

THE PREDATOR UAV

One item which did eventually find its way into the British inventory was a larger UAV with a wingspan of 50ft. This was the American MQ-1 Predator.

65. This was effectively confirmed by General Sir Kevin O'Donoghue, giving evidence to the Commons Defence Committee on 16 December 2008 (*op. cit.*). Asked whether buying an off-the-shelf Army helicopter would be cheaper, he told MPs, 'I do not actually agree with you that we could buy a helicopter which you could fly off the back of a ship and fly in the battlefield and have a common helicopter. I do not agree that we could buy that cheaper. Yes, you could buy a cheap one no doubt to fly in a land battle space. I do not think you could find an aircraft that could fly off the back of a ship much cheaper.'
66. House of Commons Defence Committee, 10 February 2009, Defence Equipment 2009 (Report).
67. Hansard, 11 July 2006: Column 1796W.
68. *The Guardian*, 25 March 2006, 'AugustaWestland given lifeline with MoD's £1bn order for Lynx'.
69. This, and the preceding narrative, was based on this author's discussions with high-level defence officials, under conditions of anonymity.

It could fly for 12 or more hours, its camera and other sensors sending a constant stream of intelligence to the ground, and could also carry Hellfire missiles, their 20lb high-explosive warheads delivering instant annihilation. Mahdi fighters were often fanatical in their disregard for death but even they might have taken the hint if, time after time, attempts on British bases had been both unsuccessful and fatal.

Predators were deployed by US forces in 2001. In six years, they had fired over 6,000 Hellfires in combat.[70] Secretly, the MoD – conscious of the failure of the Phoenix – had in 2004 joined the Predator programme. From the US Nellis Airbase, RAF personnel were controlling by satellite link leased machines which were flying over Iraq.[71] They could have turned the battle for Abu Naji. There is one report of a Predator hitting an enemy target with a Hellfire missile in al-Amarah on 9 July 2007, nearly a year after Abu Naji had been abandoned.[72] That was too late.

Nor even was this the limit of UAV and missile technology. Effective though it was, the explosive power of the Hellfire sometimes posed an unacceptable risk of collateral damage. To overcome that, the Americans had another missile, the Viper Strike. With precision guidance, its 7lb warhead could penetrate one room of a building with lethal effect, leaving the occupants of adjoining rooms unharmed.

For al-Amarah, with its network of narrow streets and alleyways, Viper Strike had another attribute – a vertical attack profile, as opposed to the relatively shallow dive of the Hellfire. Like the famous lager, it could reach parts others could not reach. The launch platform was the MQ-5 Hunter UAV, comparable with the Shadow, which had been deployed by the Americans in late 2004.[73] Latterly, the missile had been fitted to the AC-130H Spectre gunship, but this was still experimental when Abu Naji was being abandoned.[74]

THE AC-130 SPECTRE

Very far from being experimental was the Spectre itself. Based on the Hercules – the workhorse of the RAF's medium-range transport fleet – the gunship version had been first introduced into Vietnam in 1967. It packed a 105mm howitzer, two 40mm Bofors cannons and two 20mm Vulcan cannons. Highly sophisticated sensors and advanced fire control systems

70. Wikipedia, undated, MQ-1 Predator.
71. *The Sunday Times*, 3 October 2004, 'Pilotless strikes on Iraq by RAF'.
72. *Air Force News*, 9 July 2007, 'Airpower summary'.
73. *Defense Update*, 25 September, 2005, 'Viper Strike Laser Guided Weapon for UAVs'.
74. *Defence Industry Daily*, 11 August 2005, 'Viper Strike for AC-130s?'

allowed its crew to deliver ordnance with phenomenal precision.[75] In 2004, two had supported a raid on the Mahdi Army headquarters in al-Amarah, destroying five heavy-calibre mortars that were troubling the raiders. Their intervention had been decisive.[76]

While the MoD had been lukewarm about procuring Viper Strike – which it had considered too expensive – there was unanimity on the value of the AC-130. Unfortunately, these too were expensive, the latest version (the AC-130U 'Spooky') costing approximately £60 million, about the same as a Eurofighter. That left the Army entirely reliant on US resources. And, while the US was able to provide air support on occasions, Spectres were in short supply and unavailable to the troops in Abu Naji.

APACHES AND C-RAM

Notwithstanding this, the UK had a 67-strong fleet of Apache attack helicopters, costing over £4 billion. But although ordered in 1996, production had not been completed until 21 July 2004.[77] It then took until 2006 to enter operational service, too late to save Abu Naji.[78]

Elsewhere, in an attempt to counter the threat from indirect fire, the US military had been re-visiting 1970s technology, experimenting with the naval Phalanx Close in Weapons System. This was a radar-controlled, automatic 20mm gun, capable of firing at an incredible rate of 4,500 rounds a minute, in bursts of up to 100 rounds. It had been designed as a last-ditch defence against anti-ship missiles and fixed-wing aircraft at short range.[79]

On 16 December 2004, an adapted system proved able to shoot down mortar bombs. By July 2005, under the designation of Counter-Rocket And Mortar (C-RAM), it was on its way to Iraq. It scored its first intercept in March 2006 and by May 2008 the US military was celebrating its hundredth.[80] A year earlier, in May 2007, the MoD had decided to deploy the system, borrowing equipment from the Americans while it converted its own stock of redundant naval guns.[81] This had been an almost exact re-run of the RG-31 controversy. In December 2006, Ann Winterton had

---

75. FAS Military Analysis Network, undated, 'AC-130H Spectre'.

76. Sgt Dan Mills, *Sniper One, op. cit.*, pp. 139–147.

77. Augusta Westland website, 21 July 2004, 'British Army receives 67th Apache in ceremony held at the Farnborough Air Show 2004'.

78. Armed Forces website, undated, 'Army Aviation'.

79. FAS Military Analysis Network, undated, 'Mk15 Phalanx Close-In Weapons System (CIWS)'.

80. Army.mil News, 9 May 2008, 'Countering capability intercepts 100th rocket, mortar in Iraq'.

81. *Jane's Defence Weekly*, 30 May 2007, 'UK deploys Phalanx C-RAM system to protect forces in Iraq'.

asked the MoD whether it would introduce C-RAM. The response had been the usual diet of negativity.

Initial assessments … indicate that it is not appropriate for our current requirements, but we keep the operational situation under review. We have not therefore considered the adaptation of the Counter Battery Radar to provide targeting data for this system. We provide layered protection for British bases in Iraq and Afghanistan through a range of force protection methods.[82]

THE ROMP IN THE DESERT

When C-RAM finally arrived, it was 10 months too late for Labouchere's men. They, meanwhile, had been camping out in the desert and roaming the border area close to Iran in an attempt to track down arms smugglers. David Axe, a freelance journalist, likened Labouchere to T. E. Lawrence. To the very obvious approval of Axe, he had eschewed the use of 'high-tech whizbangs other coalition commanders take for granted', relying on 'speed and agility'. He travelled light in just a dozen vehicles per squadron, mostly trucks and 'speedy Land Rovers', but including 'a handful of Scimitar light tanks'.[83] That reluctance to embrace technology also extended to the Raven UAV. Of this, Axe wrote:

A couple weeks ago they sent him a Raven drone and its operators. In a rare act of indulgence, Labouchere let them demonstrate the tiny drone. But when it crashed into his Merlin, putting a dent in the prized $30-million chopper, Labouchere sent the operators packing. Who needs a drone when you spend most of the day racing across the desert, scanning the horizon with your own two eyes?

Rather contradicting this purism, Labouchere's supply arrangements relied on daily flights from the RAF's most sophisticated and expensive transport helicopter, the (now dented) Merlin, plus top-ups from the most modern of the fixed-wing transport fleet, the C-130J Hercules. On 12 February 2007, one such Hercules flew into a 'temporary landing zone' (TLZ), bringing replenishments. As it landed, it was hit by a sequence of IED arrays. Crew and passengers escaped but the aircraft was 'irrecoverable'. To avoid it getting into enemy hands, £30 million-worth of aircraft was blown up.

The Board of Inquiry report made it quite clear that failures of the Hussars, in allowing 'sufficient time for the IEDs to be placed and well concealed' and a 'lack of understanding of TLZ clearance procedures … exacerbated by lack of coherent policy and standard operating procedures …'

---

82. Hansard, 12 December 2006: Column 938W.
83. David Axe, *Defense Tech*, 13 November 2006, 'Labouchere of Arabia'.

were contributory factors in the loss. In the published version, three other contributory factors relating to Labouchere's men were obliterated.[84]

Fortunately for them, the Hussars completed their tour without casualties. Their successors, the Queen's Royal Lancers, were not so fortunate. On 19 April 2007, Cpl Ben Leaning and Trooper Kristen Turton were killed by an IED while their Scimitar was leading a convoy from one camp to another.[85] Three other soldiers were injured, one seriously. Two other vehicles were damaged. Heavy trucks in the convoy had dictated a road passage to avoid 'forbidding water crossings and rough terrain'. The ambush, described in detail by Michael Yon, was elaborate and carefully prepared, comprising 46 EFPs and two ball-bearing bombs. Yon described route clearance measures employed en route to the ambush, designed to prevent that very eventuality:

We stopped at an intersection so the soldiers could dismount from their vehicles to check for bombs or other signs of an ambush. This way, even if the bombs explode or some other type of ambush is initiated, only one or two soldiers might get killed immediately, and the other soldiers still have the vehicles and larger weapons.

He also referred to the 'furious debate about armoured vehicles in Iraq'. Our own forces had been needlessly exposed, killed by even small attacks, he wrote: 'And so we armoured up like turtles … but at a cost. Our vehicles break down more, and our Humvees have gone from being super-agile to tortoise-like contraptions that get stuck every chance.' In the environment in which the Lancers were operating, Yon argued, 'agility, firepower and other qualities often far outweigh the heavy metal'. There was still a place for unarmoured agility.[86]

Despite this, the desert groups were unsuccessful in tracking down smugglers.[87] Labouchere had expressed his 'confidence' in Iraq's border force yet, at crossing points, Iranian trucks were stopped by guards only when British soldiers appeared. When they left, they would be waved through.[88] Following on, the Lancers and then the King's Royal Hussars were similarly unsuccessful. The arms were coming in through legal border crossings under Iraqi control – lubricated by bribes.[89] This could not be remedied. On 18 April, Maysan was handed back to the Iraqis. This 'milestone' was hailed by Maj-Gen Jonathan Shaw – now commander of coalition forces in the south – as 'a moment of optimism'.[90] The battle

84. MoD website, undated, 'Board of Inquiry into Accident involving Hercules C130 Mk4 ZH876'.
85. *The Times*, 19 April 2007, 'British soldiers killed in "secure" province'.
86. Michael Yon, undated, 'Death or Glory, Part I'.
87. *The Washington Post*, 4 October 2006, 'British find no evidence of arms traffic from Iran'.
88. *The Daily Telegraph*, 12 November 2006, 'Iraqi terrorists "are being supplied with arms smuggled from Iran"'.
89. *The Times*, 18 August 2007, 'Smugglers and scorpions in the desert war Prince Harry missed'.
90. *The Daily Telegraph*, 20 April 2007, '200 killed as province returns to Iraqi control'.

group moved back to Basra. A minimal 'border support mission' was to be controlled from there.

British forces were still available if the Iraqi government requested support.[91] On 19 October, there were reports of fighting in al-Amarah after the head of police intelligence, a member of Badr, had been killed by a bomb. His family had kidnapped the teenage brother of the local head of the Mahdi Army. The Mahdi retaliated, burning down several police stations and precipitating fighting in the streets. Some 30 people were reported killed and 100 injured.

That had not been the full extent the action. On 10 October, RAF Tornados had been in action near al-Amarah, providing close-air support to troops fighting militia forces.[92] However, the 10th Division was ordered in to restore calm, while a British battle group was despatched to the outskirts of the city. It was not required. Maliki, with his interior minister, met Muqtada. A deal was stitched up, Muqtada called off his troops and Maliki did likewise. Relative peace was restored.[93, 94] British troops returned to Basra unbloodied.

91. MoD website, 18 April 2007, 'Iraqi forces take control of Maysaan Province'.
92. Air Force Link, 10 October 2006, 'Airpower summary'.
93. BBC, 21 October 2006, 'UK may return to Iraq crisis city'.
94. *USA Today* (AP), 21 October 2007, 'Relative quiet returns to Iraq's south; concerns linger over emboldened militias'.

Chapter 8 – Tipping points

Basra:
end of June–December 2006

We are now approaching the tipping point in southern Iraq. The area will either sink into the grasp of insurgents and Iranian-sponsored militias or become a beacon of hope for the rest of the country.

THOMAS HARDING, DEFENCE CORRESPONDENT,
THE DAILY TELEGRAPH, 3 NOVEMBER 2006

As the end game in al-Amarah was about to be played out, the situation in Basra was not good. The day after the horrific suicide bombing in the old peoples' home and the attack on a petrol station saw another explosion in central Basra. Ten were killed with 15 wounded and buildings were heavily damaged. Shi'a 'sectarian militias' were suspected of being behind this and the recent upsurge in bombings. And, in what had become a familiar routine, British bases were being rocketed and mortared. When the Old State Building was again targeted that night, local sources noted that the barrage had been the most violent for some time.[1]

Thus, in a matter of days, there had been manifestations of two sides of the three-corner war which was tearing Basra apart – the infighting between Shi'a and the battle against the 'occupiers'. Three days later, the third element kicked in, the 'sectarian war'. Shi'a militiamen abducted six Sunnis from their homes, one an Imam from the local mosque. Gunmen had been accompanied by men in police uniform.[2] Then they blew up a temple belonging to the Sabeans, an ancient religious group that pre-dated Islam and Christianity. Five rockets were then fired at the Shatt al-Arab Hotel. The insurgents claimed 'direct hits' which had set off violent explosions.[3]

In early July, another troubling sectarian incident was reported. Men in civilian clothing and police uniforms, in a fleet of 10 'official cars' with no licence plates, arrived at the home of a prominent Sunni. They killed him together with his son in front of other family members, moving on to kidnap five residents in the area, some of them relatives of the dead man.[4]

1. *Free Arab Voice*, 23 June 2006, Resistance Report 559.
2. *Free Arab Voice*, 26 June 2006, Resistance Report 562.
3. *Free Arab Voice*, 29 June 2006, Resistance Report 565.
4. *Free Arab Voice*, 3 July 2006, Resistance Report 569.

Nothing of this was reported in the UK. Instead, the British public was treated to Tony Blair's evidence to the Commons Liaison Committee. Asked whether life in Basra was better than pre-war, Blair argued that the few deaths actually being recorded were 'caused by the actions of a criminal minority'. He then asserted that Iraqi forces were becoming 'more capable of taking over individual provinces', linking that with 'opportunities to draw down significant numbers of British troops'.[5]

On that very day, a six-hour daily curfew was announced in Basra in an attempt to curtail the escalating violence.[6] This was not for British consumption, and neither was the way Blair's 'criminal minority' was engaged in wholesale oil smuggling, its value estimated at $4 billion a year, or about 10 per cent of the country's gross domestic product. That detail was confined to the US press.[7] Nor was the public being told that British bases were under virtual siege. Yet another rocket attack on Basra Palace was recorded on 6 July.[8]

Nevertheless, political winds were shifting in Iraq. That day brought news of an operation in Sadr City. Led by Iraqi ground forces, the US provided air cover, demonstrating that Maliki was prepared to move against Shi'a insurgents. He was not, though, confronting Muqtada, on whom he was still politically dependent. The target, a Mahdi Army commander, was accused of trying to set up a 'breakaway insurgent operation'.[9] Whether this was true or not, it had the effect of giving Maliki a 'fig-leaf'.

This device, also used by Blair in his evidence to the Liaison Committee, was frequently employed. Most often it applied to confrontations between security forces and the Mahdi Army. The Mahdi were characterised as 'criminals', 'breakaway groups' or 'rogue elements'. Sometimes, the term 'death squads' was used, reflecting what was believed to be the splintering within the militias. The implication was that individuals were setting up freelance operations which were neither controlled nor sanctioned by militia leaders. Whatever the term used, the circumlocutions were intended to avoid any suggestion that the Baghdad government was challenging or seeking to bring down Muqtada.

THE 'DISTRACTION' OF THE WAR IN LEBANON

If there was to be any real analysis in the media of, in this case, a thinly disguised move against the Mahdi – with its enormous implications for the

---

5. BBC, 4 July 2006, ' "Significant" troops home by 2008'.
6. *Aswat al-Iraq*, 4 July 2006, 'Basra to go under a six-hour daily curfew starting Friday'.
7. *Seattle Times*, 5 July 2006, 'Oil smugglers leaving Basra in disarray'.
8. *Free Arab Voice*, 6 July 2006, Resistance Report 572.
9. *The Times*, 7 July 2006, 'Arrest of Shia militia leaders marks shift of focus in Iraq'.

British sector – it was swept away. Tension had been building in southern Lebanon where Hezbollah had been preparing an attack on Israel. On 12 July, this group launched a border raid, killing three Israeli soldiers, wounding two and kidnapping two more. Five more were killed in a failed rescue attempt. Simultaneously, Hezbollah fired rockets against civilian communities. In retaliation, Israel launched a major offensive.[10] For the 34 days of the fighting and for some time afterwards, coverage of British operations in Iraq – already minimal – almost completely dried up. Unfortunately, the period of abstinence covered the withdrawal from al-Amarah.

In that period, there was also an intense political debate in Baghdad. Maliki was coming under heavy pressure – and criticism – for his failure to rein in the militias. It was covered in detail by the respected Egyptian weekly news magazine, *Al-Ahram*. Although this might have been expected to be obsessed with the Lebanon conflict, as fighting broke out it asked: 'Who rules Iraq?' 'Disbanding the militias is the only way to put an end to the sectarian killings,' it opined.[11] Even at the height of the war, *Al-Ahram* returned to the subject. US policy-makers, it said, were 'low on patience'. It reported how, when US forces had tackled Shi'a militias, particularly the Mahdi Army, Maliki had been 'quick to use vitriol to protest US actions'. The divide between US forces and the prime minister was abundantly clear.[12]

This was a pivotal period in the occupation, but the British media was not interested. Over the period, its main concern was the deaths of British soldiers, adding to the generally distorted public perception that the only thing happening in southern Iraq was that British personnel were getting killed and injured.

BIGGER RAIDS – A CHANGE IN TACTICS

The British media thus reported on 16 July that a British patrol had been hit by a bomb in the south-west of the city, with two soldiers wounded.[13] The next day, insurgents bombarded British bases, hitting Basra airport and another site with rockets and mortars. They claimed that direct hits had inflicted damage on buildings and equipment and wounded a number of soldiers.[14] This was not reported, but when Cpl John Crosby was killed and another soldier wounded, that was. Cpl Crosby had been killed during

10. Wikipedia, 2006 Lebanon War.
11. *Al-Ahram*, 13–19 July 2006, 'Who rules Iraq?'
12. *Al-Ahram*, 17–23 August 2006, 'Baghdad in the crosshairs'.
13. *The Times*, 17 July 2006, 'British soldier dies in Basra gunfight during arrest of suspected terrorist'.
14. *Free Arab Voice*, 17 July 2006, Resistance Report 583.

a major raid on a Shi'ite stronghold in northern Basra which had involved hundreds of troops supported by Warriors.[15]

The raid itself reflected the change in British emphasis, born of the new 'Security Plan'. It had targeted Sajad Abu Aya, the head of the Mahdi Army in Basra province. Intelligence gathered led troops to another location. A two-ton cache of 'more than 50 rockets, 10 rocket-propelled grenades and 150 mortars' was seized. Commanding the operation had been Major Richard Head, leading a Company-strength force from a Warrior. The response had been ferocious. In an engagement which lasted two hours, his Warrior was hit several times. An estimated 104 RPG rounds were fired at his unit. Four military vehicles were damaged, four insurgents were killed and five wounded.[16]

The seizure of the weapons cache and the capture of Abu Aya was described as 'the most significant breakthrough' since British forces had arrived in Iraq. Des Browne praised the Iraqi security forces for providing intelligence. 'The situation in Basra is still difficult, but our ability to sustain political support allows us to do this sort of thing,' he said. Nothing had been published of the ferocity of the fighting, allowing *The Daily Telegraph* to write that the involvement of Iraqi forces, 'will add weight to suggestions of an early withdrawal of British troops'. That was precisely the conclusion the newspaper was supposed to draw.[17, 18]

THE SILENCE OF THE BBC

At this time, Conservative shadow defence secretary Liam Fox intervened, but only to attack the BBC for its 'unrelentingly negative' reports. Recently in Basra, servicemen had complained to him that the BBC reported casualties 'but not if we reconnect electricity, repair sewers or rebuild a bridge'.[19] Given the minimal coverage the BBC was devoting to the constant attacks on British troops and the steady toll of injuries – to say nothing of their reverses in al-Amarah – such a complaint was misplaced. Furthermore, the BBC's silence must have been deliberate. The Corporation monitors the world's media, including Middle East sources.

By contrast, it seemed quite prepared to broadcast a 'puff' on the virtues of the Iraqi security services. The same day Fox had complained, it was applauding an Iraqi Army patrol which had discovered five rockets 'ready

15. BBC, 17 July 2006, 'MoD names soldier killed in Basra'.
16. BBC, 28 February 2007, 'Military Cross for Kent soldier'.
17. *The Daily Telegraph*, 22 July 2006, 'British capture Iraqi bombs mastermind'.
18. *Aswat al-Iraq*, 18 July 2006, 'Mahdi Army clashes with British forces in Basra, nine casualties'.
19. *The Independent*, 22 July 2006, 'Fox attacks BBC's coverage of Iraq'.

to fire at a base housing around 200 soldiers of the Light Infantry'. It cited Major Burbridge expressing how, 'Our confidence in the Iraqi army continues to grow and this demonstrates how capable [it] is becoming'.[20] Thus, in late July, before the Iraqi Army had been tested and found wanting in Abu Naji, the agenda seemed clear – 'talking up' the capabilities of the Iraqi security forces while neglecting to reveal the growing intensity of attacks against the British forces. Whether the BBC was actively complicit in this is impossible to tell.

There was another British raid on 24 July, 'with nine Mahdi army elements' detained, after 'about 30 tanks and vehicles of the British forces supported by choppers encircled al-Qebla, 8km west of Basra'. The source of the information on the number of arrests was the al-Sadr office in Basra.[21] The Multi-National Forces admitted to arresting four suspects, detained on suspicion of launching armed operations against them.

THE ATTACKS INTENSIFY

The raids and the 'professionalism' of the Iraqi Army made no difference to the intensity of attacks on the British. The same day as the latest raid, insurgents again attacked Basra airport, firing six rockets. The airport had to be closed to air traffic. For a change, the insurgents also bombed the offices of the 'Iraqi Central Intelligence Agency'.[22] The following day, the insurgents gave the base at Shatt al-Arab Hotel their attention, firing two rockets at it.[23] Then they attacked a vehicle patrol, claiming to have 'disabled a British tank' (possibly a Warrior), wounding four British soldiers, one of them severely.

With the continuous mortar and rocket attacks on British bases, it was only a matter of time before a soldier was killed. That day arrived on 1 August when Cpl Matthew Cornish was fatally wounded by a mortar bomb that landed within the perimeter of the Old State Building. Over the seven months through the summer of 2006, more than 114 mortar and rocket rounds and 47 RPGs hit the compound. There were more than 38 recorded 'contacts' involving sniper and small arms fire, and four IED attacks on patrol vehicles.[24] That there had not been more casualties was a minor miracle.

20. BBC, 22 July 2006, 'Iraqi army "saves British troops"'.
21. *Aswat al-Iraq*, 24 July 2006, 'British forces detain nine Mahdi army elements in Basra'.
22. *Free Arab Voice*, 24 July 2006, Resistance Report 590.
23. *Free Arab Voice*, 26 July 2006, Resistance Report 592.
24. Army website, undated, 'The Rifles – for gallantry and valour'.

Significantly, Squadron Leader Richard Painter, acting as spokesman for the military, said it was 'very difficult' to defend bases against such attacks. 'We do all that is reasonably possible under these circumstances.'[25] The latter assertion, in terms of the equipment and systems provided, was fair. But in terms of what could have been done it was somewhat disingenuous. Neither then nor later was the assertion challenged by either the mainstream media or MPs. Rather than trigger discussions on how best to counter the threat, Cpl Cornish's death was used to promote the withdrawal agenda. Labour MP Alan Simpson, a long-term critic of the campaigns in both Iraq and Afghanistan, argued that this was further evidence that Iraq was 'mission irretrievable'.[26]

Unsurprisingly, given the paucity of publicity, there was little awareness in the UK of the intensity of attacks against British forces. A week after Cpl Cornish had died, insurgents launched no less than nine rockets at Basra Palace.[27] Three Iraqis, including a policeman, were then wounded by an IED. The device had been intended for a British patrol.[28] The next day, the insurgents fired three 120mm mortar bombs and four rockets into the Palace compound, claiming direct hits.[29]

As an illustration of just how far security had deteriorated, on 16 August Sadr supporters from the Bani Asad tribe laid siege to the Basra government offices, lobbing mortar bombs at the building and barricading nearby bridges. They took over parts of the building, killing four policemen and wounding five. The militia used the opportunity to attack the Light Infantry base – the Old State Building. Major Head's Company fired over 3,100 rounds in one hour, accounting for up to 15 militiamen.[30]

The attack on the government building was the tribe's response to the murder of one of their Sheikhs. They were accusing the Fadhila members – from the governor's party – of his murder. The tribesmen also cut Route 6, the main road between Basra and Baghdad, and threatened to kill police who entered their tribal area in the northern suburbs. Into deserted streets, the Iraqi Army deployed in force with armoured vehicles to 'preserve order'. The populace apparently was not reassured. British troops had to intervene to support the Iraqi security forces before the siege was lifted.[31, 32]

25. BBC, 1 August 2006, 'UK soldier killed in Basra named'.
26. *The Independent*, 2 August, 'Criticism mounts as corporal dies in attack on UK base in Basra'.
27. *Free Arab Voice*, 6 August 2006, Resistance Report 603.
28. *Aswat al-Iraq*, 13 August 2006, 'Three Iraqis wounded in Basra blast'.
29. *Free Arab Report*, 14 August 2006, Resistance Report 611.
30. Army website, undated, 'The Rifles – for gallantry and valour'.
31. *Free Arab Voice*, 16 August 2006, Resistance Report 613.
32. *The Washington Post*, 17 August 2006, 'Rival Shiite militias clash in southern Iraq'.

THE MYTH OF IRAQI SECURITY FORCES
EFFECTIVENESS

By any measure, this was a significant event. With the ongoing attacks on British bases, it confounded any suggestion that Basra was under control. As significantly, it demolished the official line that Iraqi security forces were effective. But not only was their fighting prowess suspect, their deficiencies in logistics were extremely troubling. These came to the fore on 7 July when a platoon of British soldiers had returned to its base after a combined operation in the remote desert region of Maysan.

The base was shared with an Iraqi Army unit which then had not had food or water for 36 hours. The soldiers were becoming somewhat anxious, especially as their officers had left them, apparently in a bid to arrange a re-supply. When they had not returned, a group of between 10–15 armed Iraqi soldiers approached the British platoon. After a confrontation, shots were fired over the heads of the British, the ringleader then acquiring a sniper rifle and firing around British soldiers, deliberately aiming to miss. Cpl Martin Caines faced down the gunman, for which action he was awarded the George Medal.[33]

Nothing of this found its way into the media until March 2007, when it rated a brief mention in the local press. As for the Basra siege, this was covered by US media, the *New York Times* suggesting that it 'underscored the tenuous grip the Iraqi government maintains even in regions not under the sway of Sunni Arab insurgents'.[34] Despite this, there was little UK coverage. Blair's myth of improving security and more capable Iraqi security forces was remaining intact.

That myth was quite evidently supported by the military. On 22 August, an anonymous 'senior commander' was widely reported saying that handing control of Basra to the Iraqis was 'feasible' in nine months. The Iraqi Army would be ready in 9–12 months. The handover, said the officer, 'would be reliant on stable security and the support of the Iraq government', the implication being that that was assured. Thus the British could maintain 'quite a significantly smaller force than we've got now, probably in the region of 3,000–4,000 people based in a single location'. The British government would retain one or two bases around Basra to 'protect our investment'.[35]

This was not an off-the-cuff briefing. It was based on a recent MoD feasibility study that allowed for cuts 'if current conditions prevail'.[36] By

---

33. Army website, undated, Princess of Wales's Royal Regiment (Brochure).
34. *The New York Times*, 16 August 2006, 'Iraqi and British forces battle Shiite militias'.
35. BBC, 22 August 2006, 'Basra handover "feasible" in 2007'.
36. *The Daily Telegraph*, 23 August 2006, 'Britain may halve troop numbers in Iraq by next year'.

contrast, senior officials – from which Department was not specified – were saying that the situation in Iraq 'remains far too dangerous for a full pull-out in the foreseeable future'.[37] Nevertheless, to all intents and purposes, the military were setting a timetable for departure and the sequence in which disengagement would be ordered.

There was one encouraging note. Two men from the northern city of Mosul, suspected of association with al Qaeda, were arrested in Basra by the national security department. They confessed their intention to launch 'terrorist' acts in Basra.[38] This had not been the first time al Qaeda suspects had been apprehended. While this group, reinforced by foreign fighters, had caused mayhem in the US sector, particularly alongside Sunni insurgents, they were not welcomed by the Shi'a in the south. Their insurgency was a private war. Strangers were quickly turned in to the local police or militias. That was something with which the British did not have to contend.

As for the Iraqi Army, formations were clashing with Mahdi militia in the city of Diwaniyah, 80 miles south of Baghdad.[39] Within a day, they had been routed, leaving behind them at least 25 of their number dead, to add to their battle honours at Abu Naji.[40]

THE VIOLENCE GETS WORSE

Mortaring and rocketing of British bases went on and on, as did the fighting. Basra airport suffered a rocket attack on 21 August, and again on the 28th.[41, 42] That day, it was almost 2003 all over again when there had been major riots in the city centre. Throngs of Shi'a demonstrators, 'fed up with the corrupt puppet regime and its skyrocketing prices, no electricity, no running water', chanted support for Saddam Hussein.[43] The day before, oil company employees had gone on strike, halting oil shipments over demands for higher pay and profit sharing.[44] Three years on, the only change was that the violence had got worse. Just to emphasise that, two Iraqi 'military intelligence elements' were shot dead by unidentified gunmen in the Basra central town of Tannoma.[45] The corpses of four security men were found

---

37. *The Independent*, 23 August 2006, 'UK troops to stay in Iraq "to protect investment"'.
38. *Aswat al-Iraq*, 20 August 2006, 'Two Qaeda suspects caught in Basra'.
39. *The Independent*, 28 August 2006, '23 killed in clashes between Shiite militia and Iraqi army in southern Iraq'.
40. *The Independent*, 29 August 2006, 'At least 100 die as militia force Iraqi troops out of town'.
41. *Aswat al-Iraq*, 21 August 2006, 'Katyusha attack on British base in Basra airport'.
42. *Aswat al-Iraq*, 28 August 2006, 'Katyusha attack on British base in Basra airport'.
43. *Free Arab Voice*, 23 August 2006, Resistance Report 620.
44. *Free Arab Voice*, 22 August 2006, Resistance Report 619.
45. *Aswat al-Iraq*, 21 August 2006, 'Two Iraqi intelligence elements killed in Basra'.

dumped by a roadside and a motorcycle bomb ripped through the market in the al Hayaniyah area of western Basra, a Sadr stronghold. Nine people were killed and 13 wounded.[46, 47]

A British patrol vehicle was attacked on 30 August – an IED which left one soldier wounded and the vehicle damaged. And Des Browne got a welcome package when he visited Basra airport. The insurgents laid on a rocket-firing demonstration for him.[48] Shatt al-Arab Hotel took seven mortar bombs the next day. Eyewitnesses claimed hearing violent explosions inside the facility.[49] It was on the receiving end of no less than 11 bombs on 1 September, with reports that the British had been unable to halt the barrage despite helicopter patrols.[50] The insurgents returned the next day, this time with rockets, sending 10 of them towards the base, only to have them fall outside the perimeter, seriously injuring an Iraqi woman.[51] Then 4 September saw another mortar attack.[52]

For Gunners Stephen Wright and Samuela Vanua, both of 12 Regiment Royal Artillery, this was a day that ended abruptly at about 1pm. It was also their last. In support of a Danish reconstruction team close to ad Dayr, about nine miles north of Basra, both were killed in an ambush. Two more were injured – one seriously. Their badly damaged Snatch, standing upright by the side of the road, part of the rear cabin ripped open by the force of the explosion, had all the hallmarks of an EFP strike.

Major Burbridge, the duty British military spokesman, stated the obvious: 'It appears a roadside bomb was used to attack the convoy.' He also admitted: 'They were in a Snatch vehicle.' Recognising the recent and continuing controversy, he added: 'They have been designed to protect the crew against a certain threat and on occasion they have been defeated.' In an interview for *Sky News*, Burbridge claimed the attack had happened in an area where the threat had been 'relatively low'. Snatches, he argued, were 'equipped for the job' and soldiers knew they were 'at risk'. 'The equipment we have is the best that was available at the time of going on the operation … We have a very complicated operation out here. The equipment is adequate for the task and we have to get on with it.'[53] Blair called the deaths a 'terrible tragedy'.

46. *Free Arab Voice*, 26 August 2006, Resistance Report 623.
47. *Aswat al-Iraq*, 28 August 2006, 'Basra market bombing toll up to nine dead, 13 wounded'.
48. *Aswat al-Iraq*, 30 August 2006, 'British soldier wounded in Basra blast, base attacked'.
49. *Free Arab Voice*, 31 August 2006, Resistance Report 628.
50. *Free Arab Voice*, 1 September 2006, Resistance Report 630.
51. *Aswat al-Iraq*, 2 September 2006, 'Iraqi woman wounded in attack on British base in Basra'.
52. *Free Arab Voice*, 4 September 2006, Resistance Report 632.
53. *The Guardian*, 4 September 2006, 'Iraq roadside bomb kills two British soldiers'.

'RELATIVE CALM'

A British soldier had also been killed in Afghanistan. The media woke up. Patrick Cockburn, in *The Independent*, laboriously explained how the 'war on terror' had 'fuelled resentment of the West and brought new levels of death and destruction'. He also noted that, 'It may be egocentric to write only of British dead. They are but a small percentage of the casualties in the multiple crises which are now cross-infecting each other in the Middle East.'[54] In its main news section, its pages having been devoid of operational coverage of southern Iraq for many weeks, the paper then remarked: 'The latest deaths come after a period of relative calm for the British military ...'[55] In that one, offhand, unthinking remark lay a huge distortion. There had been 'relative calm'? Yet that represented the generality of the media narrative, sustained by the almost complete lack of reporting.

In *The Daily Telegraph*, Gethin Chamberlain and Aqeel Hussein gave a hint of things to come, which should have sounded alarm bells. Sistani had abandoned attempts to restrain his followers, conceding that there was nothing he could do to prevent the country sliding towards civil war. He was 'angry and disappointed' that Shi'as were ignoring his calls for calm. 'I will not be a political leader any more,' he had told his aides. 'I am only happy to receive questions about religious matters.' It was, remarked Chamberlain and Hussein 'a devastating blow to the remaining hopes for a peaceful solution in Iraq and spells trouble for British forces'.[56]

The day after Cockburn's laborious analysis, *The Guardian* reported, 'Britain forced to send more troops to Iraq'. There was no context, nor any reason offered as to why this should be necessary, other than a vague statement that the move reflected 'increasing concern' about the threat to British troops 'and the inability of local forces to take over responsibility for the country's security'.[57] It was a recognition of the reality. But it went unremarked, even when it was officially announced in Parliament on 11 September.[58] There were no demands for a debate. Members of Parliament, in their own way, were being as supine as the media.

The news certainly did not seem to interest *The Independent*. After stirring itself to report on the breaking of the period of 'relative calm', it had returned to its torpor on 5 September while, presumably, another period of 'relative calm' descended on southern Iraq. This was celebrated

---

54. *The Independent*, 5 September 2006, 'Another fatal day in the "war on terror"'.

55. *The Independent*, 5 September 2006, 'Two troops dead after bomb strike in Iraq'.

56. *The Daily Telegraph*, 4 September 2006, 'I no longer have power to save Iraq from civil war, warns Shia leader'.

57. *The Guardian*, 6 September 2006, 'Britain forced to send more troops to Iraq'.

58. Hansard, 11 September 2006: Column 111WS.

by insurgents with the delivery of another six mortar bombs – minus their wrappings – to Shatt al-Arab Hotel. Three missed their target, falling near an Iraqi police department.[59] In Qurnah on 6 September, about 40 miles north of the area where Burbridge had described the threat as 'relatively low', Gunner Lee Darren Thornton – from the same Regiment as Gunners Wright and Vanua – experienced more of *The Independent*'s 'relative calm'. He was fatally wounded by a gunshot when his unit came under fire near the building used to plan reconstruction.[60]

Five Iraqi policemen shared some of that 'relative calm' when they were wounded by an IED as they patrolled in their vehicle five miles west of Basra.[61] British soldiers enjoyed even more of the 'relative calm' when their base yet again came under attack from rockets on 9 September.[62] Ten days later, that 'relative calm' extended to Basra airport, where three rockets landed, and to central Basra, where a gunman was killed and a British soldier was wounded when a patrol was involved in a firefight.[63] The 'relative calm', in fact, was breaking out all over, embracing even the Iranian consulate – where two rockets struck the outer walls, damaging three police vehicles – and the British consulate at Basra Palace, which enjoyed another mortar barrage, adding to its growing collection of shrapnel. So calm was it there that a British spokesman would only admit that 'this sort of attack happens from time to time, every four or five days'.[64]

As September wore on, the 'relative calm' persisted, spreading on the 22nd to a translator working for the British, who was shot and killed after insurgents raided his home, and to Shaibah, which took five rockets as opposed to the mere four that were fired at Shatt al-Arab Hotel.[65] That day also an American contractor working for the US State Department was killed in Basra, in one of the rocket attacks. To reinforce this 'relative calm', the insurgents followed up with mortars on the market in Shaibah town, where British troops were occasionally allowed out to buy souvenirs, setting fire to four civilian cars and damaging a shop. The 'relative calm' was further reinforced with a rocket fired on the town.[66]

The next day, so intense had become the 'relative calm' that only one bomb exploded alongside a British patrol, on the main street in Basra running past the police headquarters, and only 10 armoured vehicles had

---

59. *Aswat al-Iraq*, 5 September 2006, 'British base attacked in Basra'.
60. BBC, 9 September 2006, 'Regiment "numbed" by Iraq death'.
61. *Aswat al-Iraq*, 6 September 2006, 'Five Iraqi policemen wounded in Basra explosion'.
62. *Aswat al-Iraq*, 9 September 2006, 'British base attacked in Basra'.
63. *Aswat al-Iraq*, 19 September 2006, 'Gunman killed, British soldier wounded in Basra'.
64. *Free Arab Voice*, 19 September 2006, Resistance Report 647.
65. *Free Arab Voice*, 22 September 2006, Resistance Report 650.
66. *Aswat al-Iraq*, 23 September 2006, 'Basra – Shelling'.

been despatched to the scene from Basra Palace. That 'relative calm' applied when routine patrols were cancelled, to allow British troops to surround the main Sadr offices in Basra while they searched several houses in the vicinity, confiscating some weapons. Also, in this 'relative calm', a Danish serviceman was killed by an IED, a Lance Corporal in the Royal Danish Air Force. Eight others were injured, one severely.[67] They had been in a three-car motorcade carrying nine members of a Danish Air Force unit assigned to protect diplomats from Denmark in southern Iraq.[68]

Clearly, this must all have conformed with *The Independent*'s definition of 'relative calm' because neither it nor any other British media outlet bothered to report any events as they happened, other than the deaths of the British soldiers. To their credit, *The New York Times* and even the *China Post* carried reports on the deaths of the Dane and the US contractor. Never better illustrated was the metric by which the British media measured the occupation in the south. In a period when a US contractor, an Iraqi translator working for the UK forces and a Danish serviceman had been killed – all in the British sector – the British media had no comment. The moment a British soldier was killed, the flood-gates opened.

If, as with any other counter-insurgency campaign, the 'home front' was an integral part of the war, the media was hugely influential. But its absence of reporting was contributing to a massively distorted picture of events. This was having and was to have very significant political effects. But these arose not only from what was reported. What was not being reported was probably of equal importance. By contrast, on 20 September, the English-language Iraqi newspaper *Azzaman* published an editorial, noting:

The current sectarian conflict is taking new and dangerous directions which all demonstrate that the country is at the doorstep of a full-scale civil war. The conflict has taken an extremely alarming turn as more deadly weapons enter into the bloody sectarian fray. Iraqis have always been armed to their teeth and under former leader Saddam Hussein one could officially take an automatic rifle, a rocket launcher or even a mortar home.

If you declared loyalty to the regime, you could easily have your way to Ba'ath party depot. [*sic*] It did not matter whether you were really loyal. However, there were no instances of Iraqis turning those guns against their neighbours because they belonged to a different sect, religion or ethnic group. True, opposition groups occasionally waged mortar and Katyusha multiple rocket launchers at the regime's security forces but we have no instances of Iraqis attacking Iraqis for sectarian, religious or ethnic reasons.

But today mortars and Katyushas are the weapons of choice for armed groups of residential quarters in mixed cities. Even villages of opposite sects resort to these deadly weapons fired indiscriminately at civilians. Only God knows how many innocent Iraqis are being killed or maimed as a result of these attacks.[69]

67. *Free Arab Voice*, 23 September 2006, Resistance Report 651.
68. Associated Press, 28 September 2006, 'Body of Danish soldier in Iraq to be returned'.
69. *Azzaman*, 20 September 2006, 'Mortar attacks signal start of civil war'.

A new and terrifying phase in the violence was opening up, of which the British public was kept almost completely unware.

A LAST THROW OF THE DICE – OPERATION SINBAD

On 27 September, despite the 'relative calm', the Army went to war. It launched an operation, codenamed Sinbad, aimed at restoring order on the streets of Basra, addressing security, the 'rogue police' issue and infrastructure problems. For the first time on a large scale, reconstruction and community action were to be fully integrated with the military effort, with the full engagement of Iraqi security forces. The operation was aimed not only at sweeping the militia out of localities but also at upgrading local environments with 'high impact' schemes. The British committed 1,000 troops, augmented by 2,000 Iraqi Army soldiers from the 10th Division. The programme was scheduled to last five months.

Typically, the bulk of the media ignored the event. Only *The Daily Telegraph* gave it a fair wind on the day. In a reprise of the 'hearts and minds' campaign of 2003, it said, 'With soft hats and shovels, troops marched onto playgrounds to level out football pitches and fix goalposts. Iraqi contractors and labourers have been hired to undertake rebuilding projects.'[70] The Iraqi paper *Mafkarat al-Islam* also covered it, reporting sourly, 'British, Iraqi puppet forces launch sweep to retake control of al-Basrah from Shi'a sectarian militias'. It then cited Tony Dunlop, 'a British officer' saying that 1,000 British troops and '2,000 Iraqi puppet soldiers' were carrying out the operation, Dunlop adding that they were pursuing Shi'a militias – whom he called 'terrorists'. Those pro-Iranian militias had been controlling 'security' in the city since the start of the year, he was claimed to have said. The paper added:

Iraqi puppet officials and also western occupation officials have made frequent references to violations of 'security' by the puppet police in al-Basrah, a force dominated by the Shi'i sectarian militias that support the occupation as a step towards expanding Shi'i sectarian rule and Iranian domination over southern and eastern Iraq. Operation 'as-Sindibad' follows numerous smaller British operations in which commanders of the Shi'i sectarian Jaysh al-Mahdi militia were arrested and large quantities of arms and ammunition supplied to them by Iran were confiscated.[71]

The Independent left it nearly two weeks before it deigned to mention the operation. When it did, it was pessimistic, writing of 'political problems' that had resulted in a series of retaliatory attacks. The paper had

---

70. *The Daily Telegraph*, 28 September 2006, '3,000 British troops try to tame Basra'.
71. *Free Arab Voice*, 28 September 2006, Resistance Report 656.

'learned' that since the start of the operation, there had been a spate of 'what appear to be co-ordinated attacks' on military convoys – about 'four or five' in number. It referred to two soldiers, 'one British and one Danish', having been killed in Basra 'last week'. The Danish soldier had been killed more than two weeks previously. At least the paper had the grace to admit that the attacks in which the soldiers had died 'were not believed to be connected to Operation Sinbad'.

What was significant about the paper's report though were comments from the ubiquitous Major Burbridge, who – contrary to local reports – denied that Badr and Mahdi militias were being targeted. The militias, he said, were 'part of the structure of Iraq, but there are elements which have broken away, and are not under their central control'. Thus, the report continued:

According to other sources, however, there were doubts on the British side about the wisdom of the operation, and as soon as it started there were protests to Baghdad from the militias. 'There was deep disquiet among British military commanders and diplomats in Iraq beforehand,' said one source. 'The Prime Minister, Nouri al-Maliki, immediately demanded that the operation be heavily restricted in scope. It virtually came to a halt after one wave of raids, which demonstrated from the highest level to local militias that they can operate with impunity.'[72]

The report was close to the truth, but that took more than two years to surface. It came in 2008 from Chief of the Defence Staff, Air Chief Marshal Sir Jock Stirrup. Increasing UK force levels had never been 'on the cards', he then said, not least because of the commitment in Afghanistan. Moreover, more troops had not been considered the answer. Their presence had been creating 'a spurious but tangible legitimacy for violence, and for Iranian interference in support of such violence'. There was little incentive for Basrawi politicians to focus on their own governance problems. They could always blame the British. Despite that, claimed Stirrup, the UK had made 'repeated attempts' to deal with the 'extremist militia violence' but efforts had been 'emasculated' because 'we simply couldn't get the agreement of the Iraqi government; their own internal politics made it impossible'.

The Iraqi government was at that stage still dependent on the political support of Muqtada al Sadr, which made decisive action against the Jaish al Mahdi somewhat problematic for them. And there was a growing desire to assert Iraqi sovereignty, manifested by increasing restrictions on our offensive activity. The latter was of course entirely understandable – and in many ways to be welcomed.

72. *The Independent on Sunday*, 8 October 2006, 'Operation Sinbad: Mission failure casts doubt on entire British presence in Iraq'.

As a result, said Stirrup, the military had found its hands tied, unable to take decisive action. Sinbad had been 'a considerably watered down version' of its predecessor. It wasn't 'the game-changing event we were after'.[73]

Just over a week before the *Independent on Sunday* had published its piece, *The Guardian* had already pointed out, confirmed by Stirrup years later, that the military wanted to concentrate its effort on the 'more worthwhile and winnable battleground in Afghanistan'. Even in Basra, the military had decided there was a limit to what could be achieved. The comfortable mantra prevailed: it was time the Iraqis took responsibility for their own security. However, political arguments, including strong US pressure, had won the day. The British troops were to remain, 'at least for the moment'.[74]

Amongst the things those troops had to contend with was a refusal by Basra local councils to cooperate with Sinbad's 'security plan'. It may have been approved by Baghdad, but not by them. In a statement that must rank alongside *The Independent*'s 'relative calm', many council members denied the need for the operation, describing Basra as 'a safe city that needs no security plan'.[75]

British bases certainly needed a security plan. As October started, Shatt al-Arab Hotel was getting its usual hammering. *Mafkarat al-Islam* noted: 'Resistance bombardments of the British base are considered natural occurrences since they take place regularly each day.'[76] What was not a 'natural occurrence' was another British soldier getting killed – L/Cpl Dennis Brady of the Royal Army Medical Corps – when three mortar bombs landed inside the base. One more RAMC soldier was badly injured. One of the 15 mortar rounds that missed the British landed on a nearby home, killing two children and injuring a third.[77] To Major Burbridge fell the unenviable task of explaining that the military conducted regular patrols in the area to protect the security of the base. 'It is a major challenge to stop these sorts of attacks,' he admitted.

The bodies of four 'kidnapped Iraqi military elements' were found in Basra on 5 October, but they were only Iraqis so they did not merit a report in the British media.[78] Neither did the death the next day of another Danish soldier, killed in al Haritha after fighting had erupted during an operation aimed at stopping the rocket bombardments on the joint British-

73. MoD website, Speech by Air Chief Marshal Sir Jock Stirrup, Chief of the Defence Staff, at Royal United Service Institute (RUSI) on Monday, 1 December 2008.
74. *The Guardian*, 29 September 2006, 'Take UK troops out of Iraq, senior military told ministers'.
75. *Aswat al-Iraq*, 3 October 2006, 'Basra council's objection to British plan unjustifiable – spokesman'.
76. *Free Arab Voice*, 3 October 2006, Resistance Report 661.
77. *The Guardian*, 2 October 2006, 'Soldier killed in Iraq mortar attack'.
78. *Aswat al-Iraq*, 5 October 2006, 'Iraqi military intelligence element killed in Basra'.

Danish military camp.[79] Nor did it matter that the Old State Building had come under rocket attack again and that there had been an incident in which British snipers had 'opened fire … killing an Iraqi customs officer and wounding another'.[80]

DANNATT SPEAKS OUT

What did interest the media was Tony Blair's comments during a radio interview about the shortage of equipment in Afghanistan. He had pledged: 'If the commanders on the ground want more equipment – armoured vehicles for example, more helicopters – that will be provided. Whatever package they want, we will do.'[81] Iraq was not mentioned. On 9 October, Max Hastings complained that military chiefs had been prevented from speaking freely to the media, suggesting that they had 'allowed themselves to be cowed into silence'.[82]

On 13 October, General Dannatt, newly appointed as Chief of the General Staff, broke that silence. Accompanied by a front-page banner headline in the *Daily Mail* proclaiming, 'We must quit Iraq says new head of the Army', he launched into 'an extraordinarily outspoken attack on Tony Blair's Iraq policy'. He called for British troops to withdraw 'soon' or risk the consequences for both Iraq and our society, warning that the Army could 'break' if kept in Iraq too long.[83]

The BBC, the same day, published a 'puff' on Operation Sinbad, but also noted:

Foreign troops now face growing threats across the spectrum of militia activities. Helicopters only fly into central Basra at night since one was shot down in May. Downtown bases are now being rocketed or mortared almost every night. And more roadside bombs are being detonated … At night, elements of the Mahdi Army militia have fought running gun battles with Multi-National Forces – in one case we witnessed last week, a Danish soldier was killed, British troops fired 5,000 rounds, calling in Challenger tanks and fighter cover.

The *Newsnight* programme later interviewed a senior Iraqi officer who said the security situation would be better if the British were not on the streets in contact with the civilian population. One British commander noted that, every day since the liberation of Iraq, consent for the British presence had gradually waned.[84] This was Maj-Gen Richard Shirreff, the

79. *Free Arab Voice*, 6 October 2006, Resistance Report 664.
80. *Aswat al-Iraq*, 7 October 2006, 'British sniper kills policeman as base attacked in Basra'.
81. *The Times*, 7 October 2006, 'Afghanistan troops "will get whatever they need"'.
82. *The Guardian*, 9 October, 'Our armed forces have allowed themselves to be cowed into silence'.
83. *Daily Mail*, 13 October 2006, 'Government stunned by Army chief's Iraq blast'.
84. BBC, 13 October 2006, 'Talk about Newsnight'.

current forces commander. But he also warned that British troops would have to remain until the Americans 'declare game over in the centre in Baghdad'. 'Where is all this leading?' asked Mark Urban, *Newsnight* diplomatic editor. 'Probably to a crunch or tipping point in 2007.'[85]

Not everyone in Basra shared the Shirreff view. Saad Karim, a mobile phone shopowner in the city, was convinced that things would deteriorate if British troops left. 'We still believe that their removal will lead to a much worse situation, because we haven't got a proper alternative yet. All these Islamic parties and militias are corrupt and ineligible to take over and run the city,' he said.[86]

The absence of consent – if that is what it was – manifested itself on 14 October. Three British bases came under attack: Shatt al-Arab, Basra Palace and the airport, the first two from mortars, the latter from rockets.[87] That morning had seen a novel explanation for the hostility from Lt-Col Simon Brown. 'We are in a tribal society in Basra,' he said. The British Army was one of those tribes, attacked simply because 'we are the most influential'. We cramped their style. An embassy official in the Palace demurred. 'I can't believe they are saying these things,' he complained. 'This whole thing is to do with politics and Tony Blair. It's not about what is happening on the ground here, but what is happening there.'[88]

One of those officials received personal attention from insurgents two days later, when his car was destroyed by an RPG as he was visiting Basra city centre.[89] Unharmed, he was luckier than British soldiers in the al-Abbasiya district. They took an 'anti-armour missile' which wounded 'between four and five'.[90] The deputy chairman of Basra municipal council then piled in, accusing British forces of destabilising security.[91]

The occupation had now become a deadly routine of patrols and raids, in between fending off the constant barrage of mortar and rocket attacks. The local media kept the score. 'British bases attacked in Basra,' reported *Aswat al-Iraq* on 21 October. It also reported another raid, this one in az Zubayr. One man was arrested.[92] On 25 October, the paper clocked up another two attacks on British bases.[93]

85. BBC, 13 October 2006, 'UK troops begin end game in Basra'.
86. *The Times*, 14 October 2006, 'Basra fears a security disaster if British leave the field to militias'.
87. *Aswat al-Iraq*, 14 October 2006, 'Three British bases attacked in Basra'.
88. *The Guardian*, 14 October 2006, 'The British officer said: "We are now just another tribe"'.
89. *Free Arab Voice*, 16 October 2006, Resistance Report 674.
90. *Aswat al-Iraq*, 16 October 2006, 'British soldiers wounded in Basra attack'.
91. *Aswat al-Iraq*, 18 October 2006, 'Basra official accuses British forces of destabilising security'.
92. *Aswat al-Iraq*, 21 October 2006, 'British bases attacked in Basra'.
93. *Aswat al-Iraq*, 25 October, 'Iraq security – highlights'.

THE 'TIPPING POINT'

A day later Basra council, playing its usual games, suspended meetings with British forces and Maliki's 'puppet Security Committee'. The reason was the 'irresponsible' actions of the British. Troops had attacked and humiliated a policeman and were regularly insulting 'the dignity of Iraqi citizens'.[94] There was no concern about the dignity of British soldiers, who were having to dive under tables when their bases were attacked. This was becoming an art form. *Aswat al-Iraq* chronicled the next episode on 27 October, its headline announcing: 'British bases in Basra attacked with mortars, katyushas.' Basra airport and Shatt al-Arab Hotel were again getting the attention of the insurgents.[95] *Mafkarat al-Islam* added the drama, reporting an 'intense rocket barrage' at the Shatt.[96] On 28 October, two bases were attacked.[97] Just to make a change, the next day Basra Palace took two separate attacks.[98]

In between all that, on 23 October, Iraq's deputy prime minister had been in London talking to Tony Blair. This brought a rush of statements. Britain intended 'to hold its nerve' in Iraq. The UK and US could not 'cut and run ...' and leave the Iraqis to face the 'difficult challenges' on its own, said Blair. Margaret Beckett proclaimed there would be no 'rash' deadlines imposed on the Iraqis. Asked what sort of Iraq she envisioned being left behind, she said one that was democratic, which could 'cope' and was 'back on its feet'.

Meanwhile, Jon Humphrys from the BBC's Radio 4 *Today* programme had been in Basra. He had interviewed Richard Shirreff, who was pinning all his hopes on Operation Sinbad. He agreed the situation was 'bad' but part of that was 'a push-back against what we are doing'. There was 'something of a paradox'. 'On the one hand,' he said, 'we are really gaining consent ... people are welcoming what we are doing. At the same time, we are squeezing those elements who don't want us here.' 'But you can't even stop your bases being rocketed and mortared,' Humphrys countered. Shirreff stressed the value of the operation:

Through Sinbad, we are very likely to see a sort of 'tipping point' where success begins to breed success, the sort of consent, the hearts and minds that we're beginning to win on the ground allows us to reduce the problems of security as well. And we're not there yet – it is hard pounding, I accept that.[99]

94. *Free Arab Report*, 26 October 2006, Resistance Report 684.
95. *Aswat al-Iraq*, 27 October 2006, 'British bases in Basra attacked with mortars, katyushas'.
96. *Free Arab Report*, 27 October 2006, Resistance Report 685.
97. *Aswat al-Iraq*, 28 October 2006, 'British soldier killed in road accident in Basra'.
98. *Aswat al-Iraq*, 29 October 2006, 'British base attacked in Basra'.
99. Author's transcript from BBC archives.

The objective was to restore security to a level where it was 'good enough' for the Iraqis to take over. Simon Jenkins, in *The Guardian*, was not convinced. 'US and UK policy in Iraq is now entering its retreat phrase,' he wrote. 'Where there is no hope of victory, the necessity for victory must be asserted ever more strongly ... officially denial is all. For retreat to be tolerable it must be called victory.' [100]

Humphrys later published his observations in diary form.[101] Before travelling to Basra Palace by helicopter, he had asked 'if we could drive: it's only six miles'. His escorts had laughed. 'Drive through the city? Might as well put your head in a mincing machine.' At the Palace, he could not avoid noticing the barrage of indirect fire, noting:

This place gets attacked all the time. I counted nine rockets last night. There are more this afternoon. One lands on the roof of my producers' pod – a couple of feet above their heads. The shrapnel tears chunks out of a building 100 yards away. But they're OK – just very badly shaken.

He had also visited Shaibah military hospital where a consultant had told him she did not approve of Snatches. She preferred soldiers to be in Warriors. Prevention was better than cure. Oddly, Humphrys observed, the soldiers seem to like the Snatches. 'Maybe,' he speculated, 'that's because sitting in the back of a Warrior is like travelling in an oven on tank tracks. It gets to 140 degrees in summer. You can cook a leg of lamb at that temperature.'

Humphrys also met an Iraqi surgeon and asked him whether the troops should be in Iraq. He cited the surgeon's response in his summing up: 'They should not have come in, but they cannot leave now.' Everyone, said Humphrys, 'thinks if they do leave now the British civil HQ will be over-run by insurgents in five minutes.' *The Observer*, which had published the diary, mirrored that sentiment in a leader. It stated: 'We have an obligation to stay in Iraq – for now.' [102] Britain, it wrote:

... made a commitment to the people of Iraq to turn tyranny to democracy. So there are only two reasons why we might leave. First, if we think that by staying we are actually making it harder for Iraq's elected government to guarantee its people security. Second, if we believe we have failed irredeemably in our mission and might as well leave the Iraqis to sort out their problems for themselves.

To argue that we are only making things worse sits ill with the wish of the Iraqi government that we stay, it suggested. Although British forces would continue to be attacked, 'the majority of the violence and the greatest threat to Iraqi civilians now comes from sectarian fighting between Sunni

100. *The Guardian*, 25 October 2006, 'We have turned Iraq into the most hellish place on Earth'.
101. *The Observer*, 29 October 2006, 'I had never tried to present a programme while wearing a flak jacket before this trip to Basra'.
102. *The Observer*, 29 October 2006, 'We have an obligation to stay in Iraq – for now'.

and Shia and among Shia factions sporting various shades of fundamentalism'. The job of the coalition forces was to support the efforts to halt the slide into civil war.

But the die was cast. The next day brought another stage of the retreat. Gone was the optimism of July 2004 when the British Ambassador had happily spoken of 'a shared vision for a peaceful, prosperous and democratic Iraq'. The Consulate was to close and the officials were moving to Basra Air Station.[103] Their spokesman insisted they were 'not bailing out'. They were – deserting a complex refurbished at a cost of £14 million, compared with the £12.5 million spent on reconstruction in Basra.[104] Unlike the military, who were equally the target of mortars and rockets, the civil servants had had hardened sleeping shelters. When they left, they took with them the keys, refusing the military use of their sanctuaries. 'We might need them again,' was the excuse. Relations between military and officials – never entirely cordial – were not thereby improved.[105]

This was the beginning of the end and everyone in Basra knew it. Had it been able, the Army would soon have followed. It was prevented by the Americans.[106]

Days later, Thomas Harding was sheltering under a table in Basra Palace, seconds after a mortar bomb had been within feet of causing carnage. He observed that 'it would have been difficult to argue that the British Army was making progress in Iraq'. From dawn till dusk, the base had been rocketed or mortared 15 times. Harding predicted that, by the end of April, it should become clear where Basra is going and whether the British investment of 120 lives and £4 billion had been worth it. 'We are now approaching the tipping point in southern Iraq,' he wrote. 'The area will either sink into the grasp of insurgents and Iranian-sponsored militias or become a beacon of hope for the rest of the country.'[107]

103. *Aswat al-Iraq*, 30 October 2006, 'Britain moves consulate to Basra airport base'.
104. *The Daily Telegraph*, 1 November 2006, 'British to evacuate consulate in Basra after mortar attacks'.
105. Personal communication.
106. *The Daily Telegraph*, 11 September 2007, 'US "delayed UK pull-out from Basra"'.
107. *The Daily Telegraph*, 3 November 2006, 'Southern Iraq approaches the tipping point'.

Chapter 9 – The road to defeat

Basra: November 2006
to September 2007

We were now in Basra to get out of Basra without Basra descending into chaos.

LT-COL JUSTIN MACIEJEWSKI, CO, 1ST BTN,
THE ROYAL GREEN JACKETS,
BASRA, NOVEMBER 2006

In early November, Lt-Col Justin Maciejewski, the Commanding Officer, 1st Battalion, The Royal Green Jackets, was penning his thoughts on the deployment of his battle group. 'We were now,' he wrote, 'in Basra to get out of Basra without Basra descending into chaos.' The heady days of delivering a secure functioning democratic Iraq underpinned by strong institutions and civic society had been replaced by realism.[1] One of his Captains was more blunt, writing: 'I perceive the main effort amongst the US and British hierarchies now is to extract ourselves with minimum humiliation and embarrassment.'[2]

As for the enemy the Green Jackets faced, there was no circumlocution from Maciejewski. 'From where we sit,' he wrote, 'we are effectively up against an organisation known as the Jaish Al Mehdi (JAM).' They were organised into company-sized semi-autonomous groupings, some 40 *sariyas*, recruited from the unemployed and radicalised youth of Basra. The enemy's methods of attack were company-sized ambushes, targeted small arms shoots against individual soldiers, roadside bombs and indirect fire against British camps using rockets and mortars up to 120mm. The battle group had been engaged in a 'toe-to-toe' mortal fight with this enemy since the very day it had arrived in Basra. 'It has kept us fully occupied,' observed Maciejewski.

THE PROPAGANDA WAR

It had, and the butcher's bill was mounting, the first of the battle group's casualties occurring on 6 November when Kingsman Jamie Hancock was

---

1. KRRC website, undated, The Royal Green Jackets, Battalion Reports 2006.
2. A Royal Green Jacket on Tour, 7 February 2007.

shot dead while on guard duty at the Old State Building.[3] But there was another battle being played out. The war had already been lost but the political battle to present it as a victory was intensifying. With the political objectives of the war having been redefined as 'holding the line' to achieve an orderly handover to the Iraqi security services, it had become essential to present a picture of improving security. That was the only way the players could declare a 'victory' that would legitimise an exit on the terms they themselves had set. In this propaganda battle, the circumstances of Kingsman Hancock's death were disturbing enough to shake the carefully constructed myth to its foundations.

The MoD press release – its usual anodyne mixture of regrets and half-truths – was reprinted almost in its entirety by *The Daily Telegraph*. It appeared online and in the print version of the newspaper.[4] With media concerns that the Shi'a had put a sniper into the fray, Major Burbridge also undertook damage limitation, telling *Sky News*: 'There were bursts of automatic fire, which is an indication that this was not a sniper … These are individual rogue elements of criminal gangs and militias who target our soldiers.' Once again, circumlocution was to the fore. The death was attributed to 'rogue elements', the suggestion being that this was just a random shooting. Later, Burbridge went into print, adding:

The incident involved a series of bursts from automatic gunfire in an attack carried out by one or more gunmen … The solder guarding the sangar was injured by the gunshots and died within a few minutes. We did not catch the gunmen as they did not hang around after the incident. They fired off a few bursts and then disappeared. It is believed AK47 assault rifles were used in the attack that was probably carried out from a window or building over-looking the British base.

Those claims were published in a *Telegraph* account written by Thomas Harding. For sure, there had been no 'sniper', but the truth was nonetheless shocking. Kingsman Hancock had been on guard in the OSB when he had come under attack from automatic weapon fire. Harding wrote:

The building comes under attack from rocket propelled grenade and automatic gunfire three or four times every 24 hours with the attacks usually occurring at night. During a recent spate of RPG attacks the 2Bn The Royal Anglians used snipers hidden in rooftops to kill 10 gunmen over a two week period. It is believed that the insurgents use the building to 'blood' young terrorists by testing their ability and courage. If the recruits pass then they are offered positions on mortar teams earning up to $300 a firing – the equivalent of almost six month's wages.

In focusing on the possibility of a sniper, Burbridge had been gliding over the bigger picture. Basra was not under control. So confident were the

---

3. BBC, 7 November 2006, 'Iraq death soldier named by MoD'.
4. *The Daily Telegraph*, 9 November 2006, 'Soldier killed on sentry duty at base in Basra is named'.

insurgents that they were targeting soldiers in a grotesque selection procedure, attacking at will a highly fortified British base. The death of Kingsman Hancock had been cold-blooded, deliberate murder and the Army had been powerless to stop it. But what gave the account its sinister dimension was that Harding's piece was not only absent from the print edition, it appeared only very briefly online before disappearing. It was replaced by the MoD copy-out. No record of it exists.[5] 'For retreat to be tolerable it must be called victory,' Simon Jenkins had asserted. This was 'official denial' in action.

DEATH ON THE SHATT AL-ARAB WATERWAY

The tragedy continued. On 12 November, Remembrance Sunday, troops had attended a ceremony to commemorate the dead of two world wars, and those who had fallen subsequently. That day, Warrant Officer Lee Hopkins, Staff Sergeant Sharron Elliott, Corporal Ben Nowak and Marine Jason Hylton joined the ranks of the fallen, blown apart by an IED. Three other soldiers sustained serious injuries. What was very different about this incident was that they had been in a boat on the Shatt al-Arab waterway.[6]

The MoD claimed they had been 'part of a routine boat patrol' travelling north towards the Shatt al-Arab Hotel.[7] It was not a 'patrol'. Boats were routinely being used to shuttle personnel between riverside bases.[8] The bomb had been placed on the eastern edge of a pontoon bridge, on an elevated section close to the bank, the only part which had sufficient clearance for a boat to pass. It was a classic ambush. Yet, despite that, the bridge had been left unguarded and no attempt had been made to check for bombs. The route had been deemed safe because – it was claimed – there had been 'no previous attempt to plant an explosive device on the bridge'.[9]

Be that as it may, the danger had been well signalled. There had been 16 'centrally recorded' attacks on British forces transiting the waterway between 15 June 2003 and 23 November 2006. Crucially, prior to the November bomb incident, soldiers patrolling the waterway had come under fire from a bridge on the waterway. Up to six gunmen had opened fire on a four-boat convoy and a ferocious gun battle had ensued. There had been speculation

5. Parts of the article were copied onto this author's blog, which formed the basis of an analysis of the incident: *Defence of the Realm*, 9 November 2006, 'We are not being told the half of it'.
6. BBC, 14 November 2006, 'Iraq boat attack personnel named'.
7. MoD website, 14 November 2006, 'Warrant Officer Class 2 Lee Hopkins, Staff Sergeant Sharron Elliott, Corporal Ben Nowak and Marine Jason Hylton killed in Iraq'.
8. *The Daily Telegraph*, 16 November 2006, 'Iraq claims second British woman'.
9. *The Times*, 20 November 2007, 'Basra death blast bridge was unguarded'.

that the terrorists had been trying to plant a bomb and the boat patrol had disturbed them.[10, 11]

The media let the government off lightly. With Staff Sergeant Sharron Elliott having been killed, much of its coverage was 'soft focus' laments about the death of the second female soldier. Why though, if the waterway route had been so vulnerable, had no alternative been available? But, with helicopters being confined to night journeys after the Lynx had been shot down, the only realistic proposition was a Snatch. The Mamba protected vehicles could have been used, but they had been sold off – and the Mastiffs had yet to arrive.[12] With only Snatches for routine transport, the boats had been a better option, with what seemed inevitable results. Yet none of the hard questions were asked.

THE FAILURE OF OPERATION SINBAD

Out of the public eye, the mortar and rocket attacks continued. And, to confound General Shirreff's public optimism about Operation Sinbad, 16 November saw something of a landmark. Every base in Basra came under rocket attack, some 26 rockets being fired.[13] Arab media also claimed that a British vehicle checkpoint had been attacked, wounding several soldiers.[14]

The main action was an attack in az Zubayr on a convoy of empty tractor-trailers from Kuwait. They were stopped at a bogus checkpoint by insurgents dressed as police. Four Americans and an Austrian were kidnapped.[15] A major raid was mounted on the insurgents' suspected hideout the following day. After a brisk gunfight, two insurgents were killed. In a separate incident, a British security guard was shot dead, apparently by Iraqi border police.[16]

The contractors were by no means the only group at risk. Alarmingly, Iraqi interpreters working with the British army were being hunted down and killed. At least 21 had been kidnapped and shot dead over the previous month, their bodies dumped in different parts of the city. Another three were missing. In a single incident, 17 interpreters had been murdered.[17]

As Basra Palace and Shaibah echoed to the sound of sirens, with yet more mortar attacks in progress, Margaret Beckett decided to announce to MPs that British forces could hand over responsibility for security in Basra

10. Hansard, 14 December 2006: Column 1257W.
11. *Soldier* Magazine, December 2006 edition.
12. *The Sunday Telegraph*, 19 November 2006, 'A taxi to death in Iraq'.
13. *Aswat al-Iraq*, 16 November 2006, 'Huge rocket attack on all British bases in Basra'.
14. *Free Arab Voice*, 16 November 2006, Resistance Report 706.
15. BBC, 17 November 2006, 'Confusion on Iraq hostages' fate'.
16. *The Times*, 17 November 2006, 'Briton shot dead as troops clash in Iraq after kidnap'.
17. *San Francisco Chronicle*, 20 November 2006, 'Interpreters for British harried, killed'.

to local authorities by the spring.[18] The progress of the current operation in Basra 'gives us confidence that we may be able to achieve transition in that province' she said. Despite that, she acknowledged the 'appalling' daily reports of murder and kidnappings which showed that the country's fate was 'hanging in the balance'. Again, she stressed, the intention was not to leave Iraq in the lurch.[19]

By now, Tony Blair was under pressure from his own Party to quit his job and hand over to Chancellor Gordon Brown. In preparation for his role as prime minister, Brown had made his first visit to Iraq on 18 November, bearing the 'gift' of £100 million in new aid for reconstruction.[20] With Blair looking to a new, lucrative career as an international statesman, the *Evening Standard* – London's evening newspaper – speculated that he wanted 'to bow out in six months on a wave of good news'.[21] The man was obsessed, in any event, with his 'legacy'. A peaceful hand-over of Basra, with reduced British casualties, was high on his personal agenda. He did not want to leave office with Iraq regarded as a failure. *The Daily Telegraph*, amongst others, had no difficulty in seeing the contradictions. It noted: 'it might seem incongruous that the Foreign Secretary should be talking about British forces relinquishing responsibility for security in Iraq when the killing of civilians has reached an unprecedented level.' Don't abandon Iraq, it intoned.[22]

There was no discernible let-up in the deaths of British soldiers. On 25 November, during a 'search and detain' operation involving 200 troops, Sgt Jonathan Hollingsworth was shot. He died later of his wounds. He 'did not die in vain', said Des Browne.[23]

As for the civilians, the night before, a Friday, there had been a major gun battle when Sunni guards had repulsed a Shi'a attack on their mosque. It had been the fourth assault on Sunni mosques and facilities in Basra in the previous 24 hours.[24] On the Sunday, the Shi'a murder gangs switched tactics. They mortared a Sunni village about 18 miles south-east of Basra killing several people in their homes. In the centre of Basra, masked men wearing 'Interior Ministry' uniforms and driving official cars raided the home of a Sunni woman in her twenties. They murdered her and three university students, kidnapped earlier, in front of a crowd of local people.[25]

18. *Aswat al-Iraq*, 22 November 2006, 'Mortars fired on two British bases in Basra'.
19. *The Times*, 22 November 2006, 'UK could hand over Basra by next spring, says Beckett'.
20. *The Independent*, 18 November 2006, 'Brown pledges £100m aid on Iraq visit'.
21. *Evening Standard*, 23 November 2006, 'Blair "to bow out on wave of good news"'.
22. *The Daily Telegraph*, 23 November 2006, 'Don't abandon Iraq' (leader).
23. BBC, 25 November 2006, 'Soldier killed in Iraq raid named'.
24. *Free Arab Voice*, 24 November 2006, Resistance Report 713.
25. *Free Arab Voice*, 26 November 2006, Resistance Report 715.

This was the city which, by spring, was going to be peaceful enough for a hand-over.

This was not what Cpl James Larsen thought. He had recently returned from his posting at Shatt al-Arab Hotel. 'Iraq is an absolute complete and utter mess,' he said, having survived more than 1,000 bomb attacks on his base. He had been just 70 yards away when L/Cpl Brady had been killed by a mortar. 'My friends have been thrown on top of me and I have been mortared from 25 metres away when the tent got hit. We had breeze blocks going round our beds. I would roll off the bed and go under it next to the breeze blocks. I soon stopped sleeping on the bed and just lay with the breeze blocks,' he said.[26]

THE MILITARY GOES THROUGH THE MOTIONS

Nevertheless, the military was going through the motions of restoring order. On 9 December, it launched a massive raid – the biggest strike operation since the invasion of Iraq – into the Mahdi stronghold of al Harta in northern Basra, a mere mortar throw from the Shatt al-Arab Hotel. Starting at three in the morning, the Army threw in 1,000 British and Danish soldiers in tanks, armoured vehicles and assault boats. American F-15 fighter jets were called in to conduct a low and fast flypast of the Iraqi position as a show of strength. Five 'top-level terrorists' were arrested, a few weapons and some bomb-making materials were seized.[27]

Spectacular it was, and undoubtedly professionally planned and skilfully executed. It was successful in that five important members of the Mahdi Army had been taken out of circulation. But it was a strategic irrelevance. Unlike Operation Motorman in July 1972 – which had set out to deprive the Provisional IRA of its no-go areas in Belfast and Londonderry – this operation left al Harta in the hands of the Mahdi. Troops had fought their way in and had to fight their way out. The Mahdi rule was unchallenged. But then, in 1972, the British Army had around 21,000 troops at its disposal.

The reason for 'Motorman' was that the existence of no-go areas created serious problems for the security forces as they provided refuge for provisional IRA terrorists. At the same time, the establishment of loyalist no-go areas made a mockery of law within Ulster.[28] Applying the lessons of

26. *North West Evening Mail*, 6 December 2006, 'Iraq is an absolute complete and utter mess'.
27. *The Daily Telegraph*, 10 December 2006, ' "Armoured fist" smashes into Basra at dawn, capturing five terrorist leaders'.
28. National Archives, Cabinet Papers 1915–1978, 'No-go areas and Operation Motorman'.

Northern Ireland, which the Army had been so enthusiastic about, the only strategy that would have made any long-term difference would have been to have replicated Motorman. The resources simply were not available.

The Army continued its raids, with another on 23 December in which a senior Iraqi policeman, who had allegedly masterminded the abduction of the two SAS soldiers in September of the previous year, was arrested. Six other police officers had also been taken when, under the cover of thick fog, 800 British troops in tanks and armoured vehicles had 'swooped' on their homes. All the police officers had come from the notorious Serious Crimes Unit.[29] Maliki ordered the SCU to be disbanded. After so many of its personnel had been implicated in multiple murders, including killing British troops, on Christmas morning it was payback time. A force of 1,000 British and Iraqi troops raided the Unit's headquarters at Jameat, releasing 127 captives who had been found in a cramped and squalid cell, some showing signs of having been tortured. Once empty, Royal Engineers blew apart the two-storey concrete building.[30]

The raids had no observable effect. Indirect fire continued, one attack closing Basra airport to air traffic for several hours.[31] Mortar attacks on all British bases continued, as did the attacks on patrols and convoys. Two Snatches were destroyed by an IED on 27 December in northern Basra, injuring seven British soldiers.[32] An attack on a Warrior close to Shatt al-Arab Hotel, on 28 December, killed its commander, Sgt Graham Hesketh.[33]

Still the ghastly tragedy continued, played out to extract the politicians and Army with 'minimum humiliation and embarrassment'. On 13 January, Kingsman Alexander Green became the first British soldier of the New Year to be killed in action.[34] The drama had started 24 hours earlier when a 60-lorry re-supply convoy had entered the city. The insurgents had seen it enter and had planted a roadside bomb on the return route. That had detonated at 8.20am on Saturday, immobilising an escorting Warrior. A relatively fortunate soldier received minor injuries and the vehicle was dragged back to base by an armoured recovery vehicle.

An hour later, Kingsman Green had been riding in another Warrior, part of the screen to protect the returning convoy. The vehicle had stopped and he had jumped down to check for roadside bombs before the Warrior could proceed. As with Sgt Hickey, flesh and blood was doing the job of the

29. *The Daily Telegraph*, 23 December 2006, ' "Rogue" police officers seized in Basra'.
30. *The Daily Telegraph*, 26 December 2006, 'Soldiers destroy Basra's "rogue" police HQ'.
31. *Free Arab Voice*, 17 December 2006, Resistance Report 736.
32. BBC, 27 December 2006, 'Back troops, says UK Iraq general'.
33. BBC, 29 December 2006, 'British soldier is killed in Iraq'.
34. BBC, 15 January 2007, 'MoD names two dead UK servicemen'.

steel of an armoured Buffalo. A hidden gunman, no more than 150 yards distant, had shot him. He died later from his wounds. As he had been brought in to Basra Palace, where a helicopter awaited to ferry him to the hospital in Shaibah, a watching soldier had muttered, 'Why the f*** are we here?'[35] To extract the politicians and Army from Basra with 'minimum humiliation and embarrassment' would not have seemed an adequate answer.

PROPAGANDA CONTINUES

Despite this, the propaganda continued. While every British base in Basra was taking a hammering, readers of the MoD website were treated to a long 'military operations news article'. Dated 15 January, it told in some detail how UK military and civilian personnel based at Basra Air Station would 'have access to improved leisure and communication facilities as a brand new welfare "village" opened its doors'.[36] One of the accompanying pictures showed Maj-Gen Shirreff – he who had been so optimistic about Operation Sinbad – visiting a 'food concession' in the village. It was heavily fortified by giant 'Hesco' sand-filled containers – to protect against mortar and rocket fire. This illustrated the divide between official sources and reality – the former determinedly 'upbeat' and devoid of any disturbing news, offering minimal information on events.

Meanwhile, the 'carnage' that Harding had so nearly observed in November came perilously closer less than a week after Kingsman Green had died. In another attack on Basra Palace, one soldier was seriously injured and five others received less serious injuries. That was on 19 January when the Palace came under fire three times from a mixture of mortars, rockets and small arms. While it was happening, Lt-Gen Graeme Lamb, deputy commander of the multi-national force in Iraq, was fending off suggestions from American journalists that British forces had been defeated in Basra. 'I don't think we're defeated in any sense,' he said, before conceding: 'Things are difficult … But I do see every reason for optimism.'[37]

Nobody recorded whether Pte Michael Tench had expressed any optimism. Had he done so in respect of his own prospects, it would have been misplaced. On 21 January, he was dead. His contribution to extracting the Army from Basra with 'minimum humiliation and embarrassment', had been to take part in a Warrior patrol from the Shatt al-Arab Hotel. It had

35. *The Daily Telegraph*, 16 January 2007, 'The last hours of young soldier shot in Iraq'.
36. MoD website, 15 January 2007, 'Brand new welfare "village" for Basrah Air Station'.
37. *The Times*, 19 January 2007, 'Six British soldiers wounded in Basra attacks'.

got but a few miles when his vehicle had been hit by an IED, killing him and injuring four other soldiers, one seriously. Tench's CO, Major Andrew Ward said: 'It is a tragedy that we have lost a young man with so much promise.'[38]

On 31 January 2007, the Army also lost a Regiment, one of many to be amalgamated under General Jackson's 'Future Army Structure'. This was the Royal Green Jackets, which was to become the 2nd Battalion, The Rifles. The battle group of which the RGJ had been part had, since it had officially deployed on 5 November, been involved in over 100 company group, battle group and brigade operations. It had made 236 small arms 'contacts', taken 20 IEDs, and suffered 122 indirect fire attacks. In addition, it had fought off 13 complex attacks. The battle group had killed or seriously injured 84 insurgents and expended over 20,000 rounds of small arms ammunition. It had sustained 45 battle casualties of varying degrees of seriousness. The level of attacks had risen exponentially since the battle group had arrived.

Just after midnight, following the evening when the Green Jacket flag had been lowered for the last time over Basra Palace, the insurgents had heralded the passing of the Regiment into history with a barrage of 12 rockets.[39] On the convoy which Kingsman Green had died protecting had been the insignia of the new Regiment into which the RGJ had been amalgamated. That was not quite in the same league as the siege of Stalingrad in 1942, when Junkers 52s from Hitler's Luftwaffe had been despatched to airdrop container-loads of Iron Crosses to the beleaguered 6th Army. But there was a certain parallel.

On 5 February, the 100th British soldier was killed in action in Iraq.[40] He was 2nd Lt Jonathan Carlos Bracho-Cooke, slaughtered by another IED as he commanded a Warrior on patrol from the Old State Building, en route to Basra Palace.[41] What had been hazardous for Snatches was no longer safe even for Warriors. Yet Snatches were still on patrol. February 9th saw the insurgents exploit its vulnerability. As it was returning from a 'routine patrol', five miles east of Basra, a Snatch was torn apart by an IED. Its driver Pte Luke Daniel Simpson was killed. Pte Chris Herbert had his leg blown off above the knee and another soldier lost his arm.[42, 43]

38. BBC, 22 January 2007, 'MoD names soldier killed in Iraq'.
39. KRRC website, undated, The Royal Green Jackets, Battalion Reports 2006.
40. *The Daily Mail*, 7 February 2007, '100th British soldier killed in action in Iraq named'.
41. MoD website, 6 February 2007, 'Second Lieutenant Jonathan Carlos Bracho-Cooke killed in Iraq'.
42. *Goole Times*, 15 February 2007, 'Howden soldier killed in Basra bomb blast'.
43. BBC, 10 February 2007, 'Iraq bomb attack soldier is named'.

THE CHARADE COMES TO AN END

The charade was coming to its bloody end. On 21 February, despite all evidence to the contrary, Blair declared to the House of Commons that Operation Sinbad was complete and 'had been successful'. Iraq's own armed forces and police were now on the way to taking charge of security in Basra. Reconstruction had followed the improved security and there had been 'real progress'. Even his own military chiefs knew this to be untrue.

There was, however, not to be a complete withdrawal. At least 4,000 British troops were to stay for another five years. Progressively, bases in Basra were to be handed over to the Iraqis, starting with the Shatt al-Arab Hotel and the Old State Building, followed by Basra Palace in the summer. That would leave a brigade at Basra Air Station – the Contingency Operating Base – 'for at least until the Americans leave Iraq'. Troops, Blair promised, would remain in Iraq 'for as long as we are wanted and have a job to do'. Diplomatically, the White House hailed the British efforts as a 'success'.[44] *The Daily Telegraph* was closer to the truth, suggesting that:

Mr Blair is anxious to be able to demonstrate that British troops are coming home before he leaves Downing Street this summer. He also hopes the announcement will give Labour a boost in the May elections to the Scottish Parliament, Welsh Assembly and English councils.[45]

It also recalled that neither the prime minister nor other VIPs had got further than Basra air base during their recent visits. The city centre had been deemed too dangerous.[46]

The Independent also took a robust line. It cited Toby Dodge, an Iraq expert at London's Institute of Strategic Studies. He roundly condemned Blair for being 'criminally irresponsible' in abandoning the people of Basra to the ravages of 'militias, criminals and a police force fighting for control'. He added: 'Once the British forces withdraw from the city, there will be no restraints at all.' Anthony Cordesman of the Centre for Strategic and International Studies in Washington, chipped in, arguing, 'The British may not have been defeated in a purely military sense, but lost long ago in the political sense'. As for Operation Sinbad, some in the military had nicknamed it 'Spinbad'. Its effects had been exaggerated and would quickly dissipate. The operation was little more than an attempt to bring Basra under enough control to justify the withdrawal. The Shi'a militias would soon be free to resume their murderous activities.[47] All that mattered for Blair, though, is

44. *The Daily Telegraph*, 22 February 2007, '4,000 troops will stay in Iraq "for five years"'.
45. *The Daily Telegraph*, 21 February 2007, 'Troops in Iraq to be cut by 3,000'.
46. *The Daily Telegraph*, 22 February 2007, 'Withdrawal from Basra brings relief … and fear'.
47. *The Independent*, 25 February 2007, 'Basra betrayed: When the British leave, will the Mahdi Army replace them?'

that he had been able to stand up in the Commons and declare his 'success' – as he had always intended.

Despite the White House tact, in Washington Blair's announcement was widely seen as an admission that the British military could no longer sustain simultaneous wars in Afghanistan and Iraq. The *Los Angeles Times* noted that Charles Guthrie, former Chief of the Defence Staff, had warned that the military was approaching 'operational failure'. It also cited Clive Jones, a senior lecturer in Middle East politics. 'Because the British army is in essence fighting a far more intensive counterinsurgency war in Afghanistan, there's been a realisation that there has to be some sort of transfer of resources from Iraq to Afghanistan,' he said. 'It's either that, or you risk in some ways losing both. It's the classic case of "Let's declare victory and get out".'[48]

The 'victory' would be too late for Rifleman Daniel Lee Coffey. Formerly of the Royal Green Jackets, on 27 February he made history by becoming the first member of the newly formed 2nd Rifles to be killed in action. He had been 'top cover' in a Bulldog on its way to the Shatt al-Arab Hotel. His convoy had been attacked by two gunmen and he had been shot, dying later that day.[49] Nor was the 'victory' soon enough for Pte Johnathon Wysoczan. On 3 March, he was also 'top cover', this time in a Warrior tasked to investigate a possible mortar firing point. He had died after being 'struck by a single round from an unobserved gunman'.[50]

THE FIRST BASE IN BASRA HANDED OVER

Thirteen days later, the Old State Building was handed over to the 10th Division, the ceremony conducted from the relative safety of Basra Air Station. To Major-General Shaw, ever optimistic in public, this reflected 'the significant progress' that had been made 'towards complete Iraqi security self-reliance'.[51] There was no repeat of Abu Naji, with militia looting the base, but two days later the Mahdi Army attacked the Fadhila headquarters, firing RPGs and rifles. Iraqi troops surrounded the area, declared a temporary curfew and later managed to restore calm. If this was part of an attempt to take over the Old State Building, it seems to have failed. But the Iraqi defence minister decided to bring forward the deployment of an extra 5,000 Iraqi soldiers to the city.[52]

48. *Los Angeles Times*, 22 February 2007, 'Britain picks its battles carefully'.
49. BBC, 28 February 2007, 'MoD names soldier killed in Iraq'.
50. MoD website, 5 March 2007, 'Private dies in UK from injuries sustained in Iraq'.
51. MoD website, 20 March 2007, 'First coalition base is handed over to Iraqi Army'.
52. *The Times*, 23 March 2007, 'Shia factions clash as British troops pull out'.

Reuters, meanwhile, was claiming that the Mahdi Army, heavily infil-trated by Iranians, was breaking into splinter groups, with up to 3,000 gunmen now financed directly by Iran and no longer under the control of Muqtada al-Sadr. This was impossible to verify but, in the murky waters of Iraqi politics, it seemed that Muqtada might be losing his grip on his own militias, his forces infiltrated by Iranians, working to a different agenda.

THE IRANIAN HOSTAGES

By then, on 23 March, attention was focused on an extraordinary drama. Out in the Northern Arabian Gulf a boarding team comprising 15 Royal Navy sailors and Royal Marines in two small boats had been abducted by Iranian Revolutionary Guards. Despatched from the Coalition Task Force command ship, *HMS Cornwall*, the team had travelled over eight nautical miles, escorted by a Lynx helicopter, to inspect a freighter moored in shallow waters offshore. Unaccountably, once the team had safely boarded the freighter, the Lynx had returned to its mother ship, leaving the team unprotected. They had then been ambushed by Iranians in heavily armed speed boats. Overmatched, the team had surrendered.[53]

Amongst other things, it emerged that the Royal Navy was no better equipped than the Army to deal with 'asymmetric' warfare. Although a powerful Type 22 frigate had been deployed, its draught of 20.7ft had prevented it from entering shallow waters to guard its boarding team. Yet the Navy had no fast – or any – inshore patrol boats.

This, though, should not have been a problem. The senior Naval officer, Commodore Nick Lambert, did not only command British assets. The effort in the Gulf was a multi-national operation known as Task Force 158, of which he held the rotating command. It comprised US Navy and Coastguard vessels, including two heavily armed Cyclone class boats, *USS Chinook* and *USS Whirlwind*, drawing 7.5ft. There was also an Australian frigate and Iraqi inshore patrol boats. Lambert, had he so chosen, could have tasked any one of 12 vessels to carry out the freighter inspection, instead of despatching *Cornwall*'s boats from a distance of eight miles. Equally, he could have ordered any one of those vessels to provide overwatch. This would have been a sensible precaution as there had been previous attempts by the Iranians in the Gulf to take coalition forces hostage.

There were dark suspicions as to Lambert's agenda. At the time of the abduction, a BBC film crew had been on board the *Cornwall*, making a

---

53. BBC, 25 March 2007, 'Concern and hope on *HMS Cornwall*'.

documentary about the Royal Navy in the Gulf. Boarding operations had been filmed previously and much had been made of the gender equality, in that the coxswain of one of the boats – now a hostage – had been a female, Leading Seaman Faye Turney. The evidence pointed to the Royal Navy, concerned that its role in the Iraqi campaign had not been appreciated, being overly concerned with publicity opportunities, the *Cornwall* taking centre stage in a prolonged PR exercise.[54] Lambert had taken his eye off the ball.

In the event, the Navy got more publicity than it had bargained for. After 13 days of captivity, the 'frightened fifteen' were suddenly released, but not before having been forced to 'confess' to straying into Iranian waters and being paraded by Iranian president Ahmadinejad in Tehran.[55] Humiliation turned to embarrassment when the former hostages were allowed to sell their stories to the press. From these, toe-curling accounts emerged of one of the hostages, Seaman Arthur Batchelor, aged 20 – dubbed 'Mr Bean' – having cried himself to sleep after his captors had stolen his iPod. The Royal Navy became a laughing stock.[56] It cannot have helped the overall war effort – British credibility, already low, took a nosedive.

THE DEATH TOLL MOUNTS AS
THE RETREAT CONTINUES

While 'Mr Bean' had been blubbing about his loss, soldiers his age and younger were fighting for their lives in Basra. On 26 March, two Warriors were damaged by an IED, north of Basra Palace. Fortunately, no one was injured.[57] On 1 April, however, Kingsman Danny Wilson died. Close to Basra Palace, he had dismounted from his Warrior vehicle to check for IEDs when he was hit by small arms fire.[58] Once again, flesh and blood had taken the place of steel. The next day, out on patrol in the al Ashshar district, Rifleman Aaron Lincoln was hit by small arms fire and died later from his wounds. Another soldier was injured.[59]

Both Wilson and Lincoln had been killed by a single shot, leading to further speculation that there was a sniper abroad. Earlier in the year, it had been feared that insurgents had obtained 100 high-powered Austrian Steyr sniper rifles and, although this proved to be unfounded, there were plenty

54. *The Sunday Times*, 15 April 2007, 'How Mr Bean sank the Navy'.
55. *The Independent*, 25 March 2007, 'Marines "confess" to Iranian captors'.
56. *The Daily Mail*, 23 April 2007, 'Iran hostage Mr Bean branded "disgraceful" by his own mother'.
57. ITN News, 26 March 2007, 'UK soldiers survive Basra attack'.
58. MoD website, 2 April 2007, 'Kingsman Danny John Wilson killed in Iraq'.
59. BBC, 3 April 2007, 'UK soldier killed in Iraq named'.

of Russian-built Druganov sniper rifles in Iraq.[60] All it needed was the skill to use one. One or more insurgents, it seemed, had learned that skill. The same problem had also been afflicting US troops. In time, counters were developed. In the meantime, soldiers – unlike 'Mr Bean' – had to die to save the military and the politicians from the 'humiliation and embarrassment' of admitting defeat.

On 5 April, four soldiers died for this cause. They were 2nd Lt Joanna Yorke Dyer, Cpl Kris O'Neill, Pte Eleanor Dlugosz and Kingsman Adam James Smith.[61] Their Iraqi interpreter was also killed and a fifth soldier was very seriously injured. They had been in the back of a Warrior, part of a patrol which had earlier repulsed an ambush, wounding one of the attackers. Moving on to Hayaniyah, a slum stronghold of the Mahdi, the armoured vehicle was ripped apart, while the patrol came under simultaneous attack from small arms and RPGs. In a second explosion, another Warrior was damaged.[62]

There was a large crater in the centre of a tarmac road, caused by an EFP 'underbelly' bomb of a type not previously seen in southern Iraq. Its concealment had been facilitated by the damage done to the road, churned up by tracked armoured vehicles. Despite its considerable armour, the Warrior's belly was lightly protected and the blast had easily ripped through it. The next day, two similar devices were discovered, one on the way to Basra Palace and the other near Basra Air Station, not far from the fatal explosion. But these had not been the first appearances of this weapon. There had been two such attacks on Israeli Merkava tanks in Gaza early in 2002.[63] Less than 48 hours after the Warrior attack, a Challenger tank was hit by a similar device. The driver lost both legs.[64]

Attacks were escalating dangerously. Lt-Col Kevin Stratford-Wright, who had taken over as Army spokesman, observed: 'There appears to be a conscious decision by the insurgents to attack British troops … They want to be able to say "we kicked the Brits out of Basra".' Movement by military convoy had become increasingly difficult. Even the shortest journey bordered on being a major operation. For want of more suitable equipment, routes had to be laboriously cleared by Army dog handlers checking the 'vulnerable points' for IEDs. Travelling the eight miles to the airport from the city centre was taking more than five hours because it was no longer possible

60. *The Daily Telegraph*, 3 April 2007, 'Fears of expert sniper in Basra'.
61. MoD website, 6 April 2007, 'Second Lieutenant Joanna Yorke Dyer, Corporal Kris O'Neill, Private Eleanor Dlugosz and Kingsman Adam James Smith killed in Iraq'.
62. *The Times*, 5 April 2007, 'Four British soldiers killed in Basra'.
63. Col. David Eshel, Defense Update, 'The EFP killer strikes again in Basra'.
64. *The Independent*, 23 April 2007, 'Iraq bomb halted heavy UK tank'.

to take the direct route. And there were fears that, once only Basra Palace remained in British hands, the insurgents could concentrate their forces. 'It is only going to get worse,' said a British officer.[65]

This did not check the retreat. On 8 April, the Union Jack was lowered for the last time at the Shatt al-Arab Hotel as it was handed over to the 10th Division.[66] Maj-Gen Shaw described the handover as a 'repositioning'. His troops had not been 'bombed out' of other bases.

Two days later, Lt-Col Maciejewski's battle group launched a raid into the 'Shi'a Flats', a notorious Soviet-style block of dense, poverty-stricken housing on the western outskirts of Basra. Codenamed Operation Arezzo, it was partly aimed at arresting suspected insurgents. In the main, it was designed to bait them into a trap and kill them. The arrest 'targets' were not at home, but the bait succeeded in pulling hundreds of fighters into a firefight which lasted over four hours. British forces killed 26–27 insurgents. Two insurgents were captured, one in police uniform. There were no British casualties. Said Lt-Col Stratford-Wright, 'We will not allow militia gunmen to control parts of Basra.' He added:

There are no 'no-go' areas for multi-national forces in Basra. Security is our responsibility and, in conjunction with the Iraqi security forces, we seek to provide as secure an environment as possible. This will inevitably involve taking on the rogue militia who blight the lives of people in Basra.[67]

This was not true. The nature of a raid, with its surprise penetration and equally rapid withdrawal before overwhelming forces had the opportunity to muster, was the very opposite of what Stratford-Wright sought to portray. It was a sign of weakness, not strength. But in the Army of April 2007, black equalled white.

Covering the raid was Michael Yon. He noted that while the Americans counted on helicopter support, the Brits were going into extremely hostile terrain, outnumbered, relying on 'timing, terrain, manoeuvrability, firepower, and sheer audacity'. Partly to make up for the absence of helicopters, snipers had been posted on the roofs.[68] Yon was also able to experience the conditions at Basra Palace, attesting to continuous mortar and rocket attacks.

It had been little different at the Shatt al-Arab Hotel. Pte Paul Barton, described a base 'under siege'. His regiment had lost one soldier but 33 more had been injured. In one mortar attack, he had been the first to arrive after one of the tents had been hit, where one of his 'mates' was in bed. The

---

65. *The Sunday Telegraph*, 7 April 2007, 'Battle for Basra will grow deadlier with retreat'.
66. MoD website, 10 April 2007, 'UK forces hand over Shatt-Al-Arab Hotel to Iraqi Army'.
67. *The Daily Telegraph*, 13 April 2007, '20 Shia gunmen die in British Basra fightback'.
68. Michael Yon, 11 April 2007, 'British forces at war: As witnessed by an American'.

top of his head and his hand was blown off. He was now brain damaged. Of the 40 tents in the base, five had remained unscathed. On his previous tour, his group had rarely been mortared. On his recently completed tour, it had been two to three times a day. 'Fifteen mortars and three rockets were fired at us in the first hour we were there,' he said. 'We were getting mortared every hour of the day. We basically didn't sleep for six months … it wore you down. Every patrol we went on we were either shot at or blown up by roadside bombs.'[69]

This account was published on 27 April. Four days earlier, Kingsman Alan Jones had been shot dead while providing 'top cover' in a Warrior, patrolling in al Ashshar, a crowded slum district in the centre of the city, over a canal from the shipyards.[70] On 29 April, as he dismounted from his Bulldog, 18-year-old Rifleman Paul Donnachie was shot, again in al Ashshar – the 12th British soldier to die in Iraq that month.[71] The day after he died, Shaibah was handed to the Iraqi Army. The event passed off without incident. That left Basra Palace and one rarely mentioned outpost, the Provincial Joint Co-ordination Centre (PJCC) in the centre of Basra.

In Basra Palace, the fears that the insurgents would concentrate their forces were coming to pass. Not only was the base under siege, re-supply had become very dangerous. In the official reports, though, there was barely a hint of this. For instance, when on 6 May Pte Kevin Thompson was killed by an IED, little information was given. Yet he had been driving a 46-ton tank transporter. It must have been a powerful blast to have 'partially disabled the vehicle' and killed the driver.[72] Pte Thompson's 'grief-stricken father' condemned Tony Blair for a 'pointless war'.[73]

THE MoD MEDIA OFFENSIVE

At last the British media was beginning to wake up to what was happening in Basra. It cannot have been a coincidence that the MoD also sprang into life, releasing a series of reports about troop activities. The first proclaimed: 'British troops lead capture of Iraqi criminals'. It told of how British soldiers from 19 Light Brigade 'had led a series of successful search and arrest operations around Basra', aimed at deterring rogue militias known to be operating there. The raid had 'resulted in the capture of four leading criminals linked with roadside bomb attacks on British Forces'.

69. *The Independent*, 27 April 2007, 'Serving British soldier exposes horror of war in "crazy" Basra'.
70. BBC, 24 April 2007, 'UK soldier killed in Iraq named'.
71. BBC, 30 April 2007, 'UK soldier killed in Basra named'.
72. MoD website, 7 May 2007, 'Private Kevin Thompson dies in UK from injuries sustained in Iraq'.
73. *Daily Mail*, 7 May 2007, 'Father of soldier killed in Iraq says: "I could strangle Tony Blair"'.

'One of the most notable successes' had been 'the capture of a criminal gang leader who has been involved in the extortion, kidnap and intimidation of the local Iraqi population.' It was then left to spokesman, Capt Ollie Pile, to explain:

Our Brigade has seen substantial progress during our tenure, not only of the improved security situation for the Iraqi people, but also the growing effectiveness and responsibility of the Iraqi Security Forces in providing for their own security.[74]

Not least of the Orwellian omissions was any reference to the Mahdi Army, especially as the raids had been carried out on notorious Sadr strongholds. The refusal officially to acknowledge that the Army was up against an organised insurgency was holding to the last.

On 10 May, Tony Blair was in his constituency in Sedgefield, announcing his decision to stand down from the leadership of the Labour Party. In a brief reference to the invasion of Iraq and the 'blowback since, from global terrorism' he cautioned that 'the terrorists, who threaten us here and round the world, will never give up if we give up'. It is, said Blair, 'a test of will and of belief. And we can't fail it.'[75] He was about to do just that.

The MoD's second 'puff' came four days later, again triumphal in tone. It announced that British troops had 'scored a double success during a series of weekend raids in and around Basra' which had 'brought the discovery of a significant number of weapons and bomb-making equipment'. Interestingly, the cache included components for making EFPs, plus two Druganov sniper rifles and telescopic sights.[76] What made the MoD's offering propaganda was what it did not publish. Later, the MoD was to explain is aims, articulated by Lt-Col Stratford-Wright:

Iraq is a huge challenge. Reporting of Iraq operations is generally negative. A win story on Iraq is a balanced one as the prospect of a positive one is generally bleak. I find reporters' inability to look past their pre-conceived ideas and to go against the prevailing direction of Iraq reporting to be hugely disappointing.[77]

Significantly, while the Media Management Group was anxious to 'balance' its accounts of the exploits of British troops, and was offering 'positive' stories about the doings of the Iraqi security forces, it had little time for the Danes. Thus, while it was celebrating on 14 May the exploits of the joint operation, 'led by the Iraqi Army', supported by British soldiers – this being no more than a diplomatic fiction – it neglected to mention something else. On the same day, another Danish soldier had been killed. Five others

74. MoD website, 8 May 2007, 'British troops lead capture of Iraqi criminals'.
75. BBC, 10 May 2007, 'Blair's resignation speech in full'.
76. MoD website, 14 May 2007, 'Basra raids net weapons and bomb-making equipment'.
77. MoD website, 10 August 2007, 'Embedding – the MOD's view'.

and an Iraqi interpreter had been injured. This had been the result of a gun battle and an IED attack – al Harthah again. With the soldiers' up-armoured M-113 (equivalent to the Bulldog) in flames, local residents gathered around it, cheering, dancing and waving a blackened military helmet in the air.

Nor did the Media Management Group report that British troops had been deployed to assist the Danes and they too had come under attack from RPGs, small arms and roadside bombs. That, presumably, would not have been 'balanced'. Nevertheless, the Danes had had enough. Three months previously, the Danish government had announced it was withdrawing its 460-strong contingent, replacing it with a token helicopter unit to be stationed at Basra airport.[78]

No doubt, though, the egregious Lt-Col Stratford-Wright would have approved of the balance in a Reuters report, published the day of the attack on the Danes. It noted the development of 'a turf war' in Basra that had 'all the ingredients of a gangster movie set in 1920s Chicago'. Sporadic militia battles, endemic corruption and death threats now scarred the once tranquil port. Peter Harling, an analyst for the International Crisis Group, said:

Everyone's trying to grab resources and make a quick profit without considering a long-term programme or attempting to establish a power base for the future. The interesting thing about violence in Basra is that it's not related to the two big factors of violence elsewhere: fighting the occupation and sectarian violence.

Residents feared that violence could be a sign of things to come, especially as British troops disengaged, the piece concluded. The 'balance' came from a spokeswoman for the British consulate, who 'played down fears'. 'The most important question is not whether there'll be trouble in Basra but whether Iraqi security forces can handle it. We have seen the Iraqis are increasingly ready and willing to assume more responsibilities,' she said.[79]

THE NEW BRITISH STRATEGY

This pointed to the new – or, at least, consolidated – British strategy: first, ignore the insurgency; second, characterise the insurgents as 'criminals' and 'rogue elements'; third, play down the extent of the violence, and position that which was evident as a reaction to the occupiers; fourth, embed the idea that withdrawal of the occupying forces would lead to a diminution of the violence; and finally, talk-up the capabilities of the security forces, especially the Iraqi Army.

78. *International Herald Tribune*, 14 May 2007, 'Danish soldier killed, 5 injured in Iraq'.
79. Reuters, 15 May 2007, 'Shi'ites battle for power in Iraq's Basra'.

It was plausible. But it was also fiction, a complex, structured falsehood that bore no relation to reality. Unfortunately, the British Army was in the thick of it, the soldiers on the ground expected to maintain the lie long enough to avoid the politicians and the 'brass' suffering the 'humiliation and embarrassment' of admitting defeat. It was a defeat that had been entrenched first in the mind of Mr Blair and then in the higher reaches of the Army, spreading through senior ranks like a virus. Never beaten on the field of battle, the Army was defeated by its own leaders.

The MoD's efforts to play down the violence were evident on 21 May when Cpl Jeremy Brookes was killed by small arms fire. We were told that he had been commanding a Bulldog involved in escorting a 'routine re-supply convoy' in the al Tuwaysa district of the city. A civilian fuel tanker involved in the convoy was also attacked, catching fire and killing the civilian driver. We were also told that the 4th Battalion The Rifles had 'recently taken over responsibility as the Basra City battle group, based at Basra Palace, from 2nd Battalion The Rifles'.[80] Harding's 'tipping point' had come and gone. His worst-case scenario was coming true.

In media coverage, it was noted that a 'cheering mob' had made victory hand signals after Cpl Brookes had been killed.[81, 82] But it took Michael Yon to reveal that, on the day of the fateful incident, the men of the 4th had already been fighting for 13 hours. With the temperature in their vehicles approaching 70°C, exhausted, drained from the heat, they were then escorting a re-supply convoy straight through the centre of Basra. As they approached the Martyr Sadr building, they were attacked by an estimated 100 insurgents with small arms and RPGs. Brookes was shot in the head and died on the spot. Others were wounded. Some of the insurgents con-centrated their fire on a fuel tanker. The driver, a Pakistani contractor, slumped and fell from the burning cab, whence an armed crowd surged into the street and dragged away his body. It was never seen again.

In order to break out of the ambush, the convoy attempted to cross a bridge over a canal, but a low-loader carrying two vehicles broke down. A Warrior moved towards the bridge, taking hits from all directions, to a dominating position. It was joined by Captain Richard Moger, the Platoon commander in his own Warrior. After two and a half hours of fighting, some of the men cooped up in the oven-like interiors of the armoured vehicles were near death from heat exhaustion. They were evacuated.

80. MoD website, 22 May 2007, 'Corporal Jeremy Brookes from 4th Battalion The Rifles killed in Iraq'.
81. *The Daily Telegraph*, 23 May 2007, 'Mob cheers as British soldier dies'.
82. *The Times*, 22 May 2007, 'British soldier is killed in Basra ambush'.

A team was urgently summoned from Basra Palace to recover the broken-down low-loader. In an unarmoured Foden truck, L/Cpls Burn and Miller were escorted the three miles to the bridge, to the middle of a 'ferocious, three-dimensional gun battle'. Warriors and Bulldogs provided cover but Moger's Warrior was running out of 30mm ammunition. Nevertheless, while the men suffering from heat exhaustion were evacuated to the Palace, he stayed in the fight. Burn and Miller, under heavy fire for 45 minutes, attempted to move the low-loader. After preparatory work, they then drove the Foden to a better position, escorted by a Bulldog, only for the Bulldog to be immobilised by an IED, injuring two men.

The recovery team could do no more. It was escorted back to base while a Warrior moved in to recover the Bulldog. Under heavy fire, tow cables were attached and it was dragged back to the Palace. Company commander Major James Bryant relieved the platoon at the bridge, taking hits from RPGs while returning fire. With one dead soldier and eight other casualties, it was now too risky to continue recovery attempts so he instructed Moger to use his last 30mm ammunition to destroy the immobilised vehicles.[83] That was one convoy on one day: two dead (one a Pakistani contractor) and eight wounded, with many more near death through heat exhaustion; three expensive military vehicles and a tanker destroyed, and one Bulldog damaged. There would have to be many more convoys before this 'pointless war' was ended.

ARMY WORRIES

Within some of the higher echelons of the Army and the MoD, there was now genuine concern that the 'retreat' and the cutbacks had gone too far. While there had been no great discussion about the withdrawal from Abu Naji, there had been some reservations about pulling out from the Shatt al-Arab Hotel. Now, with only two bases left, some senior officers were seriously questioning the wisdom of further withdrawal. Far from the retreats making things easier, the upsurge of Mahdi activity was straining the resources of the Army.

Something of that broke into the public domain in late May with Mike Smith of *The Times* retailing the fears of 'senior army officers'. They were worried that Gordon Brown – soon to become prime minister – was going to cut the number of troops in Iraq to such a low level that their effectiveness would be jeopardised and lives endangered. Unwittingly though – and without passing comment – Smith highlighted the devastating effect of

83. Michael Yon, undated, 'Men of Valour Part II'.

equipment inadequacies. He had one officer complaining: 'We are sitting ducks and have very little in the way of resources to react. If we mount an operation to deter a mortar attack it takes an entire battle group and ties up all our people.' Any further reductions in numbers, said the officer, would leave British troops 'hanging onto Basra by our finger tips'.[84]

This was the limit of the argument and the public perception. More attacks required more troops for defence or, at least, the retention of existing manpower, with an officer openly stating that it took a complete battle group – some 500 men – to 'deter a mortar attack'. Yet that task could so easily have been accomplished by a single Predator UAV armed with Hellfire missiles. It would have required no more than a few dozen men who would never have been exposed to any personal risk.

It is not as if the importance of UAVs was not understood. In November, the MoD was to announce the deployment of the first of three of the more powerful versions of the Predator, known as the Reaper. Each was capable of carrying 14 Hellfire missiles, 12 more than its predecessor, or laser-guided bombs.[85] The problem was, they were destined for Afghanistan.[86] Iraq had been written off. To add insult to injury, in January of the following year, the MoD was to order 10 more Reapers, with nine sets of Lynx 'ground scanning moving-target radar' with which to equip them. Incredibly sophisticated, these radars could pick up a man-sized target at the range of 50 miles. They too were destined for Afghanistan.

Essentially abandoned by their own Army and government, without the right equipment and enough resources, men were to continue dying. The next was Cpl Rodney Wilson. He was killed on 7 June as he tried to rescue a wounded comrade under heavy fire.[87] Another was Major Paul Harding. Stationed at the Provincial Joint Co-ordination Centre, on 20 June he had placed himself in the centre's most exposed fortified position to help secure the route in for a re-supply convoy from Basra Palace. He was hit by a mortar bomb and died instantly.[88] Two days later, Cpl John Rigby was the next to go. He was in a Bulldog returning to base when it was hit by an IED. He died two days later on his 24th birthday, his twin brother at his side.[89]

Four days on, three soldiers were killed together as they dismounted from their Warrior, hit by an IED hidden in the kerbside. A fourth was seriously injured. They had been returning to Basra airport after carrying

84. *The Times*, 27 May 2007, 'Army fear over Iraq troop cuts'.
85. MoD website, 9 November 2007, 'Reaper takes to the air in Afghanistan'.
86. MoD website, 10 January 2008, 'Reaper: The eye in the Afghan sky'.
87. BBC, 8 June 2007, 'Tributes to "selfless" UK soldier'.
88. BBC, 6 July 2007, 'Major given full military funeral'.
89. BBC, 24 June 2007, 'UK soldier died on 24th birthday'.

out a re-supply mission to Basra Palace. An Army spokesman admitted that the number of attacks had peaked at the end of February, fallen, and was now rising again. 'We believe this to be in part because of our success against rogue militia who are trying to destabilise the situation,' he said.[90] One thing was for sure. Any residual effect from Operation Sinbad had evaporated.

BLAIR RESIGNS ON A WAVE OF HYPOCRISY

The day before the three had died, Tony Blair was standing in the Commons for the last time, announcing his resignation as prime minister. He started off, as had become the custom, by offering his 'deep condolences' to the families and friends of the soldiers who had died since he had last spoken. He then made some general remarks about the armed forces. 'I have never come across people of such sustained dedication, courage and commitment,' he said, adding:

I am truly sorry about the dangers that they face today in Iraq and Afghanistan. I know that some may think that they face these dangers in vain. I do not, and I never will. I believe that they are fighting for the security of this country and the wider world against people who would destroy our way of life. But whatever view people take of my decisions, I think that there is only one view to take of them: they are the bravest and the best.[91]

Asked whether it was time to give a timetable to bring the troops out of Iraq, Blair refused to agree. Of the terrorists, he said, 'We will not beat them by giving in to them. We will only beat them by standing up to them.' Equally, he refused to accept that the troops were not properly equipped. 'Our troops are, in fact, extremely well equipped,' he declared.[92] With that, Gordon Brown moved into 10 Downing Street. On 7 July, another of Blair's 'extremely well equipped' troops died. He was Cpl Christopher Read, a military policeman, who had been engaged on a 'large scale operation'. Two other soldiers were injured in the operation, which involved 1,000 troops.[93] The same day, L/Cpl Ryan Francis was killed by an IED while driving a Warrior.[94]

BASRA AIR BASE UNDER ATTACK

After firing off rockets at Basra air base for years, on 19 July the insurgents killed three RAF soldiers. They had been conducting base security

90. BBC, 28 June 2007, 'Iraq bomb kills three UK soldiers'.
91. Hansard, 27 June 2007: Column 323.
92. Hansard, 27 June 2007: Column 328.
93. BBC, 9 July 2007, 'UK soldier killed in Iraq named'.
94. BBC, '"Heart and soul" soldier killed'.

patrols and, tragically, had been hit by a rocket while taking a break in an unprotected building.[95] Previously, two RAF airmen had been seriously injured when a barrage of four rockets hit them while they had been driving out in the open. By the time the three had been killed, C-RAM had been installed – but too late. The equipment was still being 'worked up' and had not been able to provide the vital protection.

The situation at Basra air base had become intolerable. In three months, more than 450 rockets had been fired, the insurgents using the control tower as an aiming point – visible from miles away in the desert. In 2004 there had been 26 attacks, the following year 15. Late in 2006 they had risen dramatically to 177. One officer said that in tented accommodation all people could do was put on their body armour and helmets and pray they were not hit. 'The situation is far worse than is being portrayed back home,' said one RAF officer. 'People are just relying on luck to stay alive.'[96] This was the 'layered protection' of which the defence minister had been so confident. He might not have been so confident had his own house been subjected to the same treatment. But troops in Basra were expendable.

Three days after the RAF deaths, this time from a mortar attack at Basra Palace, REME fitter L/Cpl Timothy Flowers died while working out in the open on a Warrior.[97] Cpl Steve Edwards was then killed on patrol in a Warrior on 31 July, another victim of an IED.[98] On 6 August, Pte Craig Barber was driving a Warrior on a 'counter rocket and mortar' mission when he was shot, another victim of the 'Basra sniper'.[99] On a foot patrol north of Basra Air Station to deter mortar attacks, Leading Aircraftman Martin Beard was slaughtered by an IED on 9 August.[100]

With five men having been recently killed by indirect fire and two on the fruitless task of deterring mortar attacks, the week before, USAF Predator operators had observed insurgents fire two mortar bombs then load the tube into the trunk of their vehicle. The operators launched a Hellfire from the Predator, hitting the front of the car and destroying it.[101] This was the job for which the British needed an entire battle group.

While LAC Beard had been so tragically and unnecessarily engaged on something so effortlessly achieved by a UAV, L/Sgt Chris Casey, and L/Cpl Kirk Redpath were getting murdered. This was equally pointless and unnecessary. They had been 'top covers' in a Snatch escorting a convoy of large

95. BBC, 21 July 2007, 'Servicemen killed in Iraq named'.
96. *The Daily Telegraph*, 20 August 2007, 'Rocket attacks on Basra airbase increase'.
97. BBC, 22 July 2007, 'UK soldier killed in Iraq named'.
98. BBC, 2 August 2007, 'British Basra casualty is named'.
99. BBC, 8 August 2007, 'British serviceman killed in Iraq'.
100. BBC, 9 August 2007, 'Two British soldiers die in Iraq'.
101. *Military Aviation News*, 27 July 2007, 'US Air Force airpower: Predators stop insurgents'.

trucks out from Kuwait and had been hit by an IED. Two other soldiers were seriously injured.[102] The insurgents had seen the vehicles going down and were waiting for their return.[103]

After all this time, when the Army had been losing Bulldogs, Warriors and even Challengers to IEDs, it was still sending men to die in Snatches. Mastiffs were in theatre and the soldiers' platoon commander had asked for one. Despite Mr Blair's assurances that the armed forces were 'extremely well equipped,' none had been available. For all these soldiers' sacrifice, neither had many 'hearts and minds' been won on the six-lane motorway out of Kuwait where the 'size and profile' of the Snatch had so obviously and desperately been needed.

DEFEATED IN THE SOUTH

A few days before Casey and Redpath had died, *The Washington Post* had noted:

'The British have basically been defeated in the south', a senior US intelligence official said recently in Baghdad. They are abandoning their former headquarters at Basra Palace, where a recent official visitor from London described them as 'surrounded like cowboys and Indians' by militia fighters.[104]

Predictably, Muqtada capitalised on the British defeat – as he had done with Abu Naji – proclaiming: 'The British have given up and know they will be leaving Iraq soon. They are retreating because of the resistance they have faced. Without that they would have stayed for much longer, there is no doubt.' Equally predictably, the Army hotly denied the claim, accusing Muqtada of trying to 'create the false impression that they were driving us out'. But in the war of words, perception was everything. Muqtada was articulating and amplifying the view of the 'Arab Street': the British were running.[105]

By now, proportionately, the death rate amongst British forces was higher than that of the American mission of 160,000 troops, 41 US soldiers having died compared with 29 Brits in all of 2006. But at least the pain was about to end.

On 25 August, following repeated attempts by the Mahdi Army to overrun the base, British forces evacuated the Provincial Joint Co-ordination Centre (PJCC). Officially, the small contingent of troops had been 'moved' within 'the framework of the plan for the handover of the Basra Palace to

---

102. BBC, 10 August 2007, 'UK soldiers killed in Iraq named'.
103. *The Daily Telegraph*, 14 August 2007, 'Tributes for Guardsmen killed by Iraq bomb'.
104. *The Washington Post*, 7 August 2007, 'As British leave, Basra deteriorates'.
105. *The Independent*, 21 August 2007, 'Army chiefs deny al-Sadr's claim of victory in Iraq'.

Iraqi control'. Reports then indicated that Shi'a fighters arrived and began emptying the facility. With *The Independent* quick to claim that the militia occupation 'further undermines Britain's hopes of a smooth transfer and gives the impression of a rout', the MoD claimed Iraqi police had thwarted the take-over. It seemed the militia had gathered in front of the PJCC and chanted victory slogans before withdrawing peacefully. An MoD spokesman said there was a green Shi'a flag flying on the building, not the black Mahdi Army flag.[106] Spinning to the last, the MoD added that the Iraqi forces were demonstrating that they could take the lead in the city.

THE FINAL RETREAT

By then, behind the scenes, British commanders were paving the way for the retreat from Basra Palace, striking a secret deal with Sadr's men to ensure safe passage. To cement the deal, they agreed to release more than two dozen Mahdi Army prisoners. One was Sajad Abu Aya whose capture in July 2006 had been hailed as such a coup. Now he was a pawn, played to avoid the British Army having to fight its way out of the Palace. The last thing that either the politicians or the 'brass' wanted was the 'impression of a rout'. That would have deprived them of the opportunity of claiming their 'success'.

On the streets, there was a sense of jubilation and victory. In central Arousa Square, a street was renamed after the 'martyr Jaafar Muhammad', killed in clashes with the British. 'He's one of my guys. One of the valiant heroes of the Imam Mahdi Army,' declared a bearded company commander. 'God has blessed us with victory over the occupation.'[107]

With their way clear, British troops evacuated Basra Palace on 2 September.[108] Their retreat was redolent of a similar humiliation in Aden when, in November 1967, British forces had marched out of their base six abreast with flags flying, never to return. Then, to mark their departure, the band of the Royal Marines had struck up 'Things Ain't What They Used to Be.[109] This time there were no bands, just Union Jacks and Regimental banners flying from a convoy of armoured vehicles as it wound its way through Basra to the last redoubt. The media were banned from witnessing the event, having to rely on carefully framed MoD handouts to illustrate their reports. The Mahdi Army honoured its agreement. Not a shot was fired at its defeated enemy. The mirage of 'success' was intact.

106. BBC, 26 August 2007, 'Troops withdraw from Basra base'.
107. *Christian Science Monitor*, 28 August 2007, 'As British leave Basra, militias dig in'.
108. *The Sunday Times*, 2 September 2007, 'The exit from Basra'.
109. *The Times*, 20 December 2008, 'Aden was left to its own chaos'.

Chapter 10 – Return to al-Amarah
... and beyond
The final humiliation of the British

It's insufferable for Christ's sake. He [Major General Jonathan Shaw] comes on and he lectures everybody in the room about how to do a counter-insurgency. The guys were just rolling their eyeballs.

ANONYMOUS SENIOR US OFFICIAL, AUGUST 2007

The Americans, it is fair to say, profited far more than the British from their experience in Africa, thus confirming that education is easier than re-education.

ERWIN ROMMEL[1]

Despite a very obvious and humiliating retreat in progress, the British military had learnt little from their experience. On 20 August, *The Daily Telegraph* retailed how, when America's top commanders in Iraq had held a conference with their British counterparts:

Major General Jonathan Shaw – Britain's senior officer in Basra – was quick to share his views on how best to conduct counter-insurgency operations. For much of the last four years, the Americans in the room would have listened carefully, used to deferring to their British colleagues' long experience in Northern Ireland. This time, however, eyes that would once have been attentive simply rolled ...

'It's insufferable for Christ's sake,' said one senior figure closely involved in US military planning. 'He comes on and he lectures everybody in the room about how to do a counter-insurgency. The guys were just rolling their eyeballs. The notorious Northern Ireland came up again. It's pretty frustrating. It would be okay if he was best in class, but now he's worst in class. Everybody else's area is getting better and his is getting worse.'[2]

The point was that the Americans, after making possibly every mistake in the book – and some – had learned. A milestone in their learning curve had been on December 2004 when in a remote desert camp in Kuwait there had been an extraordinary exchange between then Defense Secretary Donald Rumsfeld and Iraq-bound troops. They complained of being sent into combat with insufficient protection and ageing equipment. In stark contrast to the deferential, secretive and largely unreported debate in the British military, Specialist Thomas Wilson tackled Rumsfeld head-on. He told him that soldiers had to scrounge through local landfills for pieces of rusty scrap metal and bulletproof glass – what they called 'hillbilly armor'

---

1. Carlo D'Este, *Patton, A Genius for War* (New York, HarperCollins, 1995), p. 485 (quoting from Liddell Hart's edition of *The Rommel Papers*.)
2. *The Daily Telegraph*, 20 August 2007, 'British forces useless in Basra, say officials'.

– to bolt on to their trucks for protection. This was said openly, to cheers and applause from many of the 2,300 troops who had been assembled in a cavernous hangar to meet the secretary. And it was reported by the media.

Famously, Rumsfeld had answered, 'You go to war with the army you have, not the army you might want or wish to have at a later time'. He was then to utter the mantra which, four years later, was still being repeated. Adding more armour to trucks and battle equipment did not make them impervious to enemy attack. 'If you think about it,' Rumsfeld had said, 'you can have all the armour in the world on a tank and a tank can be blown up. And you can have an up-armoured Humvee and it can be blown up.'[3]

Even in November 2008, a retired officer from the Royal Armoured Corps with 33 years service was telling us: 'anti-tank mines do exactly what they say on the tin case; they destroy tanks, therefore no vehicle is immune from them.'[4] This was exactly Rumsfeld's thinking. Since tanks could not protect from IEDs, nothing else could. This neglected the simple fact that modern tanks had been designed primarily as anti-tank weapons, their armour optimised to protect them from the tanks they were intended to kill. To save weight and thus to enable topside armour to be maximised, their underbellies – as with the Warrior – were relatively lightly protected. Anti-tank mines and IEDs exploited that weakness with devastating effect.

More than 30 years previously the Rhodesians, attempting to deal with a vicious insurgency of their own, had developed vehicles which could shrug off such weapons. They had even adapted a Land Rover, using it for base security on airfields, a vehicle capable of resisting a mine that could destroy a tank 30 times its weight. Its protection had been optimised to deal with the specific threat, the thinking and technology then being passed to the South Africans and embodied in the RG-31 which, even as Rumsfeld was enunciating his flawed thesis, was in limited use by the USMC in Iraq.

THE MRAP PROGRAMME

Despite Rumsfeld's reservations, the US could not afford to ignore its troops' complaints. Two months before he had been so publicly challenged, an Army reserve unit in Iraq had refused to carry out a convoy supply mission. With the poor condition of their fuel trucks and the lack of armoured vehicles to escort them, they had felt it would have been 'suicide'.[5] The

---

3. *The New York Times*, 8 December 2004, 'Iraq-bound troops confront Rumsfeld over lack of armor'.
4. Intervention on an internet forum, 15 November 2008.
5. *Los Angeles Times*, 16 October 2004, 'Army reserve unit reportedly balked at risky mission in Iraq'.

immediate response was to speed up a programme of 'up-armouring' Humvees. Millions of dollars were spent, and not only on new armour. The Army also embarked on a year-long programme of clearing vegetation and debris along major routes. Military technicians equipped vehicles with ever-more sophisticated electronic counter-measures. Tactics were reviewed and improved. In spite of those efforts, deaths from IEDs rose by more than 41 per cent in the first five months of 2005 compared with the same period in the previous year. They accounted for nearly 51 per cent of the 255 US combat deaths.[6]

On the other hand, the USMC pointed out that, while US Army soldiers were dying in their hundreds, their 'MRAPs' had taken 300 IED hits without a single Marine being killed.[7] But even in the US, early initiatives to introduce MRAPs on a large scale had been defeated by a combination of military bureaucracy and inertia. An early advocate had been Marine Corps combat engineer Lt-Col Wayne Sinclair who had lived in South Africa and had seen first-hand the value of mine-protected vehicles. In 1996, then still a Captain, he had written a paper in the *Marine Corps Gazette* entitled: 'Answering the Landmine.'[8] He reported:

Although landmines have been a major weapon of war for more than a half century, the Corps continues to lag in adopting defensive measures … Perhaps the greatest advancements in the development of mine resistant vehicles came from the Rhodesian Bush War in south central Africa between 1962 and 1980 … their most effective answer was found in landmine survival measures rather than detection methods or equipment. The remoteness of the many hundreds of miles of unpaved roads made the daily task of sweeping and clearing most roads with any degree of certainty impossible. Therefore … the Rhodesian Army developed tactical wheeled vehicles that would significantly protect their occupants from a mine's blast and allow for the vehicle to be repaired and returned to service.

Sinclair had also noted that during UN operations in Somalia, between December 1992 and March 1994, at least 8 vehicles and 16 Americans had fallen victim to landmines. The contingent from Zimbabwe (formerly Rhodesia), using mine-protected vehicles developed in the 1970s, had taken no casualties. However, in a situation that was to be repeated by the British many years later, the idea of a MRAP capability was rejected on the grounds that such vehicles did not conform with the expeditionary warfare concept.

Thus, it was not until Bush replaced Rumsfeld with a new defence secretary, Robert M. Gates, in December 2006 – 10 years after the case had

6. Knight-Ridder News Agency, 10 June 2005, 'More Americans dying from roadside bombs in Iraq'.
7. *USA Today*, 2 October 2007, 'The truck the Pentagon wants and the firm that makes it'.
8. Cited in: Franz J. Gayl, 22 January 2008, 'Mine Resistant and Ambush Protected Vehicle, Ground Combat Element (GCE) Case Study', Headquarters, United States Marine Corps.

first been put for protected vehicles – that the US government woke up. It launched a massive re-equipment programme which by early 2007 had become the 'highest priority' acquisition programme in the US Armed Forces leading to orders for over 15,000 MRAP vehicles at a value of over $10 billion.[9, 10]

The mass deployment of MRAPs contributed to a huge fall in IED casualties. In August 2006, 47 troops were killed. In the same month in 2008, the number had fallen to seven. While 384 troops had been wounded by roadside bombs in August 2006, two years later that figure had fallen to 52 – an 86 per cent reduction.[11] Gates was totally vindicated. Speaking in May 2008, he revealed preliminary figures for the MRAP programme. There had been 150-plus attacks. All but six soldiers had survived. The casualty rate had been one-third that of an armoured Humvee, less than half that of an Abrams tank. 'These vehicles are saving lives,' he declared.[12] A soldier had more than twice the chance of walking away uninjured from an MRAP vehicle hit by an IED than if he had been in a 70-ton main battle tank.

As for the oft-quoted saw, that to counter better armour the insurgents would simply build bigger bombs, Major-General Rick Lynch, who had commanded a division in Baghdad, had the answer. The MRAPs did indeed force the insurgents down that route. Occasionally they succeeded. But these bombs took more time to build and hide, which gave US forces a better chance of catching the insurgents in the act.[13] And there was a limit to how big the bombs could be. In 2007, photographs were being circulated of a US Army Cougar which had taken a hit from an IED estimated at 300–500lb in weight. It had destroyed the vehicle, throwing the engine a hundred yards from the explosion site. All five of the crew had survived with only minor injuries.

Nor were MRAP vehicles used entirely in the passive, defensive sense. They formed the core of IED hunting teams, comprising the Buffalo and the Cougar. There was another component, the Meerkat mine detection vehicle and then the more powerful version, the Husky. This was based on a 1960s vehicle developed by the Rhodesians called the Pookie, fitted with under-belly sensors to undertake vehicle-borne mine detection. It replaced the laborious and dangerous process of using hand-held detectors or dogs to find mines and buried IEDs. The Meerkat and Husky brought to

---

9. *Inside Defense*, 8 May 2007, 'Gates designates MRAP Pentagon's "highest priority" acquisition program'.

10. *USA Today*, 20 December 2007, 'Military sets sights on at least 15,000 MRAPs'.

11. *Army Times*, 28 September 2008, 'IED casualties in Iraq drop sharply'.

12. Secretary of Defense Robert M. Gates, 13 May 2008, Remarks to the Heritage Foundation (Colorado Springs, CO).

13. *USA Today*, 22 June 2008, 'Roadside bombs decline in Iraq'.

the table another design feature which helped protect crews. Its wheels, fore and aft – on a vehicle which looked rather like a road grader but with a v-shaped hull – were attached by spindly frames, clear of the main body. They were designed to be blown off in the event of an explosion. The damaged wheels and suspension could be replaced within half-an-hour, spares being carried for that very purpose. This was an application of the so-called 'sacrificial' principle, losing non-vital components to a blast rather than trying to resist it through mass of armour.

The system was South African and the British – as so often – had been there first, having been the first foreign nation to acquire this equipment. It was deployed under the name of the 'Chubby' system in Bosnia in 1996. Sadly, the equipment was taken off charge in March 2001 and given to a mine-clearing charity.[14] The same system became one of the lead counter-measures used by the Americans in the war against the IED, while the British used men and dogs.

Nevertheless, the IED was not entirely defeated by such means. There were to be more deaths and injuries and the MRAPs were certainly not immune to attack. Much more went into the fight than just improved armour, not least better intelligence, both electronic and human. Improvements in tactics continued and greater use of helicopters also contributed to reduced exposure to the threat. MRAPs were not a panacea, a single solution to a complex problem. What they did was bring the casualty rate down to a more tolerable level and, as importantly, boost morale. Troops not only felt safer, they believed that their government, with its highly visible and massive investment, actually cared about them. There was a bleed-through into the home front. Military families and the public at large got the same message.

In the same way that the Snatch symbolised the reluctance of the British to address the insurgency, the US 'Humvee' came 'to represent one aspect of the US military's unpreparedness for the irregular warfare it now wages in Iraq and Afghanistan'.[15] By the same token, the MRAP programme symbolised US determination to defeat the insurgency. It gave a psychological boost and made a highly practical contribution to neutralising the IED as a *strategic* threat, helping to restore tactical mobility. These vehicles, in combination with the other measures taken, paved the way for success.

---

14. Hansard, 4 March 2008: Column 2352W.
15. Andrew F. Krepinevich and Dakota L. Wood, *Of IEDs and MRAPs: Force protection in complex irregular operations* (Center for Strategic and Budgetary Assessments, 2007).

BUSH LAUNCHES HIS COUNTER-OFFENSIVE

The appointment of Robert Gates, who then launched the MRAP re-equipment programme, was only one of three developments that drastically changed the Iraqi campaign. The second had started in March 2006 when the US Congress had appointed a 10-person bipartisan committee under the chairmanship of James Baker, a former Secretary of State, and Lee Hamilton, a former US Representative. Its remit was to review the progress of the Iraq war and to make recommendations. Called the Iraq Study Group, it published its report on 6 December to great public acclaim, with high political and popular expectations.[16]

Its substantive recommendations bore an uncanny resemblance to the strategy already adopted by the British. The Iraqi government, it said, should accelerate assuming responsibility for security by increasing the number and quality of Iraqi Army brigades. These would take over primary responsibility for combat operations. The United States should significantly increase the number of US personnel imbedded [*sic*] in and supporting Iraqi Army units. Then, by the first quarter of 2008, all US combat brigades not necessary for force protection could be out of Iraq.

Days before the Study Group had published, Bush had already ruled out US troop reductions and, in an act of great political courage, rejected the Study Group findings. This was a major turning point. Bush ignored the defeatist counsel to hand the problem over to the Iraqis and walk away, as the British were doing. Instead, he decided to go on the offensive, sending an additional 21,000 troops to Iraq for what was to become the 'surge'.[17, 18]

The number of extra troops committed was relatively modest. Extra troops, in themselves, could not prevail. What was also needed – the very thing the British had refused to countenance – was a major change in strategy. The man with a plan was General David Petraeus. Bush appointed him as Commanding General, Multi-National Force – Iraq, effectively putting him in charge of the 'surge'.

Petraeus was an interesting choice, a 'thinking man's general'. Awarded a PhD for his thesis on the lessons of Vietnam, he had held academic and military posts before commanding, with some success, the elite 101st Airborne Division in Mosul. An acknowledged expert in counter-insurgency, between 2005–2007 he was responsible for oversight of the Command and General Staff College and 17 other schools, centres, and training programmes as well as for developing the Army's doctrinal manuals. Before

---

16. US Institute of Peace, 6 December 2006, The Iraq Study Group Report.
17. *The New York Times*, 1 December 2006, 'Bush rejects troop reductions, endorses Maliki'.
18. *The Washington Post*, 14 January 2007, 'Opposition to Iraq plan leaves Bush isolated'.

taking up his new post, he had published a 'Commander's Counter-insurgency Guidance'. With his draft field manual on counter-insurgency, this became the template for the surge.[19, 20]

The studies produced by Petraeus were of the same order as the conceptual work undertaken by Liddell Hart and Gen J. F. C. Fuller, which had led to the development of *Blitzkrieg*, used to stunning effect by the Germans in 1940. They were the embodiment of a truism enunciated by *Sun Tzu*, that the prosecution of war is primarily an intellectual exercise. Experience counts for little when a concept has never been tried before or when it is not underpinned by a sound intellectual base. The British were relying on experience. The Americans were now deploying a powerful intellectual force.

Amongst the key principles Petraeus set out was the requirement to live among the people. 'You can't commute to this fight,' he told his troops. Then, areas cleared of insurgents had to be retained. People needed to know that 'we and our Iraqi partners will not abandon them'. When reducing forces, the crucial thing was gradually to thin the presence rather than handing off or withdrawing completely. As for patrolling, the advice offered was 'walk'. Move mounted, work dismounted, he counselled: 'Stop by, don't drive by. Patrol on foot and engage the population. Situational awareness can only be gained by interacting with the people face-to-face, not separated by ballistic glass.' Then, something the MoD could have read with advantage, he told his soldiers, 'be first with the truth':

Get accurate information of significant activities to the chain of command, to Iraqi leaders, and to the press as soon as is possible. Beat the insurgents, extremists, and criminals to the headlines, and pre-empt rumours. Integrity is critical to this fight. Don't put lipstick on pigs. Acknowledge setbacks and failures, and then state what we've learned and how we'll respond. Hold the press (and ourselves) accountable for accuracy, characterisation, and context. Avoid spin, and let facts speak for themselves.

In his various writings though, there is no evidence that Petraeus fully understood the significance of the IED and the devastating effect it was having on the Iraqi campaign. The references to IEDs in the field manual were few and he wrote about 'uparmoured vehicles', calling on Vietnam experience. Arguably, had his injunction to 'move mounted, work dismounted', been obeyed without the influx of MRAPs, the surge would have failed. Fortunately, thanks to Robert Gates, these vehicles were flooding into theatre, their stabilising presence enabling the grand strategy to work. It did.

19. *Military Review*, September–October 2008, 'General David H. Petraeus, a Commander's counter-insurgency guidance'.
20. Headquarters Department of the Army, Washington, DC, 16 June 2006, Field Manual No. 3-24, Counterinsurgency.

By March 2007, just as the British were retreating from the Old State Building, there was clear evidence of success. Petraeus was reporting that he had been able to walk down the streets of Ramadi, an insurgency hotspot, 'in a soft cap eating an ice cream with the mayor on one side of me and the police chief on the other, having a conversation'.[21] By September, as the British forces had hunkered down in their last redoubt, Petraeus was telling Congress that there had been sufficient progress to allow troop reductions to pre-surge levels without jeopardising gains made.[22]

MALIKI'S POLITICAL MOVES

So far then, there have been identified two elements behind this transformation. There had been the appointment of Robert Gates who in turn had kick-started the MRAP programme. Then there had been President Bush's rejection of the Study Group recommendations, his decision to mount the 'surge' and his appointment of Petraeus to implement a new counter-insurgency doctrine. But there was a third, vital element needed to ensure success: a transformation of Iraqi politics. Maliki was the central figure.

With the emergence of the Shi'a insurgency and the growing power and popularity of Muqtada al-Sadr, Maliki was under enormous pressure to sort out the problem. But as the violence had mounted through 2006, to the frustration of the US and the British, he had refused to grasp the nettle. By August 2006, there had been insistent rumours that the Bush government might be considering 'alternatives other than democracy' in order to rein in the violence.[23] Pressure on Maliki continued to intensify.[24] In October, American commentators were openly discussing the possibility of a *coup d'état* in Iraq, in order to 'salvage the war'.[25]

In early November, this had reached the Egyptian *al-Ahram* newspaper (and many foreign language newspapers, although not, it seems, the British media). Echoing a consistent line of thought, *al-Ahram* decided that one of the solutions to the problem was 'some sort of military take-over that would oust the elected government'. It would be replaced with a 'national salvation' government with the mission to re-establish security and stability in Iraq.[26]

---

21. *New York Post*, 20 March 2007, 'The Iraq surge: why it's working'.
22. American Forces Press Service, 10 September 2007, 'Petraeus: Surge in Iraq works; reductions could begin by summer 2008'.
23. *The New York Times*, 17 August 2006, 'Bombs aimed at GIs in Iraq are increasing'.
24. *Los Angeles Times*, 20 September 2006, 'Pentagon sees no troop reductions in Iraq'.
25. Robert Dreyfuss, *TomPaine.common sense*, 6 October 2006, 'Coup in Iraq?'
26. *Al-Ahram*, 1–7 November 2006, 'A volte face for Iraq?'

Maliki was in an impossible position. Ruling over a fractious, divided nation, nominally leading an unstable Shi'a coalition in which Muqtada's Sadrists held the balance of power, early moves against the Mahdi Army would have been political suicide. Even by October 2006, the 'experts' were doubtful that Maliki could prevail.[27] Gradually though, with pressure and support from the US, a process in which Bush was reportedly directly involved, he worked to marginalise Muqtada, starting negotiations with several of Iraq's major political parties across the sectarian divide.[28]

By mid-August 2007 he was able to announce a new alliance with the Kurds, weakening Muqtada's hold on the government.[29] Although the deal was openly denounced by the Sunnis, Maliki was nevertheless working with them to bring the moderate Iraqi Islamic Party on side, offering former Ba'athist party members concessions and launching a reconciliation process. A tentative deal was announced by late August, but immediately disowned by the Sunnis.[30] Behind this was something of a Catch 22 situation. To bring the Sunnis fully on board, Maliki had to demonstrate his willingness to tackle the Mahdi Army but, to tackle the Mahdi Army, he needed the support of the Sunnis.

THE BRITISH HAND BACK BASRA

On 16 December 2007, the British, in a formal acknowledgement of their reduced role, handed back the security responsibility for Basra to the Iraqi government.[31] Maliki was on his own. Building bridges with Iran, in particular Sistani, and making overtures to SCIRI, Maliki sought to position Muqtada as a pawn of the Iranians, thereby undermining his support from Iraqi nationalists which included the Sunnis. By February 2008, commentators – who had previously dismissed the man – were openly talking of Maliki's political re-birth.[32]

To an extent, Maliki was helped by the militias, who overplayed their hand. Openly bearing arms in the streets and setting up military parades, the Mahdi Army – and its many splinter groups – were also taking on the Iraqi Army and the police. Basra was becoming a war zone, punctuated by

27. Council on Foreign Relations, 24 October 2006, 'Maliki and Sadr: An alliance of convenience'.
28. *International Herald Tribune*, 11 December 2006, 'Iraqis weigh alliance to marginalize Sadr and bolster Maliki'.
29. *Radio Free Europe*, 16 August 2007, 'Iraqi leaders announce deal on political alliance'.
30. *Javano*, 26 August 2007, 'Sunni Arab Party to join new alliance – Iraq PM'.
31. *International Herald Tribune*, 16 December 2007, 'British forces hand over security responsibility for Basra'.
32. *Asia Times*, 12 February 2008, 'Maliki rises from the ashes'.

a series of running battles.[33] Sectarian violence had continued unabated and the process of creating an Islamic independent state was continuing apace, with the murder of 'westernised' women widely reported.[34] The city was descending into anarchy. After months of calm, attacks on the last British base had resumed.[35]

Tucked up securely in their base, the British seemed – as always – to be oblivious to events. Late the previous year, Gethin Chamberlain – witness to the drama in al-Amarah in 2004 – had observed that British forces were getting their information from local newspapers and from the Iraqi army, although one battalion was isolated inside the city and the other was in training outside.[36] Nevertheless, by February 2008, there was definitely a sense of Basra being a powder keg waiting to blow. A final all-out battle was seen as inevitable.[37] Despite this, the Chief of the Defence Staff, Jock Stirrup, chose the fifth anniversary of the invasion, on 20 March, to publish a 'tribute to the sacrifice and achievements of the British forces'. He then wrote:

More and more people in Basra are turning from violence on the streets to politics. Not all of them, and not as quickly as we would like. But those who continue to practise violence are being dealt with increasingly effectively by the Iraqi security forces.[38]

The British commander was now Major-General Barney White-Spunner. He too thought the situation inside the city was getting better. 'No one is saying it is ideal,' he said. 'But the indications are that the militias are losing some of their influence, and there are divisions appearing among them.' The 'divisions' were not among them – not yet. Stirrup and White-Spunner both were in the land of the fairies. Even in their own narrow little world, there was evidence of a deterioration. With the attacks on the base increasing, they had been forced to delay reducing the number of troops.

Meanwhile, an Iraqi Army Corps comprising the 10th and 14th Divisions was preparing to conduct a major operation. The British and the Americans expected it to be launched in the summer. Its commander, Major-General Mohan al-Furayji, had come down from Baghdad promising to sort out the city. His officers were not optimistic. Capt Ali Modar, of the new 14th Iraqi Division, admitted that his men needed much more time. 'Soldiers from Basra can't fight against militias,' he said. 'It is difficult

33. *Arab News*, 19 January 2008, 'Fierce battle in Basra leaves dozens dead'.
34. *The Independent*, 11 December 2007, '"Westernised" women being killed in Basra'.
35. *International Herald Tribune*, 31 January 2008, 'Violence flares in Baghdad and Basra'.
36. *The Daily Telegraph*, 29 October 2007, 'Message from Basra: "Get us out of here"'.
37. *The Observer*, 24 February 2008, 'Hopes of UK troop cuts in Basra dashed'.
38. MoD website, 20 March 2008, 'CDS: Iraqis now have a chance'.

to overcome them. We need people to come from other parts of Iraq. Soldiers from Basra know that if they arrest anyone they will be killed, or their families will be killed.' But no support was expected from the British. They were known to be unwilling to step back into the quagmire.[39]

OPERATION CHARGE OF THE KNIGHTS

Something was in the air. The Kuwaiti Arab-language newspaper *Aswan* on 22 March cited an anonymous source claiming that an operation was 'imminent'. Basra police chief, Hatem Khalaf – a Maliki appointment, six months in post – told his officers 'our patience is running out'. He warned them to prepare for the decisive battle.[40] *Aswan*'s source was correct. Maliki, having secured tentative but fragile political support across the sectarian divide, could not afford to wait until summer. Whether the Iraq Army was ready or not, he had to make an immediate move against the Shi'a insurgency or risk his work unravelling. Taking a huge gamble, he travelled to Basra personally to take charge of *Saulat al-Fursan* – Operation Charge of the Knights. The British were neither consulted nor asked for assistance. The Americans were given notice of the operation on 21 March and, despite their misgivings, mobilised support.

On 25 March, parts of Basra erupted in fighting. Iraqi troops had moved in, the action concentrated in six northern districts where the Mahdi Army was strongest. By Friday 28 March, the situation did not look good. The violence was spreading and the news agencies were carrying pictures of burnt-out Iraqi security force vehicles. Gunmen in Baghdad had seized a high-profile government spokesman from his home in a Shi'ite neighbourhood and Muqtada was not giving any ground. Maliki kept his nerve and pledged 'no retreat'. The pressure must have been phenomenal. Tens of thousands of protesters had gathered to demand his resignation and saboteurs hit the oil pipelines in Basra, striking at the heart of the Iraqi economy. All reports indicated that the militias were still controlling Basra's streets. Food and water was running out. There was a 24-hour curfew on vehicle movements, set to last until the Sunday morning.

As expected, there had been no direct involvement of British forces but, with the militias appearing to have the upper hand, *The Times* proclaimed: 'Iraqi militia success means Britain must fight – or admit failure.' Foreign editor Richard Beeston told of the battle for Basra raging on the streets

39. *The Independent*, 23 March 2008, 'British pull-out from Basra delayed after rise in rocket attacks'.
40. *Aswan*, 22 March 2008, 'Major security operation in Basra'.

showing every sign of turning into a nightmare, adding that if the Iraqi offensive failed, 'it may be necessary to reinforce the British contingent'. The only other option, he wrote, 'would be for Britain to admit finally that it has lost the fight in southern Iraq'. That, he said:

... would mean an ignominious withdrawal and handing over control of Basra to the Americans, who grudgingly would have to take over responsibility for the south. As American officers and officials have privately made clear, much of today's problems in Basra can be traced back to Britain's failure to commit the forces necessary to control Basra and southern Iraq in general.[41]

As the operation progressed, President Bush spoke of Iraq facing a new 'defining moment'. There was no official statement from Gordon Brown. In his absence, Downing Street offered the pathetic suggestion that: 'it was not really appropriate to comment on operational matters.' This left confusion as to the degree of British involvement. There had been reports of coalition forces providing air support, although it was not known whether British or US assets had been used.

In fact, both British and US aircraft were in the skies and substantial logistical support was provided by the British, plus medical assistance. On the ground, it was the Iraq forces, with the support of embedded US forces, which made the running. Bringing forward the operation from its planned summer launch, however, had forced the fielding of the raw 52nd Brigade from the 14th Division. It had graduated only five weeks earlier and, in the face of stiff Mahdi Army opposition, had cracked, precipitating mass desertions. Maliki rushed in reinforcements from some of his best units, stiffened by US forces, including a Company from the 1st Brigade, 82nd Airborne Division.

British troops, 4,000 in total, were mostly confined to barracks. Meanwhile, Damien McElroy of *The Daily Telegraph* was writing that British forces had been facing increasing pressure to intervene, with rifts growing among British officials and the military. According to McElroy, a 'British official based in Baghdad' was indicating that, 'The Army won't even listen to suggestions it might be needed'.[42] Clearly, without top-level political intervention, the factions were squabbling amongst themselves. Back on the ground, though, the real battle went on.

After five days of fighting, media, politicians and commentators alike were freely referring to the 'stalled assault'. Witnesses were reporting that the Mahdi Army had been setting up checkpoints and controlling traffic in many places. They were ringing the central district supposedly controlled

41. *The Times*, 28 March 2008, 'Iraqi militia success means Britain must fight – or admit failure'.
42. *The Daily Telegraph*, 29 March 2008, 'Rift between UK diplomats and Army in Basra'.

by the 30,000 Iraqi Army and police forces. Pessimism exuded from the media. *The New York Times* on 28 March was suggesting Maliki's military adventure had backfired. Militiamen in Basra were in open control of wide swaths of the city, using these areas to stage 'increasingly bold raids' on Iraqi government forces.[43] By 1 April, *The Times* in London was headlining: 'Nouri al-Maliki humiliated as gamble to crush Shia militias fails.'[44]

Almost without exception, the media had called it wrong. On 25 March, Maliki had given the militias a 72-hour deadline to lay down their weapons.[45] The border with Iran was closed, Basra was sealed off and there was heavy interdiction on Route 6, between Basra and al-Amarah. Considerable US air power and ground forces were employed. Although Muqtada remained defiant, his militia was deprived of weapons, ammunition and supplies. The deadline came and went and the situation seemed to be spiralling out of control. Mahdi militia were reported to be storming a state TV facility in Basra, forcing Iraqi military guards surrounding the building to flee and setting armoured vehicles on fire. They seemed to be in control, but the signs were misleading. At that point, on 30 March when all seemed lost, Muqtada called a truce, ordering his fighters off the streets.[46] They melted away.

Behind the scenes, Muqtada had been revisiting an earlier strategy, one he had employed in the 2004 uprising – running his campaign to the wire and then prevailing on Sistani to broker a truce, leaving the core of his forces intact. This time, his pleas fell on deaf ears. With his fighters desperately short of supplies, their morale plummeting, that gave him no option. He had to call off his men unilaterally or face defeat. In so doing, he hoped to gain concessions which would give him time to rebuild his strength. Maliki was unmoved and pledged to continue his military operations. By way of consolation he did offer Muqtada a fig-leaf behind which he could salve his tattered reputation. He allowed his spokesman Ali al-Dabbagh to declare that the operation, 'is not targeting the Sadrists but criminals'.

Taking advantage of Muqtada's disarray, US forces, alongside Iraqi Army units, mounted massive raids into Sadr City. In an attempt to regain the initiative, Muqtada responded with a call for a million-strong demonstration in Najaf to oppose the US presence. 'The time has come to express your rejections and raise your voices loud against the unjust occupier and enemy of nations and humanity, and against the horrible massacres committed by the occupier against our honourable people,' he stormed. But, at

43. *The New York Times*, 30 March 2008, 'Shiite militias cling to swaths of Basra and stage raids'.
44. *The Times*, 1 April 2008, 'Nouri al-Maliki humiliated as gamble to crush Shia militias fails'.
45. AFP (via al Arabiya), 25 March 2008, 'Iraq PM gives 72 hour deadline to Shiite fighters'.
46. Reuters, 30 March 2008, 'Sadr followers caught off guard by truce'.

the last minute, he changed the venue to Baghdad. Only 1,500 turned up.[47] Muqtada's influence was crumbling.

With amazing rapidity Basra returned to normality. On 25 April, *Times* reporter Deborah Haynes was in Basra recording: 'Young women are daring to wear jeans, soldiers listen to pop music on their mobile phones and bands are performing at wedding parties again.' Haynes continued:

... after three years of being terrified of kidnap, rape and murder – a fate that befell scores of other women – Nadyia Ahmed, 22, is among those enjoying a sense of normality, happy for the first time to attend her science course at Basra University. 'I now have the university life that I heard of at high school before the war and always dreamt about,' she told *The Times*. 'It was a nightmare because of these militiamen. I only attended class three days a week but now I look forward to going every day.'[48]

The power of the 'men in black' had been broken – at least for the time being. It had taken less than a month. Nor did Iraqi operations end there. Gradually, troops extended their grip, in October mounting massive sweeps throughout the province extending to the Kuwaiti border, picking up 180 'suspects', including a Pakistani al Qaeda operative. Earlier, security forces arrested an Iranian, a member of the Ramazan Corps. This was the command created by the Qods Force, the elite special operations branch of the Iranian Revolutionary Guards established to direct operations inside Iraq. Under cover of the militia violence – infiltrating local organisations rather than assuming a separate identity – it had been working to undermine the Iraqi government. With the power of the Mahdi Army diminished, the influence and activities of such groups – previously obscure – was becoming more visible. Gradually they were being mopped up.[49]

There was other unfinished business. Even at the tail end of the fighting in Basra, there had been major clashes in Nasiriya, with 85 Mahdi gunmen killed, 200 wounded and 100 arrested.[50] In the small town of Zarka, seven miles northeast of Najaf, there were several days of vicious fighting against a troublesome armed group which called itself *Jund al-Samaa* (Soldiers of Heaven). An estimated 250 gunmen were killed and hundreds of others captured. The leader of the sect was later captured in Basra.[51] Most of all, though, the city of al-Amarah beckoned, the last stronghold of the Mahdi Army, the sanctuary handed to them by the British. Even in April it was an open secret that this was Maliki's main target, his aim being the complete destruction of Muqtada's militia.[52]

47. *Long War Journal*, 9 April 2008, 'A look at Operation Knights' Assault'.
48. *The Times*, 25 April 2008, 'The men in black vanish and Basra comes to life'.
49. *Long War Journal*, 28 October 2008, 'Iraqi forces detain 180 "suspects" during Basrah raids'.
50. *Aswat al-Iraq*, 31 March 2008, '85 gunmen killed, wounded in Thi-Qar – governor'.
51. *Aswat al-Iraq*, 2 June 2008, 'Armed group's spiritual theorist captured in Basra'.
52. Iranian Press TV, 22 April 2008, 'Sadr City carnage "planned years ago"'.

OPERATION PROMISE OF PEACE

Air operations started in early May with US Air Force and Navy bombers performing 'shows of force' and precision bombing through the month and into June. At one stage an RAF Tornado joined the fray.[53] More airpower, it seems, was committed to this stage of the operation than the British had enjoyed throughout their whole tenure. As this phase started, on 10 May Iraqi Special Operations Forces detained three suspected 'Special Groups criminals' in al-Amarah.[54]

Checkpoints had also been strengthened, with productive results. On 6 May police found weapons and ammunition near the Baghdad checkpoint, north of Amarah, presumably destined for Sadr City. The find included mortar bombs, 17 missiles, 18 anti-armour missiles, and 50 landmines. Separately, the police recovered 141 mortar rounds, 99 'cannonballs', 38 missiles, and 16 landmines.[55] On 5 June, the Special Operations unit mounted another raid into the city and captured one more 'criminal'.[56] As guests of the Iraqi Army, one can only speculate on the hospitality captives were afforded – and the intelligence they offered in exchange.

Tribal chiefs were enlisted in the fight and two battalions were raised from tribal groups, a local counter to the largely urban-recruited militias. A new police chief was appointed and police activity was stepped up. One early dividend was the arrest of 'two persons driving a motorcycle in possession of 25 anti-tank landmines'. Patrols also found 15 landmines in a stream near the district centre.[57] As this was going on, Army engineers cleared the main routes of IEDs. Some of them were found 'beneath important bridges'. A total of 38 were detected and neutralised. 'A number of the anti-armour charges defused were very developed and emplaced in strategic spots,' said an Iraqi spokesman.[58]

Then, nine days after the special forces' second raid, the Iraqi Army's 10th Division, special forces units and elements of the US 10th Mountain and 1st Cavalry Divisions – some 22,000 troops in all – poured into the area, ringing the city. Other forces sealed off the border with Iran. An operation called by the Americans, *Basha'er as-Salaam* – 'Promise of Peace' – had begun.[59] The Iraqis had been less sensitive. It was part of an overall

---

53. US Air Force News, 9 May 2008 *et seq.*, Daily airpower summary.
54. Operation Iraqi Freedom website, 11 May 2008, 'ISOF detains three suspected Special Groups criminals in al-Amarah'.
55. *Aswat al-Iraq*, 6 May 2008, 'Amount of weapons, ammunition found in Missan'.
56. *Free Republic*, 7 June 2008, 'ISOF captures Special Groups criminal'.
57. *Aswat al-Iraq*, 8 June 2008, 'Police patrols arrest 2 person in possession of 25 landmines in Missan'.
58. *Aswat al-Iraq*, 17 June 2008, '38 IEDs defused in Missan'.
59. AFP, 14 June 2008, 'Iraqi forces poised for attack on Amara'.

plan called *Fardh al-Qanoon* (Imposing the Law).[60] That is what it was to be.

Maliki issued an ultimatum to the Mahdi Army. Repeating the strategy he had used in Basra, he gave them four days to lay down their arms – offering an amnesty to those who did. He also offered cash for any heavy weapons surrendered. He was, he said, giving the 'outlaws and the members of the organised crime groups a last chance to review their stance'. Iraqi and US soldiers then set up security checkpoints on the main roads in the city, distributing leaflets urging people to stay indoors and remain calm.[61] Iraqi troops backed by US forces made targeted raids into the city, seizing a large weapons and ammunition cache from an old cemetery in the city centre.[62] Twelve staff of the central prison were arrested for hiding guns and explosives inside the jail.[63] All the while US Navy Hornets made low passes over the city while US helicopters scattered leaflets featuring pictures of wanted persons.[64]

By then the Mahdi Army had sustained losses of over 2,000 in the various operations against it – over 400 in Basra. Muqtada's power was bleeding away.[65] All that was left was bravado. Even as the Iraqi forces were assembling, he proclaimed in a letter read out in mosques that he was establishing 'a new fighting force'. It was a thinly disguised climb-down. Effectively, he was disbanding the Mahdi Army as a mass movement. Resistance would be exclusively conducted by only one group. 'This new group will be defined soon by me,' he stated. Weapons would be held exclusively by this new group, to be pointed exclusively at the 'occupier'. He would forbid the group 'to target anyone else'.[66] A day later, he announced that he was withdrawing his support for the political process, pulling out from the provincial elections scheduled for late January 2009.[67] Then, faced with the overwhelming force surrounding his stronghold, he sent a delegation to al-Amarah to order his fighters to stand down.[68]

The scene was set. At 5am local time on 19 June, after Maliki's ultimatum had expired, the main force moved in. Not a shot was fired. Militia fighters were seen throwing their weapons into the canals. One of the first targets for the troops was the Mayor, who was arrested and detained with about 16 other Sadr organisation officials.[69] Moving through the rest of

60. *Aswat al-Iraq*, 16 June 2008, 'MNF's role in Missan "consultative"'.
61. *International Herald Tribune*, 16 June 2008, 'Iraqi forces mass outside southern city of Amara'.
62. *Aswat al-Iraq*, 18 June 2008, 'Big weapons cache seized in cemetery in Amara'.
63. *Aswat al-Iraq*, 18 June 2008, '12 policemen arrested in Amara'.
64. *Aswat al-Iraq*, 14 June 2008, 'Missan residents urged to stay home when security operation begins'.
65. *Gulf News*, 26 June 2008, 'Mahdi Army militia "going underground"'.
66. CNN, 13 June 2008, 'Al-Sadr: New force to fight US in Iraq'.
67. *The Washington Post*, 15 June 2008, 'Powerful Iraqi cleric recalibrates strategy'.
68. *The Times*, 17 June 2008, 'Iraq gives al-Mahdi militia deadline to surrender its weapons'.
69. *International Herald Tribune*, 19 June 2008, 'Iraqi troops move into militia-held city of Amara'.

the silent, fearful city, the Iraqi Army brought with them a secret weapon – over 10,000 halal ready-meals. Setting up distribution points in 12 neighbourhoods, they handed them out to all comers. By midday, the streets were thronging with life. Following the troops were 'community transportation improvement teams', ready to start a programme of city public works and highway sanitation.[70] Before that, teams of national police joined with the troops to conduct house-to-house searches.[71]

Far from meeting resistance, as had the British, they found enthusiastic citizens telling them where to look. Within days they had detained approximately 200 militia and collected more than 220 weapon caches, distributed in homes, businesses and public areas throughout the city. A substantial cache was found in the 'office of a representative for Shiite cleric Muqtada al Sadr', and a bomb-making factory was discovered. Another was later found in a building 12 miles east of the city, 'thanks to local residents' co-operation with security forces'.[72] Overall, the haul amounted to 2,262 mortar bombs, 1,034 mines, 971 artillery rounds, 749 rocket-propelled grenades, 598 rockets, 259 missile launchers, 176 IEDs, 259 grenades, 43 heavy machine-gun barrels, 141 EFPs and 22 missiles. After a month of occupation, the Iraqi Army had not seen a single gunfight, not one IED attack, nor received any indirect fire.[73]

Operations continued in Maysan, occasionally meeting with sporadic resistance. It was quickly suppressed. Many more caches were found and many more arrests were made. On 16 August, Iraqi and US troops discovered near al-Amarah 250 EFP plates, 125 107mm rockets, two rocket launchers, 15 120mm mortar bombs, one mortar tube and two sniper rifles.[74]

By early October, Colonel Philip Battaglia, commander of the 4th Brigade Combat Team of the US Army's 1st Cavalry Division, was confident that resistance had been broken. The weapons haul now exceeded 8,000, including about 600 EFPs. Said Battaglia, 'al-Amarah … was an area where these devices were assembled and then from there shipped to other parts of the country, into Baghdad and other places'. He added, 'We believe – we know – that we have interrupted the flow of these explosives'.

Petraeus confirmed this observation, announcing that the flow of weapons was drying up throughout Iraq. 'We think we are literally running out of

70. Operation Iraqi Freedom website, 26 June 2008, 'DoD News Briefing: Col. Charles Flynn'.
71. *The New York Times*, 20 June 2008, 'Troops move into militia-held city of Amara'.
72. *Aswat al-Iraq*, 21 June 2008, 'Sticky IEDs factory seized east of Amara'.
73. Operation Iraqi Freedom website, 22 July 2008, 'New signs of peace continue in Amarah'.
74. Operation Iraqi Freedom website, 17 August 2008, 'IA, MND-C soldiers locate large weapons cache'.

safe havens and strongholds and starting to run out of these areas where there were these very significant caches,' he said.[75] He was not exaggerating. US engineers had since late July been finding a sharp fall in the number of IEDs placed. Insurgents, short of materials, were increasingly resorting to hoaxes, placing propane tanks, tyres and water jugs on the sides of the roads.[76] The scourge of al-Amarah had ended. The reckoning – for the British – was to come.

MALIKI GETS HIS REVENGE

The nemesis – appropriately enough, given Blair's enthusiasm for international law – was the UN Security Council Mandate. It was due to run out on 31 December 2008. Without alternative arrangements, foreign forces could no longer remain in the country. Through 2008, Maliki had been negotiating with the Americans on a new deal, concluding a 'Security Framework Agreement' in the November. This allowed US forces to stay until at least 2011. Then and only then did he turn to the rest of the coalition 'partners', including the UK.

Anticipating an unfavourable outcome, in July Brown had already visited Basra. Spinning furiously, he announced a 'historic realignment' in the war on terror. Gone were the military expectations articulated in August 2006 that the British would keep troops in Basra to 'protect our investment'.[77] Consigned to the dustbin were Blair's plans announced in February 2007. Troops were not going to stay for another five years. There would be no brigade stationed 'for at least until the Americans leave Iraq'.[78] Brown set out a 'four-point plan' for a complete pull-out by the end of 2009.[79] This was, of course, not a retreat. It was a 'fundamental change of mission'. Most of the troops would be redeployed to Afghanistan.

The 'chattering classes' saw this through the filter of UK domestic politics. It was giving Brown 'a platform for a general election campaign in the spring of 2010'.[80] They were completely wrong. On 9 December a 'senior defence source' revealed another change of plan. Withdrawal would start in March 2009 with almost all the troops out in a few months. Brown was expected to announce this in the January, his rationale the 'dramatic

75. Reuters, 9 October 2008, 'US Army says it has disrupted Iraq weapons'.

76. *Long War Journal*, 2 August 2008, 'IED hunters take on insurgency in northern Iraq'.

77. BBC, 22 August 2006, 'Basra handover "feasible" in 2007'.

78. *The Daily Telegraph*, 22 February 2007, '4,000 troops will stay in Iraq "for five years"'.

79. *The Independent*, 20 July 2008, 'Brown plans to withdraw troops as he backs Obama over "war on terror"'.

80. Patrick Hennessy, *Daily Telegraph* blog, 19 July 2008, 'Gordon Brown sets sights on Iraq troops withdrawal'.

improvement in security'.[81] The real reason was rather different. Maliki was about to kick the British out. He was not even prepared to give Brown the figleaf of being able to make the announcement himself.

The news broke in *The Independent* on 14 December.[82] Maliki was 'taking his revenge' on the British for surrendering Basra to the militias. *The Times* got the point the next day. 'Britain faces a humiliating Iraq withdrawal', it headlined.[83] Troops had to cease operations by March and get out of the country by the end of July. To add to the humiliation, Britain had been lumped in with the likes of Romania, El Salvador and Estonia, included in a 'mini-agreement for the six entities', separate from the US.

Britain had wanted a separate deal but the Iraqis had dismissed the idea, saying: 'There was no way we could have done a security agreement to the same level of detail that we had with the Americans in such a short period.' Britain was just another 'entity'. A senior British official observed:

We should not forget how angry – and mistrustful of the British – Maliki is for allowing the Shia militias to take over in Basra. He regards the British as having entirely sold the pass. It is true that it suits him, for domestic political reasons, to be seen to be giving the British a hard time, but it happens to be something he feels very cross about.

The wider media response to the news was mixed. *The Guardian* contented itself with, 'Not a moment too soon'.[84] *The Times* lamented that the Americans would reap the benefits as they moved in to fill the gap.[85] Patrick Cockburn's view was that, 'Britain's long campaign in Iraq achieved almost nothing'.[86]

To many, it did not matter one way or another. They were just happy to see 'our boys' come home. Thomas Harding, who had covered so much of the story from the front line, was in Basra when the news broke. There, as half-a-dozen British officers shed their body armour and deposited themselves at a table in the once notorious Hayaniya district, Colonel Richard Stanford said: 'Last year we would have been dead at least 10 minutes ago if we had sat here.' Across the street was a long wide strip of green that had been used by insurgents for firing rockets and mortars. It had been the scene of some of the toughest street-fighting experienced by the British Army since the Second World War. 'Yet here we were,' wrote Harding, 'chatting to the locals and sipping sweetened black tea.'

General Dannatt was not impressed by the media responses, questioning 'the wisdom of some of the armchair critics'. 'We have been quite clear

81. *The Independent*, 10 December 2008, 'British troops to start Iraq pullout in March'.
82. *The Independent*, 14 December 2008, 'Maliki takes revenge over new mandate'.
83. *The Times*, 15 December 2008, 'Britain faces humiliating Iraq withdrawal'.
84. *The Guardian*, 17 December 2008, 'Troops out of Iraq: Not a moment too soon'.
85. *The Times*, 18 December 2008, 'Americans will reap benefits of withdrawal'.
86. *The Independent*, 18 December 2008, 'Our troops had few friends in Basra'.

about what we had to do and we have done it and we are going to leave in the early part of next year because the job is done,' he said. Nigel Haywood, the Consul General in Basra, argued that there would have been no Iraqi army to fight the insurgents without British training. 'We beat ourselves up about this, but the military have done an astonishing job in appalling circumstances,' he said. Harding himself concluded: 'We might indeed come to look upon Basra as a success story – but if we are to win out in the far more challenging arena of Afghanistan, then the Army had better change, and change soon.' [87]

The great problem was that the Army did not see any need to change. Since it had been victorious – as it had been in Northern Ireland – having achieved what it had set out to achieve, why should it change? Thus imbued with its sense of righteousness, it celebrated the despatch of Snatch 'Vixens' – modified Snatches with additional, bolt-on armour – to Afghanistan.

87. *The Daily Telegraph*, 12 December 2008, 'Iraq: After Basra, a new reality'.

Chapter 11 – Armchair Generals

A war lost ... another to win ...
from Iraq to Afghanistan

*We ought to be very careful about commenting from the comparative comfort
of wherever we are, when we are not out there on operations, about decisions
that operational commanders and other people make.*

DES BROWNE, SECRETARY OF STATE FOR DEFENCE
SKY NEWS, LONDON, 6 APRIL 2007

Faced with media criticisms of the Iraqi operation, Dannatt was by no
means the only one to round on 'armchair critics'. At the height of the
Iranian hostages affair in April 2007, there had been much speculation
about the apparent willingness of the boarding team to surrender without
a shot being fired. Des Browne had sprung to the team's defence, castigat-
ing the 'armchair pundits'. 'We ought to be very careful about commenting
from the comparative comfort of wherever we are, when we are not out
there on operations, about decisions that operational commanders and
other people make,' he said.

It was perhaps a little unkind to point out that, when it came to arm-
chairs, the MoD was better equipped than most. To complement the £2.3
billion refurbishment of its headquarters in Whitehall, it had purchased
over 3,000 Herman Miller Aeron chairs, described as 'the most comfortable
office chairs in the world' – at a list price of over £1,000 each. The media had
not been reticent about pointing out the cost and making comparisons,
not least noting that the Navy was considering mothballing up to half its
44 ships to save money.[1,2] The contrast between sending out lightly armed
sailors and marines in rubber boats without a warship to protect them,
while 'fatcat bureaucrats' – military and civilian – swanned around in their
luxurious headquarters, was easy to make.

On the other hand, it was easy for the military to dismiss its critics,
which it did with unfailing regularity, 'gobshite civilians' being one of the
more colourful epithets directed at those incautious enough to question
their equipment or tactics. 'Armchair generals' was another.

1. *The Times*, 7 January 2007, 'MoD spends £2.3bn on Whitehall offices'.
2. *The Daily Mail*, 8 January 2007, 'MoD spends £2.3 billion on new offices while families of soldiers
live in "squalor"'.

AN ARMY INCAPABLE OF LEARNING

This was an Army which seemed incapable of learning. For instance, with troops deployed in Afghanistan, albeit in small numbers before 2006, routine patrols in the capital Kabul had been carried out in Wolf Land Rovers. Sure enough, on 28 January 2004, a patrol was attacked by a suicide bomber, killing Pte Jonathan Kitulagoda and destroying the Land Rover.[3] As in Iraq, the Army replaced these vehicles with Snatches. Sure enough, on 4 September 2006, a patrol was attacked by a suicide bomber, killing Pte Craig O'Donnell. Four Afghani civilians were also killed and another soldier was very seriously injured.[4]

Just over a month later, on 19 October, Marine Gary Wright, 45 Commando Royal Marines, was killed in a Snatch as it left the police station in Lashkar Gah, the regional capital of Helmand Province. A suicide bomber had been waiting for his convoy. The Snatch was destroyed, one other Royal Marine was seriously injured and two children bystanders were killed.[5]

In all, up to the end of 2008, at least 10 soldiers died in Snatches in Afghanistan, culminating in an infamous incident on 16 June 2008. Then, four soldiers were killed in a Snatch, three from the SAS and one female soldier, Sarah Bryant. Another soldier was badly injured. The use of the Snatch was roundly condemned as 'cavalier at best, criminal at worst', by Major Sebastian Morley, the soldiers' CO. Having tendered his resignation, he claimed that Whitehall officials and military commanders had repeatedly ignored his warnings. Troops would be killed if they continued to allow them to be transported in this vulnerable vehicle, he had protested. He had not been alone. 'We highlighted this issue saying people are going to die and now they have died,' said a soldier who served with Major Morley, referring to a vehicle that the troops were calling 'mobile coffins'.[6]

DEFENCE OF THE SNATCH

Far from being contrite, the MoD robustly defended the Snatch. In the immediate aftermath of the June incident, Defence Minister Bob Ainsworth had in the Commons insisted that 'commanders on the ground' were telling him they still needed Land Rover-based platforms '… and they will do for the foreseeable future.'[7, 8] Weathering aggressive oral questions and

3. BBC, 29 January 2004, 'Part-time soldier dies in bombing'.
4. BBC, 4 September 2006, 'Kabul suicide bomber kills five'.
5. BBC, 20 October 2006, 'Afghanistan bombing marine named'.
6. *The Daily Telegraph*, 3 November 2008, 'SAS chief quits over "negligence that killed his troops"'.
7. Hansard, 19 June 2008: Column 1124.
8. *The Guardian*, 19 June 2008, 'Minister defends use of light armoured vehicles in Afghanistan'.

even a question to the Prime Minister, the MoD maintained its fightback.[9] This culminated in briefings to MPs and media on 16 December from none other than Lt-Gen Nick Houghton, now Chief of Joint Operations.[10] Patronising in tone and simplistic in content, Houghton's dissertation amounted to an admission that, as long as there was a tactical need for a light protected vehicle, the Snatch would have to remain in service. There was no other option. 'You may have heard of alternatives,' he said, 'but at present no acceptable alternative vehicle exists though they are being actively sought.'

THE VECTOR – A 'COFFIN ON WHEELS'

What Houghton admitted to journalists after his formal presentation, though, was that there had been an alternative. This was the Pinzgauer Vector, about which the Army had been so enthusiastic in July 2006. Then, it had prevailed upon Des Browne to buy more – its price for accepting the Mastiff which it had not wanted. A clear record of the Army's intent had been delivered in March 2007 – by Houghton himself.[11] He then told the Commons Defence Committee that once the Vector had been deployed fully, 'the more vulnerable Snatch would be withdrawn from service in Afghanistan'.[12]

There were hints of a problem in June 2008 in a published list of 'expected out-of-service dates' for a range of vehicles. The Vector was given a date of 2015.[13] In an Army that routinely kept vehicles for 30 years or more, a mere seven-year service life was unprecedented. Therein lay a tale which raises serious questions about the competence and good faith of those involved in the procurement of Army vehicles. The Vector had 'proved inadequate, unable to cope with the threat from roadside bombs'.[14]

In June 2006, when the Army ordered its first batch of 80 Vectors, at a cost of £35 million, the intention – or so it was claimed – had been 'to counter the threat posed by suicide bombers'. It had been adapted for use in 'high-risk' environments and would thus 'protect troops from automatic fire, landmines and fragmentation bombs'. Even then, it was reported, senior officers believed the greatest threat to British troops would come

9. Hansard, 5 November 2008: Column 251.
10. Nick Houghton, 19 December 2008, 'Remember the Pigs? Lessons for Snatch Landrover critics'.
11. *The Daily Telegraph*, 13 November 2008, 'Broken promise on Snatch vehicles'.
12. House of Commons Defence Committee, 3 July 2007, UK operations in Afghanistan, Thirteenth Report of Session 2006–2007, p. 32.
13. Hansard, 3 June 2008: Column WA30.
14. *The Daily Mail*, 16 December 2008, 'Government refuses to remove "killer" Snatch Land Rovers from Afghanistan and Iraq'.

from suicide bombers and insurgents 'armed with the same improvised explosive devices that have been used against lightly armoured vehicles in Iraq'.[15]

This 'armchair general', however, expressed alarm at these 'coffins on wheels'. The concern was based on the manufacturer's specifications, which claimed protection against 'two NATO L2A2 hand grenades detonating simultaneously only 150mm below the floor pan' – 350g of high explosive. The vehicle was to be deployed to one of the heaviest mined countries in the world, up against Russian anti-tank mines housing 7.5kg of high explosive.[16] More alarmingly, the Vector had a 'cab forward' layout, with the driver and the front seat passenger seated over the wheel arches. If a mine detonated under a wheel, either the driver or the passenger would be directly in the so-called 'cone of destruction', exposed to the full force of the blast.[17] At least with the Snatch and its 'engine forward' layout, there was some distance between the front wheels and the occupants of the cab, allowing, as some did, soldiers to escape the full force of a mine and survive.[18]

Had it deliberately sought out a design to maximise deaths and injuries, the Army, in selecting the Vector, could not have made a better choice. Furthermore, the vehicle was not cheap. Including the support package, each cost £437,000. They were not only 'coffins on wheels', they were very expensive coffins. The £258,000 price of a Force Protection Cougar – on which the Mastiff was based – was better value.[19]

Predictably – totally and completely predictably – within months of the Vector being deployed, a fatality was reported. This was on 25 July 2007 when L/Cpl Alex Hawkins and others, 'had been taking part in a routine patrol and were returning to their patrol base when the explosion struck their Vector'. Hawkins was killed and two soldiers were injured. The Vector had to be destroyed to avoid it falling into enemy hands.[20] *Channel 4 News* noted:

Vector, which is more suitable for rugged terrain than the army's existing Snatch patrol vehicle, was recently introduced as part of a package of measures designed to increase

15. *The Sunday Telegraph*, 29 April 2006, 'Army gets £35m vehicles to protect patrols from suicide bombers'.

16. *Defence of the Realm*, 26 June 2006, 'Coffins on wheels'.

17. Geneva International Centre for Humanitarian Demining, undated, Mechanical Study, Chapter 5, 'The protection of vehicles and plant equipment against mines and UXO'.

18. In September 2007, the then manufacturers of Pinzgauers unveiled the Pinzgauer II, known as the 'Mantis', with an engine-forward layout, thus offering an 'additional' mine blast protection capability. See: BAE Systems: Press Release, 11 September 2007, 'BAE Systems launches new Pinzgauer vehicle at DSEi exhibition'.

19. *Defence of the Realm*, 24 July 2006, 'Corporate manslaughter'.

20. MoD website, 26 June 2006, 'Lance Corporal Alex Hawkins 1st Battalion The Royal Anglian Regiment killed in Afghanistan'.

troops' safety in Iraq and Afghanistan. The first Vectors began arriving in the country in April of this year and are being phased in, set to replace most of the Snatch vehicles by late October.[21]

How many non-fatal incidents occurred we have no means of knowing but reports from serving troops recorded that the 'ambulance' section of their flights home were frequently occupied by soldiers who had lost their legs from mine blasts.[22] There is no means of knowing either how many soldiers were killed in Vectors. Conscious of the potential for damaging publicity, the MoD stopped reporting the types of vehicle involved in fatal incidents. But we do know that, from October 2007 when Snatches were supposed to have been replaced, there had been only one fatal incident involving a Snatch – killing Sarah Bryant and her colleagues – as against three known fatal Vector incidents. There has since been one more, bringing the known total to four.[23]

There was one more twist to this debacle. Another Snatch replacement could have been available. In April 2008, months before Sarah Bryant and her colleagues had died, the MoD had ordered 24 mine-protected Bushmasters, exclusively for the Special Forces. Had the British emulated the Dutch and called off vehicles directly from the Australian Army stock of 400, they could have been on a freight aircraft within weeks and been issued to units in Afghanistan by May. This vehicle could readily have resisted the attack that had killed four people and injured another.[24]

In what might be the final chapter, however, in December 2008, General Sir Kevin O'Donoghue was giving evidence about the Vector to the Defence Select Committee. Without so much as a blush, he told MPs, 'You produce a solution for the requirement of the time; the requirement changes as the threat changes, as the security architecture changes and you need to produce something else.'[25]

That 'something else' was in the pipeline. In February 2009, the MoD quietly issued – without any public statement – a request for 'expressions of interest' from manufacturers willing to supply 'up to 400 Light Protected Patrol Vehicles (LPPV)'. These had to be production-ready in 2010, for delivery into service in 2011. They were to replace 'light legacy platforms' based on the Snatch and could be used as the basis for the replacement of the Wimik. They had to provide high cross-country mobility *and* the

---

21. ITN *Channel 4 News*, 25 July 2007, 'British soldier killed in Afghanistan'.
22. Personal communications.
23. *Defence of the Realm*, 13 November 2008, 'That rarest of commodities'.
24. *Defence of the Realm*, 3 November 2008, 'The ugly face of politics'.
25. House of Commons Defence Committee, 16 December 2008, uncorrected transcript of oral evidence.

specification required them to be mine-resistant.[26] Given the time scale, the only vehicles that could have been supplied were types already available before the Vector had been purchased. Houghton's 'acceptable alternative' that did not exist seems to have existed after all.

Meanwhile, Royal Marine Commandos in Afghanistan, forced to use the Snatches which should by then already have been replaced, were complaining of being a 'laughing stock'. 'You show it to the Yanks and they are laughing at us,' said one. An RM officer, Major Reggie Turner, in defence of the vehicle, claimed that their versatility and manoeuvrability provided crucial 'situational awareness' which would be lost in bigger vehicles.[27] This brought to mind the 'immortal words' of a British officer in Iraq, who had roundly declared, 'One should never confuse situational awareness with knowing what is actually going on.'[28] Not a few people might have benefited for knowing what was 'actually going on'.

DEFENCE OF A FAILED STRATEGY

Tragically, while Snatch was getting the lion's share of attention – greater than in 2005, when so many more soldiers were being killed – troops were being killed and injured in a far more dangerous vehicle, one which had been slated as a replacement for the Snatch. No wonder the Snatch Vixen was rushed in to plug the gap. No wonder Lt-Gen Houghton and the MoD had been defensive.

There was though, more to Houghton's defensiveness. As indicated right at the start of this book, the Snatch was more than just a vehicle. It was the embodiment of a mindset. The vehicle filled an operational requirement, reflecting the Army's approach to counter-insurgency. As Houghton explained in his briefing:

In counter insurgency environments, other factors play into the desired capability mix. Most obvious amongst such factors are first the physical accessibility of vehicles in built up areas and narrow streets … Second the physical profile of the vehicle and its affect [*sic*] on the local people.

Third the ability of a vehicle to allow its occupants to interact with the local population and to allow observation of local atmospherics. And finally I would say the physical effect that a vehicle has in respect of the likelihood of it damaging local infrastructure such as mud walls and weakly constructed roads and culverts and thereby alienating the local population.

The Snatch was essential to the Army's 'hearts and minds' strategy. But what Houghton did not explain was that there were two parts to this strategy,

26. Public Sector Tenders, 17 February 2009, Contract Notice: 2009/S 32-046827.
27. *Western Morning News*, 24 February 2009, 'We're a laughing stock'.
28. *Space Review*, 12 February 2007, 'The space weapons debate, continued'.

summed up as 'go light – go heavy'. The essence was outlined in a joint US/UK study of the British approach to 'low intensity operations' in Iraq. This grouped armour into two packages. The Challengers and the Warriors were the 'heavies', the Snatch, obviously, the 'light'. Thus:

Warriors and ultimately Challengers were found to send a very strong statement whereas the use of Snatch vehicles ... sent an entirely different message. During difficult periods, having such impressive physical capabilities greatly enhanced the ability to ramp up and down between stances, maintaining British credibility as a serious fighting force.[29]

The strategy amounted to sending messages, essentially paternalistic in nature. If the citizens were good, daddy would use Snatches. If they were naughty, daddy would send out the Warriors. If they were very naughty, daddy would get *really* cross and inflict Challengers on them. If they then behaved, it was back to Snatches as a reward ... go light, go heavy – go light, exactly the rhythm to which the Staffords had been exposed in al-Amarah in 2005 with such tragic consequences. The problem, of course, was that the insurgents did not quite see things like that. Going 'light' meant offering them targets. When the British upped the ante and escorted the Snatches with Warriors, the insurgents learnt how to take out Warriors. When the Challengers appeared, they learnt how to take them out as well. After that, the British had nowhere to go, other than their bases – where they became ... targets.

One thing the study also noted was the 'instinctive reluctance of junior officers to rely heavily on technology to assist in their tactical decision-making'. Was it 'based on ill-founded conservatism or on a justified concern with how it may adversely influence their instincts?', it asked. It failed to note that, *pace* Lt-Col Labouchere, technophobia was not confined to junior officers. However, the point was made – that technology was not always part of the British force mix. More worryingly, it was not part of the intellectual make-up of the Army.

AFGHANISTAN – SAME STRATEGY, SAME ERRORS

In Afghanistan, the strategy was different, and the same. In the low population density rural areas in which the Army was now fighting, 'routine patrols' were still a major part of the work programme. 'Mowing the grass,' it was called. But, with few roads and many of them in poor condition or little more than tracks, the emphasis was on off-road performance. This

29. Department of Defense, Office of Force Transformation, Washington, DC, 20303, DGMC, Ministry of Defence, 12 February 2007, 'The British approach to low-intensity operations Part II'.

paved the way for another procurement disaster or, more specifically, another armoured round peg in a square hole.

Deployed with great fanfare in October 2006 were Viking tracked 'all terrain vehicles', developed for the Royal Marines as lightly armoured amphibious assault vehicles. At £1 million each, they were hailed uncritically by the media as giving 'far greater protection than the infamous Snatch'. Nevertheless, the ballistic protection was about the same and the mine protection was pathetic, proof against 0.5kg anti-personnel mines. Inevitably, the casualty figures mounted as these machines were ripped apart, with six dead and an unknown number of injured.[30] To counter this, the MoD propaganda machine published a gushing 'puff' in January 2007, proclaiming 'Viking vehicles are saving lives in Afghanistan', and another in the September announcing: 'Viking vehicles prove their worth in volatile Helmand.'[31, 32]

Contrasting with the MoD's heavy promotion of its favoured vehicle, it was left to freelance journalist Nigel Green to write up testimonials for the unloved Mastiff. In a regional newspaper, he wrote of soldiers' experiences in Afghanistan. One, Pte Stephen MacLauchlan, had survived four RPGs hitting his vehicle. Another, Pte Lee Ashton, had been on a mission to supply food and water to frontline troops when his Mastiff had hit an anti-tank mine. It blew off the front tyre and wheel arch but the vehicle kept driving. Then there was Pte Lee Jones. He was in a Mastiff when it hit an anti-tank mine. 'There was a big explosion and a lot of dust. It lifted the vehicle between seven and eight feet,' he said. 'It was like a car crash. It blew the front wheels off, but this vehicle is brilliant. It saved my life. It has saved a lot of lives.'[33]

Tucked away in an obscure newspaper, without analysis or given a wider context, the obvious lessons were not spelled out. But the ultimate reason for the defeat in Iraq was there, in black and white. In Afghanistan, the Mastiffs were keeping the troops moving – and safe. In Iraq, there had been too few of them and they had arrived too late.

There was still that major problem with the Mastiff. It was too big and too heavy for many roles. In that, Houghton was perfectly correct – but then the 6×6 had been the MoD's choice. There always had been lighter MRAPs available and that issue was being addressed. In an opaque statement to Parliament in December 2007, Gordon Brown announced that, at a cost of £150 million, 150 'additional protected vehicles' were to be

30. *Defence of the Realm*, 23 December 2008, 'Sooner kill than cure'.
31. MoD website, 10 January 2007, 'Viking vehicles are saving lives in Afghanistan'.
32. MoD website, 12 September 2007, 'Viking vehicles prove their worth in volatile Helmand'.
33. *The Northern Echo*, 27 August 2007, 'Soldiers tell of escapes after vehicles targeted'.

procured.[34] Defence Minister Bob Ainsworth gave them a name – Ridgebacks. There were no questions from MPs. They were more concerned with services housing and the treatment of injured troops.[35]

Almost as if it was ashamed of what it had done, the MoD offered little more information. Not until April 2008 did it emerge via the US government that the Ridgeback was the 4×4 version of the Cougar.[36] Furthermore, it was to be fitted with a 'Remote Weapon Station'. Gone was the idea of giving soldiers guns and sticking them through holes in roofs – exposing them to sniper fire and blast from IEDs. This was a remote-controlled machine gun, with a powerful visible spectrum and infra-red video camera which acted as a sight for the gun and could be used for area surveillance. Images could be viewed on a unit similar to a laptop from the comfort and safety of the (air-conditioned) armoured compartment, the gun trained and fired by a joystick that bore some resemblance to that used in computer games. The Army was catching up with the 21st century.

There was an added benefit. Similar in principle to the gun sights on US Abrams tanks, their gunners had routinely been using the infra-red capability for other purposes. On early morning patrols, before the sun had baked the ground, recently disturbed earth gave a characteristic infra-red signature, indicating the potential presence of a buried bomb.[37] Of course, the equipment was too late for Iraq. The first Ridgebacks, sent to the UK for adaptation to British military specification, arrived in August 2008.[38]

LIGHT AVIATION

Surveillance cameras with the same capabilities had been fitted to light aircraft supplied to the Iraqi Air Force – militarised two-seater, single-engined club trainers called the Sama 2000. The aircraft purchased for £363,000 each, their equipment was capable of detecting a man-sized target at two miles range from 2,000ft – or a hidden bomb. Although the aircraft were limited in their capabilities, they carried exactly the same optical equipment as the giant, four-engined Nimrod MR2 maritime surveillance aircraft, one of which was so tragically to crash in Afghanistan in September 2006. They were occasionally used to support British forces in Maysan.

34. PR Newswire, 12 December 2007, 'PM announces additional protected vehicles for Afghanistan'.
35. Hansard, 12 December 2007: Column 332.
36. Defense Security Cooperation Agency, 9 April 2008, News release: 'United Kingdom – Mine Resistant Ambush Protected (MRAP) Vehicles'.
37. Personal communication.
38. MoD website, 14 August 2008, 'Antonov delivers first Ridgbacks to Brize'.

The main support, though, was the fleet of Nimrods. They were operated out of Oman, flying up the Gulf and deep inland. Costing £30,000 an hour on sorties of 12 hours duration – more with air-to-air refuelling – three days-worth of flying set back the military budget £1 million.[39] The Samas, at a fraction of the cost, could have provided a 'good enough' solution to the problem of providing low-level airborne surveillance.[40] But that was not the British way. While 'good enough' was entirely acceptable as a military solution to Iraq, when it came to equipment it was not. There, the answer was hugely expensive adapted maritime aircraft or £30 million Future Lynx helicopters delivered in 2014 or sometime never – with very similar camera equipment. The best was the enemy of the good.

This lack of flexibility and the determination to opt for the 'best' long-term solution – even though it would not be available for many years – was to deprive the Army of crucial air support. Through the Second World War, it had enjoyed its own light reconnaissance capability with the single-engined Auster – another adapted club aircraft. Operating in far more dangerous environments than Iraq, its losses were remarkably low. The type was used in Aden and Oman, supplemented by the more powerful DHC Beaver, which also flew in Northern Ireland where it was the Army's primary surveillance platform. In other Armies, light fixed-wing aviation also had a long history. For instance, the Australian Army in the Vietnam War operated the Pilatus Porter for reconnaissance, liaison and for communications relay, the latter function carried out in Iraq by the Nimrod.

The Porter was an interesting aircraft. With exceptional short-field performance, it is still in production. Its airframe costs around £2 million and it has low operating costs (under £2,000 an hour). It, or something similar, could have provided a useful stopgap. In the early 1970s, however, the Army Air Corps had converted to an all-helicopter fleet, so a fixed-wing option could not be considered.

There were a few exceptions. One of those was the two-engined Britten-Norman Defender surveillance aircraft. Four were purchased in 2003, at a total cost of £18 million.[41] Some were deployed to Iraq but, despite extensive inquiries, no reports of their performance were ever released. They cannot have been overly successful because in May 2007 the MoD ordered replacements: four highly sophisticated Beechcraft King Air 350 aircraft – designated the Shadow R. They cost £14 million each. Not intended for service until 2010, these were far too late for Iraq.

---

39. Hansard, 26 November 2007: Column 4W.
40. *Defence of the Realm*, 5 March 2007, 'Value for money'.
41. Hansard, 29 March 2007: Column 1670W.

Meanwhile, the RAF had been waiting for five twin-jet R1 Sentinel surveillance aircraft, ordered in 1999 at a cost of just over £1 billion. Each was equipped with high-performance radar based on that used in the later versions of the U-2 'spy-plane' of Cold War fame. With it, an aircraft could detect footprints in the desert sand from an altitude of 20,000ft. Originally intended to be operational by 2005, the date was deferred to 2007 because of development problems, then to 2008 and finally to 2010, once again far too late for Iraq.[42]

This was a disease affecting the whole military establishment. With no end of high-performance kit just over the horizon, the money had been committed yet the capabilities were not available. Their effect was to block – both financially and intellectually – consideration of stopgap solutions that were 'good enough' to solve immediate problems.

DEMISE OF THE VIKING

Unfortunately, all too often, the MoD's idea of 'best' was not even 'good enough'. With so many torn apart by mines, in October 2008 it admitted defeat and announced it would replace the Viking. A new vehicle code-named 'Bronco' was to be supplied. The *Daily Mail* reported:

The £1million Viking amphibious combat vehicle was hailed as a triumph when it first arrived in Helmand Province in 2006, offering unprecedented agility as it swam across rivers and charged over the most rugged terrain, even clambering over ditches and walls. But in a sign of the increasing ferocity of the fighting against the Taliban, the Viking's armour has proved unable to protect soldiers and Marines from roadside bombs and buried mines, and at least six drivers are understood to have been killed in explosions.[43]

Nevertheless, official spokesman Colonel Charlie Clee did not demonstrate any great understanding of the reasons why the vehicle had failed. Flat bottomed with a thin-skinned underbelly, the Viking embodied all the inadequacies of contemporary military vehicle design, a reflection of the almost complete inability to take the mine/IED threat seriously. Clee's view was: 'You simply cannot protect against everything. If you built the perfectly-protected armoured vehicle it would be too heavy to move.' In December, the MoD unveiled the Bronco. It was very similar to the Viking, with the same basic design flaws – but it had heavier armour.[44]

---

42. *The Times*, 15 February 2009, 'Life-saving Sentinel R1 spy planes grounded by lack of crews'.
43. *The Daily Mail*, 29 October 2008, 'MoD forced to shell out extra £700million on tougher fighting vehicles after just two years'.
44. MoD website, 19 December 2008, 'The Warthog is on its way'.

THE RE-EQUIPMENT PACKAGE

Some lessons had been partially absorbed. The October announcement on the Viking had also heralded the purchase of a £700 million package of new armour, Des Browne's last 'gift' to the Army before he had been reshuffled to the back-benches. This included a range of 'support vehicles', some 400 in all, split into three categories, heavy, medium and light. They were code-named respectively, 'Wolfhound', 'Husky' and 'Coyote'. Canine names for armoured vehicles had become the fashion.[45]

The Wolfhound was good news. It was a cargo version of the Mastiff, developed in a mere nine weeks by its manufacturer, Force Protection Inc. On the other hand, the Husky was not good news. For inexplicable reasons, the MoD had rejected a number of sound, purpose-designed MRAP solutions and instead had opted for a conversion of an American-built civilian pick-up truck.[46] In classic style, the Army had gone for the solution adopted in 1905 by the French, for the first ever production armoured car, the Charron. It had bolted armour onto an existing commercial vehicle.[47]

The Coyote was even worse. It was to be a six-wheel version of the Army's newly introduced Jackal 'light strike vehicle', itself a partial replacement for the Land Rover 'Wimik'. Like the Snatch, the development and introduction of this vehicle illustrated another procurement debacle. This stemmed from the mid-1980s when, like virtually every other in the world, the Army had fielded an armoured car, then the Fox. However, when this equipment was retired, no replacement had been decided upon, leaving a major capability gap.

Here, the Army had no alternative but to use a stopgap, pressing into service stripped-down Land Rovers. These gradually evolved into a purpose-built conversion, lightly armoured, with roll bars, and – usually – a .50 cal machine gun on a ring mount and a secondary GPMG operated by the front seat passenger. The conversion was known as the Land Rover Weapons Mounted Installation Kit, or more conveniently as the 'Wimik'. As with the Viking and the Vector, it was not mine-protected. In Afghanistan, the Taleban extracted a terrible toll. At one time, the Army was losing more than one Wimik a week, with dozens of soldiers being terribly injured. At least 10 were killed.

With no plans to buy more Land Rovers – the manufacturer not in any event interested in building small numbers of specialist vehicles – the Army cast around for a replacement. It aimed for something more substantial, with better off-road performance, longer range and more load-carrying

45. MoD website, 29 October 2008, 'New armoured vehicles for Afghanistan'.
46. MoD website, 19 November 2008, 'Preferred bidders named for new breed of armoured vehicles'.
47. *Defence of the Realm*, 20 January 2008, 'Time to go back to basics'.

capacity. Enter the Jackal. Originally designated the M-Wimik (the 'M' standing for mobility), this made a public appearance in June 2007. It was immediately dubbed the 'Mad Max monster', resembling as it did the machines seen in the *Mad Max* films. *The Mail on Sunday* was particularly gushing, referring to its 'awesome firepower' (two machine guns, the same as the Wimik) which was to be 'unleashed' on the Taleban.[48]

In fact, the vehicle was not new. It had been developed for the SAS as a replacement for the 'Pink Panther', a stripped-down Land Rover Series 3, from which had emerged the Wimik concept. It had been in Afghanistan for at least a year.[49] Moreover, it was not a purpose-designed fighting vehicle, but a Supacat HMT 400 high-mobility truck. Once again, the Army had bought a 'truck with guns'. Alarmingly, it was completely unarmoured and, like the Vector, had a 'cab forward' design. Only the thinnest sheets of metal separated the driver and the front gunner from the wheels. The design was lethal. In the field, troops were lining their seats with 'ballistic matting' – Kevlar pads – as makeshift armour, also strapping pads on the sides of their vehicles in an attempt to overcome the obvious weaknesses. The same stratagem had been used on the original Land Rover Wimik. This was the best a 21st-century Army could do – send its troops to war in trucks with bits of armour tied onto them?

The new batch of vehicles had been specified without armour, but in April 2008 they re-emerged sporting two tons of armour around the cab and sides, bringing the weight to seven tons. It was now a truck, with guns, with bolt-on armour. This did not stop the MoD gushing that the 'awesome firepower and agility puts Jackal in a class of its own'. Major Tom Wood, 'part of the team that produced the vehicle', burbled: 'I don't think we, as an Army, have ever bought such an incredible piece of kit before. It packs as much power as some of our tanks!'[50] It had exactly the same 'power' as the secondary armament of a US World War II Sherman tank.

Soldiers, as one might expect, loved it. Compared with being cooped up in the back of a Snatch or an overheated Warrior, driving in the desert in this powerful beast was not an unattractive proposition. Criticisms of the vehicle attracted passionate rebuttals, except from the six soldiers who were blown apart by mines or IEDs, and the unknown number injured. Up to March 2009, after six months in service, 18 vehicles had been lost, out of 120 deployed. Nevertheless, with the Jackal firmly entrenched in the Army inventory, it was given a matching 'support vehicle' – so compounding the original error.

48. *The Mail on Sunday*, 23 June 200, 'The 80mph "Mad Max" monster targeting the Taliban'.
49. With Special Forces and the Special Forces Support Group. Personal communication.
50. MoD website, 8 April 2008, 'Awesome firepower and agility puts Jackal in class of its own'.

STRATEGIC ERRORS IN AFGHANISTAN

More to the point, this vehicle was a *strategic* error, reflecting – as had the Snatch in Iraq – a flawed approach to fighting the insurgency in Afghanistan. A country wracked by 30 years of war needs more than anything, repair and redevelopment. The key to that is roads – building, rebuilding and repair – on which everything else depends. With 80 per cent of the population rurally based, the primary need was for rural roads linking to the main centres and thence to the international network where maximum value could be gained from the sale of crops. Yet, of the billions in aid pouring into the country, only about 10 per cent went into rural development and, of that, only about 10 per cent went into the road programme.

Much of that money was unspent. It was in the hands of civilian agencies. They required security. With the Army unable to guarantee that, redevelopment in key areas stalled. The fatal flaw was in separating security from redevelopment, making one dependent on the other. Yet, in the longer term, it is redevelopment which brings peace. If the civilian agencies cannot work in insecure areas, the Army has to carry out redevelopment, the priority being the road network. Therefore, high-mobility patrol vehicles are not the priority. This should be combat engineers, plant and armoured road-building equipment. Rather than responding to the poor condition of the roads with off-road vehicles, the better option is to build new roads along which military – and civilian – traffic could pass.

Apart from the broad strategic advantages, this has other benefits. One of the most difficult tasks for security forces in fighting guerrillas is to bring them to battle on their terms. Building roads, with the economic and social benefits that accrue from them, presents the Taleban with targets they cannot afford to ignore – small wonder they have expended much energy on disrupting even the pitiful programme that has been undertaken. With the Army building roads, choosing the times and places, it regains the initiative. This is one of the quintessential requirements for success, one enumerated by *Sun Tzu* and by other successful generals, from Hannibal and Napoleon to Montgomery.[51]

In indulging its obsession for high-performance off-road vehicles, the Army was equipping itself for a war that it was comfortable with, rather than the war that needed to be fought. The Jackal, together with other 'boy racer' kit, indicated that the Army's strategic direction and tactics were wrong. Once again, equipment – and the procurement decisions that preceded it – were the window which revealed its underlying thinking.

51. The above analysis is based on a detailed study undertaken by the author, published in *Defence of the Realm*, 7 July 2008, 'Winning the War'.

THE 'TALISMAN' PROJECT

From the October package, there were other conclusions to be drawn. Alongside the support vehicles was a project codenamed 'Talisman', intended for mine clearance. It comprised three components, the Buffalo, more Mastiffs and vehicles described as the 'Engineer Excavator'. From the background to each, and a notable omission, there was information to be gleaned about how and why equipment was bought, on failures in the procurement system and, ultimately, how and why the Army won and lost wars – not that it had been doing any winning of late.

First, the Buffalo: ordered three years almost to the day since Sgt Hickey had died investigating the roadside for the presence of IEDs. Many more had since died doing the same thing. The Army, at last, was to obtain these life-saving machines. That it had taken so long was not just a failure of government. It was also a failure of the entire political system. Political pressure, as much as anything, had brought the Mastiff into service. A good part of that came from the opposition, focusing and ganging up on the government, insisting – with the weight of public opinion behind it – that something be done about the Snatch. That the MoD was now buying the Buffalo demonstrated that, in 2005, there had been an equally good case. Had the opposition pressed the point then and subsequently, arguably, it would have been fielded earlier.

It will be recalled that there had been, in November 2005, a call from back-bencher Ann Winterton for the Buffalo to be introduced. But there was no follow-up from the opposition front-benches. Three months later, Gerald Howarth asked about the 'South African manufactured Buffalo' but this was an armoured personnel carrier also known as the 'Buffel'.[52] In September 2006, Owen Paterson asked about the vehicle, having had two soldiers in his constituency killed by an IED. He did not get a satisfactory answer. Again there was no follow-up from the front-benches.[53]

Then there was an extremely unhelpful intervention from Conservative back-bencher Mark Lancaster. Not only an MP, he was a Major in the Territorial Army and in the summer of 2006 had been serving in Afghanistan. Thus enlightened, on 10 October 2006 – close to the first anniversary of Sgt Hickey's death – he spoke in a session of the Defence Committee. But he asked specifically for the route clearance package then in use by US forces in Afghanistan – which included the Buffalo – *not* to be purchased. It was, he said, 'completely unsuitable for Afghanistan'.[54]

52. Hansard, 27 February 2006: Column 6W.
53. Hansard, 4 September 2006: Column 1705W.
54. Select Committee on Defence, 10 October 2006, Minutes of Evidence.

The House, on this matter, did not exert itself on behalf of the troops. That was often the case. An enormous amount of time and energy was devoted to attending to the welfare of troops, their pay and conditions, their families' housing, the treatment of the injured, and diverse other matters. Important though these matters were, considerably less attention was given to the urgent task of preventing soldiers being killed. The Snatch controversy was an exception. By and large, MPs – with only a few honourable exceptions – avoided any discussions on the capabilities and weaknesses of British military vehicles.

As to the Mastiffs in the 'Talisman' package, these were not standard personnel carriers. They were going to carry bomb disposal officers and their equipment. In May 2007, however, the MoD had already bought new 'munitions disposal vehicles' for this purpose, specifically for Iraq and Afghanistan.[55] At a cost of £415,000 each – a cool £7.5 million – the MoD had obtained 18 Swiss-built trucks called the 'Tellar'. They were unarmoured vans. Like the Vector, they had a 'cab forward' design, making them extremely vulnerable to IED attack. There was only one concession to the fact that they were going into war zones. They had 'a level of riot protection' – mesh screens on the windows.

It is difficult to describe this purchase as anything other than insane – the officials responsible for its procurement totally detached from reality (the low value of the contract was below the threshold where ministerial approval was required). 'Felix wagons', as they are called by troops, are always prime targets for insurgents. One common tactic is to set up decoy explosions and then mine the area where a vehicle might be expected to park when it arrived with its crew to investigate. Another is simply to ambush the vehicles en route. Thus, the lack of protection was not an academic issue. The US was equipping its disposal teams with MRAPs – armoured, armed and self-supporting. The British, forever complaining about 'overstretch', had to keep available large numbers of mounted infantrymen to escort unarmoured and unarmed bomb disposal vehicles.

Nor was this the only area where British strength was sapped on unproductive tasks. In Afghanistan particularly, as many as 100 troops would routinely be committed to running small convoys over relatively short distances to outlying posts, taking up to four days for the outward and return journeys. For one such 40-vehicle convoy, half of them escorts or support vehicles, it was calculated that the supplies carried could have been delivered by one Mi-26 helicopter in the same period.[56, 57] These helicopters

55. MoD website, 18 May 2007, 'Newest munitions disposal vehicle is launched'.
56. MoD website, 3 May 2007, 'Convoy keeps troops supplied in southern Afghanistan'.
57. *Defence of the Realm*, 18 September 2007, 'Force multipliers'.

had been offered to the British government, flown by experienced, ex-military pilots, at £6,000 per operating hour – less than a fifth of the cost of flying an RAF Merlin. But to take up such options was not the British way. It was preferable to tie up valuable combat troops, and take the losses in men and vehicles through the inevitable mines and ambushes. Any problems could be put down to 'overstretch'.

There was another option, devised by the Americans, the GPS-guided 'smart' parachute – known as the Joint Precision Airdrop System (JPADS). This allowed high-flying transport aircraft to make precision drops of supplies to isolated outposts. So successful has this been that the USAF delivered 313,824 pounds of supplies between August 2006 and September 2007 – keeping an estimated 500-plus convoys off the roads.[58] Of course, having lost three C-130s on operations in Iraq and Afghanistan, the RAF was short of aircraft. The government, having chosen to replace part of its ageing fleet of C-130s with Airbus A400M transports, the prototype of which had yet to fly, there was no possibility of fully exploiting this technology. Thus convoys continue to soak up valuable men.

In this and many other ways is illustrated the 'drag' procurement decisions impose on operations, themselves a reflection of the inability to understand and implement sound technological solutions to basic military problems. With the Tellar, the problem has been rectified by the purchase of the new Mastiffs, but only after £7.5 million had been wasted.

Turning to the third vehicle of the 'Talisman' package, this provided illustrations of several phenomena, not least the venal and childishly superficial behaviour of the media. There was nothing wrong with the vehicle itself, properly designated the 'High Mobility Engineer Excavator' (HMEE). It had been developed for the US Army by JCB, a custom-designed military machine based on the commercial Fastrac. The British were buying an armoured version. One unanswered question, though, was why this had been included in a 'route clearance' package. No other military forces in theatre – the US and Canadians – used such a machine for this purpose. Their packages still comprised the three types – the Buffalo, the Cougar (Mastiff equivalent) as a command and EOD vehicle, and the Husky mine detector. Why the HMEE had been included, when the Husky had not – leaving a massive capability gap – has not been explained.

Also unexplained was why the MoD was purchasing a fleet of armoured excavators when it already had a fleet of 25 heavy duty Caterpillar armoured excavators, purchased at the cost of £14 million. More accurately, the MoD used to have these vehicles. They were being sold by dealers, unused,

---

58. *Popular Mechanics*, May 2008, 'Computer-guided parachutes resupply Army in Afghanistan'.

at a knock-down price of £4.5 million – a loss to the taxpayer (including dealers' commission) in excess of £10 million. The excavators, incidentally, were advertised as 'mine clearance vehicles'.[59]

Such waste, one might have thought, would have interested the media. But concern over the 'Talisman' package extended only to lurid pieces written about the HMEE. One such, by *The Daily Mail*, wrongly surmised that it was being bought to compensate for delays in the Army's 'Terrier' battlefield engineering vehicle programme. Then, picking up on the manufacturer, JCB, it charged that the Army had been 'forced to buy JCBs and paint them in camouflage colours to clear war zones'. It illustrated its story with a picture of a fleet of civilian, yellow-painted JCB excavators.[60] Unfortunately, *The Daily Telegraph* followed suit.[61]

These stories, in many ways, typified the media approach to military procurement – ill-informed, inaccurate and missing the point. Generally, like the MPs, the media rarely took any great interest in military equipment, except after the event. With the Snatches, it joined in the hullabaloo, but then only after the research had been done by others. Certainly in respect of Army equipment, almost never did it show any interest in the decisions made by the MoD which led to specific equipment being purchased. It never challenged the strategic, tactical or technical assumptions on which decisions were based. Most criticism related to cost over-runs or late delivery. Too often, it reserved comment until equipment was about to be issued, when its coverage tended to mimic the 'Boys Own' style, with gushing, uncritical 'puffs', characterised by its treatments of the Viking and the Jackal.

EQUIPMENT VERSUS INCOMPETENCE

More disturbingly, over the course of the Iraqi war, and then bleeding into the Afghani campaign, equipment – as in 'deficiencies' – became a political 'stick' with which to beat the government. Every setback and catastrophe was interpreted as the government failing to supply 'Our Boys' with the necessary kit. A classic example of this came on 20 January 2008 when *The Daily Telegraph* ran a story headed, 'Kit shortages put troops' lives at risk'.[62] This referred to the unfortunate death of Captain James Philippson

59. *Defence of the Realm*, 15 May 2008, 'The "underfunded" MoD strikes again'.

60. *The Daily Mail*, 18 December 2008, 'Army forced to buy JCBs and paint them in camouflage colours to clear warzones'.

61. *The Daily Telegraph*, 1 December 2008, 'Mine clearing vehicle that could save lives of British troops delayed for two years'.

62. *The Daily Telegraph*, 18 April 2008, 'Kit shortages put troops' lives at risk'.

of the Royal Horse Artillery, the first soldier to be killed in southern Afghanistan.

An earlier and, as it turned out, fictitious account of the Captain's death had been published in June 2006, shortly after he had been killed. This had it that, as part of a Quick Reaction Force (QRF), he had gone to the rescue of British troops who had been ambushed while on patrol in the Sangin district. The force had arrived in armoured Land Rovers to find a convoy of British vehicles pinned down by Taleban fighters who were firing from nearby buildings. Philippson and his men had jumped from their vehicles, firing their rifles as they ran to protect the convoy and to reach the wounded soldier. The injured man was successfully removed under fire, but while he was being pulled to safety a burst of Taleban gunfire hit Philippson and the other member of the Quick Reaction Force, killing the Captain and severely wounding the other soldier.[63]

In January 2008, *The Telegraph* had it that Philippson's death was in part due to the shortage of 'vital kit' such as body armour, heavy machine guns, night vision goggles and ballistic matting for Land Rovers. This theme was explored during the subsequent Coroner's Inquiry. At its conclusion, Andrew Walker, assistant coroner for Oxford, pronounced that 'totally inadequate' resources had led to the force of which Captain Philippson had been part, being 'outgunned by a bunch of renegades'. The soldiers had been defeated 'not by the terrorists but by the lack of basic equipment', Walker said. He added: 'To send soldiers into a combat zone without basic equipment is unforgivable, inexcusable and a breach of trust between the soldiers and those who govern them.'

This criticism was very widely reported in the media, not least in *The Daily Mail* which retailed the views of Philippson's understandably angry father, Anthony. He held the MoD responsible but also declared: 'The MoD was starved of cash by the Chancellor.' In the *Mail*'s article, the verdicts on the deaths of L/Sgt Casey and L/Cpl Redpath were also reported, the two soldiers who had been killed in a Snatch for want of a Mastiff. They got six lines.[64]

In the matter of the 'scandal' of Captain Philippson's death, an Army Board of Inquiry saw events differently.[65, 66] Philippson had indeed been part of a Quick Reaction Force. It had volunteered to come to the aid of

---

63. *The Times*, 14 June 2006, 'British soldier died as he saved comrade in Taleban ambush'.
64. *The Daily Mail*, 15 February 2008, 'The Para betrayed by Britain: Coroner attacks MoD over "unforgivable and inexcusable" death'.
65. *Daily Mirror*, 16 February 2008, 'Scandal of Para Captain James Philippson's death'.
66. Army Board of Inquiry Report, 8 June 2007, 'An investigation into the circumstances surrounding the death of Captain J. A. Philippson'.

a patrol which had been looking for a UAV that had crashed near its base. The patrol had not found it – a 'Desert Hawk', another of those 'toy' aeroplanes about which Labouchere had been so dismissive. On its journey back to its base, it had been ambushed by the Taleban. As to Philippson's death, he had been killed '… as a result of poor tactical decision-making, a lack of SOPs (Standard Operating Procedures) and lack of equipment'.

The Board further concluded that the decision to retrieve the downed UAV might be questionable, 'given its relatively low value, low security classification and the late hour at which the initial patrol deployed'. Had the patrol not been ordered to recover the UAV, 'it is unlikely that the incident would have occurred'. But it was clear, even from the measured tones of the BOI report and its caveats about 'hindsight', that this had not been the Army's finest hour.

The QRF had been a composite force, comprised of 30 British Army personnel from 13 different Arms who had never worked as a fighting team, plus four US personnel. As support, they had a detachment of Afghani soldiers who had not completed their training. Although a 'formed infantry unit' would have been preferable, that had not been available. Ministers had put a cap on the number of troops which could be sent to Afghanistan and the infantry units were deployed elsewhere. To that extent, there attached some political blame for the decision to send so few troops to theatre.

However, when the QRF had been set up, its commanding officer – Major Jonathon Bristow – had issued no SOPs and had carried out no rehearsals. When the contact report had come in, Bristow did not brief his patrol on the proposed route or any tactical procedures to be adopted. By his own admission, he 'had little idea about how he was going to conduct the link-up' and some members of the patrol left their base 'without any idea where they were going'.

Preparations for departure had been so rushed that the patrol, nominally nine vehicles, was on its way out of the base six minutes after the contact report, leaving behind vital Bowman radios and two of its number. The drivers could not find their ignition keys, which were in the pocket of an occupant of another vehicle. That vehicle got snarled up in barbed wire on its departure from the base. After some delay, it returned and the remainder of the vehicles followed on. The QRF was thereby split into two components.

As to the speed of response, to be ready in six minutes represented 'either a very well rehearsed drill or an ill-prepared rush'. Given the lack of rehearsals, the Board concluded it was the latter. Then, once on the road, without any clear idea of the route it was going to take, the first part of the QRF found itself on a narrow track which became too narrow for vehicles. Bristow ordered the troops to proceed on foot. By so doing, he 'significantly reduced the firepower at his disposal'.

Crucially, without Bowman radios, Bristow was not in touch with his base. Had he so been, he would have been told that the patrol he was seeking to rescue was no longer in contact with the enemy and might have decided to return. Fatefully, the patrol continued, whence it came into contact with 'between 12 and 15 people ... with what looked like small-arms weapons'. There was an exchange of fire and Captain Philippson received his fatal gunshot wound. Here, the lack of night vision goggles may have been relevant as the 20 or so men in the patrol had only three sets between them. Major Bristow, leading the patrol, did have a set. He saw the armed men and shouted a warning. Fatally, his had not been helmet-mounted, preventing him from observing and firing his rifle at the same time.

That lack had led to a short pause before Bristow had fired 'two or three rounds' in the enemy's direction. The Taleban had returned fire, one of their shots killing Captain Philippson. The lull between Bristow shouting his warning and firing, 'may have given the enemy enough time to react aggressively'. But he should not have been leading the patrol. At the very least, he should have been behind his patrol sergeant who had a rifle fitted with a night sight, and had observed the Taleban moments earlier.

On such slender grounds had Andrew Walker alleged 'betrayal', and upon his comments had the media based their stories. At the Inquiry, Bristow had been asked if his troops could have matched their attackers if they been supplied with Minimi machine guns and under-slung grenade launchers. He told the court: 'It would have made a hell of a difference. We lost the initiative through a lack of firepower and thus the Taliban had a greater weight of firepower.'

The Board agreed that the patrol had lost the initiative, but only after the death of Captain Philippson. Then, for five minutes, there had been widespread confusion. But the firepower available had been 'sufficient for dealing with the enemy action'. The patrol, in fact, did, have one General Purpose Machine Gun detached from one of the Wimiks. Had the QRF not become split, there would have been two available. More firepower, said the Board, would only 'have allowed a swifter extraction from the killing area'.

The truth is that the patrol had been ill-prepared, badly led and disorganised. Had any number of events been different, the tragic outcome could have been avoided. In this toxic mix, the role of equipment had been marginal. An 'ill-prepared rush' had led to a soldier being killed.

The deeper problem though was the narrative adopted by the coroner, by media, by the opposition politicians, by much of the public and even within the military. The Army could do no wrong. Anything that did go wrong was the fault of the 'government' or somebody else. Yet, while people will readily accept – albeit ironically – that 'military intelligence' is an oxymoron, they forget that the words 'military' and 'incompetence' are frequent bedfellows.

What we saw in Iraq, however – and continue to see in Afghanistan – is that 'fault' is a complex, multi-factoral issue. In Iraq, the Army was defeated. Indisputably, the major fault lay with the politicians, in particular, one man – Tony Blair. But the Army was not without fault. Its equipment was wrong, its tactics were wrong and, in the final analysis, it lost faith in its mission and gave up. Whether Service chiefs could have made a difference lies in the realm of speculation. The indications are that they did not try. They accepted defeat and, in so doing, made it inevitable.

Chapter 12 – Lost before it started

An occupation undermined

I think that we were a bit too complacent about our experiences in Northern Ireland and certainly on occasion we were a bit too smug about those experiences.

AIR CHIEF MARSHAL SIR JOCK STIRRUP
INTERVIEWED BY *THE ECONOMIST*, 30 JANUARY 2009

The 88 wrought havoc on the battlefield throughout the desert war because the British were slow to learn. The pre-war British Army did not appreciate the extent to which a future war would be a battle between machines, and that technology was an essential element in tactics.

STEPHEN BUNGAY (2002), *ALAMEIN*[1]

When the British Army invaded Iraq in early 2003 alongside US forces, it fought largely with 'legacy' equipment and structures designed to meet Warsaw Pact forces on the plains of Northern Europe. The war was expected to be a short, high-intensity armoured battle. Fortunately, it was. Furthermore, it was fought in the cooler months of the year when the equipment, designed for temperate climes, could still function. The occupation could not have been more different. It was a long-duration, low-intensity war, often fought in the heat of summer, which rendered much of the Army's equipment inoperable or unusable. It does not take a military genius to work out that fundamentally different structures and equipment were needed to prevail.

Yet by 2006, three years into the most vicious counter-insurgency campaign in its recent history, the Army was still fielding much of the equipment with which it had invaded Iraq. The main addition to its order of battle was the Snatch Land Rover. By contrast, three years into the Second World War, an Army which had been equipped in 1939 with the Cruiser Mk1 tank – weighing 12 tons and armed with a 2-pounder (40mm) gun – was facing Rommel in the North African Desert. It was equipped with the 30-ton Sherman tank armed with a 75mm gun. The appearance of this tank demonstrated that the Army had adapted to battlefield conditions, perforce in the face of the German Army which was better equipped and had consistently outfought its opposition. By that measure, the continued use of Snatches at a critical juncture in the Iraqi campaign suggested a failure to adapt. But the Army of 1942 had wanted to win. The Army of Iraq in 2006, fielding 14-year-old Snatches, did not.

---

1. (London, Aurum Press Ltd).

That said, the Sherman was American, in 1942 the match of the German Mk III and IVs which up until then had dominated the battlefield. But it was to remain the Allies' main tank through to the end of the War. The Germans went on to produce the Panther and the formidable 'Tiger' series. The Panther and the Tiger II featured sloped glacis plates for their frontal armour, influenced by the appearance of the Russian T-34. It was not until 1945 that the British finally produced in the Centurion a tank thus equipped.

Early British tanks lacked effective armour and a gun capable of delivering high-explosive shells. Thus they could not deal with the relatively unprotected crews of 88mm anti-tank guns. Neither did their guns have the range to counter the long reach of that deadly weapon. These deficiencies contributed considerably to the ability of the Germans often to counter overwhelming superiority and firepower, adding significantly to the casualty toll and perhaps prolonging the war.

The concept of sloped glacis plates embodied the principle of deflection. This was found to enhance the protection offered. It took the British even longer to apply the same principle to protecting against mines and IEDs. In Aden in the 1960s, however, the mine was a potent weapon. In Oman and in other theatres, it had been the major killer of men. To counter this threat, the Army in 1966 acquired several hundred Bedford RL lorries, with 'mine plate' armour, the sloped sides and 'v shaped' profile which we now recognise in the modern MRAP vehicles. Although bought to address a real need in a real war, the Army could not wait to get rid of them and revert to 'proper' lorries to fight its 'proper' wars. It was then to re-learn the lessons in Bosnia in the 1990s. Mine protection again came to the fore. Afterwards, the Army again discarded its equipment and abandoned its hard-won knowledge.

In the new war in Iraq, the Army needed to re-learn those lessons – again. It did not. Thus, it was not until mid-2006 that the politicians drove the procurement of the Mastiff. But in the teeth of Army opposition, too few of them were ordered to make any strategic difference. There was other equipment too, but nothing on any scale that could have been decisive. Imposed on the Army, the new equipment was not born of new thinking, new strategies. It was accepted grudgingly and used to reinforce existing strategies rather than to enable new directions to be forged.

To have won would have required the same degree of commitment injected by President Bush, Robert Gates and General David Petraeus. Yet, the Army – Dannatt in particular and Jackson before him – was not prepared to sanction what was required to fight a war that he and the rest of the Army no longer believed was winnable. That was the real problem. Wars are won and lost in the minds of men.[2] Even without the political drag, this war would have been lost because the Army had decided it was not worth winning. More to the point, it had decided that the price it would have to pay in order to win was unacceptable.

This notwithstanding, the proximate cause of the British defeat in Iraq was political, stemming from one man, Tony Blair. Following the successful invasion, he demanded that the military rebuild a shattered nation. At the same time, he failed to ensure that adequate resources were allocated for this monumental task. When difficulties were encountered, he pledged support to the Iraqi government while quite obviously planning a wholesale withdrawal of troops. Then, while making the withdrawal conditional on the ability of local security forces to cope, he withdrew the troops anyway, when it was manifestly obvious that the security forces were not ready.

All this was overlaid by hypocrisy. Even during his last speech in Parliament, before submitting his resignation to the Queen, he was pledging support for the fight against the 'terrorists' in Iraq, saying: 'We will not beat them by giving in to them. We will only beat them by standing up to them.' Yet withdrawal plans had been set in stone, giving in to the terrorists rather than 'standing up to them'.

Had the political framework been different and the Army had initially received the full support of Blair and his government, it still could not have prevailed without the right equipment, structures and tactics. More troops devoted to fighting an insurgency are not necessarily an answer. Without the right elements in place, they are vulnerable targets and become casualties. Then, as the Americans found to their cost in Mogadishu in 1993 – scene of the epic novel and film, *Black Hawk Down* – continued military adventures become politically unsustainable.

In Iraq in 2003 and throughout the campaign, events were to conspire to ensure that the Army was unable effectively to fight the insurgency. There were many reasons, not least the failures explored earlier in this book, in particular the tardy recognition of the fact of an organised Shi'a insurgency. But one of the main reasons was the Army's failure to re-equip. Because the need was so obvious, the unwillingness to embrace it suggests there were more issues than simply a blind refusal to do the right thing. In fact, there were two, one political and one to do with the Army itself.

---

2. The 'minds of men' effect is extensively explored in a paper written in 1980 called 'From PSYOP to mind war: The psychology of victory' by Colonel Paul E. Valley.

THE SHADOW OF EUROPE

The political die was cast in 1998, 10 years before the Army's final defeat in Basra. Tony Blair met Jacques Chirac, then French President, in St Malo, France, for a summit on defence cooperation. It was there – and in Helsinki the following year – that Blair pledged to work towards building a European Rapid Reaction Force (ERRF). This was to be a Europe-wide force of 15 Brigades or about 50,000–60,000 troops, capable of intervening rapidly in a crisis. It was to be deployable within 60 days at a distance of 2,500 miles and sustainable in the field for a year. In order to maintain such a force, with rotating replacements, the actual manpower requirement was closer to 180,000. In addition, there would need to be home-based supporting elements and logistic support.

The potential British contribution included up to 12,500 troops, 72 combat aircraft and 18 warships, with a full range of supporting capabilities.[3] Blair was in effect committing the bulk of the UK's long-term deployable forces to the venture – considerably more than he was to commit to the occupation of Iraq.

The immediate effect was to usher in an obvious but undeclared – and frequently denied – policy of 'Europe first' in procurement issues, all aimed at securing the harmonisation and 'inter-operability' of European forces. Through that, billions of pounds were wasted on European-sourced equipment which could have been obtained better and more cheaply elsewhere.[4] This was to cast a shadow over the defence budget, focusing procurement on high-value projects which soaked up funds and reduced the ability of the MoD to respond to changing circumstances. Its main political priority became to equip the British component of the ERRF.

For the Army, the effect was dramatic. The ERRF embodied what was called the 'expeditionary' concept, but with a difference. Because of the requirement for speed of deployment over distance, it needed a highly mobile, air-portable armoured force. This was a capability which – as we have seen – the British Army completely lacked.

The requirement for air-mobility created huge technical problems. Currently available military transport aircraft (the C-130 Hercules being taken as the standard) imposed severe restrictions on dimensions, particularly height. Crucially, their lifting capabilities restricted vehicle weights

---

3. Hansard, 16 January 2003: Column 703W.
4. This is explored in detail in this author's paper for the Centre for Policy Studies entitled 'The wrong side of the hill'. It was estimated that £14 billion had been overpaid on European projects when better and cheaper equipment could have been bought from Anglo-US contractors. In just one instance, £109 million was wasted on a joint Anglo-French anti-tank missile which failed to perform, resulting in the purchase of the more capable US Javelin missile, off-the-shelf.

to around 20 tons. Yet those same vehicles, once deployed, might be expected to confront main battle tanks three times their weight, with far thicker armour, and defeat them. To square the circle, an entirely new military concept emerged. This was not a vehicle as such, but a *system*. Actually, it was even more than that. It was a 'system of systems'. In British military circles, it became known as the Future Rapid Effects System or FRES.

THE FUTURE RAPID EFFECTS SYSTEM

FRES was a break from the established principles of relying on armoured vehicles, which themselves relied on a compromise between protection, mobility and firepower. It added a fourth dimension – 'situational awareness', the new religion in military thinking.

This would be achieved by flooding the battlefield with advanced electronic and other sensors, including those fitted to a new generation of vehicles. They would all be linked together by a vast electronic communications network – the military equivalent of the internet. It would allow commanders right down to the level of a four-man patrol to have a perfect overview of the battlefield. Instantaneous communication with all other units would be possible, allowing sharing of information and enabling the coordination of actions. In theory, the enemy could then be detected at a distance. At that point, the final element came into play – an array of precision-guided, stand-off weapons which could be used to neutralise hostile forces before they came close enough to inflict damage to the lightly protected vehicles deployed.

This became the Holy Grail, the search for which was shared by most other Western armies and by US forces which were working on their own version called the Future Combat System (FCS). Such ventures were of course welcomed by the military-industrial complex. It saw in the various projects opportunities for lucrative development and production contracts. There was also another dividend anticipated. The technology was seen as a 'force multiplier', allowing the 'effects' to be achieved with a vastly smaller number of men. It reduced the cost of maintaining large standing armies and the difficulties most nations were experiencing in recruiting enough personnel for their largely volunteer forces.

Absent entirely from the UK's Strategic Review of 1998, FRES was nevertheless enthusiastically embraced by the former Member of the European Parliament Geoff Hoon. In October 1999, he had been appointed Secretary of State for Defence. Despite that, no immediate progress was made. Attention was consumed by 11 September 2001 and the attacks on the World Trade Center. Only then, in the 'New Chapter' of the Strategic Defence Review, published in July 2002, ostensibly in response to the attacks, did the Government announce it was 'pursuing the concept' of FRES.[5] This was little noticed at the time, with the focus on the invasion of Afghanistan on 7 October 2001 and the invasion of Iraq on 20 March 2003.

In May 2004, though, even as British forces in Iraq were about to confront the Mahdi Army uprising, the European Union's General Affairs and External Relations Council was kick-starting the ERRF. It delivered what were known as the 'Headline Goals 2010'. These were subsequently endorsed by the European Council of 17 and 18 June 2004.[6] They were both a 'shopping list' of equipment required to fill capability gaps and a deadline set for the completion of the ERRF, the member states undertaking to be ready by 2010 to carry out 'military rapid response operations'.

In anticipation of meeting the UK commitment, there had already emerged in the Defence White Paper of July 2003 completely new plans for 'a major restructuring of the Army'. There would be a 'shift in emphasis to light and medium weight forces' based around the Future Rapid Effects System (FRES) family of vehicles. Three brigades would be equipped.[7] This was the British element of the ERRF, introduced at the very time when the Army needed to keep its options open. Instead, it was committing its intellectual, planning and financial resources to a 'major restructuring' involving an entirely new and untried system. With such a huge commitment, restructuring to meet the demands of a counter-insurgency campaign was not only inconceivable. It was beyond the financial resources of the Army and its organisational capabilities.

Whether the military could have resisted the ERRF is debatable. Certainly, the political pressure for delivery was very strong. Relations between the UK and most of the rest of her EU 'partners' had been seriously strained in the run-up to the invasion of Iraq. Post-invasion, not only did Blair want to rebuild bridges, he needed European Union support for a UN mandate to endorse the occupation. He also had hopes of member states joining the 'coalition of the willing' in Iraq. Active UK participation in ERRF preparations was necessary to send a positive signal to Brussels.

Nevertheless, there is no evidence that there was any strong resistance to this development in the Army, the implementation of which became the responsibility of the newly appointed Chief of the General Staff, General Sir Mike Jackson. He was not necessarily enthusiastic about the European

5. Ministry of Defence, Strategic Defence Review – New Chapter, July 2002.
6. Council of the European Union, 18 June 2003, Presidency conclusions.
7. Command Paper 6269, July 2003, 'Delivering security in a changing world: future capabilities'.

'project' and, in fact, warned that no army could operate properly without 'clear political authority'.[8] But the idea of a 'major restructuring', with the prospect of substantial funding for new equipment, was extremely attractive. An in-service date of 2009 was declared for FRES, in good time to be ready for service with the ERRF.[9]

Whatever the political deadline, the very idea of introducing FRES in five years – or at all – was fantasy. It was not even within the remotest realms of possibility. In 2001, enthusiasts in the Defence Evaluation and Research Agency had not expected operational readiness for at least 25 years.[10] Much of the technology needed did not exist. No one was even sure what it was, or what its final form might be. Gregory Fetter, a senior land-warfare analyst, had observed: 'It's like trying to grab a cloud of smoke.'[11] Whatever it was, there were serious doubts as to whether it was at all feasible. MP Nicholas Soames complained of defence workers who had for the past two years 'been anxiously awaiting a decision from the Government [on the FRES vehicle] ... for which there is not yet even a drawing'.[12]

Nevertheless, there were early clues to signal quite how important the project had become to the Army. Despite the completely unrealistic in-service date of 2009, the Army was strongly opposed to 'stopgap' solutions. This was forcibly put by Lt-Gen Rob Fulton to the Commons Defence Committee in May 2004. He had been asked whether, if there was going to be a delay in getting FRES, an option would be to buy something off-the-shelf for a short period to fill the capability gap. His response left no room for doubt:

> It is an option but from my perspective it would be a very unattractive option because it would divert much needed funds either from FRES or from some other programme. In other words, it would be a dead end capability. It would be a stopgap but it would be a dead end.[13]

This, writ large, was the real reason for the opposition to the Mastiff and any other MRAP-type vehicles. They were a 'stopgap' – a 'dead end capability'. More dangerously, they could 'divert much needed funds ... from FRES'. Thereby, the Army was prepared to reject much-needed equipment to deal with a real war, in favour of a fantasy project. At least in 1915 when

8. *The Guardian*, 29 March 2004, 'European army not on agenda, top general says'.
9. House of Commons Committee on Defence, 25 May 2004, Examination of Witnesses (Questions 300–319).
10. *The Independent*, 14 April 2001, 'Heavyweight tanks are defeated by plastic rivals'.
11. *National Defense Magazine*, September 2002, 'US Future Combat Vehicle sets tone for other nations'.
12. Hansard, 25 March 2004: Column 1097.
13. House of Commons Defence Committee, 24 May 2004, Examination of Witnesses (Questions 300–319).

the Army had rejected the tank, it had done so to favour its existing capability – the cavalry. But here, the Army seemed determined to reject real equipment in favour of a fantasy, the shape and nature of which appeared to be unknown.

Even the price ticket was fantasy. Originally slated at £6 billion for 900 vehicles, in a sparsely attended Westminster Hall debate held at the end of June 2005, Ann Winterton was shocked to hear Defence Minister Don Touhig read from a prepared speech that 3,500 vehicles were planned. The cost had risen to £14 billion.[14] After the debate, Touhig admitted surprise – he had seen the figure for the first time while he had been reading it out.[15] Later, the price increased to £16 billion. There does not seem to have been a formal announcement. It just appeared. One day, it was £14 billion, the next £16 billion.

Despite this – or perhaps because of the huge price ticket – General Jackson set about reorganising the Army with vigour. The existing structure of the Infantry, based on what was known as the 'Arms Plot', did need reform. It was wasteful, inefficient and disruptive. But Jackson's 'Future Army Structure' went far beyond what was necessary. He refashioned the Army to make it conform with the FRES/ERRF concept, creating a highly specialised force of mechanised infantry. In so doing, he discarded four infantry battalions, relying on the dividend gained from the supposedly more effective FRES formations. The end result was the abolition of most of the traditional regiments. This led to a huge outcry about the loss of 'cap badges' but never once did it impinge on the public debate that the restructuring was being carried out to enable the Army to fit the ERRF.

While he pursued his task of bringing FRES to fruition, there is no evidence that General Jackson actually understood what was involved. He would not have been the only one. But nor is there any evidence that he was concerned at all with the idea of FRES. There was a hidden agenda – the real agenda. Very quickly in Army circles, the term had morphed into the 'FRES family of medium armoured vehicles' (FFMAV), which was highly revealing.

This harped back to the 1980s when the Army had been planning a range of armoured vehicles on a common chassis to replace equipment such as the wheeled Saladin APC, the tracked Scimitar reconnaissance vehicle and others. To that effect, it had unveiled as an 'aspiration' in 1987 the Future Family of Light Armoured Vehicles (FFLAV). As is so often the case with defence procurement projects, this project was shelved, but not before a preferred option had been identified, the Swiss-designed Piranha

14. Hansard, 28 June 2005: Column 390WII.
15. Personal communication.

multi-role armoured personnel carrier, a platform which could be adapted to meet a variety of needs.

There was an attempt by Nato in 1991 to bring together the disparate requirements of member states in order to produce a common armoured platform. This project was named the 'Multi-purpose Base Armoured Vehicle' (MBAV) and was being discussed internationally in 1993 as a possible replacement for the then ageing M-113 series of armoured vehicles and others, such as the Piranha.[16] The United States was also carrying out studies for a replacement programme, which was provisionally named the Light Contingency Vehicle (LCV) programme, in which the possibility of a platform suitable for rapid deployment was mooted, in support of United Nations 'peacekeeping' operations. This, however, was cancelled in 1993 through lack of funding.[17]

With the United States and the British sharing some common requirements, some of this project's intended functions were incorporated in a 1996 joint UK/US project, called by the British 'TRACER'. In 2001, the British government pulled out, losing its stake of £131 million. By then, the government was looking for a 'European' solution and it poured money into a consortium with Germany and Holland to produce what it hoped might be a common European platform. Originally, France was to be a partner, but it decided to pursue its own design, which became the Nexter VBCI.[18] The tripartite project became the Multi Role Armoured Vehicle (MRAV), very similar in concept to the original FFLAV project.

However, in the 'post-Cold War era', the idea of 'rapid reaction' forces was gaining considerable currency and was beginning to dominate military thinking – later to become the template for the ERRF. This coalesced in a United Nations-sponsored conference in 2001, focused on determining the parameters for rapid military intervention.[19] For such purposes, the MRAV – which had acquired the name 'Boxer' – was too heavy for air transportation. The UK, therefore, also pulled out of that project in order to concentrate on FRES, with a loss of £57 million. This left the Army having spent probably more than £200 million on *not* replacing its medium-weight armoured capability. In FRES came the opportunity to revisit the original project. FFLAV became FFMAV. All that had changed was one letter. The Army was hankering after old dreams, cloaking them with 'new' thinking to bring them to fruition.

16. *Jane's International Defence Review*, 1 October 1993, 'MBAV, Nato's best chance for a truly co-operative vehicle programme?'
17. *Defense Daily*, 1 February 1993, 'LCV cancelled'.
18. Wikipedia, undated, 'Boxer (Armoured Fighting Vehicle)'.
19. Report from the NGO–Government Dialogue: 'Towards a rapid reaction capability for the UN: Taking stock', Ottawa, Canada, 19 November 2001.

With such a glittering prize so close, after nearly 20 years of frustration and hundreds of millions in wasted expenditure, it is hardly surprising that when a need emerged in late 2003 for new equipment in Iraq, General Jackson should have taken an easy option. Neither willing nor able even to consider something more suitable for fear of prejudicing his treasured project, he raided the stores in Northern Ireland and despatched surplus Snatch Land Rovers. A 'stopgap' was not good enough for the *real* Army, but it was good enough for Iraq. Then he turned his attention back to the project that to outsiders seemed so vague that 'a cloud of smoke' had more substance. It was not so vague inside the Army. It was a dream about to come true. In pursuing it, Jackson, his staff – and the politicians behind him who allowed it – condemned the Army in Iraq to impotence, with all the consequences that followed.

A NEW BROOM

When General Sir Richard Dannatt took over as Chief of the General Staff from Jackson in August 2006, the war in Iraq was at a critical phase. The 'repositioning' in al-Amarah was imminent and the violence in Basra was reaching fever pitch. Rather than grip the situation, however, he shared the lack of enthusiasm for mine-protected vehicles displayed by his predecessor. During the intense debates through the Browne review, he was 'barely visible'.[20] On the other hand, he did inherit Jackson's enthusiasm for 'FRES'. Then, as the Army – predictably – failed to grapple with the insurgency, Dannatt looked to the fresher fields of Afghanistan. There, he thought, the highly mobile warfare was more like the war the Army wanted to fight. Facetiously, one might say that he didn't like the war they were in, so he looked around for another, better one.

Ostensibly, the Afghan war presented a tactical opportunity for deploying a medium-weight, mobile force. This allowed Dannatt to continue his advocacy of FRES – more accurately FFLAV – which he did at any and every opportunity. In early 2007 it looked as if the project was coming 'unstuck', with suggestions that the first vehicles would not enter service until 2017.[21] But, by mid-2007, even as the US MRAP programme was moving into high gear and Gates had identified it as his 'highest priority', Dannatt declared that FRES was his 'highest equipment priority'. He was determined, he said, 'that we will make this programme a timely success – it is at the heart of the future Army'.[22] It was not a 'future army'. It was one

---

20. Personal communication.
21. *The Times*, 14 January 2007, 'Army faces 5-year wait for armoured carriers'.
22. MoD website, 8 June 2007, 'Drayson. New vehicles will have "vital part to play in the Army of the future"'.

that rested on an operational concept settled twenty years earlier for a war on another continent against a different enemy. Likely, it was based on doctrines that were even older, dreamed up by long-retired generals from another age.

Nevertheless, by July 2007, Dannatt was insisting that 'FRES' should acquire an in-service date of 2012. This, he said, was 'non-negotiable'.[23] In October, a shortlist of three vehicle types was settled. One was the Piranha. Another was the MRAV, the project from which the British had already withdrawn. But there was no longer even a pretence that this was FRES. It was what the Army had always intended it should be – a straight purchase of a new armoured vehicle. Predictably, the favourite was the Piranha. This was a later version of the very same vehicle that the Army had picked for FFLAV. In twenty years, the Army had gone full circle – its dreams were within a whisker of fulfilment.

There was absolutely no doubt about the Army's determination to acquire this particular vehicle. To meet the notional and still vague requirements for FRES, General Dynamics, the Piranha manufacturers, had offered a 'paper upgrade' of the then current version. In the 'trials of truth' which the MoD arranged in 2007 to pick a winner, it 'ticked all the boxes'. The 'paper vehicle' completely met the paper specification.

Up against it, as the third of the triumvirate in the competition, was the Nexter VBCI, very similar in concept to the Piranha and the vehicle the French had developed in preference to the MRAV Boxer, against which it was now competing. Unlike the Piranha V – as it was to be called – the VBCI was a real vehicle, in production and entering service with the French Army.

The manufacturers, formerly the state-owned Giat Industries, were very keen to secure this prestige British order. In a bid to clinch the deal, they prevailed upon the French government to agree to modify its own delivery programme to release sufficient vehicles to equip a British battle group.[24] Not only was the VBCI a real vehicle, therefore, it was available for delivery in 2011 – at a fixed price. It was the only equipment that could have permitted the MoD to meet Dannatt's preferred in-service date. In fact, it could have come into service before his deadline.

In the 'trials of truth', real vehicle confronted paper specifications. Unfortunately, it passed almost all the requirements, proving 95 per cent compliant. This was not what the Army wanted. Out on the testing ground,

---

23. *The Times*, 16 July 2007, 'Armed Forces get £30bn for new equipment in defence budget'.
24. Unpublished: VBCI and Protected Mobility for UK Forces, June 2008. A formal offer was made to the British government, to which there was no response.

therefore, diligent MoD officials failed it on a number of arcane requirements, such as the speed with which an engine could be changed in the
field. The company had been judged on a leisurely demonstration which
had not been part of the competition, despite evidence of controlled tests
which proved that the specification could be exceeded.

Such was the determination that the vehicle would fail that a general
specification unique to the British Army was also applied. This was the
'ground running test', a legacy of an Army that had become used to dealing with the unreliable tank engines with which it had historically been
provided. Before fitting it to a tank in the field, a replacement power pack
had to be capable of being set up on the ground, with the necessary fuel
and electrical connections, in order for it to run. This avoided having to
commit the labour to installing the engine, only to find that it did not
work.

With the VBCI being fitted with a modified commercial truck engine
produced by Renault, with hundreds of millions of miles behind it, Nexter
thought such a provision unnecessary. Furthermore, French Army doctrine
did not require it. With a light, wheeled armoured vehicle, the preference
was to recover the vehicle and tow it to a field workshop rather than replace
a failed engine *in situ*. Thus, there was no provision for ground running.
Had it been considered, the engineering modifications to allow it would
have been simple and cheap to provide. But, as submitted for the 'trials of
truth', the equipment lacked this element. Thus was the VBCI failed, despite
protestations that modifications could and would be made before any
vehicle went into service.[25]

The Piranha V, of course, had a provision for ground running – on
paper. By such means did the paper Piranha triumph. But for this, even
within its own published terms, the Army could have had its FRES utility
vehicle. It would have been a Nexter VBCI. This was not acceptable. Twenty
years previously, the Army had set its heart on the Piranha. Wish fulfilment
was more important than operational capability.

Unconscious of the history and clearly unaware of the recent background to vehicle procurement decisions, Michael Evans of *The Times*
noted the 'delay' in procuring 'FRES'. He thus opined that, to fill the gap,
'the MoD has had to spend £120 million to buy 200 Mastiff and Vector
armoured personnel carriers off the shelf to provide sufficient protection'.[26] That represented the extent of media understanding of what had

25. Personal communications. Interviews with Nexter technical directors and consultants, Paris,
June 2008.

26. *The Times*, 29 November 2007, 'Army forced into retreat over upgrade to ageing armoured
vehicle fleet'.

been – and was then still – one of the most closely fought procurement battles in recent times, a battle that had stretched back over twenty years. The lack of understanding extended even to the failure to distinguish between the Mastiff and the Vector.

Unsurprisingly, when the Piranha was selected in May 2008 as the preferred design for FRES – as only it could have been – very few noted the subtle change in Dannatt's position. From being his 'highest equipment priority', FRES had become his 'highest priority *after* support to operations'.[27] The born-again FFLAV was slipping through his fingers. As the campaign in Afghanistan was bogging down, with the proliferation of the IED increasingly hampering mobility, even Dannatt was having to concede that the Army would have to be equipped to fight the real war.

In February 2009 – just short of a year later – then Foreign Secretary David Miliband freely acknowledged that the Taleban had managed to create 'a strategic stalemate' in parts of Afghanistan, 'through their use of improvised explosive devices'.[28] What had happened in Iraq had come to pass in Dannatt's 'better' war, just as Ann Winterton had suggested in the Commons would happen, more than two years earlier. The fantasy Army had collided with reality.

FRES AND COUNTER-INSURGENCY

Had FRES, as originally conceived, ever been put to the test in a counter-insurgency environment, it would have been a disaster. Based on detecting the enemy before it could get close enough to do any damage, the concept was dangerously wrong.

Insurgents, as is generally known, are not always obliging enough to wear uniforms and drive around in hardware conveniently painted in military colours. Indistinguishable from the civilian population in which they operate, they rely on cheap weapons, immune to the high-tech sensors and the billion-pound weapons systems. A man with an RPG bought in the local arms bazaar for a few dollars or with two artillery shells taped together which he can bury by the roadside can get inside the 'sensor loop'. He can destroy equipment worth tens of millions of pounds, kill and injure soldiers and civilians and make the 'battlefield' untenable.

As to the Army structure required for FRES, this was also the antithesis of that needed to conduct a successful counter-insurgency. With General

27. MoD website, 8 May 2008, 'Design selected for future armoured vehicle for British Army (FRES)'.
28. *The Times*, 10 February 2009, 'David Miliband: Nato troops stuck in an Afghanistan "stalemate"'.

Jackson's Future Army Structure, the requirement was for highly specialised mechanised infantry, endowed with a very high level of technical skills and capable of operating sophisticated electronic equipment and advanced weapons systems. Crucially, proficiency required an equally high level of training, plus constant rehearsals and exercises, all to keep skills current and maintain unit cohesion – especially given the relatively high churn rate in the infantry and the low skill base of recruits.

In such an Army, training is a full-time job and one that cannot be neglected. So specialised is the task that training and deployment for entirely different counter-insurgency tasks, in two different theatres, could not help but impose enormous strains on a relatively small Army. It was this, more than anything, to which Dannatt was referring when he complained of Iraq plus Afghanistan breaking his Army. The operations did not cause the problem. Maintaining what amounted to two reinforced brigades in the field, even with manpower levels under 100,000, should have presented no insuperable difficulties. It was operations, *plus* the pressing need to maintain the 'normal' training cycle – to maintain his 'balanced force', as Dannatt liked to call it – which caused the problem.[29]

Stresses had been considerably exacerbated by the *roulement* system, where complete units were rotated into theatre for six months, before being returned. With gaps between each operational deployment of two years under the so-called 'harmony guidelines', this created a planning nightmare.

But the greater problem was the six months needed for the specialist pre-deployment training that each unit needed, and the period of 'deprogramming' afterwards. Cramming in the 'proper' training, for the FRES/balanced force capability, and then having to rebuild the skill sets and currency after they had been lost during operational deployments and their training cycles were extremely problematical. Depending on the view taken, either this requirement was breaking the Army, or the operational load was doing the damage. Dannatt believed it was the latter.

In that sense, FRES – and the commitment to the ERRF – cast a long shadow. It overstressed an Army that could perhaps have performed one function well, but could not cope with two entirely different and mutually incompatible tempos. There lay a further element to the defeat in Iraq. Forced to choose between losing the war and, in his terms, irrevocably damaging his Army – not that it was put in such blunt terms – Dannatt made what appeared to be a soldier's choice. His Army came first. In fact, it was a bureaucrat's choice. The Army as an object had become more

---

29. See, for instance: RUSI, 21 April 2006, The RDS Military Interview, General Sir Richard Dannatt. His comments, viewed in this context, take on a much deeper meaning.

important than the tasks it was to perform. There is even a name for this – it is called *self-maintenance*.

As to the FRES vehicles, Dannatt's precious Piranhas, clearly they would have provided better protection than Snatch Land Rovers. But they would probably have been no greater a success than the Warriors they would have replaced – i.e. less effective than dedicated MRAP vehicles. Here, it is possible to gain some first-hand indications as to how they would actually have performed for, while the British abandoned the FFLAV idea, the Canadian forces did not. They introduced the earlier version of the Piranha as the LAV (light armoured vehicle) which – in its numerous variants – formed the backbone of their armoured formations. With the Canadian deployment to Afghanistan also went their LAVs.

There is no reliable information on casualty rates relative to specific vehicles. The Canadians adopted as a formal policy that which exists informally in the British Army, that of declining to identify the vehicles involved in incidents, fatal or otherwise. However, before information dried up, it was evident that a considerable and distressing number of LAVs had been involved in attacks in which one or more crew members had died.[30]

What also appeared to be the case was that the bulk – if not all – of the casualties occurred on roads, where the vehicles were either in transit to or from operations, or on escort duties. In most cases, they were travelling with their armoured hatches open, either to improve visibility (and ventilation) or – in accordance with standing orders – to relieve overpressure in the event of a hull breach from a mine or IED. This can be more dangerous in the confines of an armoured vehicle than direct blast effects.

For whatever reason, most of the casualties involved either drivers or vehicle commanders, these being in the most exposed positions. Although more heavily armoured, there is no reason to suppose that the crews of later mark Piranhas would not suffer the same fate. They are not mine-protected to anything like the same extent as dedicated MRAPs and do not provide all-round, enclosed protection. In fact, the same old battle was being played out, with Defence Minister Bob Ainsworth arguing as late as June 2008 that the vehicle would have to have 'a high degree of mobility'. This, he said, 'will of course need to be set off against the essential requirement for mine protection and blast deflection to be built into the vehicle's design'.[31]

There are also the experimental Stryker Brigades deployed by the US Army in Iraq, these too being based on the Piranha platform. These are

30. *Defence of the Realm*, 25 January 2008, 'Lessons to learn'.
31. Hansard, 16 June 2008: Column 665.

perhaps closer to the model which the British vehicles would have followed, as the Brigades were set up to develop the Future Combat System (FCS), the closest parallel to FRES. Their performance is a matter of considerable debate – and dispute. The consensus, if there is one, lies in the view that the 'jury is still out'.

However, there have been reports of considerable losses. A single infantry company in Diyala province lost five Strykers in less than a week. In one of the biggest hits, six American soldiers and a journalist were killed when a huge bomb exploded beneath their Stryker on 6 May 2007. It was the biggest one-day loss for the battalion in more than two years.[32] It is perhaps significant that General Petraeus did not seek to expand the Stryker force when implementing the surge, and that MRAP vehicles now perform many of the functions previously carried out by Strykers. On that basis, the experience does not provide a comforting assurance that British deployment of Piranhas would have been successful.

The ultimate irony though is that FRES had been killed off by the very insurgency it was never meant to fight. Recognising the inherent vulnerability of FRES vehicles, designers had sought to bolt more and more armour on them, and added more systems, in a vain attempt to proof them against IEDs. They are now so heavy that they cannot be carried by standard military transport aircraft. The concept is no longer viable – not that it ever was.

Unsurprisingly, given the background, this led the chairman of the Commons Defence Committee to ask, 'Is this the most disastrously managed programme of Ministry of Defence history?'[33] He was subsequently to label it a 'fiasco'.[34] Up to the end of November 2008, the total expenditure on the FRES programme had been £155.2 million, of which some £132 million had been spent on the utility vehicle project – with nothing at all to show for the money.[35] With the money wasted on the previous projects, a hundreds-strong fleet of mine-protected vehicles could have been bought.

A DOCTRINAL SHIFT

With such a huge commitment to FRES, both in structural and equipment terms, when it was announced in October 2008, the £700 million re-equipment

32. *Defence of the Realm*, 14 May 2007, 'Warfare state to welfare state'.
33. House of Commons Defence Committee, 16 December 2008, uncorrected transcript of oral evidence.
34. House of Commons, 26 February 2009, Defence Committee publish equipment report (Press release).
35. *The Daily Mail*, 20 January 2009, 'Axed military truck costs Ministry of Defence £132 million'.

package was not just a matter of buying new equipment. Coming less than 18 months after Dannatt had declared FRES his 'highest equipment priority', it represented – in part – a doctrinal shift. It was also a recognition that FRES, and the underlying concept of an air-mobile expeditionary fighting force, was dead.

Robert Gates, the US Defense Secretary, got there before Dannatt, accusing his own Generals of 'Future-war-itis', a propensity to look to the next war (rather than the last, as Generals are so often accused of doing). This would be a high-tech war full of exciting new kit, computer screens and 'networks' in which the enemy would be defeated by the power of technology rather than by flesh and blood, and boots on the ground. The only problem was, Gates observed, that future wars were more likely to be the same as the ones already being fought. They, not some future dream, should dictate the priorities. In fact, Gates was wrong. The Generals had been thinking of old wars, dressed up in new clothes.

Even then, as we have seen, the 'package' was far from optimal. Technophobia, and the technical illiteracy that goes with it, is strongly embedded in this man's Army. In the advocacy of FRES, upheld as the ultimate in technological modernity, there had appeared to be a paradox. But that was more apparent than real. In reality, the Army had always been more interested in acquiring new 'toys with wheels' than complex systems. Whatever the interest though, it did not focus on that messy, real war going on in Iraq. Thus did Stirrup, in a moment of candour, tell *The Economist*:

I think that we were a bit too complacent about our experiences in Northern Ireland and certainly on occasion we were a bit too smug about those experiences. You're only as good as your next success not your last one. You can never rest on your laurels and I think we may have done that. I think we may have been guilty of doing that here. That's not the case at the moment. We are in the throes of a fundamental reappraisal of our doctrine and training and our structures for counter-insurgency. But I would accept the charge that for a while there we were perhaps too slow in doing that.

This is exactly what the head of the Islamic Party in Basra had been saying back in February 2006, but nobody had been listening then and they barely were in 2009. Then, Stirrup was asked about the production of an updated counter-insurgency doctrine, he replied: 'One of the problems of course is that we are learning all the time and that was something that perhaps we were a bit slow to recognise four or five years ago, we needed to do.' [36]

36. *The Economist*, 30 January 2009, 'Jock Stirrup on Britain's military'.

A 'bit slow' encompasses a period longer than the European phase of the Second World War. Glacial might be a better word. The problem is that, in the hierarchy of military planning, the statement of objectives should come first – the strategy – and then follows the doctrine, the detailed exposition of how the objectives are to be achieved. Then, in an ideal world – one in which wars are actually won – comes the functional equipment designed to enable troops to implement the doctrine. Four or five years down the line – closer now to six – for want of new doctrines, the equipment 'tail' had been wagging the Army 'dog'. Both strategy and doctrines had been dictated by what equipment had been available, not the other way around.

In this sense, there was never anything wrong with the Snatch Land Rover or any of the other equipment on the Army inventory. The problem was not the equipment but the thinking behind it – or lack of it. If military equipment is, or should be, the ultimate in functionalism, the logical progression in equipping an army starts with strategy, from which follows doctrine and then comes the equipment and the tactics, the latter two closely inter-related. In Iraq, the situation was reversed. The tactics and equipment were imported from another world, unrelated to the realities of the insurgency in Iraq, and with them the second-hand doctrines from Northern Ireland. These in turn dictated what could (or, in this case, could not) be achieved – the strategy.

There is an obvious truth in Rumsfeld's assertion that, 'You go to war with the army you have'. If intelligence and forward planning has been good, then that army will be equipped to deal with the enemy it encounters. More likely, it will not. But if the intention is to win, that army does not stay the same for very long. Rapid and extensive changes are very often seen once an army is committed to a campaign, a victorious army often emerging in a very different state from when it started.

What should have happened in Iraq was that, once the strategy had been fixed, the planners, tacticians and designers should have gone to work. New doctrines should have been forged and the Army should have been re-equipped and re-structured accordingly. In the way of war, as the situation developed, there would then have occurred a process of defining and redefining both equipment and tactics to meet new challenges.

What actually happened was that, barring small changes of no strategic importance, equipment and doctrines were effectively fixed. Thus, the main variables were (minor) changes in tactics, and changes in strategy. The only real option was to redefine the strategy. It started with grand ambitions of rebuilding the nation, bringing peace and democracy, to 'holding the line' so that there could be an 'Iraqi solution to an Iraqi problem'. When even that could not be achieved, the politico-military establishment decided to withdraw the troops, letting the Americans fill the gap, while claiming credit for the results.

The progression was utterly dishonest. Now that same establishment is doing its best to convince itself – and the public – that the 'holding the line' strategy was the one they had decided all along. By that measure, because the Iraqis eventually succeeded (in part, and with a great deal of help from the Americans) the campaign was a success. Stirrup thus got away with his extraordinary admission, untouched by the defeat he helped bring about.

Even now, the tail continues to wag the dog. The Army has identified a need for off-road vehicles – and while one might argue about the relative priorities, such a capability is part of the toolkit of any army – it is still well behind the curve. In the dismally limited vision of so many British 'experts', protection and mobility were still seen as mutually incompatible. Having learned absolutely nothing, they remain fixed on the idea that you can have one only by sacrificing the other – even if the MoD was very belatedly recognising both were possible. Yet, the US, with the recognition that the current MRAP vehicles lack the necessary off-road performance, was fortunately deprived of the experts' views and was no longer beguiled by Northern Ireland experience. The Department of Defense was well advanced with a programme to develop 'high mobility' MRAPs. In the real world, mobility and protection were no longer regarded as incompatible.

The continuing tragedy is that, over 30 years ago, the Rhodesians were already there. Recognising exactly the same need, in 1978 they produced the 'Mine Protected Combat Vehicle' (MPCV), offering mine protection and significant cross-country capabilities. For 30 years, military vehicle designers for the Western armies have sat on their hands, ignoring earlier lessons and experience, designing the equipment they want to build and their customers want to buy, rather than what is actually needed. And, much to its surprise, when the Army met 'soldiers' who did not care whether they lived or died, and were ignorant of the rules by which the Western powers had decided wars would be fought, it was defeated.

By 2009, then, some lessons were beginning to be learned, but not fast enough to have avoided the 'strategic stalemate' that David Miliband observed earlier in the year. With the Army having only recently escaped the shadow of FRES – the October equipment package was not due to start coming on-stream until late 2009, with deliveries continuing into 2010, while high-mobility mine-resistant patrol vehicles would not be available until at least 2011.

UNDERFUNDING

Then there was the issue of funding. Back in 2007, when L/Sgt Casey and L/Cpl Redpath had just been killed in their Snatch, Colonel Bob Stewart – 'former UN commander of British troops in Bosnia' – ventured that the Army was taking the casualties because: 'we cannot dominate the ground'. The options, he said, were to 'retake and dominate the ground, or abandon it'.[37]

Liam Fox, shadow defence secretary, saw things differently. He said the Army was paying for the government's mistake of not investing enough men, equipment or money into reconstruction at the time of the invasion. 'It's tragic that our Armed Forces are paying the price of a lack of political care and planning,' he said.[38] Six months later, Redpath's girlfriend, Sharon Hawkes, echoed this theme: 'It was underfunding by the Government that killed him,' she said.[39] But she had been pre-empted by Lord Rees-Mogg, who observed:

Throughout the Iraq war, our Forces have been short of suitable armoured vehicles. For years, the Basra palace run had to be performed in vulnerable Snatch vehicles; these have only recently been replaced by the Warrior, which is itself vulnerable to roadside bombs. Unlike American vehicles, the Warrior is not air-conditioned and can get unbearably hot in the sun.[40]

These problems, Rees-Mogg – together with hundreds of the *commentariat* – attributed to 'underfunding', thus illustrating the shallowness of the public debate. The Army had been turning down immediate funding in order to pursue the Eldorado of its £16 billion fleet of medium-weight armoured vehicles, an issue that had almost completely escaped attention.

Even at a more prosaic level, Rees-Mogg was out of touch. Warriors had been available since before the occupation and the use of the Snatch had been a policy issue. There had been no funding issues. Not least, the cost of operating Warriors was £250 per track mile, in normal peacetime use.[41] Aside from the far better protection afforded by the Mastiff – which was also fitted with powerful and highly effective air conditioning – this vehicle was far cheaper to run. Arguably, the operational savings alone would

---

37. BBC Radio 4 *Today* Programme, author's transcript.
38. *The Daily Telegraph*, 10 August 2007, 'Record death toll of British troops in Iraq'.
39. *The Daily Telegraph*, 17 February 2008, 'Troops killed "by lack of basic equipment"'.
40. William Rees-Mogg, *The Times*, 27 August 2007, 'Blood on a budget: our soldiers betrayed'.
41. Hansard, 17 July 2006: Column 214W.

have justified their use. And, compared with buying a basic FRES utility vehicle at an estimated £8 million each, the Mastiff – and Ridgeback – comes out at one-eighth of the cost, with far more durability and real-world capability.

Significant savings have been demonstrated by US forces, primarily through reduced long-term medical care, rehabilitation, and death benefit payments arising from the lower casualty rate. Additionally, many damaged MRAPs could be repaired and returned to service while conventional vehicles would often have to be written off. Vehicles with add-on armour were also suffering reduced serviceability and shorter lives. MRAPs lasted considerably longer. These factors, together with the decrease in force replacement costs due to casualties and improvements in operational effectiveness, made the MRAP significantly less costly than legacy vehicles.[42]

Thus, underfunding was not the issue – it never has been. Waste has been – not least because the Army was having to pay twice for protected patrol vehicles – while the obsession with buying absurdly expensive 'toys' certainly had contributed much to the failure to obtain the right equipment. Underfunding is too easy an excuse. The real causes of failure ran much deeper but even now few understand or want to address them. The British could not 'dominate the ground' as Colonel Stewart counselled because, every time they left their bases, they were brought down by IEDs and the constant attacks. When they stayed in their bases, the insurgents killed troops there as well. When the British left their bases in an attempt to track down and destroy their attackers, they were also killed. It had become a vicious circle, one that could have been broken had the Army applied its mind to the problem, but it chose not to. The Generals wanted their new 'toys'.

42. Franz J. Gayl, 22 January 2008, Mine Resistant and Ambush Protected Vehicle, Ground Combat Element (GCE) Case Study, Headquarters, United States Marine Corps.

Epilogue
Could it have been different?

It was our fault, and our very great fault – and now we must turn it to use.
RUDYARD KIPLING, THE LESSON

... authoritarian organisations are past masters at deflecting blame. They do so by denial, by rationalisation, by making scapegoats, or by some mixture of the three.

NORMAN DIXON (1976), *ON THE PSYCHOLOGY OF MILITARY INCOMPETENCE*

Blair's decision to throw his lot in with the Europeans – compensating, many believe, for his failure to deliver the UK into the embrace of the single currency – seriously hampered the ability of the Army to deal with the insurgency. And, having pledged the nation's armed forces to the Europeans and Iraq, he offered troops to reinforce the campaign in Afghanistan. That made a tight situation worse.

Even then, defeat was not inevitable. Looking at the campaign in the round, the single most egregious failure was the decision to abandon al-Amarah, walking out on a half-trained and poorly equipped 10th Division. That was a major strategic error. The decision itself was not initiated by the politicians but by the military. Strangely, there was very little discussion or debate. Equally, there was virtually no evaluation of the strategic consequences. Then, the 'retreat' was an administrative decision. The 'road map' had already been revealed by General Houghton in March, over three months earlier. But 'repositioning' in order to concentrate on Basra was putting the cart before the horse. Al-Amarah was the Mahdi Army's major armoury and it would have made more strategic sense to have cut off the supply of arms at source before dealing with the problem of Basra.

Of course, to have maintained forces at Abu Naji would have required dealing with the indirect fire. Here, the main problems were the lack of suitable equipment, in particular UAVs, helicopters and MRAPs, plus C-RAM for base defence. Even at a late hour, had General Dannatt been able to break free of the Army's obsession with FRES, he could have negotiated a major MRAP package. In exchange for scrapping FRES or putting it on the back-burner, substantially larger numbers of Mastiffs could have been bought, together with other, smaller MRAP vehicles. When this happened anyway in October 2008, it was too late for Iraq – and maybe too late for Afghanistan.

As to helicopters, the Army was again partly the author of its own misfortune. Many times, cheaper options than the Future Lynx were offered, and rejected. Had the Army been intent on acquiring tactical helicopters rapidly, it could have had them. It was occasionally able to borrow US Blackhawks and the Americans also provided medivac helicopters, but this was not a reliable foundation on which to carry out planning. It had been offered a new fleet of Blackhawks off-the-shelf. It had turned them down. As for UAVs, the MoD already had in place a replacement programme for the Phoenix, called Watchkeeper. They were modified Israeli Hermes 450s – with deliveries scheduled for 2010. The modifications, incidentally, were part of FRES, which included extra communications systems to fit in with the proposed 'network' that was at the heart of the system.

Because of the urgency of providing the Army with a UAV capability, in May 2007 the programme was brought forward with the purchase of the basic Hermes system off-the-shelf, direct from Israel. What was done then could have been done earlier, but for the determination to incorporate FRES modifications. Similarly, with C-RAM being ordered by the MoD in 2007, and temporary measures taken to ensure its early deployment, it is not untoward to argue that this equipment too could have been procured earlier.

With suitable equipment, holding the base at Abu Naji could have been tenable, buying time further to train and equip the Iraqi Army 10th Division. That perhaps could have allowed the Army, with existing resources, to back the Iraqis in recovering the city that much earlier, possibly as early as February/March 2008. Instead, the Army having committed its main strength to Basra, in September 2006 launched Operation Sinbad. Stirrup then complained that the action lacked support from the Iraqi politicians, particularly Maliki. But the British had misread the political situation and had acted prematurely. Maliki had not by then secured his political base. He could not have taken the same robust line that he took in 2008. The British would have been well advised to have husbanded their resources until a more propitious moment.

There were, though, the dangerous and debilitating attacks on the bases in Basra, but what held for al-Amarah could equally have applied to them – with the probability that, without Abu Naji having been abandoned, the pressure on Basra would not have been as strong. Then, given the change in the balance of political power in Baghdad, a move on al-Amarah would have made dealing with Basra an easier proposition.

Arguably, instead of Basra becoming the battlefield in Charge of the Knights and al-Amarah being taken without a shot fired, the situation might have been reversed. The battle would have been at al-Amarah. By June 2008, Muqtada was a busted flush and with British support, again using existing resources, the 10th/14th Iraqi Divisions could have walked into the Sadr strongholds in Basra without a shot being fired. The British, instead of skulking in their base in Basra airport, would have been central to the action, with a wholly different outcome to the one that has come to pass.

THE ROLE OF THE MEDIA

So much for the politicians and the military. But there was that other player, the media. It was almost completely oblivious to the strategic play in southern Iraq. It will be remembered that only one newspaper reported the retreat from al-Amarah. Again, there was minimal coverage of Operation Sinbad. Nowhere was there any detailed analysis or discussion of strategy, much less tactics.

On the other hand, the media was only too keen to use 'underfunding' as a tool to indulge in its favourite sport – politician-baiting. It was less keen to explore the underlying issues, understanding the complexities of military funding and coming up with ideas of its own. Still less did it trouble itself with any serious evaluation of military tactics, the equipment fielded or the manifest deficiencies in the inventory. For sure, it would retail the comments of opinionated and often ill-informed coroners, but it would never initiate its own discussions and debate. On the issue of FRES and its implications, the media did not even get off the starting blocks. Its coverage was pitiful.

As for the reporting of the occupation generally, while some were better than others, from no single source would it have been possible to develop a clear narrative, or to have gained any comprehensive – or any – understanding of what was going on. It is unlikely, therefore, that many journalists themselves had a good understanding of the situation. But with the British public thus ill-informed, it was deprived of an opportunity to engage in the strategic debate. It could not because there was not one – the options on offer were for the Army to stay in Iraq, take the pain and achieve nothing, or quit. Small wonder that most people opted for the latter. A 'third way' – i.e. winning – was not even considered. In that single sense, the media's failure was every bit as profound as the politicians of which it was so often critical. It failed in its most fundamental task of reporting the news, and its analysis was too often trivial or non-existent.

By contrast, the US media hosted vibrant and very public debates on strategy, tactics and equipment. The discussion on the Iraq Study Group was intense and the media coverage on equipment paved the way for Robert Gates to set up the MRAP programme. In popular newspapers and on television there was considerable comment and discussion on the relative merits of different equipment, at a level which would be found in the UK only in specialist magazines, and perhaps not even then. Instead, the media gorged on the mantras. In addition to 'underfunding', the legend of 'overstretch' was frequently rehearsed.

The trivial superficiality of the modern media compares poorly with earlier eras. When more and better warships were needed to counter the threat from the Imperial German Navy, in 1909 the press took up the cry 'we want eight and we can't wait', demanding eight dreadnoughts. In 1935, Lord Rothermere campaigned through his newspapers, *The Daily Mail* and *Bristol Evening News*, to force the Air Ministry to issue a specification for a modern, high-speed bomber. It was then that he purchased a Bristol Type 142 at a personal cost to himself of £18,500, naming it 'Britain First'. In a grand public display, he presented the aircraft to the nation for the Air Ministry to use as a test aircraft.[1] In March 1939, we saw lengthy and learned discussions from Captain Basil Liddell-Hart, engaged in earnest technical debate in the pages of *The Times*, exploring the merits of conscription and the acute difficulties of training and equipping impressed troops.[2]

Throughout our martial history, the press – and then the 'media' as broadcasting was included – had always taken a keen interest in our Armed Forces, and played an important role in ensuring they were adequately equipped. The modern UK media did not. Yet there was no need for leaked memos or insider information. All it needed was an examination of the equipment the army was fielding, against what it could have had. From that, it could easily have been divined that the Army leadership had 'sold the pass'.

Equipment, we asserted near the beginning of this book, is the window which reveals the underlying thinking. But it is also the window into the very soul of an army. The equipment deployed in Iraq provided such a window. There, the failure of the Army is a matter of record, no matter how the military and the politicians try to spin it. It was visible at the time, when many other things were not. But the media went to sleep. Thus, while it is conscious now of the failure in Iraq, it has no idea why it happened. More to the point, it took little part in trying to make things different.

1. *FLIGHT*, 12 February 1960, 'Fifty Bristol years'.
2. For instance, see *The Times*, 24 March 1939, Letters.

MoD PROPAGANDA

Whatever the failings of the media, the MoD performed even worse. It was in any event partly responsible for the lack of news reaching the media. Not only was it often economical with the truth, major actions went unrecorded simply because the MoD never gave any details of them.

Neither, in this internet age, was the MoD reliant on the media to distribute its message. It had its own websites on which it could easily post news of the campaign. While the Army was complaining of being unappreciated, it was the MoD that was most often silent about its exploits. Even its own 'successes', like the rapid acquisition of C-RAM once it had made up its mind to buy it, the procurement of the Ridgeback and the record of the Mastiff, it kept under wraps. Thus, the many 'resistance' sites became sources of information. Although very often exaggerating the outcome of engagements, they were surprisingly accurate in their reporting of the dates and locations of events. The enemy told us more about British activities than did the MoD.

Instead of a portal for information, the MoD chose to use its resources for propaganda, distorting rather than illuminating. It never set out clearly to explain its strategies, or offer anything in the way of a narrative. Too often, it relied on the great god 'OPSEC' (operational security) to justify its silences. This became so entrenched that, in December 2007, it refused to publish any information on an ongoing operation to recover Musa Qala in Helmand province. Yet newspapers were offering detailed reports, based in part on telephone interviews with Taleban fighters in the besieged town. Once again, the enemy was a better source of information.[3]

If the MoD has any complaints as to the way information was handled, it needs only look at itself.

HOPE AND DENIAL

Through the strength and constancy of the Americans, and the bravery of the Iraqis, the struggle to rebuild Iraq now looks as if it could be successful. The provincial elections of late January – the first electoral test of prime minister Maliki after the military operations in Basra and al-Amarah – brought a sweeping victory, in which voters themselves rejected the destructive embrace of Muqtada al-Sadr.

In Basra, Maliki's 'State of Law' coalition took 37 per cent of the vote. Although the Sadr party did not contest the elections, a Sadrist-supported

---

3. Hansard, 12 December 2007: Column 300.

coalition scored a mere 5 per cent, coming fourth in the league table. In Maysan Province, the result was closer. Maliki took nearly 18 per cent of the vote, with the Sadrist coalition at just over 15, coming second. In a city that Muqtada once called his own, having taken 87 per cent of the vote in 2005, it was still a victory.[4] Though many problems remained, this was a very hopeful sign.

Despite that, the British cannot claim a victory. The best that can possibly be allowed is that, having had their objectives redefined, the men and women on the ground carried out their tasks with skill, professionalism and dedication – and enormous courage. But, as we pointed out in the introduction, the campaign did not achieve the objectives originally set, or meet its international legal obligations. To that extent, it was a failure – in military terms, a defeat. How much of that was avoidable is debatable. What precisely was needed to recover the situation is also debatable. We have explored some of the issues.

Most tendentious is the issue of 'boots on the ground'. Many will argue that, without more troops, the campaign could never have succeeded. Allan Mallinson, former soldier, writer and military historian, argues thus. He may be right. But he also argues that the strategy must be right. 'Without a coherent strategy,' he says, 'even the best tactics are futile: casualties just mount.' He then adds: 'But there is no getting round it: strategy needs troops on the ground.'[5] That remains his considered view.[6]

One can agree with that, but also suggest that the troops did not have to be British. In the successful operations to recover Basra and then al-Amarah, the bulk of the troops were Iraqi. They had strong American support but the US Army committed just 2,500 troops to southern Iraq – less than the British fielded throughout the occupation. The fault lies in handing over to the Iraqis before they were ready – and indeed before Maliki had secured his political base and could commit them to the battle with the Mahdi Army.

For what they did achieve, British troops – and the personnel of all the services – can be proud. Their reputations stand and we have the greatest admiration for them. But that should not prevent their leaders exploring, honestly and openly, the issues, and working out what could have been done better. Should they then conclude – with more evidence than I have been able to gather – that there was very little more that could have been done – then so be it.

---

4. *The New York Times*, 5 February 2009, 'Election: Preliminary results'.
5. *The Times*, 10 February 2009, 'Afghanistan: It will be tougher than we think'.
6. Personal communication.

But what seems grotesque – and is in many ways an insult to those who tried so hard and the many who died – is to pretend that the campaign was entirely successful and, by inference, that there is nothing to learn from it. Bizarrely, as the preliminary results of the provincial elections came through, Maj-Gen Andy Salmon, then UK forces commander, pronounced that the 'peaceful elections met the latest of Prime Minister Gordon Brown's goals for removing Britain's 4,000 troops from Iraq by the end of July' – seemingly unaware that UK forces had been instructed to leave, come what may.[7] The Deputy Commanding General Multi-National Force Iraq, Lt-Gen John Cooper, then spoke in glowing terms of the 'success', refusing to debate 'what has gone on before'. The key, he said, 'is that we were deployed and given a task to do and we've done that pretty well. Now we will extract in good order. Our losses will be vindicated in the same way our losses in Northern Ireland were.'[8]

This delusional behaviour lies not in the realms of military strategy or politics. An explanation lies in the black art of psychology, for which we have to turn to a practitioner for guidance. The Army, we are thus informed – for all its outward modernity – is an authoritarian organisation. A sad feature of such organisations, we learn, is:

> ... that their nature inevitably militates against the possibility of learning from experience through the apportioning of blame. The reason is not hard to find. Since authoritarianism is itself a product of psychological defences, authoritarian organisations are past masters at deflecting blame. They do so by denial, by rationalisation, by making scapegoats, or by some mixture of the three. However it is achieved, the net result is that no real admission of failure or incompetence is ever made by those who are really responsible; hence nothing can be done about preventing a recurrence.[9]

If we look past the denial, we see the bloodstained wreckage of Snatch Land Rovers, the icon of defeat. The Army's soul is bared and the word victory will not be engraved there until it exorcises the ghost of those Snatches and learns again how to think – and faster. A 'bit slow' is not good enough. Not only is the British Army being out-manoeuvred, it is being out-thought by an internet-savvy enemy which can develop ideas and distribute them faster than the MoD can get a memo from one end of its luxurious headquarters to another.

The MoD and especially the Army must explore its failures and learn from them. In particular, it must start to specify equipment attuned to the wars it is fighting, rather than to the ones it wants to fight. It must wake up

---

7. Reuters, 2 February 2009, 'UK troops have met conditions for Iraq withdrawal'.
8. *The Times*, 16 February 2009, 'Lieutenant-General John Cooper: Death of 179 troops is price worth paying for our success'.
9. Norman Dixon (1976), *On the Psychology of Military Incompetence* (London, Random House).

to the intellectual – and political – dimensions of warfare and act accordingly. These latter issues are the most important. There is a war to fight in Afghanistan. But Afghanistan is not Iraq – or Vietnam. The political, economic, geographical and social dynamics of the two countries are very different. What might have worked in one will not necessarily work in the other. It is pointless, therefore, slavishly applying 'lessons learned' from minor tactics and equipment deployed. The lesson needed is how to respond to the situation, moulding doctrine, tactics and equipment to the realities on the ground. While a UAV in the right place and the right time might have been a 'war winner' in Iraq, an armoured digger could be a better option in Afghanistan.

Most of all, though, we have to expunge the taste of defeat. Only then will those who have had their bodies so cruelly ripped apart by that foul weapon, the IED, be able to rest in peace. Only then will the British Army, victorious in el-Alamein and in every campaign afterwards to the end of the Second World War, regain the habit of winning. The politicians are beyond redemption.[10] The Army, we hope, is not.

---

10. With, of course the exception of Des Browne, who brought the Mastiff to the Army and engineered the 'October package' for Afghanistan.

Index

Index

Index

Index

Index